Tafsīr al-Qurṭubī

Vol. 5

Juz' 5: Sūrat an-Nisā' 23-176

Tafsīr al-Qurṭubī

The General Judgments of the Qur'an and Clarification of what it contains of the Sunnah and *Āyah*s of Discrimination

Abū 'Abdullāh Muḥammad ibn Aḥmad ibn Abī Bakr ibn Farḥ al-Anṣārī al-Khazrajī al-Andalusī al-Qurṭubī

Vol. 5

Juz' 5: Sūrat an-Nisā' 23 – 176

translated by

Aisha Bewley

Diwan Press

Classical and Contemporary Books on Islam and Sufism

Published by: Diwan Press Ltd.

Website: www.diwanpress.com

E-mail: info@diwanpress.com

By: Ab 'Abdullah Muhammad ibn Ahmad al-Qurtubi

Translated by: Aisha Abdarrahman Bewley

Edited by:Abdalhaqq Bewley

A catalogue record of this book is available from the British Library.

ISBN13: 978-1-908892-89-8 (Paperback)
978-1-908892-90-4 (Casebound)
978-1-908892-98-0 (ePub & Kindle)

Contents

Table of Transliterations

ء	ʼ
ا	a
ب	b
ت	t
ث	th
ج	j
ح	ḥ
خ	kh
د	d
ذ	dh
ر	r
ز	z
س	s
ش	sh
ص	ṣ
ض	ḍ
ط	ṭ
ظ	ẓ
ع	ʻ
غ	gh
ف	f
ق	q
ك	k
ل	l
م	m
ن	n
ه	h
و	w
ي	y

Long vowel

ا	ā
و	ū
ي	ī
أَوْ	aw
أَيْ	ay

Short vowel

ـَ	a [*fatḥah*]
ـُ	u [*ḍammah*]
ـِ	i [*kasrah*]

Translator's note

The Arabic for the *āyats* is from the Algerian State edition of the *riwāyah* of Imam Warsh from the *qirā'ah* of Imam Nāfi' of Madina, whose recitation is one of the ten *mutawātir* recitations that are mass-transmitted from the time of the Prophet ﷺ.

There are minor omissions in the text. Some poems have been omitted which the author quotes to illustrate a point of grammatical usage or as an example of orthography or the usage of a word, often a derivative of the root of the word used in the *āyah*, but not the actual word used. Often it is difficult to convey the sense in English. Occasionally the author explores a grammatical matter or a tangential issue, and some of these may have been shortened. English grammatical terms used to translate Arabic grammatical terms do not have exactly the same meaning, sometimes rendering a precise translation of them problematic and often obscure.

The end of a *juz'* may vary by an *āyah* or two in order to preserve relevant passages.

Sūrat an-Nisā' – Women 23 – 176

حُرِّمَتْ عَلَيْكُمْ أُمَّهَٰتُكُمْ وَبَنَاتُكُمْ وَأَخَوَٰتُكُمْ وَعَمَّٰتُكُمْ وَخَٰلَٰتُكُمْ وَبَنَاتُ ٱلْأَخِ وَبَنَاتُ ٱلْأُخْتِ وَأُمَّهَٰتُكُمُ ٱلَّٰتِىٓ أَرْضَعْنَكُمْ وَأَخَوَٰتُكُم مِّنَ ٱلرَّضَٰعَةِ وَأُمَّهَٰتُ نِسَآئِكُمْ وَرَبَٰٓئِبُكُمُ ٱلَّٰتِى فِى حُجُورِكُم مِّن نِّسَآئِكُمُ ٱلَّٰتِى دَخَلْتُم بِهِنَّ فَإِن لَّمْ تَكُونُوا۟ دَخَلْتُم بِهِنَّ فَلَا جُنَاحَ عَلَيْكُمْ وَحَلَٰٓئِلُ أَبْنَآئِكُمُ ٱلَّذِينَ مِنْ أَصْلَٰبِكُمْ وَأَن تَجْمَعُوا۟ بَيْنَ ٱلْأُخْتَيْنِ إِلَّا مَا قَدْ سَلَفَ إِنَّ ٱللَّهَ كَانَ غَفُورًا رَّحِيمًا ۝

23 Forbidden for you are: your mothers and your daughters and your sisters, your maternal aunts and your paternal aunts, your brothers' daughters and your sisters' daughters, your foster mothers who have suckled you, your foster sisters by suckling, your wives' mothers, your stepdaughters who are under your protection: the daughters of your wives whom you have had sexual relations with (though if you have not had sexual relations with them there is nothing blameworthy for you in it then), the wives of your sons whom you have fathered, and marrying two sisters at the same time – except for what may have already taken place. Allah is Ever-Forgiving, Most Merciful.

Forbidden for you are: your mothers and your daughters

This means it is unlawful for you to marry your mothers and daughters. In this *āyah*, Allah mentions which women are lawful and which are unlawful as He has already mentioned the prohibition of marrying a father's wife. Allah forbade seven on account of lineage and six on account of suckling and marriage. The *Sunnah* adds a seventh, which is being married to a woman and her aunt at the same time, and there is consensus on that. It is confirmed that Ibn 'Abbās said,

'Lineage forbids seven and marriage seven,' and he recited this *āyah.* 'Amr ibn Sālim, the freedman of the Anṣār, said the like of that and said, 'The seventh is in Allah's words: "*married women*" (in the next *āyah*).'

The seven by lineage are: mothers, daughters, sisters, paternal aunts, maternal aunts, brothers' daughters and sisters' daughters. The seven forbidden by marriage and suckling are: foster mothers by suckling, foster sisters by suckling, the mothers of wives, stepdaughters, the wives of sons, and being married to two sisters at the same time. The seventh are women your fathers have married.

Aṭ-Ṭaḥāwī said, 'All of this is confirmed judgment and agreed on. The consensus is that it is not permitted to marry any of them except the mothers of wives with whom the marriage was not consummated. Most of the early generations held that the mother was forbidden by the contract with the daughter but that the daughter only forbidden by consummation with the mother. This is the position of most of the imams who give fatwa.' One group of the early generations said, 'Mothers and foster daughters are the same: they are only made unlawful by virtue of consummation with the other.' They said that *'your wives' mothers'* means mothers of the wives with whom you have consummated marriage. In respect of the words: *'your stepdaughters who are under your protection, the daughters of your wives whom you have had sexual relations with,'* they claim that the condition of consummation refers to both mothers and stepdaughters. Khilās related that from 'Alī ibn Abī Ṭālib. It is related from Ibn 'Abbās, Jābir, and Zayd ibn Thābit, and it is the position of Ibn az-Zubayr and Mujāhid. Mujāhid said that that is meant in both cases.

The position of the majority is contrary to this. The people of Iraq were severe and said, 'Even if he has intercourse with her by fornication, or kisses or touches her with lust, her daughter is forbidden for him.' According to us and ash-Shāfi'ī, she is forbidden by a valid marriage, and the unlawful does not make the lawful unlawful. The *ḥadīth* which Khilās cites from 'Alī is not evidence and its transmission is not considered sound by the people with knowledge of *ḥadīth.* What is soundly reported from him is like the position of the Group.

Ibn Jurayj said, 'I asked 'Aṭā', "If a man marries a woman and then does not see her or have intercourse with her before he divorces her, is her mother lawful to him?" "No," he replied, "she is parted from him whether or not he has consummated it." I then said to him, "Did not Ibn 'Abbās recite, 'the mothers of your wives with whom you have had sexual relations'?" "No, no," he said.' Sa'īd related from Qatādah from 'Ikrimah from Ibn 'Abbās that 'wives' mothers' is undefined, and a woman becomes unlawful simply by virtue of a contract with her daughter. This is similar to what Mālik related in the *Muwaṭṭā'* from Zayd ibn

Thābit. 'Zayd said, "No. The mother is prohibited unconditionally. There are conditions, however, about foster-mothers."' Ibn al-Mundhir said, 'This is sound since all mothers of wives are included in the expression.'

This is supported in terms of syntax by the fact that when two predicates have a different regent, what they describe is not the same. According to grammarians, it is not permitted to say, 'I passed by your wives, and I fled from Zayd's wives, who were elegant' when 'elegant' is an adjective describing 'your wives' and 'Zayd's wives'. That is also the case in the *āyah*: it is not permitted for '*allātī*' to describe both of them because there are different predicates. It is. However, permitted if it means: 'I mean'. [ILLUSTRATIVE POEM]

There is an explicit *ḥadīth* in which the Prophet ﷺ said, 'When a man marries a woman, it is not lawful for him to marry her mother, whether or not he has consummated the marriage with the daughter. When he marries the mother and does not consummate the marriage and then divorces her, if he so wishes, he can marry her daughter.' If this is confirmed and established, then you know that the prohibition does not describe individuals, as they are not the subject of general legalisation or prohibition, but is a general obligation of commanding and forbidding connected to the actions or inaction of those who have legal responsibility. When that is connected to individuals, it alludes to the general ruling and judgment. It is connected to it metaphorically as an allusion to what is lawful in action.

'Your mothers' is a general prohibition in every case and not specific to a particular aspect the matter. This is why the people of knowledge call it 'undefined', meaning that there is no definitive opening to it nor any means to bar the prohibition. It is the same with the prohibition of daughters, sisters and the other categories of forbidden women mentioned. *Ummahāt* (mothers) is the plural of *ummahah.* It is said that *umm* and *ummahah* mean the same. The Qur'an uses both and this was explained in the commentary on the *Fātiḥah.* It is said that the root of '*umm*' is '*ummahah'* on the measure of *fu''alah*, like *qubbarah* and *ḥummarah* for two birds (lark and dove). The letter is dropped but returns in the plural. [POEM] It is said that root of *umm* is *ummah.* [POEM] If that were the case, its plural would be *ummāt.* [POEM]

The word 'mother' is a term that comprises every female responsible for your birth, and that includes your actual mother, her mother and her grandmothers, and her father's mother and her grandmothers. 'Daughter' is used for every female in whose birth you have a part, and so the prohibition applies to every female whose lineage derives from you, which would include daughters, their daughters, and also the daughters of your sons. 'Sister' applies to every female connected to you via one or both parents. The plural of *ukht* (sister) is *'akhawāt'*.

A 'paternal aunt' is every female who shares with your father or grandfather in one or more of his parents and includes the sister of your father's mother. The term 'maternal aunt' applies to every female in whose parents or parent your mother shares. So that includes the sisters of your father's mother. A 'brother's daughter' is every female in whose birth your brother played a part, directly or indirectly and the same is true of a 'sister's daughter'. These seven are forbidden by lineage.

In the variant of Abū Bakr ibn Abī Uways Nāfi' recited *'akhkh'*.

your foster mothers who have suckled you

'Abdullāh recited *'ummahātukumu'llāya'* without *tā'*. [EXAMPLES]

They are forbidden in the the same way as the others already mentioned. The Prophet ﷺ said, 'What is unlawful by lineage is unlawful by suckling.' So when a woman suckles a male child, she is forbidden to him because she is his mother, her daughter is forbidden because she is his sister, her sister because she is his aunt, her mother because she is his grandmother, the daughter of her husband because she is his sister, his sister because she is his paternal aunt, and his mother because she is his grandmother, as well the daughters of his sons and daughters because they are daughters of his brothers and sisters.

Abū Nu'aym 'Ubaydullāh ibn Hishām al-Ḥalabī said, 'Mālik was asked whether a woman may perform *ḥajj* with her brother by suckling. "Yes," he said.' Abū Nu'aym also said, 'Mālik was asked about a woman who married and her husband consummated the marriage and then a woman came who claimed that she had suckled both of them. He said, "They are separated and what she took from him is hers and he does not have to pay anything he still owes." Then Mālik said, "The Prophet ﷺ was asked about a similar situation and commanded that. They said, 'Messenger of Allah, she is a weak woman.' The Prophet ﷺ said, 'Will it not be said that so-and-so has married his sister?'"'

The prohibition based on suckling occurs when the suckling is in the first two years, as was mentioned in *al-Baqarah*. With us, there is no difference between a little and a lot of suckling as long as it reaches the stomach, even a single swallow. Ash-Shāfi'ī makes that conditional on two things. One is that it happens five times, based on the *ḥadīth* of 'Ā'ishah: 'Part of what Allah Almighty revealed of the Qur'an is that ten known breast-feedings make unlawful and then that was abrogated by five known ones. When the Messenger of Allah ﷺ died that was in what is recited of the Qur'an.' The evidence is that ten was abrogated by five, and if less than five had created the prohibition, that would also have had to have been abrogated. On this basis, a single report would not be accepted and there is no analogy because they are not abrogated. We find in the *ḥadīth* of Sahlah, 'Suckle him five times and you will be forbidden to marry him.'

The second condition is that it occurs in the first two years. If it is after that, it has no effect since Allah says: '*...two full years – those who wish to complete the full term of nursing.*' (2:233). There is nothing after completion. Abū Ḥanīfah allowed six months after two years. Mālik said a month or so. Zafar said, 'As long as the child only drinks milk and is not weaned, he is nursing, even if it is three years old.' Al-Awzā'ī said, 'When it is weaned after a year and remains weaned, there is no suckling after that.'

Al-Layth ibn Sa'd alone among scholars says that suckling an adult brings about the prohibition. It is the position of 'Ā'ishah and is related from Abū Mūsā al-Ash'arī, but something is also related from him indicating that he retracted that. Abū Ḥuṣayn reported that Abū 'Aṭiyyah said, 'A man came with his wife to Madīnah and she became pregnant and her breasts swelled. He began to suck it and spit it out but some of it went into his stomach. He asked Abū Mūsā who said, "She is separated from you. Go to Ibn Mas'ūd and tell him." He did that and Ibn Mas'ūd then brought the Bedouin back to Abū Mūsā al-Ash'arī and said, "Do you think this grey-haired man is a suckling child! It is the suckling which produces flesh and bone which makes marriage unlawful." Al-Ash'arī remarked, "Do not ask me about anything while this scholar is among you."' This indicates that he retracted his position.

'Ā'ishah's evidence was the story of Sālim, a man who was the *mawlā* of Abū Ḥudhayfah. The Prophet ﷺ told Sahlah bint Suhayl, 'Suckle him.' The *Muwaṭṭā'* and other sources transmitted it. One group took an aberrant view and considered the prohibiting number of sucklings to be ten, holding to what was revealed. It is as if the abrogation had not reached them. Dāwūd said that a woman only becomes forbidden after three sucklings. He cited as evidence the words of the Prophet ﷺ, 'She is not made unlawful by one or two sucklings.' Muslim transmitted it. It is related from 'Ā'ishah and Ibn az-Zubayr. That is the position of Ahmad, Ishāq, Abū Thawr and Abū 'Ubayd. It is holding to something on the basis of a statement, and it is disputed.

A number of the imams of *fatwā* say that the prohibition is achieved by just one suckling, which is the minimum to which the name of suckling can be applied and this was the practice in Madīnah and is analogous to in-lawship for the reason that it is something new which demands perpetual prohibition and no number is stipulated, as is also the case with in-lawship. Al-Layth ibn Sa'd said, 'The Muslims agree that both a little and a lot of suckling make unlawful in the cradle that which breaks the fast.' Abū 'Umar said, 'Al-Layth did not come across the disagreement about that.'

There is a clear text about this: 'One or two sucks does not bring about prohibition.' Muslim transmitted it in the *Ṣaḥīḥ*. This explains the meaning of Allah's words in this *āyah*. It means that the number of sucklings is three times or more, since it is possible that it did not reach the stomach. That is the reason for the words, 'ten known sucklings' and 'five known sucklings'. They are described as 'known' to avoid what is doubtful or where it is uncertain that it has reached the stomach. It is deduced from the words that if the number of the instances of suckling are not known, then they do not make someone unlawful. Allah knows best.

Aṭ-Ṭaḥāwī mentioned that [the report about] one or two sucklings is not confirmed because sometimes it is related by Ibn az-Zubayr from the Prophet ﷺ, sometimes from 'Ā'ishah, and sometimes from his father. Such confusion annuls it. It is also related from 'Ā'ishah that seven sucklings make someone unlawful. It is also related from her that she instructed her sister Umm Kulthūm to suckle Sālim ibn 'Abdullāh ten times. The same is related from Ḥafṣah. Three times is also related from her as is five times, as ash-Shāfi'ī said and is related from Isḥāq.

This *āyah* also indicates negation of the effect of milk produced by a male which does not create the prohibition. Sa'īd ibn al-Musayyab, Ibrāhīm an-Nakha'ī and Abū Salamah ibn 'Abd ar-Raḥmān said, 'Milk produced by a male does not render anyone unlawful.' Most say that the words indicate that the male is the father because the milk is ascribed to him and is a result of his child. This is weak. A child is created from the fluids of the man and woman together and milk emerges from the woman and not the man. All that the man did was to engage in sexual intercourse which is the cause of the emission of fluid from him. When the child is weaned, Allah creates milk without any ascription to the man in any way whatsoever. That is why the man has no right with respect to milk. Milk belongs to the woman. So it is not possible to make that analogous to any other fluid. The words of the Messenger of Allah ﷺ, 'Suckling makes unlawful what lineage makes unlawful,' make it clear that the prohibition is on account of suckling, and there can be no ascription of suckling to the man in the way that the ascription of the fluid to him is evident. Suckling is the business of the woman. Indeed, the basis of it is found in the *ḥadīth* of az-Zuhrī and Hishām ibn 'Urwah from 'Urwah in which 'Ā'ishah said that Aflaḥ, the brother of Abu-l-Qu'ays came and asked permission to visit her after the veil had been lowered, and he was her paternal uncle by suckling. She said, 'I refused to give him permission to enter. When the Prophet ﷺ came, I told him about what I had done and he said, "Let him enter. He is your uncle!"' Abu-l-Qu'ays was the husband of the woman who had nursed 'Ā'ishah. This is a single report. It is possible that Aflaḥ and Abū Bakr were milk siblings and that is why he said, 'Let him enter. He is your uncle!'

In general, the position regarding this matter is unclear and knowledge rests with Allah. However, the normative practice is based on it and it is better to be cautious regarding the prohibition although the words of Allah: *'Apart from that He has made all other women lawful for you,'* strengthen the position of the one who disagrees.

your foster sisters by suckling,

This means full sisters by the same mother and father, which means the woman suckled them both by the milk generated by the pregnancy caused by the father, whether it is at the same time or if she was born before or after him. It also includes a sister by the same father but from another mother. In other words, one who was suckled by [another] wife of the father. It also includes a sister by the same mother who was suckled by the milk caused by a pregnancy from a different man.

your wives' mothers,

Then Allah mentions the prohibition caused by marriage and says, *'your wives' mothers.'* Four come under this heading: the wife's mother, her daughter, the wife of the father and the wife of the son. The wife's mother is made unlawful by virtue of a sound contract, as already stated.

your stepdaughters who are under your protection: the daughters of your wives whom you have had sexual relations with

This is a separate category and does not pertain to the first group. It refers to stepdaughters. A stepdaughter is the daughter of a man's wife by another man. She is called that (*rabībah*) because she is raised (*rabbaba*) in his care. So it means 'cared for' (*marbūbah*). *Fuqahā'* agree that a stepdaughter is unlawful to her mother's husband when the marriage has been consummated, even if the daughter is not actually in his care.

Some early scholars and the literalists took an aberrant position and said that a man's stepdaughter is not unlawful for him unless she was actually in his care when he was married to her mother. If she was in another town and separate from her mother after he consummated the marriage with her, then he is permitted to marry her. They cited this *āyah* as evidence and said that Allah only made stepdaughters unlawful under two conditions. One is that she is in the care of the man married to her mother. The second is that the marriage with her mother has been consummated. If either of these conditions is missing, then there is no prohibition. They also cited as evidence the words of the Prophet ﷺ: 'Even if she had not been my stepdaughter in my care she would not be lawful for me since she is my milk niece.' So he made care of her a condition.

It is related that 'Alī ibn Abī Ṭālib allowed that. Ibn al-Mundhir and aṭ-Ṭaḥāwī said, 'As for the *ḥadīth* of 'Alī, it is not firm because it is related by Ibrāhīm ibn 'Ubayd from Mālik ibn Aws from 'Alī. Ibrāhīm is not recognised. Most of the people of knowledge accuse him of repudiation and disagreement.' Abū 'Ubayd said, 'It is refuted by his words, "Do not display your daughters or sisters to me." It is undefined and he did not say, "those in my care". He made them all the same with respect to prohibition.' Aṭ-Ṭaḥāwī said, 'Their ascription to "care" (literally "laps") is because that is usually the case with stepdaughters; they are not unlawful when they are not like that.'

though if you have not had sexual relations with them there is nothing blameworthy for you in it then.

The pronoun '*them*' here refers to the mothers and the subsequent '*it*' refers to marrying their daughters if you divorce them, or they die, before consummation takes place. Scholars agree that when a man marries a woman and then divorces her or she dies before consummation, it is lawful for him to marry her daughter. They disagree about the definition of consummation with the mothers by which the prohibition of stepdaughters occurs. It is related that Ibn 'Abbās said that consummation means sexual intercourse, which is the position of Ṭāwūs, 'Amr ibn Dīnār and others. But Mālik, ath-Thawrī, Abū Ḥanīfah, al-Awzā'ī, and al-Layth agree that if he touches her lustfully, her mother and daughter are prohibited for him, and she is prohibited for his father and son. It is one of two positions of ash-Shāfi'ī.

There is disagreement where looking is concerned. Mālik said, 'When a man looks at her hair, breast, or some of her beauties for pleasure, her mother and daughter are forbidden to him.' The Kufans said, 'If he looks lustfully at her private parts, it is like touching her with lust.' Ath-Thawrī said, 'The prohibition comes about if he deliberately looks at her private parts or touches her,' and he did not mention lust. Ibn Abī Laylā said, 'She is not forbidden by looking until he actually touches her,' and that is the position of ash-Shāfi'ī. The evidence for looking bringing about a prohibition is that it is a type of enjoyment and so is like sexual intercourse. Judgments are connected to meanings not words. It is possible to say that it is a type of union through enjoyment. The look is a form of joining and encounter and enjoyment is experienced by lovers through it. Poets went to great lengths about that as in the following:

Does not night join us to Umm 'Amr? That brings us close.
Yes, she sees the crescent moon as I see it. Day is over her as it is over me.

So then how much is that the case with looking, sitting together, talking together and the pleasure of that?

The wives of your sons whom you have fathered

Ḥalā'il is the plural of *ḥalīlah* which means wife. She is called that because she stops (*ḥalla*) with her husband where he stops. Az-Zajjāj and some people believed that it is derived from *ḥalāl* (lawful) and so it means that she is made lawful. It is said that it is because each of them can undo (*ḥalla*) the waist-wrapper of his partner.

Scholars agree on the prohibition of fathers marrying after sons or sons after fathers, whether there is sexual intercourse after the contract or not, because Allah says: *'Do not marry any women your fathers married'* (4:22) and: *'the wives of your sons whom you have fathered.'* If one of them marries with an invalid marriage contract, that creates the same impediment that a sound contract would do, because an unsound contract can be agreed to be unsound or that can be disputed. If it is agreed to be unsound, then it does not oblige a ruling and it is the same whether it exists or not. If it is disputed, then the same prohibition is connected to it that is connected to a sound contract because of the possibility that it is a marriage and therefore included under the generality of the term. In this sort of case, when there is a conflict between prohibition and lawfulness in respect of private parts, prohibition dominates, and Allah knows best. Ibn al-Mundhir said, 'All reputable scholars from the various regions agree that if a man has sexual intercourse with a woman in an unsound marriage, she is unlawful to his father, son, grandfathers and grandchildren.

Scholars also agree on another issue. The purchase of a slavegirl by a man does not make her unlawful to his father or son, but if a man buys a slavegirl and touches or kisses her, then she becomes unlawful to his father and son, and I do not know of any disagreement about that. There is disagreement about whether the prohibition arises by merely looking at her without touching, and so that is not permitted because of the disagreement. Ibn al-Mundhir said, 'Nothing different to what we said is confirmed from any of the Companions of the Messenger of Allah ﷺ.' Ya'qūb and Muḥammad said, 'When a man looks at the private parts of a woman with lust, she is unlawful for his father and son and her mother and daughter are unlawful to him.' Mālik said, 'When a man has sex with a slavegirl or goes to her with that intention, even if he does not complete it, kisses her, touches her or presses her with pleasure, she is then not lawful for his son.' Ash-Shāfi'ī said, 'She becomes unlawful by touch but not a glance without touching.' That is the view of al-Awzā'ī.

There is disagreement about sexual intercourse in fornication and whether that creates the prohibition or not. Most of the people of knowledge say that if a man fornicates with a woman, marriage with her is not forbidden by that nor is marriage with her mother or daughter. It is enough that the *ḥadd* punishment is carried out on him and then he consummates with her as his wife. If someone fornicates with a woman and then wants to marry her mother or daughter, that is not unlawful for him. One group say that it does create a prohibition, and this position is related from 'Imrān ibn Ḥuṣayn and it is the position of ash-Sha'bī, 'Aṭā', al-Ḥasan, Sufyān ath-Thawrī, Aḥmad, Isḥāq and the People of Opinion. It is related from Mālik that fornication renders both the mother and daughter unlawful, just as is the case with a lawful marriage. That is also the position of the people of Iraq.

The sound position of Mālik and the people of the Hijaz is that fornication has no bearing here because Allah says: *'the mothers of your wives,'* and fornication plays no part in that. That is the position of ash-Shāfi'ī and he said because in fornication there is no dowry, *'iddah,* inheritance or paternity as there is in legal marriage, and the *ḥadd* punishment is mandatory. Ad-Dāraquṭnī related from az-Zuhrī from 'Urwah that 'Ā'ishah said, 'The Messenger of Allah ﷺ was asked about a man who fornicates with a woman and wants to marry her or her daughter and he said, "The unlawful does not make the lawful unlawful. The prohibition is created by marriage."'

Part of the argument for the other view is found in the report of the Prophet ﷺ about Jurayj in his words, 'Boy, who is your father?' and he answered that it was a certain shepherd. This would indicate that fornication makes unlawful what lawful marriage makes unlawful. So neither the mother nor the daughters of a woman are lawful to the fathers or sons of the man who fornicated with her. That is transmitted by Ibn al-Qāsim in the *Mudawwanah*, and it is also used as evidence that a female, who is the result of fornication, is not lawful to the man who committed fornication with her mother. That is well known. The Prophet ﷺ said, 'Allah will not look at a man who looks at the private parts of both a woman and her daughter,' and he did not make a distinction between lawful and unlawful. He ﷺ also said, 'Allah will not look a man who removes the covering of both a woman and her daughter.' Ibn Khuwayzimandād said, 'That is why we said that kissing and other forms of enjoyment bring about prohibition.'

'Abd al-Malik ibn Mājishūn said, 'She is lawful. That is sound based on the words of the Almighty: *"It is He Who created human beings from water and then gave them relations by blood and marriage."* (25:54) This means sound marriage as will be explained in *al-Furqān*. The manner in which one holds to the *ḥadīth* about those two questions is that the Prophet ﷺ related that Jurayj ascribed the bastard to the fornicator and Allah affirmed his relationship by a miracle in which the infant spoke and testified to that, and the Prophet ﷺ reported that from Jurayj as praise and making his miracle known. That ascription was sound because Allah affirmed the truth and the Prophet ﷺ reported that. It confirmed Prophethood and its rulings. If it is said that, on this basis, the rulings of Prophethood and paternity proceed in inheritance, guardianship and other matters, when there is agreement among the Muslims that they do not inherit from one another, so how can this ascription be valid, the answer to that is that what we mentioned obliges this and the consensus concurs about the rulings we excepted, while the rest remain on the basis of that evidence. Allah knows best.

Scholars also disagree about sodomites in this context. Mālik, ash-Shāfi'ī, and Abū Ḥanīfah and his people say that marriage is not forbidden on account of sodomy. Ath-Thawrī says, 'If someone plays with a boy, then the boy's mother is forbidden to him.' That is the position of Aḥmad ibn Ḥanbal who said, 'When someone commits sodomy with a woman's son, father or brother, that woman is unlawful for him.' Al-Awzā'ī said, 'When someone commits sodomy with a boy who later fathers a daughter, the man is not permitted to marry her because he is the daughter of someone he has had sex with.' That is also the position of Aḥmad ibn Ḥanbal.

The phrase *'whom you have fathered'* is a specification that excludes adopted sons. When the Prophet ﷺ married the ex-wife of Zayd ibn Ḥārithah, the idolaters said, 'He has married his son's wife!' since the Prophet ﷺ had adopted him. This will be explained in *al-Aḥzāb*. The wife of a milk son is unlawful, even though there is no direct lineage, based on the consensus which derives from the statement of the Prophet ﷺ about suckling making unlawful what lineage makes unlawful.

marrying two sisters at the same time

The expression is general and includes combining them either through marriage or by virtue of the right of ownership. The Community agree that it is forbidden to include them in the same marriage contract based on this *āyah* and the words of the Prophet ﷺ, 'Do not offer me your daughters or your sisters.'

There is disagreement about two sisters when they are both slaves. Most believe that it is not permitted to combine them when ownership also entails sexual intercourse, while the consensus is that it is permitted to own them both. The same applies to marrying a woman and her daughter in the same contract. There is disagreement about a marriage contract with the sister of a slavegirl with whom one has had sexual intercourse. Al-Awzā'ī said, 'If someone has sexual intercourse with a slavegirl on the basis of ownership, he is not permitted to marry her sister.' Ash-Shāfi'ī said, 'Ownership does not prevent marriage with a sister.' Abū 'Umar said, 'If someone makes a marriage contract like a sale, he allows it. If someone makes it like sexual intercourse, he does not allow it.' They agree that on the basis of the *āyah* it is not permitted to marry a wife's sister. The literal words of the *āyah*, 'combining two sisters,' means marrying both. Therefore, stop at what they agree on and then what is correct with respect to their disagreement will be clear to you, Allah willing. Allah knows best.

The Ẓāhirī School takes an aberrant position and allows combining two sisters in sexual intercourse by virtue of ownership in the same way that it is permitted to own both of them. Their argument is based on what was related from 'Uthmān about owning two sisters: 'One *āyah* makes them unlawful and one *āyah* makes them lawful.' 'Abd ar-Razzāq mentioned it from az-Zuhrī from Qabīṣah ibn Dhu'ayb that 'Uthmān ibn 'Affān was asked about having sex with two sisters whom one owned. He said, 'I neither permit nor forbid you. One *āyah* makes them unlawful and one *āyah* makes them lawful.' The one who asked left and met one of the Companions of the Messenger of Allah ﷺ – Ma'mar said, 'I think that it was 'Alī.' – He asked him, 'What did you ask 'Uthmān about?' He told him what he had asked him and the fatwa he was given. He told the man, 'But I forbid you. If I had had a way against you, I would have made you a punitive example!' Aṭ-Ṭaḥāwī and ad-Dāraquṭnī mentioned a similar position of 'Uthmān from Ibn 'Abbās and 'Alī. The *āyah* that makes them lawful is the words of Allah: *'Apart from that He has made all other women lawful you.'*

None of the imams of fatwa pay any attention to this position because they understand that what the Qur'an means is not that and they do not believe that it is permitted to twist the interpretation. The Companions who stated that included 'Umar, 'Alī, Ibn Mas'ūd, 'Uthmān, Ibn 'Abbās, 'Ammār, Ibn 'Umar, 'Ā'ishah,

Ibn az-Zubayr and those who have knowledge of the Book of Allah. Those who oppose them deviate in interpretation. Ibn al-Mundhir mentioned that Isḥāq ibn Rāhawayh considered having sex with both of them to be unlawful and most of the people of knowledge dislike it. He said that Mālik was one of those who disliked it. There is no disagreement that it is permitted to own both of them. That same is true of a woman and her daughter.

Ibn 'Aṭiyyah said, 'It comes from the position of Isḥāq that he would stone someone who had sex with both of them and dislike is found in the position of Mālik when he said, 'When he has sex with one of them and then with the other, he stops from having sex with them until one of them is unlawful. Then the *ḥadd* punishment is not obliged for him.' Abū 'Umar said, "Alī said, "I would have made you a punitive example" and not "I would have given you a *ḥadd* punishment for fornication." That is because it is part of interpretation of an *āyah* or *sunnah*, and the man did not have sex thinking that it was unlawful, and so the consensus is that he is not a fornicator and that he erred – unless someone claims that when there is no excuse for his ignorance.' The statement from the early Companions that one can have sexual intercourse with two sisters on the basis of ownership, 'One *āyah* makes them unlawful and one *āyah* makes them lawful,' is known and recorded. So how can someone receive the *ḥadd* punishment for fornication when there is considerable uncertainty like this. Success is by Allah.

Scholars disagree about what happens when a man has sexual intercourse with one and then wants to have it with the other. 'Alī, Ibn 'Umar, al-Ḥasan al-Baṣrī, al-Awzā'ī, ash-Shāfi'ī, Aḥmad and Isḥāq said that it is not permitted until the first is no longer lawful to him by virtue of selling her, freeing her, or giving her in marriage. Ibn al-Mundhir said that there is a second position from Qatādah who says that he must just intend to prohibit the first woman to himself. If he does go near her, he then refrains from both of them until the waiting period of the first ends whereupon he can have sexual intercourse with the other. There is a third view which is that when he owns two sisters, he does not go near either of them. That is the position of al-Ḥakam and Hammād, and something like that is related from an-Nakha'ī.

The position in the school of Mālik is that when a man owns two sisters, he can have sexual intercourse with whichever of them he wishes and then refraining from the other is a trust for him. If he wants to have intercourse with the second, he must forbid himself the first by the action of giving her in marriage, selling her, freeing her, a *kitābah* contract, or long service. If he has sexual intercourse with the second without doing that, he must refrain from both of them and cannot approach either until he makes one of them forbidden and it is no longer left to his trust because he is suspect which he was not before when he had only had sex with one.

The position of the Kufans with regard to this is that ath-Thawrī and Abū Ḥanīfah and his people said that if he has sexual intercourse with one of his two slavegirls, he may not have it with the other. If he sells the first or gives her in marriage and then she returns to him, he must refrain from the other. He can have sexual intercourse with her while her sister is in the *'iddah* for divorce or being widowed, but not after the end of that period until someone else can legally have sex with her. That is related from 'Alī. They said that the reason for that is that ownership which prevents having sex with the slavegirl exists in the beginning and there is no difference between her being returned to him and her remaining in his possession.

The position of Mālik is good because it is a sound prohibition in the situation and does not oblige taking the end into account. It is enough that sexual intercourse with a sister is unlawful by a sale or marriage for her to be immediately unlawful for him. There is no disagreement about emancipation because in it he has no disposal at all. As for a slavegirl with a *kitābah*, if she cannot fulfil it, she reverts to being his property.

If a man has sex with a slavegirl and then marries her sister, there are three positions about the marriage. In the third position, we find in the *Mudawwanah* that he must stay away from her when there is a marriage contract until one of them is unlawful even though there is dislike for this marriage since it is a contract for a situation in which sexual intercourse is not permitted. This indicates that ownership does not prevent marriage, as was already mentioned from ash-Shāfi'ī. There is another view about this matter, which is that the marriage is not contracted, and that is the idea that al-Awzā'ī expressed. Ashhab said in *Kitāb al-Istibrā'* that a marriage contract with one sister makes sexual intercourse with the other one unlawful.

Scholars agree that when a man divorces a wife with a revocable divorce, he cannot marry her sister or a fourth wife until she has completed her *'iddah*. They disagree about what happens when it is an irrevocable divorce. Some say that he cannot marry her sister or a fourth wife until the end of her *'iddah*, and that is related from Zayd ibn Thābit and is the position of Mujāhid, 'Aṭā' ibn Abī Rabāḥ, an-Nakhā'ī, Sufyān ath-Thawrī, Aḥmad ibn Ḥanbal and the People of Opinion. Another group said that he can do that, and that is related from 'Aṭā' and also from Zayd ibn Thābit. It is the position of Sa'īd ibn al-Musayyab, al-Ḥasan, al-

Qāsim, 'Urwah ibn az-Zubayr, Ibn Abī Laylā, ash-Shāfi'ī, Abū Thawr and Abū 'Ubayd. Ibn al-Mundhir said, 'I reckon that it is the position of Mālik.'

except for what may have already taken place

It is possible that this refers to women their fathers married, and there is another possible idea which is permission for what has already taken place. It is that combining sisters in the Jāhiliyyah was a valid marriage. When Islam came, according to what Mālik and ash-Shāfi'ī said, a man had to choose between the two sisters. The contracts were not according to Islam and what is demanded by the Sharī'ah, whether it was a single contract which combined them or they were combined in two separate contracts. Abū Ḥanīfah voided their marriage if they were married in the same contract.

Hishām ibn 'Abdullāh related that Muḥammad ibn al-Ḥasan said, 'The people in the *Jāhiliyyah* recognised as forbidden all the women who were mentioned in this *āyah* except for two: marrying a father's wife and marrying two sisters at the same time. Allah knows best.

وَالْمُحْصَنَاتُ مِنَ النِّسَاءِ إِلَّا مَا مَلَكَتْ أَيْمَانُكُمْ كِتَابَ اللَّهِ عَلَيْكُمْ
وَأُحِلَّ لَكُم مَّا وَرَاءَ ذَٰلِكُمْ أَن تَبْتَغُوا بِأَمْوَالِكُم مُّحْصِنِينَ
غَيْرَ مُسَافِحِينَ فَمَا اسْتَمْتَعْتُم بِهِ مِنْهُنَّ فَآتُوهُنَّ أُجُورَهُنَّ فَرِيضَةً
وَلَا جُنَاحَ عَلَيْكُمْ فِيمَا تَرَاضَيْتُم بِهِ مِن بَعْدِ الْفَرِيضَةِ إِنَّ اللَّهَ كَانَ
عَلِيمًا حَكِيمًا ﴿٢٤﴾

24 And also married women, except for those you own as slaves. This is what Allah has prescribed for you. Apart from that He has made all other women lawful for you provided you seek them with your wealth in marriage and not in fornication. When you consummate your marriage with them give them their prescribed dowry. There is nothing wrong in any further agreement you might come to after the dowry has been given. Allah is All-Knowing, All-Wise.

And also married women

This is added to the prohibited women and those mentioned before. *Tahaṣṣun* means 'securing'. *Ḥiṣn* (stronghold) comes from it because it protects, as is *ḥiṣān* for a horse because it protects its rider from destruction. *Ḥasān* is a chaste women because she guards herself from destruction. The verb is *ḥaṣanat*, *taḥṣunu*, and she is *ḥaṣān*. It is like the verb *jabunat* (to be cowardly) and she is *jabān*. Ḥassān said in describing 'Ā'ishah:

Chaste (*ḥaṣān*), honourable, free of suspicion,
morning finds her free from having eaten the flesh of chaste women.

The verbal nouns are *ḥaṣānah* and *ḥiṣn*.

What is meant by '*muḥṣanāt*' here are those with husbands. '*Muḥṣinah*' also means 'free'. An example of that usage is: '*Free women (*muḥṣanahāt*) from among the believers and free women (*muḥṣanahāt*) of those given the Book.*' (5:5) It can also mean 'chaste' as in Allah's words: '*as married/chaste women, not in fornication.*' (4:25) 'Chaste' means prevented from indecency and freedom prevents a free woman from doing what slaves do. Allah says in *Surah an-Nur*: '*...those who make accusations against chaste/free women*' (24:4). This refers to free women, because in the Jāhiliyyah slave-girls were known for fornication. Do you not see what Hind bint 'Uqbah said to the Prophet ﷺ when she gave allegiance to him? She said, 'Does a free woman fornicate?' Having a husband also prevents her from marrying another husband. The basis root of the verb means prevention as we already mentioned.

The term *iḥṣān* is used in Islam because it protects and prevents. It comes in the Sunnah and the Prophet ﷺ said, 'Granting security precludes slaying without warning.' Part of that is the words of al-Hudhalī:

Umm Mālik, it is not like the treaty with the house,
but it includes lives and chains.

A poet said:

She said. 'Come to conversation!'
I said, 'No, Allah and Islam refuse you.'

Suḥaym said:

White hair and Islam are enough of a prohibiter for a man.

If this is confirmed, scholars disagree about the interpretation of this *āyah*. Ibn 'Abbās, Abū Qilābah, Ibn Zayd, Makḥūl, az-Zuhrī, and Abū Sa'īd al-Khudrī said that it means captured women with husbands, in other words such women are forbidden except those you own by capture from the abode of war. Such women are lawful for the person who receives them in his share of the booty. Ash-Shāfi'ī says that capture cuts off the tie of marriage. Ibn Wahb and Ibn 'Abd al-Ḥakam said that, and that is reported from Mālik, and Ashhab also said that.

That is indicated by what Muslim reports in his *Ṣaḥīḥ* from Abū Sa'īd al-Khudrī that in the Battle of Ḥunayn the Messenger of Allah ﷺ sent an army to Awṭās and they fought the enemy and defeated them and took captives. Some of the Companions of the Prophet ﷺ refrained from sexual intercourse with them because they had husbands among the idolaters and so Allah revealed this to show that they were lawful for them after they had completed their *'iddah*. It is a sound clear text that the *āyah* was revealed about the Companions who refrained from sexual intercourse with captives who had husbands and so Allah sent down this *āyah* to answer that. That is what is stated by Mālik, Abū Ḥanīfah and his people, ash-Shāfi'ī. Aḥmad, Isḥāq and Abū Thawr. That is the sound position, Allah willing.

They disagree about the *istibrā'* (waiting period for slavegirls). Al-Ḥasan said that the Companions of the Messenger of Allah ﷺ used to wait one menstrual period in the case of a captive. That is related from the *ḥadīth* of Abū Sa'īd al-Khudrī about the captives of Awṭās: 'Do not have sexual intercourse with a pregnant woman until she has given birth nor one who is not pregnant until she has menstruated.' He said that the prior marriage had no bearing and she observes the *'iddah* as a slave, although al-Ḥasan ibn Ṣāliḥ says that she should observe an *'iddah* of two periods if she has a husband in the abode of war. All scholars agree that she must observe *istibrā'*, and if she has no husband, the waiting period is one menstrual period.

The well-known position in the school of Mālik is that there is no difference between whether a couple are captured together or separately. Ibn Bukayr reports that if they are captured together and the man lives, the marriage is affirmed. In that he thought that his survival was based on being owned because he has a contract and his wife is part of what he owns and so they are not parted. That is the position of Abū Ḥanīfah and ath-Thawrī, and Ibn al-Qāsim said that and reported it from Mālik. The sound position is the first because of what we mentioned and because Allah says: *'except for those you have taken in war'*. So ownership is what has an effect and the ruling is connected to it in general and by causation unless there is something specified by evidence.

There is a second view expressed about the *āyah* taken by 'Abdullāh ibn Mas'ūd, Sa'īd ibn al-Musayyab, al-Ḥasan ibn Abī-l-Ḥasan, Ubayy ibn Ka'b, Jābir ibn 'Abdullāh and Ibn 'Abbas, as transmitted by 'Ikrimah. It is that what is meant are women with husbands: they are unlawful to you unless a man buys a married slavegirl and then her sale constitutes her divorce. Giving her away as *ṣadaqah* constitutes her divorce as does her being inherited. Ibn Mas'ūd said, 'If a slavegirl who has a husband is sold, then her buyer is more entitled to her, as is the case with someone captured. All of that obliges separation between her and her husband.' They said, 'When that is the case, then the slavegirl must be sold to bring about her divorce because the private parts of two are forbidden in one situation according to the consensus of the Muslims.

This is refuted by the *ḥadīth* of Barīrah because 'Ā'ishah purchased Barīrah and set her free. Then she informed the Prophet ﷺ. Barīrah had a husband and the consensus is that she was given a choice about remaining married to her husband Mughīth after 'Ā'ishah had purchased her and set her free. This is evidence that the emancipation of a slavegirl is not a divorce. That is the position of most of the *fuqahā'* of all regions among the People of Opinion and the People of Hadith. The divorce is up to her. Some of them argue by the general nature of the words of the *āyah* and make it analogous to captives. What we mentioned about the *ḥadīth* of Barīrah defines it and refutes that: that is particular to captured women based on the *ḥadīth* of Abū Sa'īd. That is correct and the truth, Allah willing.

There is a third position reported by ath-Thawrī from Mujāhid from Ibrāhīm that Ibn Mas'ūd said that it is about women with husbands from among the Muslims and idolaters. 'Alī ibn Abī Ṭālib said, 'Women with husbands among the idolaters.' We find in the *Muwaṭṭā'*: 'Sa'īd ibn al-Musayyab said, "The *muḥṣanāt* among women are those who have husbands."' That referred to the fact that Allah has made fornication unlawful. One group said that *muḥṣanāt* in this *āyah* means chaste women and they are called *muḥṣanāt* whether or not they have husbands since the words demand that.

except for those you own as slaves.

The literal Arabic is '*what your right hands own*', which means by marriage or purchase. This is the position of Abu-l-'Āliyah, 'Abīdah as-Salmānī, Ṭāwūs, Sa'īd ibn Jubayr and 'Aṭā'. 'Abīdah reported from 'Umar that they included marriage under ownership of the right hand, and so it includes those with whom you have the bond of marriage. So the *āyah* means 'those whom you own through the bond of marriage and those you own as slaves through purchase'. So it is as if there is possession in both cases. Everything outside of these two categories is fornication. This is a good position.

Ibn 'Abbās said, '*Muḥṣanāt* are chaste women of the Muslims and People of the Book.' Ibn 'Aṭiyyah says that, on this basis, it refers to the prohibition of fornication. Aṭ-Ṭabarī reported that a man asked Sa'īd ibn Jubayr, 'Do you not see that when Ibn 'Abbās was asked about this *āyah*, he did not say anything about it?' Sa'īd said, 'Ibn 'Abbās did not know it.' He also reported that Mujāhid said, 'If I had known someone who could explain this *āyah* to me, I would have beaten camels to reach him.' Ibn 'Aṭiyyah said, 'I do not know how he attributed this position to Ibn 'Abbās nor what led Mujāhid to say that.'

This is what Allah has prescribed for you.

The prohibition of these women was prescribed for you by Allah. *'Unlawful for you'* means 'Allah has prescribed for you.' Az-Zajjāj and the Kufans said that it is in the accusative for instigation (*ighrā'*) and means: 'Cling to the Book of Allah' or 'The Book of Allah is prescribed for you.' There is some disagreement about it which Abū 'Alī mentioned. Grammatically, in the case of 'instigation', it is not permitted for the noun in the accusative to precede the particle. This is true when the noun is connected to *'alā*, but when an elided verb is implied, then it is permitted. It can also be in the nominative, meaning: 'This is the Book of Allah and what it makes obligatory.'

Abū Ḥaywah and Muḥammad ibn as-Samayfa' recited *'kataba'llāh'* based on the past tense of the verb whose subject is the name of Allah Almighty. It means: 'Allah has prescribed for you the prohibition He recounted.' 'Abīdah as-Salmānī and others said that His words indicate what is confirmed in the Qur'an when He says: *'two, three or four.'* (4:3). This is unlikely. What is apparent is that His words indicate the prohibition against what the Arabs used to do.

Apart from that He has made all other women lawful for you

Ḥamzah, al-Kisā'ī and 'Āṣim in the variant of Hafṣ read *'uḥilla'* (are made lawful), referring to *'Unlawful to you,'* while the rest read *'aḥalla'* (He has made lawful), referring back to *'prescribed for you.'* This would demand that only those women mentioned are unlawful, but this is not the case. Allah has forbidden others on the tongue of His Messenger ﷺ who are not mentioned in the *āyah*, and they are added to them, since Allah says: *'Whatever the Messenger gives you you should accept and whatever he forbids you you should forgo.'* (59:7) Muslim and others reported that the Messenger of Allah ﷺ said, 'Do not marry a woman together with her paternal aunt or a woman together with her maternal aunt.' Ibn Shihāb said, 'We think the great aunt is in the same position.' It is also said that that prohibition is taken from the *āyah* itself because Allah forbade two sisters at the same time, and marrying a woman and her aunt comes under the same heading, or it is because the maternal aunt has the meaning of a mother and paternal aunt. The sound position is the first because the Book and the *Sunnah* are like a single thing. It is as if He were saying, 'I have made lawful to you what is other than what We have mentioned in the Book, and I have completed the clarification of what is apart from that on the tongue of Muḥammad ﷺ.'

The view of Ibn Shihāb is: 'We think that the paternal and maternal aunts of a woman's father are in the same position. That is the case because the paternal and maternal aunts are undefined. That is because paternal aunt is a term for any female who shares with your father, fully or partially, and the same is true of maternal aunts as we made clear. We find in the *Muṣannaf* of Abū Dāwūd and elsewhere from Abū Hurayrah that the Messenger of Allah ﷺ said, 'Do not marry a woman when you are already married to her paternal aunt, nor a paternal aunt when already married to her brother's daughter, nor a woman when already married to her maternal aunt, nor a maternal aunt when already married to her sister's daughter. Do not marry the elder while married to the younger, nor the younger while married to the elder.' Abū Dāwūd also transmitted from Ibn 'Abbās that the Prophet ﷺ disliked someone being married to both a paternal and maternal aunt, or two paternal aunts or two maternal aunts. 'Joining' conveys the legal nature and contains the prohibition of doing it. This *ḥadīth* agrees on the practice of being married to the two mentioned at the same time. The Khārijites permitted marrying two sisters and marrying a woman and her aunt. However, their disagreement is not considered because they left the *dīn* and because they opposed the firm *Sunnah*.

His words ﷺ about not being married to two paternal aunts or two maternal aunts are unclear to some of the people of knowledge who were confused about it, to the point that they applied it to what is not permitted or what is unlikely. They say that the meaning of two paternal aunts is metaphorical and means a paternal aunt and her brother's daughter. They are called 'two paternal aunts' in the way that you can say, 'The *sunnah* of the two 'Umars: Abū Bakr and 'Umar'. The same is true of 'two maternal aunts.' An-Naḥḥās remarked, 'This is arbitrariness whose like is almost never heard of. In addition to the arbitrariness of it, it is repetition of words without any benefit, because when the prohibition of combining a paternal aunt and the daughter of her brother, and then not combining two paternal aunts, means the paternal aunt and the daughter of her brother, it is pointless repetition. Furthermore, if it had been as he said, it would oblige that the same be said about maternal aunts. The *ḥadīth* is not like that because the *ḥadīth* forbids combining a paternal aunt with a maternal aunt.' What is obliged from the words of the *ḥadīth* is to not combine two women, one of whom is the paternal aunt of the other or the maternal aunt of the other.'

An-Naḥḥās continued, 'This follows a sound understanding. A man and his son marry a woman and her daughter. The man marries the daughter and the son marries the mother. Each of them has a daughter by their wife and so the father's daughter is the paternal aunt of the son's daughter, and the son's daughter is the maternal aunt of the father's daughter. As for combing two maternal aunts, this obliges that no one is married at the same time to two women, each of whom is the maternal aunt of the other. As for combining two paternal aunts, it must be that he does not combine two women, each of whom is the paternal aunt of the other. That would be when a man marries a man's mother who in turn marries the mother of the first man. Each of them has a daughter and the daughter of each of them is the paternal aunt of the other. This is what Allah forbade on the tongue of His Messenger Muḥammad ﷺ.'

When this is confirmed, scholars assumed that there was a good contract in the case of the one who said that it was forbidden to combine the two women in marriage. Mu'tamir ibn Sulaymān related from Fuḍayl ibn Maysarah from Abū Ḥarīz: 'Ash-Sha'bī said, "When one of the two women has a male relative in the same proximity as the other, it is not permitted for someone married to one of them to marry the other one. So being married to both of them is void." I asked him, "Who did you get this from?" He answered, "From the Companions of the Messenger of Allah ﷺ."' Sufyān ath-Thawrī said, 'We believe that its explanation is in respect of lineage, not the position of a woman and her husband's daughter who may be combined if someone wishes.' Abū 'Umar said, 'This is according to the school of Mālik, ash-Shāfi'ī, Abū Ḥanīfah, al-Awzā'ī and the rest of the *fuqahā'* of the regions from the People of Hadith and others. As far as I know, there is no disagreement about this.'

Some of the early people disliked a man to be married at the same time to the daughter of a man and his wife because if one of them had been a male, it would not have been lawful for him to marry the other. Scholars believe that there is no harm in that and what one takes account of is lineage rather than any other aspect of married relations.

Then some reports call attention to the reason for forbidding the combination of those mentioned, in that combining might lead to cutting off close relations owing to the hatred and evil that arises between co-wives because of jealousy. It is related that Ibn 'Abbās said, 'The Messenger of Allah ﷺ also forbade a man to marry a wife's paternal or maternal aunt. He said, "If you do that, you will sever bonds of kinship."' Abū Muḥammad al-Aṣīlī in *al-Fawā'id*, Ibn 'Abd al-Barr and others mentioned it. We find in the *Marāsīl* of Abū Dāwūd that 'Īsā ibn Ṭalḥah said, 'The Messenger of Allah ﷺ forbade a man to marry the sisters of his wife out of the fear of causing severance.' Some of the early generations rejected this reason and forbade combining a woman and her close relative, whether it is the daughter of paternal uncle or aunt or the daughter of a maternal aunt. That was related from Isḥāq ibn Ṭalḥah, 'Ikrimah, Qatādah, and 'Aṭā' in the transmission of Ibn Abī Najīh. Ibn Jurayj related from him that there is nothing wrong with that. It is sound.

Ḥasan ibn Ḥusayn ibn 'Alī married, on the same night, the daughter of Muḥammad ibn 'Alī and the daughter of 'Umar ibn 'Alī, and so combined two daughters of a paternal uncle. 'Abd ar-Razzāq mentioned that. Ibn 'Uyaynah added, 'In the morning the wives did not know to which of them he would go.' Mālik disliked this, but did not think that it was forbidden. Ibn al-Qāsim said: 'Mālik was asked about marrying two daughters of paternal uncles at the same time and answered, "I do not know that it is unlawful." He was asked, "Do you dislike it?" He replied, "Some people are fearful regarding it."' Ibn al-Qāsim stated, 'It is lawful and there is no harm in it.' Ibn al-Mundhir said, 'I do not know of anyone who considers such a marriage invalid.' The two are included in the sum of what is permitted in marriage, not outside of it by the Book, Sunnah or consensus. The same is true of combining two daughters of paternal aunts or two daughters of maternal aunts.

As-Suddī said that the words: '*...apart from that He has made all other women lawful for you*' refers to sexual activity other than vaginal. It is said that it means that female relatives other than these are lawful for you. Qatādah said that it refers to slaves in particular.

provided you seek them with your wealth in marriage and not in fornication.

The expression covers both marriage and purchase. The particle '*an*' is in the accusative as an appositive for *mā*. According to the reading of Ḥamzah, it is in the nominative, and it is possible that it means: 'because (*li*)' or 'through (*bi*)' and the participles are elided and so it is in the accusative. '*In marriage*' is in the accusative for the *ḥāl*. It means being free of fornication. The word *safāḥ* means fornication, taken from *safḥ*, which is the spilling of water. An example of it can be seen from the words of the Prophet ﷺ when he heard the tambourines at a wedding, 'This is marriage, not fornication (*safāḥ*) nor secret marriage.'

It is said that the words of the *āyah* here can have two meanings. We have mentioned the first, which is chastity (*iḥṣān*) by the marriage contract, meaning: 'Seek sexual pleasure with your wealth in marriage, not fornication.' So the meaning is general. It is also possible that '*muḥṣinīn*' means that the women have this quality, implying marry them provided they are chaste. The first is more appropriate because, whenever possible, the *āyah*s are taken in a general way and the second meaning would also result in a fornicatress not being lawful to marry, and that is contrary to consensus.

Allah allowed access to private parts through *ḥalāl* wealth, even if the details of that are not spelled out. When sexual gratification is obtained without *ḥalāl* wealth, then the permission is not granted, because it is without the condition which allows it, as is the case when someone makes any contract based on wine or pigs or anything else that is not sound. It refutes the position of Aḥmad that emancipation can constitute a dowry, because then there is no handing over of wealth since it is merely a cancellation of ownership. If the husband does not give the woman anything, he is not entitled to anything. He has simply destroyed his property and it is not a dowry. This is clear since Allah says: *'Give women'* (4:4). That command is an obligation, so granting freedom is not sound as dowry. He also says: *'If they are happy to give you some of it, make use of it'* (4:4), and it is impossible to do that with emancipation. So a dowry is only possible with actual wealth as Allah makes clear here.

There is disagreement about the amount involved. Ash-Shāfi'ī makes it undefined and says that any amount is permitted as a dowry, and that is sound. That is reinforced by what the Prophet ﷺ says in the *ḥadīth* of the woman who gave herself when he mentioned, 'even an iron ring' and 'marry the unmarried.' It was asked, 'What is the tie between them, Messenger of Allah?' He said ﷺ, 'What the families agree upon, even if it is a stick of arak.' Abū Sa'īd al-Khudrī said, 'We asked the Messenger of Allah ﷺ about the dowry of women and he said, "It is what her family agree to."' Jābir reported that the Prophet ﷺ said, 'If a man gives a woman a handful of food, that makes her lawful.' Ad-Dāraquṭnī transmitted it in the *Sunan*.

Ash-Shāfi'ī said, 'Everything that has a price, or for which there is a wage, is permitted as a dowry.' This is the position of the majority of the people of knowledge. A group of the People of Hadith among the people of Madīnah and others allow any dowry, whether it is a little or a lot. That is the position of 'Abdullāh ibn Wahb, Mālik's companion, and Ibn al-Mundhir and others preferred it. Sa'īd ibn al-Musayyab said, 'If he gives her a whip, she is lawful for him.' He married his daughter to 'Abdullāh ibn Wadā'ah for two dirhams. Rabī'ah said marriage is permitted on the basis of one dirham. Abu-z-Zinād said, 'It is that with which both families are content.'

Mālik said, 'There is no dowry less than a quarter of a dinar or three dirhams.' One of our people said that the reason for that is that it is the same as the least for which the hand is cut off, because the genitals are a limb as the hand is a limb, and it is made lawful by a certain amount of money. That is a quarter of a dinar or three dirhams. Mālik made the genitals analogous to the hand. Abū 'Umar said, 'Abū Ḥanīfah preceded him in this and made the dowry analogous to cutting off the hand, and the hand is only cut off for a gold dinar or ten dirhams in measure. He believes that there is no dowry less than that. That is the position of most of his companions and the people of his school in respect of the amount for which the hand is cut off, not for the minimum dowry. When Mālik said that there is no dowry less than a quarter of a dinar, ad-Darāwardī said to him, 'You have lessened the amount, Abū 'Abdullāh,' in other words followed the path of the people of Iraq.'

As evidence for this Abū Ḥanīfah used the *ḥadīth* from Jābir in which the Messenger of Allah ﷺ said, 'There is no dowry less than ten dirhams.' Ad-Dāraquṭnī transmitted it. Its *isnād* contains Mubashshir ibn 'Ubayd who is abandoned. It is related from Dāwūd al-Awdī that ash-Sha'bī related that 'Alī said, 'There is no dowry less than ten dirhams.' Aḥmad ibn Ḥanbal said, 'Ghiyāth ibn Ibrāhīm dictated to Dāwūd al-Awdī from ash-Sha'bī. An-Nakha'ī said that it is forty dirhams; Sa'īd ibn Jubayr said fifty dirhams and Ibn Shubrumah said five. Ad-Dāraquṭnī related from Ibn 'Abbās that 'Alī ؓ said, 'There is no dowry less than five dirhams.'

When you consummate your marriage with them give them their prescribed dowry

Consummation is enjoyment. The word '*ujūrahunna*' (lit. their wages) here means their dowry. The dowry is called a wage because it is the wage for enjoyment as it is to legalise the enjoyment of the private parts. Since it is a benefit, it is called a wage. Scholars disagree about whether the contract is about the body of the woman, sexual use or making lawful. It is clear that all three aspects are involved, and Allah knows best. Scholars disagree about the meaning of the *āyah*. Al-Ḥasan, Mujāhid and others said the meaning is, 'When you enjoy and have sexual intercourse with women in sound marriage, give them their dowries.' So one act of sexual intercourse obliges the payment of the full dowry if it is specified, or a suitable dowry if it is not specified.

If the marriage is invalid, transmissions from Mālik vary about whether the woman is entitled to a suitable dowry or the specified one. He said once that it is the specified dowry, and that is his apparent position. That is because what they agreed to is clear. There is *ijtihād* regarding a suitable dowry and they must consult what they are certain about because there is no entitlement to property based on doubt. One aspect of 'a suitable dowry' is that the Prophet ﷺ said, 'If a woman marries without the permission of her guardian, her marriage is invalid. If it is consummated, she receives a suitable dowry which would allow intercourse with her.'

Ibn Khuwayzimandād said that it is not permitted to apply the *āyah* to the permission for *mut'ah* (temporary marriage) because the Prophet ﷺ forbade the *mut'ah* marriage and prohibited it, and because Allah says: *'Marry them with their owners' permission,'* (4:25) and it is known that marriage with the permission of the families is refers to legal marriage with a guardian and two witnesses. The *mut'ah* is not like that. The majority say that *mut'ah* marriage existed at the beginning of Islam and then the Prophet ﷺ forbade it. Ibn 'Abbās, Ubayy and Ibn Jubayr recited, 'When you consummate your marriage with them to a fixed term…' and then the Prophet ﷺ forbade it.

Sa'īd ibn al-Musayyab said that *mut'ah* was abrogated by the *Āyah* of Inheritance because *mut'ah* entailed no inheritance. 'Ā'ishah and al-Qāsim ibn Muḥammad said, 'It was forbidden and abrogated in the Qur'an by Allah's words: "*…those who guard their private parts – except from their wives or those they own as slaves, in which case they are not blameworthy.*" (23:5) *Mu'tah* is neither marriage nor ownership.' Ad-Dāraquṭnī reported that 'Alī ibn Abī Ṭālib said, 'The Messenger of Allah ﷺ forbade *mut'ah* and said, "It was for the one who had no means to marry. When marriage, divorce, *'iddah* and inheritance between the husband and wife were revealed, it was abrogated."'

It is reported that 'Alī said, 'The fast of Ramaḍān abrogated every fast. Zakāt abrogated every *ṣadaqah*. Divorce, *'iddah* and inheritance abrogated *mut'ah*. Sacrifices abrogated every slaughter.' Ibn Mas'ūd said, '*Mu'tah* was abrogated by divorce, *'iddah* and inheritance.' Ibn 'Abbās said, '*Mu'tah* was only a mercy from Allah Almighty to His slaves. Were it not for 'Umar's prohibition of it, only a wretch would fornicate.' Scholars disagree about how often it was allowed and abrogated. In *Ṣaḥīḥ Muslim*, 'Abdullāh said, 'We used to go on expeditions with the Messenger of Allah ﷺ and had no women. We said, "Shall we castrate ourselves?" He forbade us that and then he allowed us to marry a woman for a price for a term.' In his *Ṣaḥīḥ* Abū Ḥātim al-Bustī said that the words 'Shall we castrate ourselves' is evidence that the *mut'ah* was forbidden before it was allowed. If it had not been forbidden, they would not have asked this. Then it was forbidden to them in the year of Khaybar and then allowed in the year of the Conquest and then forbidden after three days and now remains forbidden until the Day of Rising.

Ibn al-'Arabī remarks that *mut'ah* is one of the odd things in the Sharī'ah because it was allowed at the beginning of Islam, then forbidden at Khaybar and then allowed in the Awṭās expedition and then forbidden again after that. The only thing similar in the Sharī'ah is the question of the *qiblah* because abrogation also occurred twice in respect of that. Some combine the paths of the transmission of hadiths about it and say that there were seven times. Ibn Abī 'Amrah related that it was at the beginning of Islam. Salamah ibn al-Akhwa' related that it was in the year of the Awṭās expedition. 'Alī related that it was forbidden in the year of Khaybar. Ar-Rabī' ibn Sabrah related that it was allowed in the year of the Conquest of Makkah. All these paths of transmission in *Ṣaḥīḥ Muslim* and elsewhere from 'Alī report that it was forbidden in the Tabūk expedition. Isḥāq ibn Rāshid related it from az-Zuhrī from 'Abdullāh ibn Muḥammad ibn 'Alī from his father from 'Alī. Isḥāq ibn Rāshid is not corroborated in this transmission from Ibn Shihāb. Abū 'Umar stated that.

We find in the *Muṣannaf* of Abū Dāwūd from ar-Rabī' ibn Sabrah that it was forbidden in the Farewell Hajj. Abū Dāwūd believed that this is the soundest of what is related about that. 'Amr said that al-Ḥasan said, 'The *mut'ah* was only allowed for three days in the Fulfilled *'Umrah*, not before or after.' That is also related from Sabrah. These are seven instances in which it was either made lawful or unlawful.

Abū Ja'far aṭ-Ṭaḥāwī said, 'All of those who related permission for it from the Prophet ﷺ reported that it was on a journey and the prohibition was connected to it after that journey. No one reported that it was while he was resident. That is like what was related from Ibn Mas'ūd.' As for what is related from Sabrah about the Prophet ﷺ permitting it during the Farewell Hajj, it is outside of all the meanings. We consider this to be deviation and have only found it transmitted by 'Abd al-'Azīz ibn 'Umar ibn 'Abd al-'Azīz alone. Ismā'īl ibn 'Ayyāsh related it from 'Abd al-'Azīz ibn 'Umar ibn 'Abd al-'Azīz and he mentioned that it was during the conquest of Makkah when they complained about being spouseless and he allowed them that during it. It is impossible for them to have complained about being spouseless in the Farewell Hajj because they were performing hajj with their wives and it was possible to marry wives in Makkah. That was not the case in the earlier expeditions mentioned. It is possible that it was the custom of the Prophet ﷺ to repeat that during his expeditions and in gathering places. He mentioned its prohibition in the Farewell Hajj because people gathered in it to listen to him when they had not before, and he stressed it so that no one would be in doubt and suppose that it was lawful and because the people of Makkah used to practise it often.

Al-Layth ibn Sa'd related from Bukayr ibn al-Ashajj that 'Ammār, the client of ash-Sharīd, said, 'I asked Ibn 'Abbās whether *mut'ah* was fornication or marriage. He replied, "Neither fornication nor marriage." "So what is it?" I asked. He said, "*Mu'tah* was as Allah Almighty said." I asked, "Is there an *'iddah* for it?" "Yes," he replied, "one menstrual period." "Do they inherit from one another?" I asked. "No," he replied.' Abū 'Umar said, 'There is no disagreement among scholars, early and modern, that the *mut'ah* entails no inheritance and separation occurs at the end of the term without divorce.'

Ibn 'Aṭiyyah said, '*Mu'tah* was that a man married a woman with two witnesses and the permission of a guardian for a fixed term on the basis that there would be no inheritance between them and she would be given an agreed amount. When the period ended, he had no way to her and she would observe *istibrā'* because the child was attached to him without doubt. If she was not pregnant, then she was lawful for another. An-Naḥḥās said that this is an error and there was no attachment of paternity in the *mut'ah*.' This is understood from what an-Naḥḥās said. He said that the *mut'ah* consisted of the man saying to a woman, 'Shall I marry you for a day (or the like of that) on the basis that you do not have to observe an *'iddah* afterwards, there is no inheritance between us, no divorce, and no witness to testify to that?' This is fornication and was not permitted at all in Islam. That is why 'Umar said, 'When I am brought a man who has married in a *mut'ah*, I will make him disappear under stones.'

Our scholars disagree about whether someone who contracts a *mut'ah* is subject to the *ḥadd* punishment and the child not attached to him, or whether the *ḥadd* is averted by doubt and the child connected to him, but he is excused and punished. Today the child in a *mut'ah* marriage is attached to the father according to some scholars, even though it is unlawful, so how can the child not be attributed at that moment in which it was permitted? That indicates that *mut'ah* marriage was treated as a valid marriage, but differs from it in respect of having a fixed term and lack of inheritance. Al-Mahdawī related from Ibn 'Abbās that *mut'ah* marriage is without *walī* or witnesses. There is weakness in what he related because of what we mentioned.

Ibn al-'Arabī said, 'Ibn 'Abbās used to say that it was permitted. Then it is confirmed that he retracted that. The consensus is that it is forbidden. If someone does it, the dominant position of the School is that he is stoned. Another transmission from Mālik is that he is not stoned because a *mut'ah* marriage is not unlawful. It is based on another principle of our scholars which is unusual and they hold whereas other scholars do not. It is the question of whether what is forbidden by the Sunnah is like what is forbidden by the Qur'an or not? One of the transmissions of the one of the Madinans from Mālik is that they are not the same, but this is weak.'

Abū Bakr aṭ-Ṭarṭūsī said, 'The only ones who give an allowance for the *mut'ah* marriage are 'Imrān ibn Ḥuṣayn, Ibn 'Abbās, some Companions and some of the People of the House. A poet said about the words of Ibn 'Abbās:

I say to the caravan when the stop has been long,
'Companion! Do you have the fatwa of Ibn 'Abbās?

Plump, loose-limbed, soft.
You remain until the people return.'

The rest of the scholars and *fuqahā'* among the Companions, Tābi'ūn and righteous Salaf say that this *āyah* is abrogated and that *mut'ah* is unlawful.' Abū 'Umar said, 'The Companions of Ibn 'Abbās from the people of Makkah and Yemen all think that *mut'ah* is lawful according to the school of Ibn 'Abbās. The rest of people consider it to be unlawful. Ma'mar said that az-Zuhrī said, 'People have increased their abhorrence for it until a poet said:

When the *ḥadīth* scholar sat for a long time, he said,
'Companion! Do you have the fatwas of Ibn 'Abbās?'

'Their dowry (lit. wages)' includes property and other things, so the dowry can consist of specific benefits (such as teaching a *sūrah* of the Qur'an). Scholars disagree about this. Mālik, al-Muzanī, al-Layth, Aḥmad, and Abū Ḥanīfah and his people forbid it, although Abū Ḥanīfah said that if the marriage is conducted on that basis, it is permitted. It is like a marriage in which the dowry is not specified and she receives a suitable dowry if the marriage is consummated. Otherwise, she has a gift. Ibn al-Qāsim disliked it and Aṣbagh allowed it. Ibn Shās said, 'If it occurs, it is carried out according to most scholars, and Aṣbagh transmitted it from Ibn al-Qāsim.' Ash-Shāfi'ī said that the marriage is confirmed and he must teach her what has been stipulated for her. If he divorces her before consummation, he has two views. One is that she has half the wage for teaching that *sūrah* and the other is that she has half of a suitable dowry. Isḥāq said that it is permitted.

Abu-l-Ḥasan al-Lakhmī said, 'The position that all is permitted is better.' The wage and *ḥajj* are like other properties which can be owned and bought and sold. Mālik disliked that because he preferred that the dowry be immediate, and hire and *ḥajj* are delayed. The people who hold the first position use as evidence the fact that Allah says: '*with your wealth*'. Wealth can bring things that one desires and is considered as useful. The profit from a slave in hire and teaching is not 'wealth'.

Aṭ-Ṭaḥāwī said, 'The principle which is agreed upon is that if a man hires another man to teach him a certain *sūrah* from the Qur'an for a dirham, it is not permitted, because hire is only permitted for one of two things: either for particular work, like sewing a garment and the like, or for a known period of time. If he hires him to teach a *sūrah*, that hire is neither for a known time nor known work. He is hiring him to teach and that can take a shorter or longer time, and a large amount or a small amount. So, if someone sells another his house in exchange for teaching him a *sūrah* from the Qur'an, it is not allowed for the reasons which we mentioned about hire. Since 'teaching' cannot bring about ownership of uses or particular property, it is confirmed that it cannot be used to gain rights to the private parts. Success is by Allah.'

Those who allow it use as evidence the *ḥadīth* of Sahl ibn Sa'd about the woman who offered herself. In it he said, 'Go. I have married her to you for what you have of the Qur'an.' Another variant has: 'Go. I have married her to you. Teach her some of the Qur'an.' They said, 'This is evidence of contracting marriage while delaying the dowry, which is teaching.' This is taking his words literally: 'for what you have of the Qur'an.' They say that it is *bā'* of substitution as in 'Take this for that.'

The words in the other variant are a simple command to teach. The context indicates that it is on account of marriage and one does not pay attention to the words of the one who says that that is honouring the man for what he knows of the Qur'an, in which case the *bā'* means 'on account of'. The second *ḥadīth* clearly states the difference. There is no evidence in what is related about when Abū Ṭalḥah proposed to Umm Sulaym. She said: 'If you become Muslim, I will marry you.' He became Muslim and she married him. There is no known dowry nobler than her dowry, which was Islam. That is particular to him. Furthermore, he did not give her any benefits in the form of teaching or anything else. The Prophet Shu'ayb married his daughter to Mūsā in exchange for herding his sheep as part of her dowry as we see in *Sūrat al-Qaṣaṣ*.

It is related from the *ḥadīth* of Ibn 'Abbās that the Messenger of Allah ﷺ asked one of the Companions, 'Have you married?' 'No,' he answered, 'I do not have the wherewithal to marry.' He said, 'Do you not have "Say: He is Allah, One"

(*Sūrat al-Ikhlāṣ*)?' 'Yes,' he answered. He said, 'A third of the Qur'an. Do you not have the Throne Verse?' 'Yes, indeed!' he said. He said, 'A quarter of the Qur'an. Do you not have: *"When comes the help of Allah"*?' 'Yes,' he answered. He said, 'A quarter of the Qur'an. Do you not have *"When the earth shakes"*?' 'Yes, indeed,' he answered. He said, 'A quarter of the Qur'an. Marry! Marry!'

Ad-Dāraquṭnī transmitted the *ḥadīth* of Sahl from Ibn Mas'ūd. It contains an addition which clarifies what Mālik and others used as evidence. In it that the Messenger of Allah ﷺ said, 'Who will marry this woman?' A man stood up and said, 'I will, Messenger of Allah.' 'Do you have any wealth?' he asked. 'No, Messenger of Allah,' he replied. He asked, 'Do you recite any of the Qur'an?' 'Yes, *Sūrat al-Baqarah* and the *Mufaṣṣal suras*,' he answered. The Messenger of Allah ﷺ said, 'I have married you to her provided that you recite it to her and teach it to her. When Allah ﷺ gives you wealth, then compensate her.' So the man married her on that basis. This is a text, if it is sound, that teaching is not dowry. Ad-Dāraquṭnī said, 'Only 'Utbah ibn as-Sakan has it. His hadiths are abandoned. *Farīḍah* is in the accusative by the verbal noun and means 'obliged'.

There is nothing wrong in any further agreement you might come to after the dowry has been given

This means any increase or decrease in the dowry. That is allowed with mutual consent. What is meant is the woman forgoing the dowry or the man paying it in full if he divorces before consummation. Some say that it refers to what they agreed to regarding an extension of the period of a *mut'ah* at the beginning of Islam. For example, a man would marry a woman for a month for a dinar and at the end of the month, he might say, 'Give me a longer term and I will increase the dowry.' It was clear that this was permitted with mutual consent.

وَمَن لَّمْ يَسْتَطِعْ مِنكُمْ طَوْلًا أَن يَنكِحَ ٱلْمُحْصَنَٰتِ ٱلْمُؤْمِنَٰتِ فَمِن مَّا مَلَكَتْ أَيْمَٰنُكُم مِّن فَتَيَٰتِكُمُ ٱلْمُؤْمِنَٰتِ وَٱللَّهُ أَعْلَمُ بِإِيمَٰنِكُم بَعْضُكُم مِّنْ بَعْضٍ فَٱنكِحُوهُنَّ بِإِذْنِ أَهْلِهِنَّ وَءَاتُوهُنَّ أُجُورَهُنَّ بِٱلْمَعْرُوفِ مُحْصَنَٰتٍ غَيْرَ مُسَٰفِحَٰتٍ وَلَا مُتَّخِذَٰتِ أَخْدَانٍ فَإِذَآ أُحْصِنَّ فَإِنْ أَتَيْنَ بِفَٰحِشَةٍ فَعَلَيْهِنَّ نِصْفُ مَا عَلَى ٱلْمُحْصَنَٰتِ مِنَ ٱلْعَذَابِ ذَٰلِكَ لِمَنْ خَشِيَ ٱلْعَنَتَ مِنكُمْ وَأَن تَصْبِرُواْ خَيْرٌ لَّكُمْ وَٱللَّهُ غَفُورٌ رَّحِيمٌ ۝

25 If any of you do not have the means to marry free women who are believers, you may marry slavegirls who are believers. Allah knows best about your faith; you are all the same in that respect. Marry them with their owners' permission and give them their dowries correctly and courteously as married women, not in fornication or taking them as lovers. When they are married, if they commit fornication they should receive half the punishment of free women. This is for those of you who are afraid of committing fornication. But being patient is better for you. Allah is Ever-Forgiving, Most Merciful.

If any of you do not have the means to marry free women who are believers, you may marry slavegirls who are believers.

Allah points out a dispensation in respect of marriage, which is marrying a slavegirl in the case of someone who does not possess the means to marry a free woman. Scholars disagree about the meaning of '*means*' (*ṭawl*) here, and there three positions regarding it. The first is that it means plenty and wealth. Ibn 'Abbās, Mujāhid, Sa'īd ibn Jubayr, as-Suddī, Ibn Zayd and Mālik in the *Mudawwanah* said that. The verb *ṭāla, yaṭūlu* is used for giving and power. Someone who has '*ṭawl*' has power over his wealth. *Ṭūl* (height) is the opposite of shortness. The meaning here, according to most of the people of knowledge, is that he is able to pay a dowry. Ash-Shāfi'i, Aḥmad, Isḥāq and Abū Thawr said that. Aḥmad ibn al-Mu'adhdhal said that 'Abd al-Malik said that it is all that is settled on for the marriage in money, goods, or delayed debt. He said that all that can be sold or hired constitutes '*means*'. He said, 'Neither the wife nor the couple nor three are *ṭawl*.' He added, 'I heard that from Mālik.' 'Abd al-Malik said, 'Because the spouse is not married by it nor is she given to another since she is not wealth.' Mālik was asked about a man who marries a slavegirl when he is someone who has means, he said, 'I think they should be separated.' He was told, 'He fears fornication.' He said, 'He is whipped.' Then he lightened that later.

The second view is that *ṭawl* means freedom. The position of Mālik varies about whether a free woman is *ṭawl* or not. He said in the *Mudawannah*, 'The existence of a free wife when a man has means does not prevent him marrying a slavegirl when he does not have enough for another and fears fornication.' What he said in the *Book of Muḥammad* would demand that a free woman is in the position of *ṭawl*. Al-Lakhmī said, 'It is the literal text of the Qur'an.' Something similar is related from Ibn Ḥabīb. Abū Ḥanīfah also said that. This means that a man who is married to a free woman is not permitted to marry a slavegirl, even if he lacks means and fears fornication, because he seeks to satisfy lust when he already has a wife. Aṭ-Ṭabarī said that and used it as evidence. Abū Yūsuf said that it is the existence of a free wife to whom he is married. When he has a free wife, he has *ṭawl* and it is not permitted for him to marry a slavegirl.

The third view is that *ṭawl* is patience and steadfastness for the one who wants a slavegirl and desires her so that he cannot marry anyone else. He can marry the slavegirl if he cannot control his passion for her and fears he will commit fornication with her, even if he has the means in terms of wealth to marry a free woman. This is the position of Qatādah, an-Nakha'ī, 'Aṭā' and Sufyān ath-Thawrī. So according to this, the words: *'those of you who are afraid of committing fornication'* refer to lack of patience. According to the first, there are two conditions for marrying a slavegirl: lack of wealth and fearing fornication, and it is only sound with both of them. This is the position of the school of Mālik in the *Mudawwanah* from Ibn Nāfi', Ibn al-Qāsim, Ibn Wahb, and Ibn Ziyād.

Muṭarrif and Ibn al-Mājishūn said, 'It is not generally lawful for a man to marry a slavegirl and it is only allowed when both conditions are met, as Allah says.' That is the position of Aṣbagh and this is reported from Jābir ibn 'Abdullāh, Ibn 'Abbās, 'Aṭā', Ṭāwūs, az-Zuhrī, and Makḥūl. It is stated by ash-Shāfi'ī, Abū Thawr, Aḥmad and Isḥāq. Ibn al-Mundhir and others preferred that. If someone has sufficient wealth for a dowry but not maintenance, Mālik said in the *Book of Muḥammad* that a man is not permitted to marry a slavegirl. Aṣbagh said that it is allowed since the maintenance of the slavegirl is up to her people when he does not join her to him.

There is a fourth position about the *āyah*. Mujāhid said that it extends marriage in this community to a slavegirl and Christian girl, even if a man is wealthy. Abū Ḥanīfah also said that, and did not make fear of fornication a condition when a man is not married to a free woman. They said that that is because wealth which will enable someone to marry a slave girl also enables him to marry a free woman, and so according to this the *āyah* is the basis for allowing marriage to a slavegirl in general. Mujāhid said that that is the position of Sufyān. He said, 'I asked him about marrying a slavegirl and he related to me from Ibn Abī Laylā from al-Minhāl from 'Abbād that 'Alī said that when a free woman marries someone when he is already married to a slavegirl, the free woman has two days to the slave's one. 'Alī did not see anything wrong with it.'

The argument for this position is the general nature of Allah's words: *'Apart from that He has made all other women lawful for you'* and: *'If any of you do not have means … This is for those of you who are afraid of committing fornication.'* All agree that a free man can marry four wives, even if he fears that he will not be fair. Similarly, he can marry a slavegirl even if he has means and does not fear fornication. It is related from Mālik that someone who has the means to marry a free woman can marry a slavegirl even though he has the ability to marry a free woman. That is weak in his position. He said another time that it is clearly undesirable, even if it is permitted.

The sound position is that a free Muslim can marry a non-Muslim slavegirl in any case, but a Muslim slavegirl only with the two prescribed conditions that we mentioned. *'Anat* means fornication. If someone lacks the means but does not fear fornication, then he is not permitted to marry a slavegirl. That is also the case if he has the means and fears fornication. There is another question about whether he has the means to marry a Kitābī free woman.

There is disagreement among scholars about marrying a slavegirl. It is said that if someone marries a slavegirl, it should be a Muslim girl. A believing slavegirl is better than a free idolatress. Ibn al-'Arabī prefers that. It is said that he can marry a Kitābī woman because even if a slavegirl is preferred because of her faith, the unbeliever is preferred by freedom. She is a wife. Furthermore, any children of hers are free and not enslaved whereas the child of a slavegirl is a slave. This is the course of things based on the basic principle of the School.

Scholars disagree about a man who marries a free woman while married to a slavegirl and she does not know about it. One group said that the marriage is confirmed. That is what was stated by Sa'īd ibn al-Musayyab, 'Aṭā' ibn Abī Rabāḥ, ash-Shāfi'ī, Abū Thawr and the People of Opinion. It is related from 'Alī. It is said that the free woman is given a choice when she is informed. Then there disagreement about what she is given a choice about. Az-Zuhrī, Sa'īd ibn al-Musayyab, Mālik, Aḥmad and Isḥāq said that it is about her remaining with him or being separated from him. 'Abd al-Malik said that it is about the marriage to the slavegirl being confirmed or invalidated. An-Nakha'ī said, 'When a free woman marries a man already married to slavegirl, the man must part from the slavegirl unless he has a child by her. If that is the case, they are not parted.' Masrūq said, 'The marriage to the slavegirl is invalidated because it is something permitted due to necessity, like eating carrion. When the necessity is removed, the permission is removed.'

If a man is married to two slavegirls and the free woman knows about one of them but not the other, then she has a choice. Do you not see that when a free woman is content when her husband marries a slavegirl together with her, and then is content when he marries another slavegirl and then objects when he does it again, that she can do that? That is also the case when she only knows about one of the two slavegirls. Ibn al-Qāsim said that Mālik said, 'We assign choice to the free women regarding this matter based on what scholars before me said.' He meant Sa'īd ibn al-Musayyab, Ibn Shihāb and others. Mālik said, 'Were it not for what they said, I would have said that it was lawful because it is lawful in the Book.' If the free woman is not enough for him and he needs another and is unable to pay her dowry, he is permitted to marry a slavegirl until he reaches the number of four by the literal text of the Qur'an. Ibn Wahb related it from Mālik. Ibn al-Qāsim related that his marriage is rejected.

Ibn al-'Arabī said, 'The first has a sounder proof. That is how it is in the Qur'an. If someone is satisfied with a reason that is the cause, then he should also be satisfied with the resulting effect. Is it not the case that she does not have choice because she knew that he could marry four and knew that if he could not marry a free woman, he could marry a slavegirl? Allah did not make stipulations for her as she did for herself and her knowledge is not considered to be one of the stipulations of Allah.' This is ultimate summation of this subject and fairness in it.

Muḥṣanāt means free women as is clear by the context which distinguishes between them and slavegirls. One group said that it means chaste women, but this is weak because slavegirls can have sex with him. So they permit marrying slavegirls who are People of the Book and forbid whores among the believers and Kitābīs. That is the position of Ibn Maysarah and as-Suddī.

Scholars disagree about what is permitted with regard to marrying slavegirls for a free man who does not possess the means and fears fornication. Mālik, Abū Ḥanīfah, Ibn Shihāb, az-Zuhrī and al-Ḥārith al-'Uklī said that he may marry four. Ḥammād ibn Abī Sulaymān said that he may not marry more than two slavegirls. Ash-Shāfi'ī, Abū Thawr, Aḥmad and Isḥāq said that he may only marry one slavegirl. That is the position of Ibn 'Abbās, Masrūq and a group. Their argument is Allah's words: *'This is for those of you who are afraid of committing fornication.'* This fear is removed by marrying one. The *'slavegirls'* referred to in this context must belong to someone else. There is no disagreement that it is not permitted to marry one's own slavegirl because of the conflict of rights.

'Fatayātikum' means 'slavegirls', the plural of *fatāh*. In Arabic, *fatā* is used for a slave and can also be applied to free young men. This usage is seen in the sound *ḥadīth*: 'One of you should not say, "my slave (*'abdī*)" or "my slavegirl (*amatī*)", but rather should say *"fatāya"* and "*fatātī*".' The terms are also applied to free people who are youths while, in the case of slaves, it is applied to young and old.

The term *'believing women'* makes it clear that it is not permitted to marry a Kitābī slavegirl. This is a condition with Mālik and his people, ash-Shāfi'ī and his people, ath-Thawrī, al-Awzā'ī, al-Ḥasan al-Baṣrī, az-Zuhrī, Makḥūl and Mujāhid. A group of the people of knowledge, including the People of Opinion, said that it is permitted. Abū 'Umar said, 'I do not know any of the early generations who held this position except for 'Amr ibn Shuraḥbīl who said that the slavegirls of the People of the Book have the same status as their free women.'

They said '*believing women*' is a description of excellence, not a condition that does not permit others, so this is in the same position as Allah's words: *'If you are afraid of not treating them equally, then only one.'* (4:3) If he fears that he will not be fair then he is permitted to marry more than one, but it is better that he does not do so. So here it is better that he only marries a believing woman, but if he marries another, then it is permitted. They argue based on analogy with free women. That is because Allah's words: '*believing women*', about free women does not prevent marriage with Kitābi women, and so neither do they prevent a man marrying Kitābī slavegirls.

Ashhab said in the *Mudawwanah*: 'A Muslim slave is permitted to marry a Kitābī slavegirl.' He believes that the prohibition implies that it is preferable to marry a free Muslim woman. There is no disagreement among scholars that it is not permitted for a Muslim to marry a Magian or pagan woman. Since it is unlawful by consensus to marry either of them the same holds true by analogy and reflection for having sexual intercourse with them on the basis of ownership. It is related that Ṭāwūs, Mujāhid, 'Aṭā' and 'Amr ibn Dīnār said that there is nothing wrong in marrying a Magian slavegirl on the basis ownership. That is an aberrant view to which none of the *fuqahā'* of the regions pay any attention. They said that it is not lawful to have sexual intercourse with her until she becomes Muslim. This issue was discussed extensively in *al-Baqarah.* Praise be to Allah.

Allah knows best about your faith:

This means that Allah best knows the inward matters, while you have access to the outward. All of you are the sons of Ādam, and the noblest of you in the sight of Allah is the one with the most *taqwā*. Do not spurn marrying a slavegirl if necessary, even if she is newly captured or mute or the like of that. This calls attention to the fact that the faith of a slavegirl may be better than that of some free women.

you are all the same in that respect

This means: 'You are all sons of Ādam,' or 'You are all believers.' It is said that there is a change of order in the words, meaning: 'Whoever among you cannot marry free women, should marry one another: this one to a slavegirl and this one to a slavegirl.' According to this, '*ba'ḍukum*' is in the nominative by a verb, implying, 'Marry...'

This is to make marriage to slavegirls acceptable because some Arabs disdained it and would disapprove of the children of slavegirls, criticising them and calling them 'base'. When the Sharī'ah stated that it was permissible to marry them, they knew that there was no sense in that disdain, even though a slavegirl has a lower status and it is only permitted to marry her in case of necessity, because that leads to the child being a slave and also because a slavegirl is only partially devoted to her husband because she is busy serving her master.

Marry them with their owners' permission

Both slavegirls and male slaves may only marry with the permission of their owners. That is because a slave is property and lacks authority and their entire body is owned. The difference is that if a male slave marries without his owner's permission and the owner allows the marriage, then it is permitted. This is the position of Mālik and the People of Opinion. It is also the position of al-Ḥasan al-Baṣrī, 'Aṭā' ibn Abī Rabāḥ, Sa'īd ibn al-Musayyab, Shurayḥ and ash-Sha'bī. If a slavegirl marries without her master's permission, the contract is invalid and cannot be validated by the master, because the deficiency of femininity in the slavegirl prevents her forming a contract. One group said that if a male slave marries without his master's permission, the marriage is invalid. This is the position of ash-Shāfi'ī, al-Awzā'ī and Dāwūd ibn 'Alī. They said that the permission of the owner is not allowed on the basis that he was present at the marriage because it is not valid to authorise an invalid contract. If a slave wants to marry, he is directed to the correct way to do it.

There is, in fact, a consensus among Muslim scholars that it is not permitted for a slave to marry without their owner's permission. Ibn 'Umar considered that a slave who did that was committing fornication and imposed the *ḥadd* punishment on him. This is the position of Abū Thawr. 'Abd ar-Razzāq mentioned from 'Abdullāh ibn 'Umar from Nāfi' from Ibn 'Umar, and from Ma'mar from Ayyūb from Nāfi' from Ibn 'Umar that he punished a slave of his for marrying without his permission and imposed the *ḥadd* punishment on him, separated him from the woman and invalidated her dowry. He also said that Ibn Jurayj reported from Mūsā ibn 'Uqbah from Nāfi' that Ibn 'Umar thought that a slave marrying without his owner's permission was fornication. He thought that he should receive the *ḥadd* punishment. He also punished those who had married the couple. He further said that Ibn Jurayj reported from 'Abdullāh ibn Muḥammad ibn 'Aqīl who said that Jābir ibn 'Abdullāh said that the Messenger of Allah ﷺ said, 'Any slave who marries without his owner's permission is a fornicator.' 'Umar ibn al-Khaṭṭāb said, 'It is an unlawful marriage. If he marries with his owner's permission, divorce is in the hand of the one who makes the private parts lawful.' Abū 'Umar said, 'This is the position of the *fuqahā'* of the cities in the Hijaz and Iraq. There is no disagreement that Ibn 'Abbās reported that divorce is in the hand of the owner. He was corroborated in that by Jābir ibn Zayd and a group. According to scholars, it is aberrant and expanded upon. I think that Ibn 'Abbās was interpreting the words of Allah: *'Allah does make a metaphor: an owned slave possessing no power over anything.'* (16:75)

The people of knowledge agree that when a slave has his owner's permission, the marriage is permitted. If he marries in an unsound marriage, ash-Shāfi'ī said, 'If it is not consummated, there is nothing because of it. If he consummates the marriage, then he pays the dowry when he is freed.' This is the sound position in his school. It is the position of Abū Yūsuf and Muḥammad: that he does not owe the dowry until he is freed. Abū Ḥanīfah said, 'When he consummates the marriage, she is owed the dowry.' Mālik and ash-Shāfi'ī said, 'When a slave is owned by two men and one of them gives him permission to marry and he does so, the marriage is void. If a slavegirl asks her people for permission to marry and they grant it, it is permitted, even if she does not directly make the contract but entrusts someone to make it for her.'

give them their dowries correctly and courteously

This is proof of the obligation of a dowry for marriage and that it is mandatory for slavegirls as well. The phrase *'correctly and courteously'* means according to the Sharī'ah and *Sunnah*. This means that they and not their owners are entitled to their dowries, and that is the position of Mālik. He said in the chapter on pledges: 'The owner cannot take the dowry of his slavegirl and leave her without equipment.' Ash-Shāfi'ī said, 'The dowry goes to the owner because it is recompense and, therefore, not for the slavegirl. Its basis is hiring the use of the slave. It is mentioned because dowry is obligatory in itself.' Qāḍī Ismā'īl said, 'Some Iraqis claim that when someone lets his slave marry his slavegirl, there is no dowry. This is contrary to the Book and the *Sunnah*.'

as married women (*muḥṣanāt*), not in fornication or taking them as lovers.

This means chaste women. Al-Kisā'ī recited *muḥṣināt* throughout the Qur'an except for 4:24. The rest recite *muḥṣanāt* throughout the Qur'an. The expression *'not in fornication'* means not openly fornicating because the people of the Jāhiliyyah used to have women who fornicated openly and had banners erected, *'or taking them as lovers,'* meaning as friends in lewdness. *Khidn* or *khadīn* is an intimate friend. He is someone who associates with you. A man is called '*khudanah*' when he has close friends. Ibn Zayd said that. It is said that a *musāfiḥah* is someone who openly commits fornication, someone who hires herself out for that purpose. The term '*dhāt al-khidn*' is used for a woman who fornicates in private. It is also said that a *musāfiḥah* is a woman who offers herself and *dhāt al-khidn* is a woman who fornicates with only one man. The Arabs used to censure doing fornication openly but not the taking of secret lovers. Then Islam removed all of that. Allah revealed about that: '*...that you do not approach indecency – outward or inward.*' (6:151) Ibn 'Abbās and others said that.

When they are married

This is read as *aḥṣinna* in the reading of 'Āṣim, Ḥamza and al-Kisā'ī and then means 'become Muslim'. The rest read it as *uhsinna*, meaning 'are married'. If a Muslim slavegirl fornicates, she receives half the lashes of a freewoman. The word *iḥṣān* indicates her Islam in the position of the majority, including Ibn Mas'ūd, ash-Sha'bī, az-Zuhrī and others. According to this, an unbelieving woman is not flogged when she fornicates. That is the position of ash-Shāfi'ī, according to Ibn al-Mundhir. Others said that the word *iḥṣān* indicates her marriage to a free man. If a Muslim slavegirl, who has not been married, fornicates, she incurs no *ḥadd*. That was stated by Sa'īd ibn Jubayr, al-Ḥasan and Qatādah, and it is related from Ibn 'Abbās and Abu-d-Dardā' and it is the position of Abū 'Ubayd. He said that 'Umar was asked about the *ḥadd* punishment of a slavegirl and said, 'Slavegirls have their heads uncovered outside the house.' Abū 'Ubaydah said that it means: 'She does not have a veil or head covering and goes everywhere her people send her and cannot refuse to do that and cannot prevent lewdness from occurring. That is in things like herding sheep, paying the levy and the like. Therefore, she receives no *ḥadd* punishment in case of indecency based on this understanding.'

One group said that marriage makes her *muḥṣanah*. The *ḥadd* punishment is obliged for an unmarried Muslim slavegirl by the *Sunnah*. We find in the *Ṣaḥīḥ* collections of al-Bukhārī and Muslim: 'It was asked, "Messenger of Allah, what about a slavegirl who fornicates and is not *muḥṣanah*?"' He obliged the *ḥadd* punishment for her. Az-Zuhrī said, 'A married woman received the *ḥadd* punishment based on the Qur'an and an unmarried Muslim woman receives it on the basis of the *ḥadīth*.'

Qāḍī Ismā'īl said that *uhsinna* means 'become Muslim'. That is unlikely because they were already mentioned in Allah's words: *'slavegirls who are believers'*. As for those who say that *uhsinna* means 'are married', and that a slavegirl does not receive the *ḥadd* until she has been married, they take the literal meaning of the Qur'an and I think that they did not know about the *ḥadīth*. What happens with us is that when a slavegirl fornicates and is *muḥṣanah*, she is flogged by the Book of Allah. When she fornicates and is not *muḥṣanah*, she is flogged by the *ḥadīth* of the Prophet ﷺ and not stoned because stoning cannot be halved. Abū 'Umar said, 'The literal meaning of the words of Allah is that no *ḥadd* is imposed on a slavegirl, even if she is Muslim, until she has been married. Then the Sunnah stated that she should be flogged even if she is not *muḥṣanah*. That is further elucidation.' The back of a believer is protected and only open to flogging if there is certainty, and there is no certainty when there is disagreement were it not for what has come in the sound Sunnah about flogging. Allah knows best. Abū Thawr said in what Ibn al-Mundhir mentioned, 'Those who disagree about stoning them say that they are stoned if they are *muḥṣan*. If there is a consensus, the consensus is more appropriate.'

Scholars disagree about who carries out the *ḥadd* punishment on them. Ibn Shihāb says that the past custom was that their owners carry it out for fornication unless the matter is brought to the ruler. That is demanded by the words of the Prophet ﷺ: 'When one of your slavegirls of fornicates, impose the *ḥadd* punishment on her.' 'Alī said in an oration: 'People! Impose the *ḥadd* on your slaves, both those who are *muḥṣan* and those who are not. A slavegirl of the Messenger of Allah ﷺ fornicated and he commanded me to carry out the *ḥadd* on her. She was reciting in a state of lochia and I was afraid that I would kill her if I flogged her. I mentioned that to the Prophet ﷺ and he said, "You did well."' Muslim transmitted it *mawqūf* from 'Alī. An-Nasā'ī has its *isnād* and has under the title: 'The Messenger of Allah ﷺ said, "Establish the *ḥadd* punishments on those whom you own, both those who are *muḥṣan* and those who are not."'

This is a text authorising owners to impose the *ḥadd* punishments on their slaves, both those who are *muḥṣan* and those who are not. Mālik said, 'An owner imposes the *ḥadd* punishments on his slaves for fornication, drinking wine and slander when there are witnesses to that, but does not cut off their hands for theft. It is the ruler who amputates.' That is the position of al-Layth. It is related that a group of the Companions carried out the *ḥadd* punishments on their slaves, including Ibn 'Umar and Anas. None of the Companions opposed them in that. It is related that Ibn Abī Laylā said, 'I met the surviving

Anṣār and they would flog in their gatherings any of their slavegirls who had fornicated.'

Abū Ḥanīfah said, 'It is the ruler and not the owner who carries out the *ḥadd* punishments on slaves for fornication and other things. That is the statement of al-Ḥasan ibn Ḥayy. Ash-Shāfi'ī said, 'An owner carries out the punishment for every *ḥadd* and amputates.' He cited as proof the hadiths that we mentioned. Ath-Thawrī and al-Awzā'ī said that he imposed the *ḥadd* for fornication, and that is what is demanded by the hadiths. Allah knows best. Exiling slaves was already discussed in this *sūrah.*

If a slavegirl fornicates and then is set free before her master has flogged her, he cannot carry out the flogging. The ruler does that if the matter is confirmed in his presence. If she fornicates and then marries, her owner cannot flog her since that would harm her husband. This is the position in the Māliki school if the husband is not the slave of her owner. If he is a slave of her owner, he is permitted to do that because he has the right of the ownership of both of them.

If a slave confesses to fornication and the master denies it, the *ḥadd* is obliged on the slave by his confession and no attention is paid to the denial of the master. There is a scholarly consensus on this. That is also the case with a *mudabbar, umm walad, mukātab* and someone partially freed. There is also consensus that if a slavegirl fornicates and then is freed, she receives the *ḥadd* of a slave. If she fornicates not knowing that she has been freed and then learns it, the full *ḥadd* punishment of a free woman is carried out on her. Ibn al-Mundhir mentioned that.

There is disagreement about an owner pardoning a male or female slave for fornication. Al-Ḥasan al-Baṣrī says that he can do that while others say that there is no way to avoid the *ḥadd*, just as a ruler cannot pardon someone guilty of a *ḥadd* crime if he knows that to be the case. Similarly, an owner cannot pardon his slavegirl if she merits a *ḥadd*. This is according to the school of Abū Thawr. Ibn al-Mundhir said, 'That is what we say.'

they should receive half the punishment of free women.

Here 'punishment' means flogging and 'free women' means free virgins because a woman who has been married is stoned, and that cannot be halved. Here the word '*muḥṣanah*' is used for a virgin even though she has not yet married because she can become *muḥṣanah*, just as a sacrificial animal is called that before it is actually sacrificed and a cow can be described as tilling before it actually does it. It is said that *muḥṣanāt* are married women because flogging is applied to them, as is stoning in the *ḥadīth*, and stoning cannot be halved. So it refers to half the penalty of flogging.

The point in reducing their *ḥadd* punishment is that they are weaker than free women. It is also said that it is obliged commensurate with blessing. Do you not see that Allah says to the wives of the Prophet ﷺ: *'O wives of the Prophet! If any of you commits a clear act of indecency she will receive double the punishment'* (33:30)? Their blessing was greater and so the punishment was greater. Since the blessing for slavegirls is less, their punishment is lessened.

Even though female slaves are mentioned in particular in the *āyah* and male slaves are not mentioned here, the same halved punishment of fifty lashes applies to them as well, and it is also half for slander and drinking wine: forty lashes. That is because the *ḥadd* imposed on a slavegirl reflects the reduction as a result of slavehood and male slaves are included in that because they are also owned, just as slavegirls are also included in the words of the Prophet ﷺ: 'Anyone who frees his share of a slave.' This is what scholars call analogy based on the import of the basic principle. Another example of that is the words of Allah: *'Those who make an accusation against their wives…'* (24:6) That includes husbands as will be explained in *Sūrat an-Nūr*, Allah willing.

Scholars agree that the owner does not have to sell a fornicating slavegirl. It is his choice since the Prophet ﷺ said, 'If the slavegirl of one of you fornicates and her fornication is clear, flog her with the *ḥadd* and do not blame her. Then if she fornicates again, flog her with the *ḥadd* and do not blame her. If she then fornicates a third time and her fornication is clear, then sell her, even for only a hair rope.' Muslim transmitted it from Abū Hurayrah. The literalists, including Dāwūd and others, say that it is mandatory to sell her the fourth time because he ﷺ said, 'Sell her' and 'then sell her, even for a rope.' Ibn Shihāb said, 'I do not know whether it is after the third or the fourth time. *Ḍafīr* means rope. When he sells her, he makes known her fornication because it is a fault and it is not lawful for him to be silent about it. If it is said that the intent of the *ḥadīth* is to exile the fornicatress, and if the one who is obliged to sell her is obliged to announce her fornication, then no one would buy her because she is someone who must be sent into exile, the answer to that is that she is property and she, by virtue of being property, should not be wasted because of the prohibition against wasting property. She is not exiled because that would tempt her into fornication and enable her to do it. She is not permanently confined as that would invalidate her service for her master. All that is left is to sell her. Perhaps the second master will make her chaste or be effective in preventing her from doing that. In general, the change of ownership will alter her circumstances. Allah knows best.

But being patient is better for you.

Being patient as a bachelor is better than marrying a slavegirl because it leads to the child of the marriage being a slave. Lowering the self and patience are noble qualities which are better than being spendthrift. It is related that 'Umar said, 'If a free man marries a slave, he has enslaved half of himself,' meaning that his child will be a slave. Patience is better than that in that it prevents a child from being a slave. Sa'īd ibn Jubayr said, 'Marriage to a slavegirl is close to fornication as Allah has said: *"being patient is better for you."*' In the *Sunan* of Ibn Mājah, aḍ-Ḍaḥḥāk ibn Muzāḥim said that he heard Anas ibn Mālik say that he heard the Messenger of Allah ﷺ say, 'Anyone who wants to meet Allah pure and purified should marry free women.' Abū Isḥāq ath-Tha'labī related that Yūnus ibn Mirdās, a servant of Anas, added that Abū Hurayrah said that he heard the Messenger of Allah ﷺ say, 'Free women are the goodness of the house and slavegirls are the destruction of the house (or 'the ruin of the house).'

يُرِيدُ ٱللَّهُ لِيُبَيِّنَ لَكُمْ وَيَهْدِيَكُمْ سُنَنَ ٱلَّذِينَ مِن قَبْلِكُمْ
وَيَتُوبَ عَلَيْكُمْ ۗ وَٱللَّهُ عَلِيمٌ حَكِيمٌ ﴿٢٦﴾

26 Allah desires to make things clear to you and to guide you to the correct practices of those before you and to turn towards you. Allah is All-Knowing, All-Wise.

Allah desires to make things clear to you

He is clarifying for you the matter of your *dīn* and your best interests and what is lawful and unlawful for you. That indicates the impossibility of any gap occurring in the judgment of Allah as Allah says: *'We have not omitted anything from the Book.'* (6:38) And He says after this: *'Allah desires to make things lighter for you.'* He uses '*an*' when the first statement uses *lām*. Al-Farrā' said, 'The Arabs alternate the *lām* of "in order to" and "*an*" and use the *lām* with this meaning in place of "*an*" in "I wanted to" and "I commanded that." So you can say either "*aradtu an taf'ala*" or "*aradtu li-taf'āla*" because they both concern the future. It is not permitted to say, "*ẓanantu li-taf'ala*" (I thought that you should do) because you say, "*ẓanantu an.'* We find this usage in the Revelation.' [EXAMPLES & POEM] An-Naḥḥās said, 'Az-Zajjāj was wrong when he said, "If the *lām* had meant '*an*', another *lām* would have been added to it."' [EXAMPLES & POEM] It implies: 'He desires to make things clear to you.' It is said that it means: 'Allah desires to make clear to you.' It is said that it means: 'Allah desires because of this to make clear to you.'

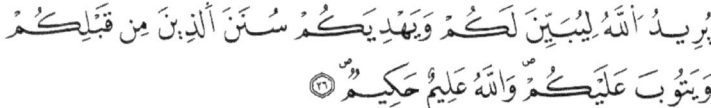

and to guide you to the correct practices of those before you

This means those before you among the People of the Truth. It is said that the word *'guide'* means 'to make clear to you the paths of those before you among the people of truth and the people of falsehood'. One of the people of reasoned thought said, 'This contains evidence that all that Allah made forbidden for us before this *āyah* was also forbidden to those before us.' An-Naḥḥās said, 'This is an error because it is a matter of meaning and Allah is clarifying the business of those before them who avoided what they were forbidden.' It can also mean that Allah is making it clear to you as He made it clear to the Prophets before you without indicating any one in particular.

It is said that the words *'Allah desires'* is the beginning and the meaning is: 'Allah desires to make it clear to you how to obey Him.' He is informing you of what was the end result of those before you when they abandoned the practices they were given. He is saying: 'If you do that I will not punish you, but I will turn to you.' Allah knows those who repent and is Wise in accepting repentance.

وَاللَّهُ يُرِيدُ أَن يَتُوبَ عَلَيْكُمْ وَيُرِيدُ الَّذِينَ يَتَّبِعُونَ الشَّهَوَاتِ
أَن تَمِيلُوا مَيْلًا عَظِيمًا ﴿٢٧﴾ يُرِيدُ اللَّهُ أَن يُخَفِّفَ عَنكُمْ وَخُلِقَ
الْإِنسَانُ ضَعِيفًا ﴿٢٨﴾

27 Allah desires to turn towards you, but those who pursue their lower appetites desire to make you deviate completely. 28 Allah desires to make things lighter for you. Man was created weak.

Allah desires to turn towards you,

Allah desires to accept your repentance and to overlook your wrong actions and He desires to make things lighter for you. It is said that this applies to all the rulings of the *Sharī'ah* and that is sound. It is said that it means to lighten things by allowing marriage to slavegirls, in other words, 'We knew you were too weak to forgo women and so We lightened things by allowing you to marry slavegirls.' Mujāhid, Ibn Zayd and Ṭāwūs said that. Ṭāwūs said, 'There is nothing that man is weaker in than the matter of women.'

but those who pursue their lower appetites desire to make you deviate completely.

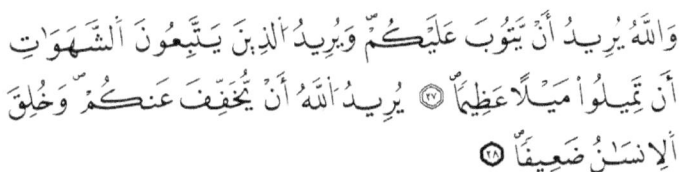

There is disagreement about who is intended by the words: *'those who pursue their lower appetites.'* Mujāhid said that they are fornicators. As-Suddī said that they are Jews and Christians. One group said that they are Jews because they wanted to follow the Muslims in marrying their father's sisters. Ibn Zayd said that it is general, and that is sounder. The meaning of '*deviate*' is to turn away from the Straight Path. Those who do that also desire those like them to do the same so that no blame will attach to them.

Man was created weak.

His desires and appetites make him deviate and his anger unsettles him. This is the most intense weakness and requires things to be made easier. Ṭāwūs said that this is only about desire for women. It is related that Ibn 'Abbās recited this and said that it means a man cannot endure not having women. Ibn al-Musayyab said, 'I am eighty-years-old and one of my eyes is gone and my sight is dim in the other and my member is dumb but I still fear the temptation of women.' Something similar is related from 'Ubādah ibn aṣ-Ṣāmit who said, 'You see me in a state in which I can only stand when supported, only eat mushed-up food, and my member (Yaḥyā said that it means the penis) has died a long time ago? Yet I am not happy to be alone with a woman who is not lawful to me. I fear that the sun might rise on me when Shayṭān has provoked me!' This was when he could neither hear nor see!

يَـٰٓأَيُّهَا ٱلَّذِينَ ءَامَنُوا۟ لَا تَأْكُلُوٓا۟ أَمْوَٰلَكُم بَيْنَكُم بِٱلْبَـٰطِلِ إِلَّآ أَن
تَكُونَ تِجَـٰرَةً عَن تَرَاضٍ مِّنكُمْ ۚ وَلَا تَقْتُلُوٓا۟ أَنفُسَكُمْ ۚ إِنَّ ٱللَّهَ كَانَ
بِكُمْ رَحِيمًا ٢٩

29 You who believe, do not consume one another's property by false means, but only by means of mutually agreed trade. And do not kill yourselves. Allah is Most Merciful to you.

do not consume one another's property by false means,

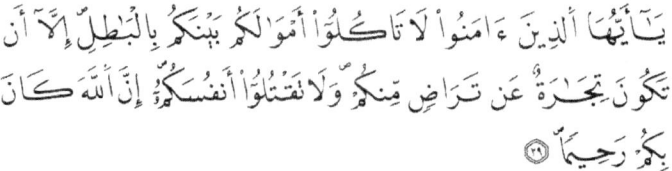

The expression *'by false means'* means without legal right. There are many aspects of that, as we will explain, and this matter was already discussed in *al-Baqarah*. An example of consumption of property by false means is the *'urbān* (deposit). It is that someone takes goods from you or rents an animal from you, giving you a dirham or more, on the condition that, if he sells it or rides the animal, it is part of the price or rental, and if he does not buy or rent, what he paid is yours. This is not correct nor permitted by most of the *fuqahā'* of the cities among the Hijazis and Iraqis because it pertains to the principle of the uncertain sale and hazard, and the consumption of property neither for recompense nor as a gift. The consensus is that it is wrong and that the transaction is void whether it occurs before or after possession. The goods are returned if they still exist or otherwise the value of the goods on the day the transaction took place. It is reported that some people, including Ibn Sīrīn, Mujāhid, Nāfi' ibn 'Abd al-Ḥārith and Zayd ibn Aslam, permitted the *'urbān* sale as described. Zayd ibn Aslam stated, 'The Messenger of Allah ﷺ allowed it.' Abū 'Umar said, 'This is not known from the Prophet ﷺ by any sound path.' There is a *mursal ḥadīth* from Zayd, which is not used as evidence.

It is possible, according to the interpretation of Mālik and the *fuqahā'* with him, that a type of *'urbān* is permitted, which is a deposit which is then reckoned to be part of the price when he chooses to conclude the sale. There is no disagreement that this is permitted by Mālik and others. In the *Muwaṭṭā'*, Mālik reports from someone he considered reliable from 'Amr ibn Shu'ayb from his father from his grandfather that that Messenger of Allah ﷺ forbade transactions in which non-refundable deposits were paid. (31.1.1) Abū 'Umar said, 'People spoke about who the reliable person was in this context. What is most likely is that Mālik took it from Ibn Lahī'ah, or from Ibn Wahb from Ibn Lahī'ah, because Ibn Lahī'ah listened to 'Amr ibn Shu'ayb and related from him. Ibn Wahb and others related from Ibn Lahī'ah. Ibn Lahī'ah was a man of knowledge, although it is said that his books were burned and that when he related after that from memory, he would sometimes err.' Some of them consider what Ibn al-Mubārak and Ibn Wahb related from him to be sound. Some of then consider all of his hadiths to be weak. He possessed vast knowledge and many hadiths, although his state was as we have described.

but only by means of mutually agreed trade.

This is a separated exception: but by mutually agreed trade. Trade consists of buying and selling as Allah says: *'But Allah has permitted trade and He has forbidden usury.'* (2:175) The word *tijārah* is recited in the nominative, meaning 'unless there is trade'. Sībawah quoted about this usage:

May my she-camel be a ransom for the sons of Dhuhl ibn Shaybān
when it is a day (nom.) of difficulties and cold.

It is also recited in the accusative and is complete because it is not complete by the noun without the predicate. So its noun is implied in it, and if you wish, you can assume it, i.e. 'property should only be the property of trade.' The *muḍāf* is elided and replaced by the *muḍāf ilayhi*. This usage was already mentioned in 2:280.

Regarding the word *'trade'*, linguistically *tijārah* implies exchange, and is also used metaphorically for what Allah gives the person in reward for his righteous actions. Allah says: *'You who believe! shall I direct you to a transaction (tijārah) which will save you from a painful punishment?'* (61:10) He says: *'...they hope for a transaction (tijārah) which will not prove profitless'* (35:29) and: *'Allah has bought from the believers their selves and their wealth.'* (9:111) All buying and selling is called that by way of metaphor like the contracts for drinks and sale goods by which desires are obtained.

There are two types of trade. There are transactions which are made while resident, without involving transportation over distance, and this involves storing while waiting [for prices to rise] which those of worth dislike and those with rank rarely do. The second is transfer of goods through travel and moving them to other places. This is better for the people of manliness and has a more general use and benefit, but more risk and uncertainty. The Prophet ﷺ said, 'A traveller and his property are in danger except for what Allah guards.' It means that he is in jeopardy. It is said that the Torah says: 'Son of Ādam! Start a journey and I will bring about provision for you.' Aṭ-Ṭabarī said, 'This *āyah* is the greatest proof of the unsoundness of what is said by ignorant Sufis who object to seeking provision through trade and crafts.'

Know that every exchange with any kind of recompense is trade, except when it is *'by false means'*. False means includes all transactions not legally permitted: usury, ignorance, or estimation of invalid goods, such as wine, pork and so on. Also outside that is every permitted contract which does not entail recompense, such as loans, *ṣadaqah*, and gifts. Contracts of gifts are permitted by other evidence which will be mentioned. These are agreed upon, as is an invitation to eat. Abū Dāwūd related from Ibn 'Abbās about this *āyah*, 'A man was forbidden to eat with other people after this *āyah* was revealed and then that was abrogated by another *āyah* in *an-Nūr*: *'There is no objection to the blind, no objection to the lame, no objection to the sick nor to yourselves if you eat in your own houses...'* (24:61) A rich man would then invite a man from his family to eat and he would say, "I am forbidden to eat from it," adding, "The poor are more entitled to it than I am." So then it was lawful for them to eat from anything over which the Name of Allah had been mentioned, and the food of the People of the Book was made lawful.'

If you buy something in the market and, before the sale, the owner tells you, 'Taste and you are within the lawful,' do not eat from it because his permission for you to eat is for the sake of the sale and the sale may not take place and then that eating will be something doubtful. If he describes it to you and you buy it and do not find it to be that, you have the option to cancel.

The majority agree on the permissibility of inequality in the exchange, as, for instance, when someone sells a ruby for a dirham when it is in fact worth a hundred. That is permitted and the proper owner is permitted to sell a lot of property for a small price. There is no disagreement about this among scholars if the seller knows its worth, just as it is permitted for someone to give a gift. They disagree about it when the person does not know the value of the thing sold. Some people say that it is permitted whether he knows it or not, provided he is sane, free and adult. Another group said that if the inequality exceeds a third, it should be rejected, but is permitted when things are close and known in sales. As for when the inequality is greatly exorbitant, then it is not. Ibn Wahb, among the Mālikīs said that. The first position is sounder because the Prophet ﷺ said about the fornicating slavegirl, 'Sell her, even for a rope.' He told 'Umar, 'Do not buy it (referring to a horse) even if he gives it to you for one dirham.' He said, 'Let people be. Allah provides for them from one another.' He said, 'Someone resident should not sell to a bedouin.' None of these statements distinguishes between a little, more than a third, or any other amount.

The word *tarāḍī* (mutually agreed) is the reciprocal form of the verb because a sale is a transaction between two people. Scholars disagree about the definition of mutual consent. One group says that it is complete when the parties separate after the transaction or one of them says to the other, 'Choose,' and he replies, 'I have chosen.' That is also after the contract and is absolute, even if they have not parted physically. A group of Companions and Followers said that. Ash-Shāfi'ī, ath-Thawrī, al-Awzā'ī, al-Layth, Ibn 'Uyaynah, Isḥāq and others said that. Al-Awzā'ī said that the choice of withdrawal is theirs as long as they have not parted except in three sales: the ruler selling booty, partnership in inheritance and partnership in trade. When there is a transaction in these three categories, the sale is obliged and there is no option to withdraw. He said, 'The definition of separation is one of them disappearing from the sight of the other.' This is the position of the people of Syria. Al-Layth said, 'The separation is that one of them gets up to go.' Aḥmad ibn Ḥanbal said, 'They always have the option as long as they have not physically parted from the place, no matter what they may have said.' Ash-Shāfi'ī also said this, and it is sound in the position according to the hadiths reported on this matter, and it is also reported from Ibn 'Umar, Abū Barzah and a group of scholars. Mālik and Abū Ḥanīfah said, 'The sale is complete when it is verbally contracted and it is obliged by that and the option ceases.'

Muḥammad ibn al-Ḥasan ash-Shaybānī said, 'The meaning of the *ḥadīth*, "The two have the option as long as they have not parted" is that when the buyer says, "I have sold to you," he can retract it as long as the buyer has not said, "I have accepted."' That is the position of Abū Ḥanīfah, and Mālik also states it. Ibn Khuwayzimandād related that. He cannot then retract. That was discussed in *al-Baqarah*. The first group use as evidence what is confirmed by the *ḥadīth* that Samurah ibn Jundub, Abū Barzah, Ibn 'Umar, 'Abdullāh ibn 'Amr ibn al-'Āṣ, Abū Hurayrah, Ḥakīm ibn Ḥizām and others related from the Prophet ﷺ: 'They both have the option as long as they have not parted or one of them said to his companion, "Choose."' Ayyūb related it from Nāfi' from Ibn 'Umar. The meaning of the words of the Prophet ﷺ, '...one of them said to his companion, "Choose"', is clarified by what is found in another transmission, 'except in the sale with an option' and 'unless they conclude the sale with the proviso of an option' and the like.

This means that after the conclusion of the sale one of them says to the other, 'Choose to have the sale carried out or voided.' If he chooses to conclude the sale, it is concluded, even if they have not parted. When Ibn 'Umar, the relator of the *ḥadīth*, made a sale transaction with anyone and wanted the sale to be concluded, he walked away a short distance and then came back. We read in *al-Uṣūl*: 'If someone relates a *ḥadīth*, he has the best knowledge of its interpretation, especially the Companions since they had better knowledge of what was said and the situation.'

Abū Dāwūd and ad-Dāraquṭnī related that Abu-l-Waḍī' said, 'We were on a journey as part of an army and a man came with a horse and one of our men said, "Will you sell this horse for this price?" He answered, "Yes." So he made the sale and spent the night with us. In the morning he went to his horse and our companion said to him, "What are you doing with the horse? Didn't you sell it to me?" He answered, "I have no need of this sale." He retorted, "You cannot do that! You sold it to me!" The people said to them, "Are you two content with the judgment of the Messenger of Allah ﷺ?" They answered, "Yes." He said, "The Messenger of Allah ﷺ said, 'The two who make a sale have the option as long as they have not yet parted.' I see that you two have not parted."' These two Companions knew the import of the *ḥadīth* and acted accordingly. This was the action of the Companions.

Sālim said that Ibn 'Umar said, 'When two of us make a trade transaction, each of us has an option to withdraw as long as we have not parted.' He said, "Uthmān and I made a transaction, and I sold him what I had at al-Wādī for what he had at Khaybar. When I had made the sale with him, then I began to withdraw out of the fear that 'Uthmān would go back on the sale before I left him.' Ad-Dāraquṭnī transmitted it and then said, 'Linguists differentiate between *faraqa* and *farraqa* (which both mean separate), saying *faraqa* is for words and *farraqa* for bodies.' Aḥmad ibn Yaḥyā Tha'lab said, 'Ibn al-A'rābī told me that al-Mufaḍḍal said, "*Faraqa* is for distinguishing between two words so that they are distinct (*iftiraqā*) and *farraqa* is for separating two bodies so that they are parted (*tafarraqā*)." So *iftirāq* is for words and *tafarruq* is for bodies.'

The Mālikīs use as evidence the prior explanation found in the *Āyah* of Debt and Allah's words: *'Fulfil your contracts.'* (5:1) These two have made a contract and this *ḥadīth* would appear to invalidate the contract. They say that separation can be verbal as is the case in the marriage contract and divorce which Allah calls 'separation' when He says: *'If a couple do separate, Allah will enrich each of them from His boundless wealth'* (4:130) and: *'Do not be like those who split up and differed.'* (3:105) The Prophet ﷺ said, 'My community will split up,' and he did not say with their bodies.

Ad-Dāraquṭnī and others transmitted from 'Amr ibn Shu'ayb who heard Shu'ayb say that he heard 'Abdullāh ibn 'Amr say that he heard the Messenger of Allah ﷺ say, 'If any man buys something from someone else, each of them has the option to withdraw until they part from where they are, unless it is a sale with an option. It is not lawful for anyone to leave his companion out of the fear that he will cancel it.' They said that this indicates that the sale has actually been concluded between them before they part because cancellation can only validly take place once a sale has been concluded. They said that the meaning of the words, 'The two parties to the sale have the option', means that they both have the option as long as the have not made a contract. When they have made a contract, then the option in it void.

The answer to this is that as for the pretext of verbal separation, that really pertains to debts as we explained in *Āli 'Imrān*. Although it is valid in some situations, it is not valid in this situation. Its explanation is that it was said, 'They told us about the words by which agreement was reached and the sale concluded and whether or not they were words by which separation is meant. If they said that it is not, then they cede and bring what is not logical because there were no other words.' If it is said that that these are the exact words, then they are told, 'How can the words by which they meet and conclude the sale be the words by which they part? This is completely impossible and unsound.'

As for the words of the Prophet ﷺ, 'It is not lawful for anyone to leave his companion out of the fear that he will cancel it,' if they are sound, they constitute a recommendation as evidenced by his words ﷺ, 'Whoever lets a Muslim rescind, Allah will undo his error.' The consensus of the Muslims is that that is lawful for the one who does it, which is contrary to the literal meaning of the *ḥadīth*. They also have a consensus that it is permitted for the sale to proceed and it is only rescinded it if he so wishes. They also agree that he can cancel it by the transmission, 'It is not lawful.' Then the aspect of this report is not recommendation. Otherwise it is void by consensus.

As for the interpretation of 'two parties' being the two bargainers, that deviates from the literal words of the *ḥadīth*. It means that the two people who conduct the sale have an option for as long as they are sitting together except for a sale in which one of them says to his fellow, 'Choose,' and he chooses. Then the option between them ends, even if they have not parted. If the option is assumed, then it means: 'except for the sale with an option. Then the choice remains after they have physically parted. The conclusion of this topic is found in the books about disagreements.

'Amr ibn Shu'ayb's words, 'I heard my father say', is evidence of the soundness of his *ḥadīth*. Ad-Dāraquṭnī said that Abū Bakr an-Naysābūrī related that Muḥammad ibn 'Alī al-Warrāq said, 'I asked Aḥmad ibn Ḥanbal, "Did Shu'ayb hear anything from his father?" He replied, "He said, 'My father related to me.'" I said, "So his father heard directly from 'Abdullāh ibn 'Amr?" "Yes," he replied, "I think that he heard directly from him."' Ad-Dāraquṭnī said that he heard 'Amr ibn Shu'ayb say, 'I heard Abū Bakr an-Naysābūrī say that he is 'Amr ibn Shu'ayb ibn Muḥammad ibn 'Abdullāh ibn 'Amr ibn al-'Āṣ. It is sound that 'Amr ibn Shu'ayb listened to his father, Shu'ayb, and Shu'ayb listened to his grandfather, 'Abdullāh ibn 'Amr.'

Ad-Dāraquṭnī transmitted from Ibn 'Umar that the Messenger of Allah ﷺ said, 'A truthful, trustworthy Muslim merchant will be with the Prophets, the truly sincere and the martyrs on the Day of Rising.' It is disliked for a merchant to swear an oath in order to promote sales or to say the prayer on the Prophet ﷺ regarding his goods, by saying, for instance, 'May Allah bless Muḥammad! How excellent this is!' It is recommended that merchants do not let their trade distract them from performing the obligatory prayers on time. They should stop trading when the time of the prayer comes so that they may be among the people of this *āyah*: *'there are men not distracted by trade or commerce from the remembrance of Allah.'* (24:37) This *āyah* and the hadiths refute those ignorant, false Sufis who dislike to seek nourishment by trade and crafts. That is because Allah has forbidden consuming provision by false means but has allowed it by trade. This is clear.

And do not kill yourselves.

The people of interpretation agree that this applies to the prohibition of people killing one another and also prohibits suicide. It also prohibits people from allowing desire for this world or seeking wealth to lead them to exposing themselves to any danger which might lead to their deaths. Another possible meaning is, 'Do not let a state of exasperation or anger bring about your death.' The prohibition applies to all these things. 'Amr ibn al-'Āṣ used this *āyah* as evidence when deciding not to wash with cold water on account of *janābah* in the Dhāt as-Salāsil expedition and the Prophet ﷺ affirmed his argument and laughed without saying anything. Abū Dāwūd and others transmitted it.

وَمَن يَفْعَلْ ذَٰلِكَ عُدْوَٰنًا وَظُلْمًا فَسَوْفَ نُصْلِيهِ نَارًا ۚ وَكَانَ
ذَٰلِكَ عَلَى ٱللَّهِ يَسِيرًا ٣٠

30 As for anyone who does that out of enmity and wrongdoing, We will roast him in a Fire. That is an easy matter for Allah.

The word '*that*' here refers to killing because it is the most immediate thing mentioned. 'Aṭā' said that. It is also said that it refers to both consuming wealth by false means and killing the self because the prohibition is about both of them. The threat is according to the prohibition. It is also said that it is general to all things that are forbidden from the beginning of the *sūrah* up to the words: '*As for anyone who does that.*'

Aṭ-Ṭabarī said that '*that*' refers to everything that has been forbidden up to the final threat except for: '*You who believe! it is not lawful for you to inherit women...*' (4:19) because there is a threat about all that is forbidden from the beginning of the *surah* except this. There is no threat after it.

The word '*enmity*' here means to exceed the limits and '*wrongdoing*' (*ẓulm*) is to put a thing in other than its proper place. The threat is connected to enmity and wrongdoing to separate it from those actions which are the result of forgetfulness or error. Both enmity and wrongdoing are mentioned although their meanings are close because the words differ and it is good in language to mention things in pairs as is frequently done in Arabic as is said:

He finds her words to be a lie and an untruth.

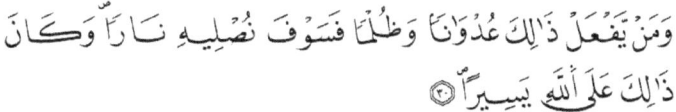

It is good to use a conjunction between them because the words are different. One says, '*bu'dan wa suḥqan*' (distant and far away). An example of that is the words of Ya'qūb: *'I make complaint about my grief and sorrow to Allah.'* (12:86) It is good because of the difference in the words.

We will roast him in a Fire.

This means that its heat will touch him. We already explained the meaning of joining these *āyahs* and the *ḥadīth* of Abū Sa'īd al-Khudrī about rebels and people of major wrong actions and there is no need to repeat it. Al-A'mash and an-Nakha'ī recited *'naṣlīhi'* from *ṣaliya* (roast at a fire). We find in a report a sheep described as *'maṣlīyah'*.

إِن تَجۡتَنِبُواْ كَبَآئِرَ مَا تُنۡهَوۡنَ عَنۡهُ نُكَفِّرۡ عَنكُمۡ سَيِّـَٔاتِكُمۡ
وَنُدۡخِلۡكُم مَّدۡخَلٗا كَرِيمٗا ﴿٣١﴾

31 If you avoid the serious wrong actions you have been forbidden, We will erase your bad actions from you and admit you by a Gate of Honour.

When Allah forbade great wrong actions in this *sūrah*, He promised, for those who avoid them, lessening the weight of their minor wrong actions. This indicates that wrong actions are divided into major ones and minor ones. This is the position of the people of interpretation and a group of *fuqahā'*. Touching and looking are definitely expiated by avoiding the major wrong actions, by His true promise and word, not because is mandatory on Him to do that. An explanation of words similar to these was dealt with earlier when the acceptance of repentance was discussed in reference to (4:17): *'Allah only accepts the repentance…'* So Allah forgives minor wrong actions by the avoidance of the major ones but with the condition that they are accompanied by something else: fulfilment of one's obligations. Muslim reported from Abū Hurayrah that the Prophet ﷺ said, 'The five prayers and one *Jumu'ah* to the next and one Ramaḍān to the next expiate what is between them if major wrong actions are avoided.'

Abū Ḥātim al-Bustī reports with a sound *isnād* from Abū Hurayrah and Abū Sa'īd al-Khudrī that the Messenger of Allah ﷺ sat down on the minbar and then said, 'By the One Who has my soul in His hand' three times. The *ḥadīth* continues, 'Then he was silent and every one of us bowed his head and wept because of the oath of the Messenger of Allah ﷺ.' Then he said ﷺ, 'There is no slave who performs the five prayers, fasts Ramaḍān and avoids the seven major wrong actions but that eight gates of the Garden will be opened to him on the

Day of Rising until they are shut.' Then he recited this *āyah.* So both the Book and *Sunnah* agree about the expiation of minor wrong actions such as a lustful glance and similar things. The Sunnah also makes it clear that the word 'avoid' does not mean total avoidance of wrong actions. Allah knows best.

The Uṣūlīs said that it is not a certainty that minor wrong actions will be expiated by avoiding the major ones. It is only a possibilty and a strong hope and firm expectation. Otherwise it would indicate that if someone avoids the major wrong actions and obeys the obligations, we would be able to declare definitively that his minor actions are forgiven, and that would be like making them allowable with no consequences. That would, in turn, lead to undoing the *Sharī'ah.* We believe that there are no minor wrong actions. 'Abd ar-Raḥīm al-Qushayrī said, 'The sound position is that all wrong actions are major ones, but some are worse than others. The wisdom lies in not distinguishing and that the person should avoid all actions which constitute disobedience to Allah.'

Whoever looks at the disobedience itself says, as one of them said, 'Do not look at whether a wrong action is small or not, rather look at the one who commits it. For him, all wrong actions are great.' It is in this vein that Qāḍī Abū Bakr ibn aṭ-Ṭayyib, Abū Isḥāq al-Isfarāyinī, Abu-l-Ma'ālī, Abū Naṣr 'Abd ar-Raḥīm al-Qushayrī and others said, 'Some wrong actions are worse than others.' One could say, for example, that fornication is minor compared to disbelief and a forbidden kiss is small compared to fornication. We do not consider that any wrong action is forgiven by the avoidance of another. All of them are great and forgiveness of their perpetrator is subject to the Divine Will, except for *shirk,* since Allah says: *"Allah does not forgive partners being attributed to Him but He forgives whomever He wills for anything apart from that."* (4:48)'

They use as evidence the reading of the *āyah* which has 'a serious wrong action' in the singular as evidence for *tawḥīd*, the serious wrong action being *shirk.* They say that when it is in the plural, it indicates all forms of disbelief. The *āyah* defines what was undefined in 4:48. They cite as evidence a *ḥadīth* that Muslim and others related from Abū Umāmah in which the Messenger of Allah ﷺ said, 'If someone takes the right of another Muslim by his oath, Allah has obliged the Fire for him and forbidden him the Garden.' A man asked him, 'Messenger of Allah, even if it something insignificant?' He answered, 'Even if it is a tooth stick.' So there is a strong threat in connection with minor as well as major wrong actions. Ibn 'Abbās said, 'Major wrong actions consist of every wrong action which Allah seals with the Fire, curse or punishment.' Ibn Mas'ūd said, 'The major wrong actions are those which Allah forbids in the thirty-three *āyahs* of this *sūrah* and that is confirmed when He says: *"If you avoid the serious wrong actions you have been forbidden."'*

Ṭāwūs said, 'A man asked Ibn 'Abbās, "What are the seven major wrong actions?" He replied, "They are closer to seven hundred than to seven, although there is no major wrong action with asking forgiveness, nor minor one with persistence in it."' Sa'īd ibn Jubayr said, 'A man asked Ibn 'Abbās, "Are the major wrong actions seven?" He answered, "They are closer to seven hundred than to seven, although there is no major wrong action with asking forgiveness, nor minor one with persistence in it."' It is reported that Ibn Mas'ūd said, 'There are four major wrong actions: despairing of Allah bringing relief, despairing of Allah's mercy, feeling safe from the plotting of Allah, and *shirk* in Allah, as indicated by the Qur'an.' It is reported from Ibn 'Umar that they are nine: taking a life, consuming usury, consuming an orphan's property, slandering a chaste woman, false testimony, disobedience to parents, fleeing from battle, magic, and heresy in the Sacred House.

Scholars in general consider major wrong actions to include gambling, theft, drinking wine, cursing the righteous early generations, turning judges from the truth, following lower desires, false oaths, despairing of Allah's mercy, a person cursing his parents by cursing another man so that that man in turn curses his parents, and causing corruption on the earth. There are many more which are mentioned in the Qur'an and in the *ḥadīth*s related by the Imāms. People disagree about their number because there are different things reported about them. I say that what is reported in sound and excellent *ḥadīth*s does not intend to restrict them to a certain number, but some of them are worse than others in respect of the harm they do.

Shirk is the worse of all since, by Allah's statement, it is not forgiven. After that comes despair of Allah's mercy because that is to deny the Qur'an in such *āyah*s as: *'My mercy extends to all things.'* (7:156) If someone says that Allah will never forgive them, they have placed restriction on His unbounded Vastness. This is when they really believe that. That is why Allah Almighty says: *'No one despairs of solace from Allah except for people who are unbelievers.'* (12:87) After that comes despair as the Almighty says: *'Who despairs of the mercy of his Lord except for misguided people?'* (15:56)

After that is feeling safe from the plotting of Allah so that one allows oneself to commit acts of disobedience while relying on Allah's mercy without any good actions to back that up. Allah Almighty says: *'Do they feel secure against Allah's devising? No one feels secure against Allah's devising except for those who are lost'* (7:99) and: *'It is that thought you had about your Lord that has destroyed so now you find yourselves among the lost?'* (41:22) Then comes killing because it is removing life and existence, sodomy, since it prevents procreation, fornication because of confusing lineages, and wine because of removing rationality, which is the source of responsibility. Then comes abandoning the prayer and the *adhān* which is ceasing to display the outward tokens of Islam. Then comes false testimony which leads to making bloodshed, illicit sexual relations and property lawful, as well as other things that entail clear harm. Every wrong action, which Divine punishment is threatened for, is major when its harm in existence is great, as we mentioned. It is great and other things are minor. This is why this section is ordered for you and precise. Allah knows best.

admit you by a Gate of Honour.

Abū 'Amr and most of the Kufans read '*mudkhal*' and so it can be a verbal noun meaning admission. It means: 'We will definitely admit you to the Garden.' It is also possible that it means a place, and so is passive. The people of Madīnah read it *madkhal*, which can be a verbal noun, stressing admission, meaning 'We will admit you by an entrance,' or it can be the name of a place and would imply: 'We will admit you to a noble place,' which is the Garden.

Abū Sa'īd ibn al-A'rābī said that he heard Abū Dāwūd as-Sjistānī say, 'I heard Abū 'Abdullāh Aḥmad ibn Ḥanbal say, "All of the Muslims will be in the Garden." I asked him, "How?" He answered, "Allah Almighty says: '*If you avoid the serious wrong actions you have been forbidden, We will erase your bad actions from you and admit you by a Gate of Honour,*' which means the Garden. The Prophet ﷺ said, 'I have stored up my intercession for those of my Community who committed serious wrong actions.' If Allah forgives everything except major wrong actions and the Prophet ﷺ intercedes for major wrong actions, what wrong action remains for the Muslims?"'

Our scholars have said that according to the people of the *Sunnah* major wrong actions are forgiven if someone refrains from them before he dies, and a Mụslim who dies while still committing them may also be forgiven, as Allah says: '*He forgives whomever He wills for anything apart from that.*' (4:48) So what is meant are those who die still committing the wrong action. If He had meant those who repent before they die, there would be no difference between *shirk* and anything else. The one who repents of *shirk* is also forgiven.

It is related that Ibn Mas'ūd said, 'There are five *āyahs* of *Sūrat an-Nisā'* which I love more than the entire world. They are: "*If you avoid the serious wrong actions you have been forbidden...*" "*Allah does not forgive anything being associated with them but He forgives...*" (4:48), "*Anyone who does evil or wrongs himself...*" (4:110), "*If there is a good deed Allah will multiply it...*" (4:40), and "*Those who believe in Allah and His Messengers...*" (4:152).'

Ibn 'Abbās said: 'There are eight *āyah*s in *Sūrat an-Nisā'* which are better for this community than everything on which the sun rises and sets: "*Allah desires to make things clear to you...*" (4:26); "*Allah desires to turn to you...*" (4:27); "*Allah desires to make things lighter for you...*" (4:28); "*If you avoid the serious wrong actions you have been forbidden, We will erase your bad actions from you.*" (4:31); "*Allah does not forgive anything being associated with Him...*" (4:48); "*Allah does not wrong anyone by so much as the smallest speck.*" (4:40); "*Anyone who does evil or wrongs himself...*" (4:110); and "*Why should Allah punish you?*" (4:147)'

وَلَا تَتَمَنَّوْا۟ مَا فَضَّلَ ٱللَّهُ بِهِۦ بَعْضَكُمْ عَلَىٰ بَعْضٍ لِّلرِّجَالِ نَصِيبٌ مِّمَّا
ٱكْتَسَبُوا۟ وَلِلنِّسَآءِ نَصِيبٌ مِّمَّا ٱكْتَسَبْنَ وَسْـَٔلُوا۟ ٱللَّهَ مِن فَضْلِهِۦٓ
إِنَّ ٱللَّهَ كَانَ بِكُلِّ شَىْءٍ عَلِيمًا ﴿٣٢﴾

32 Do not covet what Allah has given to some of you in preference to others – men have a portion of what they acquire and women have a portion of what they acquire; but ask Allah for His bounty. Allah has knowledge of all things.

At-Tirmidhī reported that Umm Salamah said, 'The men go out on expeditions and the women do not and we only have half the inheritance.' Allah revealed: '*Do not covet what Allah has given to some of you in preference to others.*' Mujāhid said that the *āyah*: '*Muslim men and Muslim women...*' (33:35) was revealed about her. Umm Salamah was the first woman who came to Madīnah in emigration in a sedan. Abū 'Īsā said that this is a *mursal ḥadīth.* One of them related it from Ibn Abī Najīḥ from Mujāhid as *mursal* that Umm Salamah said that. Qatādah said, 'In the Jāhiliyyah women and children did not inherit. When they were given inheritance and the male was given twice the portion of the female, the women wanted their shares to be the same as those of the men. The men said, "We hope that we are better than the women in the Next World by our good deeds as we are better than you in inheritance," and then this was revealed.'

Do not covet what Allah has given to some of you

Coveting (*tamannā*) is a type of desire connected to the future as regret is a type of desire connected to the past. Allah forbade the believers to covet because it constitutes an attachment of the mind and forgetfulness of the final goal. Scholars disagree about whether *ghibṭah* (positive envy) is included in that, which is that a man wishes that he were like his companion, but does not wish his companion's state to change. The majority, Mālik and others, say that *ghibṭah* is permitted. What is meant by some of them is from the words of the Prophet ﷺ, 'There should be no envy (*ḥasad*) except of two: a man to whom Allah gives the Qur'an and he stands reciting it during the night and the day, and a man to whom Allah gives wealth and he spends it the night and the day.' The meaning of 'no envy' is 'no positive envy' which is greater and better than these two things. Al-Bukhārī called attention to this in a chapter entitled: 'Envy for knowledge and wisdom.'

Al-Muhallab said, 'Allah makes it clear in this *āyah* that it is not permitted to covet, and that means coveting the goods of this world and the like.' Ibn 'Aṭiyyah said, 'As for having great desire for righteous actions, that is good. If a man hopes from something from Allah which is not accompanied by anything which we have mentioned, that is permitted. We find in a *ḥadīth*: "I wish that I could be brought to life and then killed again."' This *ḥadīth* in *Ṣaḥīḥ Bukhārī* indicates wishing for good and righteous actions and the desire for that. It mentions the superiority of martyrdom over all other good actions because the Prophet ﷺ wished for it rather than anything else because of its high station and the honour granted to its people and the fact that Allah provides for them as he said ﷺ, 'The bite [of poisoned lamb] that I took at Khaybar continues to revisit me now and my aorta is almost severed by it.'

We find in the *Ṣaḥīḥ:* 'It is said to the martyr: "Wish!" and he says, "I wish that I could return to the world so that I could be killed in the Path of Allah again."' The Messenger of Allah ﷺ used to wish for Abū Ṭālib to believe, for Abū Lahab to believe, and for the leaders of Quraysh to believe, even though he knew that that would not happen. All of this indicates that wishing is not forbidden when it does not lead to envy and mutual hatred. That is the kind of wishing that is forbidden in this *āyah.* It includes a man wishing to have the same state as another in his *dīn* or this world or removing it from the other man, whether or not he wishes for that to come to him or not. This is envy. It is that about which Allah says: *'Or do they in fact envy other people for the bounty Messenger of Allah has granted them?'* (4:54) This also includes a man proposing to a woman when another man has proposed to her or making a sale to override his sale, because that leads to envy and hatred.

Some scholars even dislike positive envy (*ghibṭah*) and include it in the prohibition. The truth is that it is permitted as we have explained. Aḍ-Ḍaḥḥāk said, 'It is not lawful for anyone to wish for someone else's property. Have you not heard the words of the Almighty: *"If only we had the same as Qārūn has been given..."* (28:79) and so forth? Then the earth swallowed up him and his wealth.' Al-Kalbī said, 'A man should not wish for his brother's property, wife, servant or mount, but he should say, "O Allah, provide me with its like."' It is like that in the Torah and it is like the words of Allah: *'Ask Allah for His bounty.'*

Ibn 'Abbās said, 'Allah forbade a man to wish for his brother's property and family, and commanded His believing servants to ask Him for His bounty.' Evidence of that among the majority is found in the *ḥadīth*: 'This world has four types of people: a man to whom Allah gives wealth and knowledge and he fears Him in it, maintains his ties of kinship and knows that Allah has a right in it. This is the best of stations. Then there is a man to whom Allah gives knowledge but not wealth, but he has a sincere intention and says, "If I had wealth, I would do with what so-and-so does." He is according to his intention and they have the same reward...' At-Tirmidhī transmitted it and says that it is sound. Al-Ḥasan said, 'No one should wish for wealth. He does not know whether he would be destroyed by it.' This is true when he desires it for the sake of this world. If it wants it in order to do good, the *Sharī'ah* permits that and someone can wish for the means to reach his Lord and then Allah will do whatever He wishes.

men have a portion of what they acquire and women have a portion of what they acquire:

This refers to reward and punishment. It is the same for women. Qatādah said that. A woman has a reward for a good action ten times over just like a man. Ibn 'Abbās said that what is meant by this is inheritance. According to this view, 'acquiring' means receiving, and a male has twice the portion of two females. Allah forbade wishing in this instance since it is part of envy and because Allah has the best knowledge of people's best interests and so He made the division as He did.

but ask Allah for His bounty.

At-Tirmidhī related from 'Abdullāh that the Messenger of Allah ﷺ said, 'Ask Allah for His bounty. He likes to be asked and the best worship of the slave is waiting expectantly for opening.' Ibn Mājah also transmitted from Abū Hurayrah that the Messenger of Allah ﷺ said, 'Allah is angry at the one who does not ask of Him.' This indicates that the command to ask of Allah is mandatory. One scholar said about this:

Allah is angry if you stop asking Him.
But when the son of Ādam is asked, he gets angry.

The Mālikī faqīh, Abu-l-Faḍl Aḥmad ibn al-Mu'adhdhal, said:

Seek provision from the One
who has no chamberlain,

He Who is angry with the one who fails to ask of Him,
and pleased with the one who seeks from Him.

When He speaks, His words are carried out
without that being written down by any scribe.

We have spoken at length on this subject in *Kitāb qam' al-ḥirṣ bi-z-zuhd wa-l-qanā'ah*. Sa'īd ibn Jubayr said that the word '*bounty*' here means worship, not the business of this world. It is said that it means: 'Ask Him for success in doing what pleases Him.' 'Ā'ishah said, 'Ask your Lord until you are satisfied. If Allah does not grant ease, there is no ease.' Sufyān ath-Thawrī said, 'He only commanded asking so that He could give.'

Al-Kisā'ī and Ibn Kathīr recite *'salū'llāh'* without a *hamzah* throughout the Qur'an. The rest have it with a *hamzah*. Allah knows best.

وَلِكُلٍّ جَعَلْنَا مَوَالِيَ مِمَّا تَرَكَ الْوَالِدَانِ وَالْأَقْرَبُونَ ۚ وَالَّذِينَ
عَقَدَتْ أَيْمَانُكُمْ فَآتُوهُمْ نَصِيبَهُمْ ۚ إِنَّ اللَّهَ كَانَ
عَلَىٰ كُلِّ شَيْءٍ شَهِيدًا ﴿٣٣﴾

33 We have appointed heirs for everything that parents and relatives leave. If you have a bond with people, give them their share. Allah is a witness of all things.

Allah makes it clear that every human being has heirs and *mawālī*. Each of them benefits from the inheritance Allah has allotted to them and should not desire the property of another. Al-Bukhārī reports in the Chapter on Shares from Sa'īd ibn Jubayr that Ibn 'Abbās said about this *āyah:* 'When the Muhājirūn came to Madīnah, an Anṣārī would inherit from a Muhājir to the exclusion of relatives because of the brotherhood established between them by the Messenger of Allah ﷺ.' When this was revealed, he said that it abrogated: *'those with whom you have a bond.'* Abu-l-Ḥasan ibn Baṭṭāl said that there is general abrogation by the words: *'We have appointed heirs for everything'* and it abrogated the previous *āyah*. So the correct position is that the *āyah* is abrogating. Aṭ-Ṭabarī transmitted that. It is related from the group of the early generations that the *āyah* abrogates the *āyah* in *al-Anfāl* (8:75). It is related from Ibn 'Abbās, Qatādah and al-Ḥasan al-Baṣrī. It is confirmed by Abū 'Ubaydah in his book, *an-Nāsikh wa-l-Mansūkh.*

There is another position related from Sa'īd ibn al-Musayyab who said that Allah was instructing those who had adopted children in the Jāhiliyyah and then were subject to the rules of inheritance to give those children a share by bequest while the actual maternal and paternal relatives would inherit through their obligatory share. One group said that it is not abrogated and that Allah is instructing the believers to give their allies their shares of help, good counsel and aid. Aṭ-Ṭabarī mentioned that from Ibn 'Abbās who said, 'It is help, good counsel, aid and making a bequest to them when the inheritance has passed.' That is also the position of Mujāhid and as-Suddī and an-Naḥḥās preferred it and related it from Sa'īd ibn Jubayr, in which case there is no abrogation. Combining is valid as Ibn 'Abbās made clear in what aṭ-Ṭabarī mentioned. Al-Bukhārī related it in the Chapter on *Tafsīr.* Inheritance will be further mentioned in *al-Anfāl.*

The word *'kull'* in Arabic has an encompassing and general meaning. All grammarians say that if it is in the singular, there must be an elision of words, as it is permitted to say, 'I passed by all.' It is like saying 'before' or 'after'. The elision implies: 'We have assigned heirs to everyone.' The expression *'those with a bond'* means those with whom you have an an alliance, as Qatādah said. That is because when one man made an alliance with another, he would say, 'My blood is your blood. My destruction is your destruction. My revenge is your revenge. My war is your war and my peace is your peace. You inherit from me and I inherit from you. You seek by me and I seek by you. You pay my blood money and I pay yours.' Before this allies would receive a sixth of the inheritance, but that was abrogated.

'Mawālī' is the plural of *mawlā* which is a word that has various meanings. A freed person is called a *mawlā* as is the freer and one refers in this context to 'the upper and lower *mawlā*.' A helper is called *mawlā* as the Almighty says: *'The unbelievers have no helper.'* (48:11) A nephew can be a *mawlā* as can a neighbour. Here it means the *'aṣabah* (paternal relatives) since the Prophet ﷺ said, 'As for the remainder of the shares, it goes to the male paternal relatives.' It goes to the upper *'asabah'*, not the lower, according to the position of scholars because what is understood is that the freer blesses the freed almost as if he gives him sustenance, and so he deserves his inheritance for that reason.

Aṭ-Ṭaḥāwī related from al-Ḥasan ibn Ziyād that the lower *mawlā* inherits from the upper one and he cites as evidence that it is related that a man freed a slave and then died without any relatives except the man he set free and the Prophet ﷺ gave him his estate. Aṭ-Ṭaḥāwī said that there is no opposition to this *ḥadīth* and so one must accept it. It is also possible to affirm the inheritance of the *mawlā* on the premise that he is someone who gave another person existence as a legal entity, and so he is like a father and the lower *mawlā* is like a son. That demands equality between them in terms of inheritance. The basis is that the connection is undefined. A report says, 'The *mawlā* of a people is one of them.' The majority, who oppose this view, say that entitlement to inheritance only comes through kinship which the freed slave does not possess, although we affirm that the emancipator does have inheritance by virtue of his favour to the one he emancipated. So recompense for the blessing demands repayment. The reverse is not true for the lower *mawlā*. A son is the person most entitled to be his father's successor and take his place. Someone freed is not entitled to take the place of the one who freed him. The emancipator blessed him and this does not exist in the lower *mawlā* and so the difference between them is clear. Allah knows best.

If you have a bond with people,

'Alī ibn Kabshah related from Ḥamzah the verb '*have a bond*' as '*aqqadat* but what is better known from Ḥamzah is '*aqadat* without the doubled *qāf*. That is also the reading of 'Āṣim and al-Kisā'ī. The former is an unlikely reading because the bond is only between two or more people. Abū Ja'far an-Naḥḥās said, 'The reading of Ḥamzah is permitted, based on some obscurity in the Arabic which implies: 'those with whom you have contracted bonds of alliance.' So it is transitive with two objects, implying, 'your bonds have contracted alliance for them' and the *lām* (connected to them) has been elided, as we see in 83:3 where the second object is elided.

Allah is a witness of all things.

Allah witnesses the bond which you form with them and He likes people to fulfil their contracts.

ٱلرِّجَالُ قَوَّٰمُونَ عَلَى ٱلنِّسَآءِ بِمَا فَضَّلَ ٱللَّهُ بَعْضَهُمْ عَلَىٰ بَعْضٍ
وَبِمَآ أَنفَقُوا۟ مِنْ أَمْوَٰلِهِمْ ۚ فَٱلصَّٰلِحَٰتُ قَٰنِتَٰتٌ حَٰفِظَٰتٌ
لِّلْغَيْبِ بِمَا حَفِظَ ٱللَّهُ ۚ وَٱلَّٰتِى تَخَافُونَ نُشُوزَهُنَّ فَعِظُوهُنَّ
وَٱهْجُرُوهُنَّ فِى ٱلْمَضَاجِعِ وَٱضْرِبُوهُنَّ ۖ فَإِنْ أَطَعْنَكُمْ فَلَا تَبْغُوا۟
عَلَيْهِنَّ سَبِيلًا ۗ إِنَّ ٱللَّهَ كَانَ عَلِيًّا كَبِيرًا ﴿٣٤﴾

34 Men have charge of women because Allah has preferred the one above the other and because they spend their wealth on them. Right-acting women are obedient, safeguarding their husband's interests in his absence as Allah has guarded them. If there are women whose disobedience you fear, you may admonish them, refuse to sleep with them, and then beat them. But if they obey you, do not look for a way to punish them. Allah is All-High, Most Great.

Men have charge of women because Allah has preferred the one above the other

The phrase *'Men have charge* (qawwāmūn) *of women'* means that they undertake (*yaqūm*) to provide for them and to defend them. Also they are judges, rulers and go on expeditions which women do not do. One says either *qawwām* or *qayyim*. The *āyah* was revealed about Sa'd ibn ar-Rabī' whose wife Ḥabībah bint Zayd disobeyed him and he slapped her. Her father said, 'Messenger of Allah! Is my daughter going to sleep with him when he slaps her!' The Prophet ﷺ said, 'Let her take retaliation from her husband.' She went with her father to take retaliation and the Prophet ﷺ said, 'Come back. Jibrīl has come to me.' This *āyah* was revealed and the Prophet ﷺ remarked, 'We desired one thing and Allah desired another.' In one variant, 'I wanted one thing but what Allah desires is better.' He reversed the first decision. It is said that it was about this rejected ruling that Allah revealed: *'Do not rush ahead with the Qur'an before its revelation to you is complete.'* (20:114)

Ismā'īl ibn Isḥāq mentioned from Ḥajjāj ibn al-Minhāl and 'Ārim ibn al-Faḍl that Jarīr ibn Ḥāzim heard al-Ḥasan say, 'A woman came to the Prophet ﷺ and said, "My husband slapped my face." He said, "There is retaliation between you." Then Allah revealed: *"Do not rush ahead with the Qur'an before its revelation to you is complete."* So the Prophet ﷺ held back until the *āyah*: *"Men have charge of women..."* was revealed. Abū Rawq said that it was revealed about Jamīlah bint Ubayy and her husband Thābit ibn Qays. Al-Kalbī says that it was revealed about 'Amīrah bint Muḥammad and her husband Sa'd ibn ar-Rabī'. It is also said that it was because of what Umm Salamah said about the women's complaint about the difference in inheritance. Then Allah explained that their preference over them in inheritance was due to what the men have to pay of dowers and maintenance, and so the benefit of that preference in fact reverted to the women.

It is said that men have preference over them with respect to intellect and management and so they have the duty of supporting them because of that. It is said that men are stronger in themselves and nature because the nature of man is hot and dry, which implies strength and force, and the nature of women is cold and wet, which implies softness and weakness, and that is why they have the duty of supporting them and because *'they spend their wealth on them.'*

The *āyah* indicates that men are permitted to discipline their wives. If women observe their husbands' rights, men must not behave badly towards them. *Qawwām* is an intensive form of *qiyām*, which caring for a thing and having a monopoly over attending to it and preserving it by effort, and so this is the charge that men have over women. They manage them, teach them and keep them at home. The woman must accept as long as that does not entail disobedience to Allah. The reason for that is virtue, maintenance, intelligence, strength in *jihād*, inheritance, and commanding the right and forbidding the wrong. Some of them see the beard as the preference, but this is baseless. Someone can have a beard and still possess none of the qualities we mentioned. This refutation was dealt with in *al-Baqarah*.

From Allah's words: *'because they spend their wealth on them,'* some scholars understand that when a man is unable to support them, then he does not have charge over them. If he does not have charge over them, then the contract is void since the aim for which marriage was legislated is removed. It contains clear evidence for the fact that the marriage can be nullified when there is inability to clothe and support the wife. That is the position of the schools of Mālik and ash-Shāfi'ī. Abū Ḥanīfah said that it is not abrogated because Allah says: *'If someone is in difficult circumstances, there should be a deferral.'* (2:280) This was already discussed earlier in this *sūrah*.

Right-acting women are obedient, safeguarding their husbands' interests

What is the meant by this is obedience to the husband and attending to his right regarding her person and his property when he is absent. Abū Dāwūd aṭ-Ṭayālusī reported from Abū Hurayrah that the Messenger of Allah ﷺ said, 'The best of women is the one who gives you joy when you look at her, obeys you when you command her, and guards her person and your property when you are absent.' Then he recited this *āyah*. He said to 'Umar, 'Shall I inform you of the best treasure a man can have? A righteous woman. When he looks at her she delights him, and when he commands her she obeys him and when he is absent from her she is mindful for him.' Abū Dāwūd transmitted it. The copy of the Qur'an of Ibn Mas'ūd has *'aṣ-ṣawāliḥu qawānitu ḥawāfiẓ'* in the feminine form. Ibn Jinnī said, 'The broken pattern is closer to the meaning since it means 'many' and is what is meant here.

as Allah has guarded them.

This is by Allah's preservation of them. It can mean 'which'. Abū Ja'far recites *'bimā ḥafiẓa-llāha'* in the accusative. An-Naḥḥās says that the nominative is clearer. It can mean they preserve things when their husband is absent by Allah's preservation and help. It is said that it might refer to what Allah has preserved in respect of their dowries and company. It is also said that the meaning is: 'By what Allah has made them preserve with regard to handing over trusts to their husbands.' If it is recited in the accusative, it means, 'by their being mindful of Allah through their guarding the affairs of their husband and their *dīn*.' It is said that it implies: 'by the way they are mindful of Allah.' It is said that it means 'by Allah's preservation' or 'by fear of Allah' as you say, *'ḥafiẓtu-llāh'* (I was mindful of Allah.)

If there are women whose disobedience you fear,

'Allātī' is the plural feminine possessive pronoun as we already mentioned. Ibn 'Abbās said that the word '*fear*' here means 'know and are certain of'. It is said that it can actually mean 'fear'. The term *nushūz* means disobedience and is derived from *nashz*. It is what rises from the earth, as when a man is sitting and then stands up. An example of that is found in Allah's words: *'When you are told, "Get up (anshuzū)," get up (fa-nshuzū).'* (58:11) It means: 'get up and rise for a war or command from Allah.' The basic meaning is: 'If you fear that they will disobey and rise and abandon the obedience to their husbands that Allah has made mandatory on them.' Abū Manṣūr al-Laghawī said, '*Nushūz* is disliked in both spouses. It is bad companionship.' Ibn Fāris said, 'A woman disobeys when she makes things difficult for her husband and a husband is disobedient to her when he hits her and is harsh to her.' Ibn Durayd said that the verbs *nashaza*, *nashasa* and *nashaṣa* mean the same.

you may admonish them,

This is with the Book of Allah, by reminding them what Allah has obliged for them of good company and comradeship for their spouses, and acknowledging the degree they have over them. The Prophet ﷺ said, 'If I were to command anyone to prostrate to anyone, I would command a wife to prostrate to her husband,' 'She should not deny herself (to him), even if she is on the back of camel,' and 'When a woman spends the night spurning her husband's bed, the angels curse her until morning.' One version has 'until she returns and places her hand in his.' Other similar things are said.

refuse to sleep with them,

Ibn Mas'ūd, an-Nakha'ī and others recited it in the singular (*maḍja'*) as a generic noun which refers to the plural. The word *hajr* (separation) in beds implies that he sleeps with her but turns his back on her and refuses to have sexual intercourse with her, as Ibn 'Abbās and others said. Mujāhid said that it means to avoid their beds altogether. If so, there is elision, meaning 'avoid them by refusing their beds,' and this is supported by that fact that the word comes from *hijrān*, which means distance. The verb '*hajarahu*' means 'separate and go far from him.' Distance is only possible by not sleeping with her. Ibrāhīm an-Nakha'ī, ash-Sha'bī, Qatādah and al-Ḥasan al-Baṣrī said something along those lines. Ibn Wahb and Ibn al-Qāsim related it from Mālik, and Ibn al-'Arabī preferred it. They said, 'They apply the command to the most prevalent, and this statement is like, "Avoid him for Allah."' This is the basic position of Mālik. It is a good position. When the husband turns from her bed, if the woman loves the husband, that is hard on her and she will revert. If she hates him, her disobedience to him will be clear.

It is said that it comes from *hujr*, which means ugly words, in other words speak harshly to them. That is what Sufyān said, and it is related from Ibn 'Abbās. It is also said that it means, 'Detain them in their houses,' from the expression 'Tie the camel,' i.e. tie with the *hijār*, which is a camel rope. That is preferred by aṭ-Ṭabarī and he attacks the other positions. What he says on this topic is questionable. Qāḍī Abū Bakr ibn 'Arabī refuted him in *al-Aḥkām* saying, 'What a slip from a man who knows the Qur'an and the *Sunnah*! What moved him to take this position is a *gharīb ḥadīth* related by Ibn Wahb from Mālik that Asmā' bint Abī Bakr aṣ-Ṣiddīq, the wife of az-Zubayr ibn al-'Awwām, used to go out until he was criticised for allowing that. He rebuked her and her co-wife and tied their hair together and then beat them. The co-wife was better at dissembling but Asmā' did not dissemble, and she got more of a beating. She complained to her father, Abū Bakr and he said to her, "My daughter, be patient. Az-Zubayr is a righteous man, and he may be your husband in the Garden. I heard that when a man marries a virgin, he will marry her in the Garden." So the view about tying is with the probable expression combined with the action of az-Zubayr and so he preferred this explanation.'

Scholars say that this shunning can last a month, as the Messenger of Allah ﷺ did when he confided something to Ḥafṣah and she told it to 'Ā'ishah and they helped one another against him. It should not reach the four months which Allah has set as a term of the *īlā'*.

and then beat them.

Allah commands that one begin first with admonition, and then with shunning, and then if that does not work, with beating. It is that which will correct her and impel her to fulfil her duty to him. Beating in this *āyah* is one of discipline and not severe. It must not break any bones or mar a limb like might result from a blow with a fist or the like. What is meant is only putting right and nothing more. It is certain that if it leads to death, he is answerable for that. That is also the position in the case of a teacher who beats his student in order to teach him the Qur'an and manners. We find in *Ṣaḥīḥ Muslim*: 'Fear Allah regarding women. You take them by the trust of Allah and make their private parts lawful by the Word of Allah. Your right from them is that they do not let anyone you dislike sleep in your beds. If they do that, beat them, but not severely.'

This is taken from a long *ḥadīth* of Jābir about the *ḥajj*. It means: 'They should not let anyone you dislike enter your houses, whether relatives, other women or non-relatives.' This is the probable meaning of what at-Tirmidhī transmitted from 'Amr ibn al-Aḥwaṣ who was present with the Messenger of Allah ﷺ during the Farewell *Ḥajj*. He said, 'He praised Allah and reminded and admonished. He said, "I command you to treat women well. They are as captives in your possession. You have no rights over them except that [i.e. physical enjoyment and that they protect their husband's interest in respect of themselves and his property]. If they act licentiously in an open way, then leave them alone in their beds and beat them but not severely. If they obey you, you have no way against them. You have rights that your women owe you and your women have rights that you owe them. Your right from them is that they do not allow into your bed those you dislike and do not permit those you dislike to enter your house. Their right from you is that you are good to them in respect of their clothes and food.' At-Tirmidhī said that it is a sound *ḥasan ḥadīth*. 'Licentiously in an open way' means: 'they do not admit those their husbands dislike or hate.' It does not mean fornication. That is forbidden and there is a *ḥadd* punishment for it. The Prophet

ﷺ is reported as saying, 'Beat women if they disobey you in what is correct, but not severely.' 'Aṭā' said, 'I asked Ibn 'Abbās what this meant and he said, "With a *siwāk* and the like."' It is related that 'Umar beat his wife and was censured for that and said, 'I heard the Messenger of Allah ﷺ say, "Do not ask a man why he beat his wife."'

But if they obey you, do not look for a way to punish them.

If they abandon *nushūz*, do not harm them by word or deed. This is a prohibition against wronging them after confirming preference over them. It is said that its meaning is do not oblige them to love you. That is not up to them.

Allah is All-High, Most Great.

This indicates that husbands should be kind and gentle, implying that if they have power over them, remember the power of Allah. His power is above every authority and no one should think himself higher than his wife. Allah is on the watch. That is why it is good to connect it to highness and greatness. This being established, know that Allah did not command anything explicit in His Book about beating except here and in major *ḥudūd,* and so their disobedience of their husbands is on a par with the disobedience of major wrong actions. The husbands are in charge of that rather than rulers and judges, and without witnesses, as a trust from Allah to the husbands. Al-Muhallab said, 'It is permitted to beat wives to when they refuse to have sex. There is disagreement about the duty to beat them to make them serve. Analogy would allow that if it is permitted to beat them for refusing to have sexual intercourse, it is permitted to do so in respect of the service obliged by normal custom.'

Ibn Khuwayzimandād said, '*Nushūz* cancels maintenance and all rights.' He says that it is permitted to beat a wife to discipline her but not severely, and to employ admonition and separation until she stops. When she stops, her rights resume. There is also a difference in the type of discipline the husband is permitted to use and the situation varies in the case of woman of high standing and one of low standing. A woman of high standing should be disciplined by admonition and a woman of low standing by beating. The Prophet ﷺ said, 'May Allah have mercy on someone who hangs up his whip and disciplines his wife.' He also said, 'Abū Jahm does not put down the cane on his shoulder.' Bashshār said:

A free man is censured and the cane is used for the slave.

Ibn Durayd said:

Censure is an abiding deterrent for a free man,
but a slave is only deterred by a cane.

Ibn al-Mundhir said, 'The people of knowledge agree that husbands are obliged to maintain their wives when they are adult except for a wife who is disobedient.' Abū 'Umar said, 'If, after consummation, someone's wife is disobedient, he does not have to maintain her unless she is pregnant.' Ibn al-Qāsim disagreed with the majority of *fuqahā'* about the maintenance of a disobedient wife and said that it was mandatory. When she returns to her husband, then he is obliged to support her in the future. A wife's maintenance is not discontinued for anything except disobedience. It is not discontinued on account of illness, menstruation, lochia, fasting, ḥajj, the husband's absence, whether that is for a duty or for injustice. Allah knows best.

وَإِنْ خِفْتُمْ شِقَاقَ بَيْنِهِمَا فَابْعَثُوا حَكَمًا مِّنْ أَهْلِهِۦ وَحَكَمًا مِّنْ
أَهْلِهَآ إِن يُرِيدَآ إِصْلَٰحًا يُوَفِّقِ ٱللَّهُ بَيْنَهُمَآ إِنَّ ٱللَّهَ كَانَ عَلِيمًا
خَبِيرًا ٣٥

35 If you fear a breach between a couple, send an arbiter from his people and an arbiter from her people. If the couple desire to put things right, Allah will bring about a reconciliation between them. Allah is All-Knowing, All-Aware.

If you fear a breach between a couple,

The meaning of the term *shiqāq* was already mentioned in *al-Baqarah.* A breach is when each of the couple take a side other than the other's, in other words a different side. What is meant is when you fear a split between them, and the verbal noun is attributed to an adverbial usage. It is as you say, 'I like the course of the moonlit night' and 'fasting the day of 'Arafah.' The usage is also seen in the Revelation: '*scheming night and day.*' (34:33) It is said that '*bayna*' (between) acts as nouns do and the adverbial quality is removed from it since it means 'their situation and company', so it means: when you fear that their companionship and company will become alienated. The verbs '*fear*' and '*send*' are based on the prior difference.

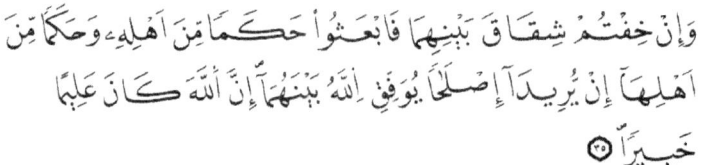

Sa'īd ibn Jubayr said that the ruling is that a husband first should admonish his wife. If she does not respond, he should shun her. If she still does not respond, he should beat her. If she still does not respond, then the judge sends an arbiter from her family and an arbiter from his family. They look to see who is at fault. A *khul'* can take place at that point. It is also said that he can beat her before admonition takes place. The first position is sounder because of the order in the *āyah*.

The majority of scholars said that those addressed here are the arbiters and rulers. The words *'If you fear'* refer to the judges and rulers. In the words *'reconciliation between them,'* what is meant is between the two arbiters according to Ibn 'Abbās, Mujāhid and others, meaning that the arbiters put things right and Allah brings about reconciliation between the couple through them. It is also said that what is meant is the couple themselves, meaning that the couple return to settlement and friendship and inform the arbiters of that, as Allah has brought about reconciliation between them. It is said that it is addressed to the guardians, meaning when you know that there is discord between the couple.

The reason that the arbiters must be from the people of each of the couple is that they have more knowledge of the circumstances of the couple; and they should also be people of justice, good investigation and insight into *fiqh*. If none exist in their families who qualify, then others with knowledge and fairness should be sent for. That is when their business is uncertain and it is not known who is behaving badly. If the wronging party is known, the right of the other party is taken and he or she is compelled to remove the harm.

It is said that the arbiter from the husband's family withdraws with him and says, 'Tell me what you want so that I know what it is.' If he says, 'I have no need of her. Take whatever you can from her and divorce us,' then he knows that the disobedience is on his part. If he says, 'I desire her, so satisfy her from my wealth whatever you wish and do not separate us,' then it clear that the fault is not his. The arbiter from her family asks her, 'Do you want your husband or not?' If she says, 'Separate us and give him whatever you wish of my property,' he knows that the recalcitrance is on her part. If she says, 'Do not separate us, but encourage him to increase my maintenance and be good to me,' he knows that the fault is with him. When they know which party is at fault, they admonish and rebuke that party. That is what is intended by the *āyah* here.

Scholars said that this *āyah* grants women their share of intelligence because they can either obey or disobey. If they sort things out the couple are left, based on what an-Nasā'ī reported. He said that 'Aqīl ibn Abī Ṭālib married Fāṭimah bint 'Utbah ibn Rabī'ah. When he went to her, she said, 'Banū Hāshim! By Allah, my heart will never love you! Where are those whose necks like silver jars! Whose noses turn before their lips! Where is 'Utbah ibn Rabī'ah? Where is Shaybah ibn Rabī'ah?' So he was silent until one day when he was cross, she said to him,

'Where is 'Utbah ibn Rabī'ah?' He retorted, 'On your left in the Fire when you enter it.' She threw her garment on and went to 'Uthmān and told him what he had said. He sent for Ibn 'Abbās and Mu'āwiyah. Ibn 'Abbās said, 'I will separate them.' Mu'āwiyah said, 'I will not separate two shaykhs of the Banū 'Abd Manāf.' They went to them and found that they had shut their door and put things right.

If the arbiters find that they disagree and do not put things right and matters come to a head, they strive to reconcile them and remind them of Allah and the need for good companionship. If they repent and return, they are left. If that does not happen and the arbiters think that they should part, they are separated. It is permitted to separate the couple, whether the judgment of the *qāḍī* is in conformity with that or against it, whether or not the couple gave them the authority to do that. Divorce is that case is final. Some people say that they cannot divorce them unless the husband has given them authority to do that and they must inform the ruler. This is based on them being messengers and witnesses. Then the ruler separates the couple if he wishes or commands the arbiter to do this. This is one of the positions of ash-Shāfi'ī and the Kufans said that. It is the position of 'Aṭā', Ibn Zayd and al-Ḥasan, as well as Abū Thawr.

The sound view is the first: an arbiter is permitted to divorce without delegation. That is the position of Mālik, al-Awzā'ī, and Isḥāq, and it is related from 'Uthmān, 'Alī, Ibn 'Abbās, ash-Sha'bī, and an-Nakha'ī, and it is one position of ash-Shāfi'ī because Allah says: '*...send an arbiter from his people and an arbiter from her people,*' and that is a text from Allah that they are judges, not agents or witnesses. The term '*wakīl*' (agent) has a name and meaning in the Sharī'ah and '*ḥakam*' (arbiter) has a name and a meaning in the Sharī'ah. Allah makes each of them clear so there should be no divergence.

Ad-Dāraquṭnī related from Muḥammad ibn Sīrīn from 'Abīdah about this *āyah*: 'A man and woman came to 'Alī, each with a group of people and he commanded them to send an arbiter from his people and an arbiter from her people. He asked the arbiters, "Do you know what you must do? If you think that they should separate, separate them." The woman said, "I am pleased that the Book of Allah should judge for me or against me." The husband said, "No separation." 'Alī said, "You lie. By Allah, you will not go until you affirm what she affirms."' This has a sound firm *isnād* related from 'Alī from firm paths from Ibn Sīrīn from 'Abīdah. Abū 'Umar said that. If they were two agents or two witnesses, he would not have asked them, 'Do you know what you must do?' This is clear. Abū Ḥanīfah argued by 'Alī's words to the husband, 'You will not go until you affirm what she affirms.' This indicates that the position of his school is that they only separate with the husband's permission and that the basic principle agreed upon is that divorce is in the hand of the husband or in the hand of the one to whom he assigns to do it. Mālik and those who follow him include it under the heading of divorce by the ruler in the case of the *īlā'* or someone impotent. If the arbiters disagree, their statement is not acted on; nothing is obliged regarding the situation unless they agree. The same applies to two arbiters concerning any matter. If one of them judges separation and the other does not, or one judges payment of money and the other refuses, nothing is decided on until they both agree.

Mālik said if that the arbiters decide on a treble divorce, then one divorce is obliged and not more than one. That is the position of Ibn al-Qāsim. Ibn al-Qāsim also said that three is obliged if they agree on that. Al-Mughīrah, Ashhab, Ibn al-Mājishūn and Aṣbagh also said that. Ibn al-Mawwāz said that if one judges one and the other judges three, then it is one. Ibn Ḥabīb related from Aṣbagh that it no consequence.

It is permitted to send only one arbiter because, although Allah judged that there must be four witnesses in adultery, the Prophet ﷺ sent Unays alone to the adulterous woman and told him, 'If she confesses, stone her.' 'Abd al-Malik also said that in the *Mudawwanah*. If one is sent and the couple grant the power of arbitration to one arbiter, that is allowed and that is more fitting since they both agree to that. The instruction that arbiters should be sent comes from Allah rather than from the couple themselves. If the couple were to send two arbiters who judged, then the judgment would be carried out since that is permissible and the judgment reached is carried out in every case. This is when they are both fair. If the arbiter is not fair, 'Abd al-Malik says that the judgment is rescinded because they have ventured into an area of uncertainty which is not appropriate.

Ibn al-'Arabī said, 'The sound position is that the judgment is carried out, since if they delegate the arbiter as an agent, the action of the agent should be implemented, and if it is a matter of legal judgment, then they have put him in charge of themselves and there is no effective uncertainty just as there is no uncertainty in the matter of delegation. There is always some uncertainty where this subject is concerned. It is not obliged for the arbiter to have full knowledge of what is being judged which will lead to a judgment.'

Ibn al-'Arabī also said, 'Allah has given us a text about the two judges and that is used when there is discord and disagreement between the couple. It is an immense matter on whose basic principle the Community agree while they disagree on the details. It is extraordinary that the people of our land ignore the Book and the *Sunnah* regarding that and just say, "They have been put into the hands of a trustworthy person." This is unconcealed divergence from the text. They are not implementing the Book of Allah or an allowed analogy. I recommended that, but they did not agree to send two arbiters in case of a rift, but only a single *qāḍī*. There is no judgment by an oath with a witness without the other party being present. If Allah gives me power, I will implement the appropriate *Sunnah*.'

The people of our land love nothing but ignorance. But I wonder at the fact that Abū Ḥanīfah does not have any report about two arbiters. And I wonder twice over at ash-Shāfi'ī who said, 'It appears from the the literal reading of the *āyah* that it is general and applies to both parties of the couple so that their states resemble one another other.' He said, 'That is because I find that Allah allows for putting things right between the couple when the wife is disobedient, and He allows the *khul'* when they fear that they will not establish the limits of Allah. That appears to be with the woman's consent. It is forbidden for a man to take anything when he wants to exchange one wife for another. When Allah commands that there be two arbiters when we fear schism between a couple, it indicates that their ruling is not the ruling of the spouses. If that is the case, that is why an arbiter is sent from his family and an arbiter from her family. Only two trustworthy arbiters are sent with the consent of the couple and they are delegated to bring them together or separate them if they think that is correct. That indicates that the two arbiters are agents of the couple.' Ibn al-'Arabī said, 'This is ash-Shāfi'ī's final word about the matter, and his people are happy with it. It does not, however, contain anything that one pays attention to nor does it comply with his place in knowledge. It was refuted by Qāḍī Abū Isḥāq, but he was mostly not fair to him.'

His words, 'It appears from the literal reading of the *āyah* that it is general and applies to both parties of the couple,' are not sound. There is indeed a text. It is one of the clearest *āyah*s of the Qur'an. Allah Almighty says: *'Men have charge of women'* (4:34), and if someone fears that his wife will be disobedient, he admonishes her. If she does not turn from it, then he shuns her in her bed. If she still does not desist, he beats her. If she continues, then two arbiters go to them. This is what the case is. If this is not a text, then there is no clarification in the Qur'an! Leave off the idea that it is not a text. It is evident. As for what ash-Shāfi'ī said about it 'appearing from the literal reading,' we do not know what is meant by it appearing from the literal reading.

Then he said, 'He allows the *khul'* when they fear that they will not establish the limits of Allah. That appears to be with the woman's consent.' Indeed it is mandatory that it is like that and it is from the text. He then said that when Allah commands that there be two arbiters, that indicates that the ruling of the arbiters is not the ruling of the spouses, it is obliged that someone other than the couple carries it out on them without their choice and so 'otherness' is achieved. If the arbiters implement what the couple have told them to do and do not judge by any other criterion, then there is no 'otherness' (and no point in having arbiters).

Ash-Shafi'i's words, '...with the consent of the couple and they are delegated,' is a clear error. When schism is feared between the couple, Allah is addressing someone other than the couple by sending two arbiters. If someone other than the couple is addressed how can that be by the couple's delegation or for the ruling not to be sound for them except when it is that on which they agree? This is fairness and precision in refuting him.

This *āyah* contains evidence for the confirmation of arbitration, and it is not as the Khārijites say about there being no arbiter other than Allah. This is a true statement by which they meant something false.

وَاعْبُدُوا اللَّهَ وَلَا تُشْرِكُوا بِهِ شَيْئًا وَبِالْوَالِدَيْنِ إِحْسَانًا
وَبِذِي الْقُرْبَىٰ وَالْيَتَامَىٰ وَالْمَسَاكِينِ وَالْجَارِ ذِي الْقُرْبَىٰ وَالْجَارِ
الْجُنُبِ وَالصَّاحِبِ بِالْجَنبِ وَابْنِ السَّبِيلِ وَمَا مَلَكَتْ أَيْمَانُكُمْ
إِنَّ اللَّهَ لَا يُحِبُّ مَن كَانَ مُخْتَالًا فَخُورًا ﴿٣٦﴾

36 Worship Allah and do not associate anything with Him. Be good to your parents and relatives and to orphans and the very poor, and to neighbours who are related to you and neighbours who are not related to you, and to companions and travellers and your slaves. Allah does not love anyone vain or boastful.

Scholars agree that this *āyah* is agreed to be one of judgment and none of it is abrogated. It is something common to all the Revealed Books. Even if that had not been the case, it would be logically known, even if there were no revelation about it. The meaning of worship was already discussed. It entails humility and need of the One Who has judgment and choice. Allah commanded His slaves to be humble to Him and sincere. The *āyah* is the basis for making actions sincerely for Allah Almighty and purifying them of the impurity of showing-off and other such defects. Allah Almighty says: *'So let him who hopes to meet his Lord act rightly and not associate anyone with the worship of his Lord.'* (18:110) This is so much the case that some scholars said that when someone performs *wuḍū'* with cold water or fasts to heat his intestines, and intends worship by that, it is not valid because it is mixed with a worldly intention and is not sincere for Allah, as Allah says: *'Indeed is the sincere* dīn *not Allah's alone?'* (39:3) Allah also says: *'They were only ordered to worship Allah, making their* dīn *sincerely His.'* (98:5) The same applies when an imām begins *rukū'* and senses that someone has joined the prayer. He should not wait for him because waiting for him removes his sincerity for Allah. We find in *Ṣaḥīḥ Muslim* that Abū Hurayrah reported that the Messenger of Allah ﷺ said that Allah says, 'I am He who is least in need of a partner. If anyone does an action, making other than Me a partner in it, I leave him to his partner.'

Ad-Dāraquṭnī reported from Anas ibn Mālik that the Messenger of Allah ﷺ said, 'On the Day of Resurrection sealed pages will be brought and set up before Allah Almighty. The Almighty will say, "Throw these aside and accept these." The angels will say, "By Your might, we only see good!" Allah Almighty will say, "This was done for other than My sake, and I only accept what was done for My sake."' It is related from aḍ-Ḍaḥḥāk ibn Qays al-Fihrī that the Messenger of Allah ﷺ said, 'Allah Almighty says, "I am the best Partner. If someone associates another with Me, he goes to the partner he associated with Me." People! Make your actions sincere for Allah Almighty. Allah only accepts that which is done sincerely for Him. Do not say, "This is for Allah and for my kin." If it is for kin, then none of it is for Allah. Do not say, "This is for Allah and for your sakes." If it is for your sakes, none of it is for Allah.'

Point. When this is affirmed, know that our scholars say that *shirk* has three levels and all of them are forbidden. The basis of it is believing that Allah has a partner in His divinity. That is the great *shirk*, and the *shirk* of the Jāhiliyyah. It is what is meant by His words: *'Allah does not forgive anything being associated with Him but He forgives whoever He wills for anything other than that.'* (4:48) This is followed in rank by believing that Allah has a partner in terms of action. That is the words of anyone who says that any existent thing other than Allah Almighty is independently capable of producing an action and bringing it into existence, even if he does not believe that it is a god. That is like what the Qadariyyah, the Magians of this Community, assert. Ibn 'Umar declared himself free of them, just as we find in the *ḥadīth* of Jibrīl. The third level of association in worship is showing off. That is when someone performs an act of worship, which Allah has commanded be done for Himself alone, for other than Him. As is made clear in many *āyah*s and *ḥadīth*s, this is something that is forbidden and it invalidates actions. It is hidden and not every stupid, ignorant person recognises it. May Allah be pleased with al-Muḥāsibī who made it clear in his book *ar-Ri'āyah* and explained how it invalidates actions.

We find in the *Sunan* of Ibn Mājah that one of the Companions, Abū Sa'īd ibn Abī Faddālah al-Anṣārī, reported that the Messenger of Allah ﷺ said, 'When Allah gathers the first and the last on the Day of Resurrection, a day of which there is no doubt, a caller will call out, "Whoever associated someone else in his actions for Allah should seek his reward from them. Allah has no need of any associate."' It is also reported that Abū Sa'īd al-Khudrī said, 'The Messenger of Allah ﷺ came out to us while we were discussing the False Messiah and he said, "Shall I inform what I fear for you more than the False Messiah?" We said, "Yes, Messenger of Allah!" He said, "Hidden *shirk*. It is that a man stands and prays and decks out his prayer striving to be seen by the people who look at him."' Shaddād ibn Aws reported that the Messenger of Allah ﷺ said, 'What I most I fear for my community is associating others with Allah. I do not say that you will worship the sun, the moon or an idol, but actions will be done for other than Allah and for a hidden appetite.' At-Tirmidhī al-Ḥakīm transmitted it. What a hidden appetite is will be explained in *Sūrat al-Kahf*. Ibn Lahī'ah related that Yazīd ibn Abī Ḥabīb said, 'The Messenger of Allah ﷺ was asked about hidden appetite and said, "It is that a man learns knowledge by which he hopes that people will sit around him."'

Sahl ibn 'Abdullāh at-Tustarī says, 'There are three aspects to showing-off. One is to believe that the basis of the action belongs to other than Allah and yet by it to desire to let it be known that it is for Allah. This is a form of hypocrisy and doubt in faith. The second that a person begins the action for Allah and then, when someone other than Him sees him, he becomes more energetic in it. When such a person repents, he should to repeat all he did. The third is that he begins the action with sincerity and produces it for Allah, and then is known for that and praised for it and so is pleased with their praise. This is the showing off which Allah has forbidden.' Sahl also said, 'Luqmān told his son, "Showing off is to seek the reward for your action in this world. The actions of the People of Allah are for the Next World." He was asked, "What is the cure for showing off?" He replied, "To conceal your action." He was asked, "How does one conceal action?" He replied, "In those actions which you are obliged to display, only enter them with sincerity. As for actions you are not obliged to show, I prefer that only Allah knows about them."' He further said, 'Any actions which creatures are aware of do not count as actions.' Ayyūb as-Sakhtiyānī said, 'The one who wants his position with respect to action to be known is not intelligent.'

Sahl's statement: 'The third is that he begins the action with sincerity...' is when a person's joy and peace of mind lie in obtaining a position in the hearts of people so that they praise and esteem him, and he obtains what he wants from them in the form of wealth or other things. This is blameworthy because his heart is filled with joy because they look at him, even if they look at him after he has finished. If Allah makes people look at someone and he does not want them to know and delights in the action of Allah and His favour to him, then his joy in the favour of Allah is obedience as Allah says: *'Say: "It is in the favour of Allah and His mercy that they should rejoice. That is better than anything they accumulate."'* (10:58)

This is treated in full in al-Muḥāsibī's book and it can be consulted there. Sahl was asked about the *ḥadīth* of the Prophet ﷺ, 'I conceal an action and it is seen and I am pleased.' He said, 'His pleasure is due to thankfulness to Allah who displayed it,' or similar words.

Be good to your parents

It was already mentioned at the beginning of this *sūrah* that one aspect of charity is to set them free. Filial duty will be fully dealt with in *Sūrat al-Isrā'*.

Ibn Abī 'Ablah recited *iḥsān* in the nominative, i.e. 'It is mandatory to be good to them.' The rest read it in the accusative, meaning: 'Be good to them.'

Scholars say, 'Those most entitled to gratitude, goodness, kindness, obedience and submission after the Creator are your parents. Allah has connected sincerity in worship, obedience and thankfulness to Himself to thankfulness to them. He says: *"Thank Me and Your parents."* (31:14)' 'Amr ibn al-'Āṣ reported that the Messenger of Allah ﷺ said, 'The Lord is pleased when parents are pleased and angry when parents are angry.'

and relatives and to orphans and the very poor,

This was discussed in *al-Baqarah*.

and to neighbours who are related to you and neighbours who are not related to you,

Allah commands us to protect our neighbours and give them their right, and He gives us responsibility for their care both in His Book and on the tongue of His Prophet ﷺ. Do you not see that after Allah mentions parents and relatives, He says: *'neighbours who are related to you'* (lit. with nearness), meaning related, and 'not related' (lit. distant) who are unrelated? Ibn 'Abbās said that, and that is the linguistic usage. Someone who is *ajnabī* is a foreigner. Similarly *janābah* also means distance. Linguists quote:

Do not deny me obtainment after distance (*janābah*).
I am a man who is an exile in the midst of the tents.

Al-A'shā said:

I came to Ḥurayth as a visitor from afar (*janābah*),
and Ḥurayth was unresponsive to my gift.

Al-A'mash and al-Mufaḍḍal recited *'wa-l-jāri-l-janb'*. They are two dialectical usages. One says *janb* and *junub*, and *ajnabu* and *ajnabī* when there is no kinship (*qirābah*, which comes from the root meaning 'nearness') between them. The plural is *ajānib*. It is said that it implies an elided *muḍāf*, meaning the neighbour with distance. Nawf ash-Shāmī said, 'The near neighbour is the Muslim and the far is the Jew and Christian.' According to this, the command regarding neighbours is recommended, be they Muslims or unbelievers, and that is sound. *Iḥsān* (being good) can means charity, and it can also mean good conduct, not causing injury and protecting. Al-Bukhārī reported from 'Ā'ishah that the Prophet ﷺ said, 'Jibrīl continued to advise me to be good to my neighbour until I thought that he would have me make him my heir.' Abū Shurayḥ reported that the Prophet ﷺ said, 'By Allah, he does not believe! By Allah, he does not believe! By Allah, he does not believe!' It was asked, 'Who is that, Messenger of Allah?' He answered, 'Someone whose neighbour is not safe from his mischief!' This is general to every neighbour, and the Prophet ﷺ stressed it by making three oaths, meaning that someone who harms his neighbour does not possess full faith. So a believer must be careful about his neighbour and refrain what Allah and His Messenger have forbidden and should desire what pleases Allah and His Messenger.

It is reported that the Prophet ﷺ said, 'There are three categories of neighbour: a neighbour with three rights, a neighbour with two rights, and a neighbour with one right. The neighbour with three rights is a Muslim relative who is a neighbour, who has the right of neighbourhood, kinship and Islam. A neighbour with two rights is the Muslim neighbour who has the right of Islam and neighbourhood. A neighbour with one right is the unbeliever who has the right of neighbourhood.' Al-Bukhārī reported that 'Ā'ishah said, 'I said, "Messenger of Allah, I have two neighbours. To which of them should I give?" He replied, "To the one whose door is nearer to you."' Some scholars believe that this *ḥadīth* explains what is meant by 'near neighbour' here that is the one physically closest to you and the 'far neighbour' also refers to physical distance.

They use this as evidence for the obligation of granting pre-emption in property to a neighbour along with the words of the Prophet ﷺ, 'A neighbour is more entitled by his proximity.' There is no real evidence in that because 'Ā'ishah asked the Prophet ﷺ about giving to neighbours and he told her that the closest was the most entitled. Ibn al-Mundhir said that this indicates that the term 'neighbour' can be used for more than the one who is right next door. Abū Ḥanīfah abandoned the literal words of this *ḥadīth* and said, 'When an adjacent neighbour gives up pre-emption and the one next to him seeks it, but has no wall or road adjacent to the house, he has no pre-emption.' Most scholars say that a man can instruct that pre-emption be given to adjacent and other neighbours except for Abū Ḥanīfah who differs from the general view of scholars and says that it may only be given to an adjacent neighbor.

People disagree about the definition of what constitutes neighbours. Al-Awzā'ī says that it is forty houses on every side, and Ibn Shihāb also says that. It is related that a man came to the Prophet ﷺ said, 'I have settled in a district and my nearest neighbour does me the greatest harm.' The Prophet ﷺ sent Abū Bakr, 'Umar and 'Alī to shout at the doors of the mosques, 'Up to forty houses are neighbours. Someone whose neighbour is not safe from his mischief will not enter the Garden!' 'Alī ibn Abī Ṭālib said, 'Whoever can hear your call is a neighbour.' One group said, 'Anyone who hears the *iqāmah* of the prayer is a neighbour of that mosque.' Another group said, 'Anyone who lives in the quarter or the town is a neighbour.' Allah says: *'If the hypocrites do not desist… Then they will only be your neighbours there a very short time.'* (33:60) So Allah deemed that their being gathered together in Madīnah made them neighbours.

There are ranks in being neighbours, some closer than others. Your closest neighbour is your spouse. One aspect of honouring one's neighbour is found in what Muslim reports from Abū Dharr that the Messenger of Allah ﷺ said, 'O Abū Dharr, if you cook a stew put a lot of water in it, keeping your neighbours in mind.' The Prophet ﷺ encouraged noble character since it results in love, good companionship, and averting need and corruption. A neighbour may be harmed by the aroma coming from his neighbour's pot. They may have children who are made hungry by it and they feel pain and regret because it, and this would be worse if they are weak or it is a widow. It is said that this is like the suffering of Ya'qūb in being parted from Yūsuf. All of this is averted by giving them share of some of what is cooked. This is why the Prophet ﷺ encouraged giving to a close neighbour since he will see what is in the house of his neighbour and what goes in and out of it and will wish to share in it. You should also be quick to respond to your neighbour when he turns to you unexpectedly with a need. That is why you begin with the closest house, and Allah knows best. Scholars say that 'putting a lot of water in it' is to make the business easy for the ungenerous as the increase, which is water, will not cost them anything. That is why he did not say to put a lot of meat in it since that would not be easy for everyone. How excellent is what a poet said!

My pot and the neighbour's pot are the same.
The pot is lifted to him before me.

You should not give an insignificant amount since the Prophet ﷺ said, 'The people of a house should look at the house of their neighbours with the intention of giving them what is correct and proper.' This means an amount that is customarily given. If a small amount is something that is given, it is not in that position [i.e. what is customary]. If only a little is all that can be given, then you should, nevertheless, give it and not discount doing it it. The one to whom it is given should accept it since the Prophet ﷺ said, 'O believing women, none of you should consider even a roasted sheep's trotter too small to give to her neighbour.' Mālik transmitted it in the *Muwaṭṭā'* (49.10.35). That is how we defined it: 'O believing women' in the nominative without *iḍāfah*. It implies, 'O you who are believing women' as you say, 'O noble men' when the vocative noun is elided. It would be *'ayyuhā'*. 'Women' is implied to be the adjective of *'ayyuhā'* and 'believing' is an adjective of 'women'. It is said that 'women' and 'believing' is in *iḍāfah*, but the first is more frequent.

Part of honouring a neighbour is not preventing them from fixing a piece of wood to a wall for a use they have for it. The Messenger of Allah ﷺ said, 'No neighbour should prevent his neighbour from inserting a piece of wood in his wall.' Then Abū Hurayrah said, 'Why do I see that you are averse to this? By Allah, I will hurl it at you between your shoulders!' It is related that *khashabahu* and *khashabah*, in the plural and singular, and 'shoulders' is related as *'aktāfikum'* and *'aknāfikum'*. 'Hurl it' is with words and in the story.

Is this mandatory or just recommended? Scholars disagree about that. Mālik and Abū Ḥanīfah and their people believe that it is a recommendation to be good to the neighbour and tolerant to him, but not an obligation, since the Prophet ﷺ said, 'The property of a Muslim man is not lawful except with his consent.' They said that its meaning is the same as that found in the words of the Prophet ﷺ: 'When the wife of one of you asks for permission to go to the mosque, do not forbid her from doing so.' So doing this is recommended, not obligatory. It is recommended because of the good and benefit in it. Ash-Shāfi'ī, Aḥmad ibn Ḥanbal, Isḥāq, Abū Thawr, Dāwūd and the group of the People of Ḥadīth believe that it is mandatory. They said that if Abū Hurayrah had not understood what he heard from the Prophet ﷺ to be tantamount to an obligation, he would have been imposing on them something that was not obligatory. That was also the position of 'Umar ibn al-Khaṭṭāb. He judged against Muḥammad ibn Maslamah in favour of aḍ-Ḍaḥḥāk ibn Khalīfah about a large body of water passing through the land of Muḥammad ibn Maslamah. Muḥammad ibn Maslamah said, 'No, by Allah!' and 'Umar said, 'By Allah, he will pass it through, even if it is over your belly!' 'Umar ordered him to allow its passage and aḍ-Ḍaḥḥāk did so. Mālik transmitted it in the *Muwaṭṭā'*. (36.26.33)

In *Kitāb ar-Radd*, ash-Shāfi'ī claimed that Mālik did not relate any disagreement from the Companions about this matter. He denied that Mālik related it and included it in his book. He did not accept it and refuted it based on his opinion. Abū 'Umar said, 'It is not as ash-Shāfi'ī claimed because the opinion of Muḥammad ibn Maslamah about that differed from 'Umar's opinion. The opinion of the Anṣār also differed from that of 'Umar. That was also the case with 'Abd ar-Raḥmān ibn 'Awf in the story about the stream and moving it. When there is disagreement among the Companions, it is necessary to resort to a careful examination of the matter, and the result of that examination makes it clear that the lives, property and honour of Muslims are prohibited to one another except that about which they consent. This is confirmed by the Prophet ﷺ.' The disagreement about it is indicated by the words of Abū Hurayrah, 'Why do I see that you are averse to this? By Allah, I will hurl it at you between your shoulders!'

The answer of the early Muslims is that giving judgment about a particular benefit [being mandatory] is not part of the Sunnah that can be taken from the words of the Prophet ﷺ, 'The property of a Muslim man is only lawful with his consent' because this refers to ownership and consumption. Benefit, however, is not part of that because the Prophet ﷺ distinguished between them in ruling. One should not combine things that the Prophet ﷺ separated. Mālik related that there was a *qāḍī* in Madīnah called Abu-l-Muṭṭalib who used to give that judgment [i.e. that granting benefit was mandatory.] They argue by the *ḥadīth* from al-A'mash that Anas said, 'One of our lads was martyred in the Battle of Uḥud and his mother began to wipe the dust from his face, saying, "Good news! Enjoy the Garden!" and the Prophet ﷺ told her, "How do you know? Perhaps he spoke about what did not concern him and denied what would not have harmed him."' It is not sound that al-A'mash listened to Anas. Allah knows best. Abū 'Umar said that.

A comprehensive *ḥadīth* about neighbours is reported from the Prophet ﷺ by Mu'ādh ibn Jabal who said, 'We asked, "Messenger of Allah, what is the right of the neighbour?" He said, "If he asks you for a loan, you should lend to him. If he asks for your help, you should help him. If he is in need, you should give to him. If he is ill, you should visit him. If he dies, you should attend his funeral. If something good happens to him, it should delight you and you should congratulate him. If he is afflicted by a disaster, it should grieve you and you should console him. You should not afflict him with the aroma of your cooking pot without ladling out some of it for him. You should not build higher than him enabling you to look down on him and block the breeze from him without his permission. If you buy fruits, give him some of them. Otherwise bring them in secretly and do not let your child take any of them outside, which might trouble his children. Do you understand what I am saying to you? Only a very few of those to whom Allah shows mercy will fulfil the right due to their neighbours."' This is a comprehensive *ḥadīth* which is *ḥasan*. Its *isnād* contains Abu-l-Faḍl 'Uthmān ibn Maṭar ash-Shaybānī who is not satisfactory.

Scholars say that the *ḥadīth*s which deal with honouring neighbours are generally applicable and not limited, including even unbelievers, as we have made clear. In a report, people asked, 'Messenger of Allah, should we feed them from the meat of our religious sacrifices (*nusuk*)?' He replied, 'Do not feed idolaters from the religious sacrifices (*nusuk*) of the Muslims.' The fact that he forbade feeding them the religious sacrifices of the Muslims may stem from the fact that an obligatory sacrifice may be one from which the sacrificer himself is not permitted to eat nor can the wealthy eat it. It is permitted to feed *dhimmīs* what the wealthy are entitled to eat. When 'Ā'ishah divided the meat of the sacrifices (*aḍḥiyah*), the Prophet ﷺ told her, 'Begin with your Jewish neighbour.' It is related that a sheep was slaughtered for the family of 'Abdullāh ibn 'Amr. When he came, he asked three times, 'Did you give some to your Jewish neighbour?' Then he said, 'I heard the Messenger of Allah ﷺ say, "Jibrīl continued to command me to give to neighbours until I thought that he would make them inherit from me."'

and to companions

This means your companions on a journey. Aṭ-Ṭabarī reported that the Messenger of Allah ﷺ was with one of his Companions and they were on two mounts. The Messenger of Allah ﷺ entered a thicket and cut two staffs, one of which was crooked. He came out and gave his companion the straight one. He said, 'Messenger of Allah, you are more entitled to this!' He said, 'No, every companion of another person is responsible for his company, even if only for an hour of a day.' Rabī'ah ibn Abī 'Abd ar-Raḥmān said, 'There is good character (*murū'ah*) on a journey and good character when resident. Good character on a journey is demonstrated by spending on provision, not arguing with your companions and a lot of jesting which does not anger Allah. Good character while resident is going constantly to mosques, reciting the Qur'an and having a lot of brothers in Allah.' One of the Banu Asad, said to be Ḥātim aṭ-Ṭā'ī, said:

When my comrade is not behind my she-camel,
he has a better mount and my foot is not carried.

If he does not have half of my provisions,
I am not with provision and not one with excellence.

Two partners in what we are in.
I see that I had better than him by what he obtains of my gift.

'Alī, Ibn Mas'ūd and Ibn Abī Laylā said that this means your wife. Ibn Jurayj said that it is the one who accompanies you and stays with you, desiring to benefit from you. The first opinion is sounder, and it is the position of Ibn 'Abbās, Ibn Jubayr, 'Ikrimah, Mujāhid and aḍ-Ḍaḥḥāk. The *āyah* can also be taken as general. Allah knows best.

and travellers

Mujāhid said that it is the one who travels with you. Part of being good to him is giving to him, being kind to him and guiding him.

and your slaves.

Allah instructs people to be good to their slaves, and the Prophet ﷺ explained how to do that. Muslim and others reported that al-Ma'rūr ibn Suwayd said, 'I saw Abū Dharr at ar-Rabadha wearing a thick cloak and his slave was wearing one like it. We said, "Abū Dharr, if you would take what your slave is wearing and put it with this one, it would make a set." He replied, "I was exchanging insults with a slave whose mother was a foreigner and I insulted him on account of that and he complained about me to the Prophet ﷺ. I met the Prophet ﷺ and he said, 'Abū Dharr, you are a man who still has some of the Jāhiliyyah in you.' I said, 'Messenger of Allah, whoever insults men insults their father and mother.' He said, 'Abū Dharr, you are a man who still has some of the Jāhiliyyah in you. They are your brothers whom Allah has placed under your authority. Anyone who has authority over his brother should feed him from what he eats and clothe him from what he wears and should not oblige his brothers to do what is too much for them. If you ask that of them, then give them a hand.'"'

Abū Dāwūd transmitted from Abū Dharr that the Messenger of Allah ﷺ said, 'As for those of your slaves whom you find acceptable, you should feed them from what you eat and clothe them from what you wear. As for those you do not find acceptable, sell them. Do not torture Allah's creation.' It is related that Abū Hurayrah was riding a mule one day and his slave was riding behind him. Someone said to him, 'You should have him walk behind your animal.' Abū Hurayra said, 'I would prefer to have two faggots of fire burn me than to have my slave walk behind me.' Muslim related from Abū Hurayrah that the Messenger of Allah ﷺ said, 'A slave has his clothing and food and is only obliged to do such work as he is capable of doing.' The Prophet ﷺ said, 'None of you should say, "my slave" or "my slavegirl," but should say, "my lad" or "my girl".' This will be further explained in *Sūrat Yūsuf.*

The Prophet ﷺ recommended that masters of slaves should have noble character and singled them out for that. He guided them to the best and to the path of humility so that they should not think that they have any prerogative over their slaves since all belongs to Allah and all wealth is the wealth of Allah. But He subjected some people to others and let some of them own others to perfect the blessing and implement wisdom. If they feed them less than they themselves eat and clothe them in garments lesser in value and appearance than they themselves wear, they are permitted to do that provided that they carry out what is obliged for them. There is no disagreement about that. Allah knows best.

Muslim related from 'Abdullāh ibn 'Amr that when Qahrmān came to him, he went in and said, 'Have you given the slaves their food?' 'No,' he answered. He said, 'Go and give them their food. The Messenger of Allah ﷺ said, "It is enough sin for a man to keep food from those he owns."' It is confirmed that the Prophet ﷺ said, 'If someone beats his slave as a *ḥadd* punishment when he did not commit the crime or slaps him, his expiation is to set that slave free.' It means when someone beats his slave to the extent of a *ḥadd* punishment when the *ḥadd* was not obliged for him. It is related that some of the Companions took retaliation on a slave on account of a child by beating him and then they freed the slave since retaliation was not justified. The Prophet ﷺ said, 'Anyone who falsely accuses his slave of fornication will have the *ḥadd* punishment for slander – eighty lashes – carried out on him on the Day of Rising.' He ﷺ also said, 'Someone who is bad to slaves will not enter the Garden.' He said, 'Bad character is misfortune. Good ownership is growth. Maintaining ties of kinship increases the length of life. *Ṣadaqah* protects against an evil death.'

Scholars disagree about who is better: a slave or a free person. Muslim related from Abū Hurayrah said, 'The Prophet ﷺ said, "A slave who puts things right has two rewards."' Abū Hurayrah said, 'By the One Who has the soul of Abū Hurayrah in His hand, if it had not been for *jihād* in the Way of Allah, *ḥajj* and dutifulness to my mother, I would have liked to die as a slave.' Ibn 'Umar related that the Prophet ﷺ said, 'When a slave is faithful to his master and worships Allah well, he has his reward twice over.' They use these and similar reports as evidence for the superiority of slaves because they are accountable in two respects: the worship of Allah and the service of their master. This is what was believed by Abū 'Umar Yūsuf ibn 'Abd al-Barr an-Namirī and Abū Bakr Muḥammad ibn 'Abdullāh ibn Aḥmad al-'Āmirī al-Baghdādī.

Those who think that the free person is superior say that free people have full disposal of the *dīn* and this world whereas slaves do not. A slave is like a tool used with force and best compelled by force. That is why slaves are removed from positions of testimony and most positions of guardianship. Their *ḥadd* punishments are less than those of free people which indicates a lesser value. The duties demanded of a free man are greater in one respect and his toil is more and so his reward is greater. Abū Hurayrah indicated this when he said, 'If it had not been for jihad and ḥajj,' meaning, 'Were it not for the deficiency connected to a slave in missing out on these things.' Allah knows best.

Anas ibn Mālik reported that the Prophet ﷺ said, 'Jibrīl continued to advise me to be good to my neighbour until I thought that he would have me make him my heir. He continued to advise me to be good to women until I thought that he would prohibit divorcing them. He continued to advise me to be good to slaves until I thought he would set a period at which they would be automatically freed. He continued to advise me to use the *siwāk* stick until I thought my mouth would be chafed. He continued to advise me to pray at night until I thought that the best of my community would not sleep at night.' Abu-l-Layth as-Samarqandī mentioned it in his commentary.

Allah does not love anyone vain or boastful.

Allah is not pleased with nor does He love such a person. This means that Allah does not show the effects of His blessing on him in the Next world when he is like this. This is a sort of threat. The vain (*mukhtāl*) is someone with pride and arrogance. Boastful means that he is proud about his virtues. Vanity is haughtiness and insolence. These two qualities are mentioned because they lead the person to have disdain for poor relatives, poor neighbours and others mentioned in the *āyah*. Therefore, he would fail in Allah's command to be good to them.

'Āṣim, in what al-Mufaḍḍāl related from him, recited, *'wa-l-jāri-l-janb'*. Al-Mahdawī said that it implies an elided *muḍāf*, i.e. the neighbour with distance. Akhfash recited:

People are distant and the amīr is distant.

It means far from kinship. Allah knows best.

ٱلَّذِينَ يَبْخَلُونَ وَيَأْمُرُونَ ٱلنَّاسَ بِٱلْبُخْلِ وَيَكْتُمُونَ مَآ
ءَاتَىٰهُمُ ٱللَّهُ مِن فَضْلِهِۦ ۗ وَأَعْتَدْنَا لِلْكَٰفِرِينَ عَذَابًا مُّهِينًا ۝٣٧

37 As for those who are tight-fisted and direct others to be tight-fisted, and hide the bounty Allah has given them, We have prepared a humiliating punishment for the unbelievers,

As for those who are tight-fisted and direct others to be tight-fisted.

'Those' is in the accusative as an appositive for *'man'* in *'man kāna'*. It is not an adjective because *'man'* and *'mā'* are not described or used as a description. It can also be in the nominative as an appositive for what is implied in 'boastful'. It can also be in the nominative and *'those who spend their wealth to show off'* is added to it. It can also be an inceptive whose predicate is elided, i.e. 'those who are tight-fisted will have...' or the predicate is: *'Allah does not wrong anyone by so much as the smallest speck'*. It is in the accusative by an implied 'I mean' and so the *āyah* is about the believers. The *āyah* can have this interpretation because the miserly are denied Allah's love, and so the believers should do good. Allah does not love those lacking in that quality. The blameworthy tightfistedness in the Sharī'ah is refusing to pay what Allah has made it obligatory to pay, illustrated by His words: *'Those who are tight-fisted with the bounty Allah has given them should not suppose...'* (3:180) This was discussed there.

The people referred to in this *āyah,* according to Ibn 'Abbās and others, are the Jews. They were characterised by vanity, boasting, miserliness and they concealed what Allah revealed in the Torah of the description of Muḥammad ﷺ. It is said that what is meant are the hypocrites whose spending and faith were mere dissembling. It means: 'Allah does not love anyone vain or boastful nor those who are tight-fisted' according to the previously mentioned syntax.

We have prepared a humiliating punishment for the unbelievers.

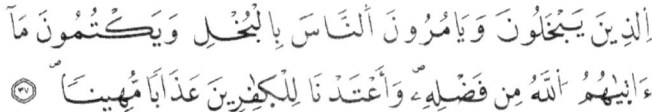

Allah warns miserly believers with the warning directed at the unbelievers by condemning the first to lack of love, and the second to a humiliating punishment.

وَالَّذِينَ يُنفِقُونَ أَمْوَالَهُمْ رِئَاءَ النَّاسِ وَلَا يُؤْمِنُونَ بِاللَّهِ وَلَا بِالْيَوْمِ الْآخِرِ
وَمَن يَكُنِ الشَّيْطَانُ لَهُ قَرِينًا فَسَاءَ قَرِينًا ﴿٣٨﴾

38 and also for those who spend their wealth to show off to people, not believing in Allah and the Last Day. Anyone who has made Shayṭān his comrade, what an evil comrade he is!

This *āyah* is added to '*Those who are tight-fisted*' and describes the unbelievers, and so it is in the genitive. Those who think that there is an extra *wāw* permit the second to be a predicate of the first.

The majority say that it was revealed about the hypocrites since 'showing off' is mentioned, and that is an aspect of hypocrisy. Mujāhid said that it is about the Jews, but aṭ-Ṭabarī says that that is weak because Allah negated belief in Allah and the Last Day for this group, but that is not the case with the Jews. Ibn 'Aṭiyyah pointed out that their belief in the Last Day will not help them. It is also said that it was revealed about those who paid out on the Day of Badr, namely the leaders of Makkah who paid people to go forth for the Battle of Badr. Ibn al-'Arabī said that what is paid in order to show off to people is included in the rulings since it is not rewarded. That is indicated in Book where Allah says: '*Say: "Whether you give readily or reluctantly, it will not be accepted from you."*' (9:53)

Anyone who has made Shayṭān his comrade, what an evil comrade he is!

A comrade (*qarīn*) is a close companion and a close friend. It is the measure *fa'īl* from *iqrān*. 'Adī ibn Zayd said:

Do not ask about a man. Rather ask about his comrade.
Every comrade follows the one he is connected to.

The *āyah* means: if anyone obeys Shayṭān in this world, he is his companion. It can also mean that he will be joined as a companion to Shayṭān in the Fire. Shayṭān is an evil comrade. It is in the accusative for distinction.

وَمَاذَا عَلَيۡهِمۡ لَوۡ ءَامَنُواْ بِٱللَّهِ وَٱلۡيَوۡمِ ٱلۡأٓخِرِ وَأَنفَقُواْ مِمَّا رَزَقَهُمُ ٱللَّهُۚ وَكَانَ ٱللَّهُ
بِهِمۡ عَلِيمًا ٣٩

39 What harm would it have done them to have believed in Allah and the Last Day and to have given of what Allah has provided for them? Allah knows everything about them.

Mā is in the nominative for the inceptive and '*dhā*' is its predicate and means 'which'. *Mā* and *dhā'* can also be single noun. According to the first, it implies, 'What harm would it have done them', and according to the second, 'What burden would it have been' if they had affirmed the necessity of the existence of Allah and the Last Day and the details of the Next World which the Prophet ﷺ brought.

إِنَّ ٱللَّهَ لَا يَظۡلِمُ مِثۡقَالَ ذَرَّةٖۖ وَإِن تَكُ حَسَنَةٗ يُضَٰعِفۡهَا وَيُؤۡتِ مِن لَّدُنۡهُ
أَجۡرًا عَظِيمٗا ٤٠

40 Allah does not wrong anyone by so much as the smallest speck. And if there is a good deed Allah will multiply it and pay out an immense reward direct from Him.

Allah does not wrong anyone by so much as the smallest speck.

He does not stint them nor decrease the reward of their action by even the weight of an atom that is owed to them by way of reward. What is meant is that Allah does not wrong in any way at all, neither a little nor a lot, as Allah says: *'Allah does not wrong people at all.'* (10:44). *Dharrah* is a red ant. Ibn 'Abbās and others said that it is the smallest of ants, or that it is the head of an ant. Yazīd ibn Hārūn said that they state that a *dharrah* is something that has no weight. It is said that a man placed bread and then a *dharrah* on top of it and the *dharrah* did not increase its weight at all. The Qur'an and *Sunnah* indicate that a *dharrah* does have some weight, as does a dinar, and Allah knows best.

Some say that it is a mustard seed, referring to what Allah says: *'No self will be wronged in any way. Even if it be no more than the weight of a mustard seed, We will produce it.'* (21:47) Other things are said. What it alludes to is the smallest and least of things. In *Ṣaḥīḥ Muslim*, Anas reported that the Prophet ﷺ said, 'Allah does not wrong a believer for a good deed. He gives to him in this world and repays him in the next World. As for the unbeliever, he eats by the good actions he does for

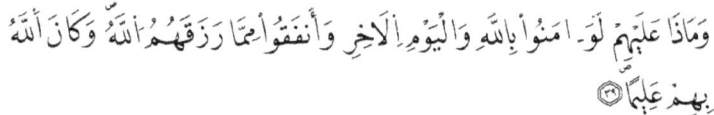

Allah in this world and when he goes to the Next world, he has no good deeds for which he is rewarded.'

And if there is a good deed Allah will multiply it

He will make its reward greater. The people of the Hijaz recite *'ḥasanah'* in the nominative while the rest have it in the accusative. According to the first, *'taku'* means 'occurs', and it is complete. According to the second, it is imperfect and implies: 'if your deed is a good deed'. Al-Ḥasan recited it with a *nūn* as *'nuḍā'ifhā'* ('We will multiply it') while the rest recite it with a *yā'*, which is sounder since Allah uses the third person after that. Abū Rajā' recited *'yuḍa''ifnā'* while the rest have it in Form III. They are two dialectical forms both of which mean to make more. Abū 'Ubaydah said that Form III means to make it many times more and Form II means to double it.

and pay out an immense wage direct from Him.

There are four dialectical forms of 'direct': *ladun*, *ludnu*, *ladu* and *ladā*. When they ascribe it to themselves, there is a double *nūn*. *'Min'* is added to it since *'min'* is added to the commencement of the limit. The same is true of *'ladun'*. When they are similar, it is good to add *'min'* to it. That is why Sībawayh said about *ladun*: 'Its position is the beginning of the commencement.'

'An immense wage' is the Garden. We find in *Ṣaḥīḥ Muslim* the long hadith of intercession narrated by Abū Sa'īd al-Khudrī in which it says: 'When the believers are saved from the Fire, by the One who has my soul in His hand, not one of you will be more insistent on the Day of Rising than the believers in entreating Allah for their brothers who are in the Fire. They will say, "Our Lord, they used to fast with us, pray and make *ḥajj!*" They will be told, "Bring out those you know from it and their forms will be forbidden to the Fire." They will bring out many people, some of whom the Fire had taken to the thighs and some to the knees. Then they say, "Our Lord, none of those You commanded us to bring out remain in it." He will say, "Go back and bring out anyone in whose heart there is a dinar of good," and they will bring out many people. Then they will say, "Our Lord, none of those You commanded us to bring out remain in it." Then He will say, "Go back and bring out anyone in whose heart there is a half a dinar of good," and they will bring out many people. Then they will say, "Our Lord, none of those You commanded us to bring out remain in it." Then He will say, "Go back and bring out anyone in whose heart there is a speck of good," and they will bring out many people. Then they will say, "Our Lord, no one with any good at all in him

remains there."' Abū Sa'īd al-Khudrī said, 'If you do not believe me about this *ḥadīth*, then recite: *"Allah does not wrong anyone by so much as the smallest speck. And if there is a good deed Allah will multiply it and pay out an immense reward direct from Him."'*

It is related from Ibn Mas'ūd that the Prophet ﷺ said, 'A person will be brought on the Day of Rising and made to stand. A caller will call out in front of people, "This is so-and-so the son of so-and-so. Whoever is due something from him should come for his right." Then He will say, "Give them what they are due." He will say, "Lord, how can I do that when the world is gone?" Allah Almighty will say to the angels, "Look at his righteous deeds and give them some of them." If the amount of a mustard-seed remains, the angels will say, "O Lord (and He knows that better than they do), "Everyone who is owed something has been given his due and a speck of good deeds (*dharrah*) still remains." Allah will tell the angels, "Multiply it for My slave and admit him to the Garden by My mercy." Its confirmation is His words: *"Allah does not wrong anyone by so much as the smallest speck. And if there is a good deed, Allah will multiply it."* If it is someone wretched, the angels will say, "Our God, his good actions are used up and only his evil deeds remain. There are still many making demands." Allah will say, "Take some of their evil deeds and add them to his evil deeds." Then they will beat him into the Fire.'

According to this interpretation, the *āyah* is about litigation. Allah Almighty will not wrong one litigant in respect to what he is owed by the smallest speck and he will not be wronged by the slightest speck in what remains for him. Instead, he will be rewarded for it and it will be multiplied for him. That is what it says here. Abū Hurayrah reported that he heard the Messenger of Allah ﷺ said, 'Allah will give the believer a hundred thousand good deeds for one good deed.' Then he recited this. Abū Hurayrah said, 'An immense reward is one which cannot be estimated.' Ibn 'Abbās and Ibn Mas'ūd said, 'This is one of the *āyah*s that is better than everything that the sun rises on.'

فَكَيْفَ إِذَا جِئْنَا مِن كُلِّ أُمَّةٍ بِشَهِيدٍ وَجِئْنَا بِكَ عَلَىٰ هَٰؤُلَاءِ شَهِيدًا ﴿٤١﴾

41 How will it be when We bring a witness from every nation and bring you as a witness against them?

'Idhā' (when) is an adverb of time and its regent is 'We bring'. Abu-l-Layth as-Samarqandī mentioned from al-Khalīl ibn Aḥmad from Ibn Manī' from Abū Kāmil from Fuḍayl from Yūnus ibn Muḥammad ibn Faḍālah from his father that the Messenger of Allah ﷺ came to them among the Banū Zafar and sat on a

stone there with Ibn Mas'ūd, Mu'ādh and some other people. He asked a reciter to recite. When he reached the *āyah*: *'How will it be when We bring a witness from every nation and bring you as a witness against them?'* the Messenger of Allah ﷺ wept until his cheeks were wet and said, 'O Lord, this is against me! Who am I among them and how will it be when I have not seen them?'

Al-Bukhārī reported that 'Abdullāh said, 'The Messenger of Allah ﷺ told me, "Recite to me." I asked, "Shall I recite to you when it was sent down to you?" He replied, "I want to hear it from someone other than myself." So I recited *Sūrat an-Nisā'* to him. When I reached: *"How will it be when We bring a witness from every nation and bring you as a witness against them?"* he said, "Stop," and tears were flowing from his eyes.' Muslim related it, and instead of 'Stop,' he said, 'I raised my head' or 'A man beside me nudged me and I lifted my head and saw his eyes flowing with tears.' Our scholars say that the Prophet ﷺ wept because of the huge implications this *āyah* contains regarding the terror of the Presentation (of actions) and the magnitude of the matter, since the Prophets will be brought as witnesses against their communities as to whether they are lying or telling the truth and he ﷺ will be brought as a witness on the Day of Rising.

The words *'against them'* refer to the unbelievers of Quraysh and other unbelievers. Qurayshī unbelievers are mentioned in particular because the burden of punishment will be more severe for them than others since they were obdurate in the face of miracles and breaking of normal patterns that Allah manifested at the hands of the Prophet ﷺ. The import of this question is: 'What do you think will be the fate of these unbelievers on the Day of Rising: *'when We bring a witness from every nation and bring you as a witness against them?'* Do you think they will be punished or blessed? The question entails a stern rebuke. It is said that it involves all of his community. Ibn al-Mubārak said that it was reported to him that Sa'īd ibn al-Musayyab was heard to say, 'No day passes without his community being presented to the Prophet ﷺ morning and evening and he knows them by their mark and their actions. That is why he will testify against them. Allah says: *"How will it be when We bring a witness from every nation"* – meaning their Prophets – *"and bring you as a witness against them."'*

'How' is in the accusative by an implied verb. It implies: 'What will their state be,' as we mentioned. The verb implied fills the need of '*idhā*'. The regent is '*idhā*' is 'We bring' and 'witness' is a *ḥāl*.

The *ḥadīth* contains the understanding that it is permitted for a student to recite and read to his Shaykh just as the reverse is permitted. This will be explained in the *ḥadīth* of Ubayy in a later *sūrah*, Allah willing.

يَوْمَئِذٍ يَوَدُّ ٱلَّذِينَ كَفَرُوا۟ وَعَصَوُا۟ ٱلرَّسُولَ لَوْ تُسَوَّىٰ بِهِمُ ٱلْأَرْضُ وَلَا يَكْتُمُونَ ٱللَّهَ حَدِيثًا ﴿٤٢﴾

42 On that day those who disbelieved and disobeyed the Messenger will wish that they were one with the level earth. They will not be able to hide a single circumstance from Allah.

There is a *ḍammah* on the *wāw* in *'aṣawu'* because of the meeting of two silent letters. It is also permitted with a *kasrah*. In this Nāfi' and Ibn 'Āmir read *'tassawwa'*, Ḥamzah and al-Kisā'ī read *'tasawwa'* and the rest *'tusawwa'* based on the passive with the subject not named. The meaning is: 'If Allah had made them level with the earth.' Another meaning is: 'They will wish that Allah had not raised them and that the earth was levelled over them because they will be transported from the earth.' According to the first two readings, the earth is the subject and the meaning is: 'they will wish that the earth had been opened for them and that they could sink into it.' Qatādah said that. It is said that *bā'* means 'over, on'. It means they will wish that it would split open and be levelled over them. Al-Ḥasan said that. The reading with a double *sīn* is based on *idghām*, and the single *sīn* is based on the elision of the *tā'*. It is said that they will wish for this when they see the animals become dust and know that they will be eternally in the Fire. This is the meaning of Allah's words: *'The unbeliever will say, "Oh, if only I were dust!"'* (78:40)

It is said that they will wish this when this community testifies on behalf of the Prophets as already mentioned in 2:143. The past communities will say, 'There are fornicators and thieves among them, so do not accept their testimony!' The Prophet will declare their integrity and the idolaters will say: *'By Allah, our Lord, We were not idolaters.'* (6:23) Their mouths will be sealed and their hands and feet will testify to their errors. That is why they will wish that the earth had swallowed them up. Allah knows best.

They will not be able to hide a single circumstance from Allah.

Az-Zajjāj said that some of them said that this is a new sentence because what they did will be evident to Allah and they will not be able to conceal it. Others said that it is added to what is before it and means: they will want the earth to be level with them but they will not be able to hide anything because their lies will be evident. Ibn 'Abbās was asked about this *āyah* and about the words: *'By Allah, our Lord, We were not idolaters'* (6:23), and he said, 'When they see that only the people of Islam will enter the Garden, they will say: *"By Allah, our Lord, We were not idolaters."*

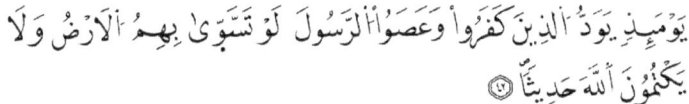

Allah will seal their mouths and their hands and feet will speak and they will not be able to hide a single circumstance from Allah.'

Qatādah and al-Ḥasan said, 'The Next World consists of different places: these will be in some and those in another.' It means when it is clear to them and they are reckoned, then they will not conceal anything. Allah willing, this will be further explained in *al-An'ām*.

يَٰٓأَيُّهَا ٱلَّذِينَ ءَامَنُواْ لَا تَقۡرَبُواْ ٱلصَّلَوٰةَ وَأَنتُمۡ سُكَٰرَىٰ حَتَّىٰ تَعۡلَمُواْ مَا تَقُولُونَ
وَلَا جُنُبًا إِلَّا عَابِرِي سَبِيلٍ حَتَّىٰ تَغۡتَسِلُواْۚ وَإِن كُنتُم مَّرۡضَىٰٓ أَوۡ عَلَىٰ سَفَرٍ
أَوۡ جَآءَ أَحَدٞ مِّنكُم مِّنَ ٱلۡغَآئِطِ أَوۡ لَٰمَسۡتُمُ ٱلنِّسَآءَ فَلَمۡ تَجِدُواْ مَآءٗ فَتَيَمَّمُواْ صَعِيدٗا
طَيِّبٗا فَٱمۡسَحُواْ بِوُجُوهِكُمۡ وَأَيۡدِيكُمۡۗ إِنَّ ٱللَّهَ كَانَ عَفُوًّا غَفُورًا ٤٣

43 You who believe! do not approach the prayer when you are drunk, so that you will know what you are saying, nor in a state of major impurity – unless you are travelling – until you have washed yourselves completely. If you are ill or on a journey, or any of you have come from the lavatory or touched women, and you cannot find any water, then do *tayammum* with pure earth, wiping your faces and your hands. Allah is Ever-Pardoning, Ever-Forgiving.

You who believe! do not approach the prayer when you are drunk, so that you will know what you are saying,

Allah singled out the believers for this instruction because they used to perform the prayer when they had drunk wine and their minds were disordered and so they were singled out for this, since the unbelievers did not perform the prayer, whether sober or drunk. Abū Dāwūd reported that when the prohibition of wine was revealed, 'Umar ibn al-Khaṭṭāb said, 'O Allah, give us an adequate clarification about wine,' and so the *āyah* in *al-Baqarah* was revealed: *'They will ask you about intoxicants and gambling.'* (2:219). 'Umar was summoned and it was read to him and he said, 'O Allah, give us an adequate clarification about wine!' Then this *āyah* in *an-Nisā'* was revealed. When the one who announced the prayer for the Messenger of Allah ﷺ called the prayer, he would say, 'No one drunk should come near the prayer.' 'Umar was called and it was read to him. Again he said, 'O Allah, give us an adequate clarification about wine,' and then the *āyah* was revealed: *'So will you then give them up?'* (5:91) 'Umar said, 'We have given up.'

Sa'īd ibn Jubayr said, 'The people continued what they used to do in the *Jāhiliyyah* until there was a command or prohibition about it. They used to drink at the beginning of Islam until Allah revealed: "*They will ask you about intoxicants and gambling. Say, 'There is great wrong in both of them and also certain benefits for mankind.'* (2:219)." They then said, "We drink it for the benefit, not the prohibition." So a man would come to the prayer and recite, "Say, 'O unbelievers, I worship what you worship' (instead of 'I do not worship')" and so the *āyah*: "*You who believe! do not approach the prayer when you are drunk...*" was revealed. They said, "Then (it is all right) in other than the prayer itself." 'Umar said, "O Allah, O Allah, give us an adequate clarification about wine," and: "*Shayṭān desires...*" (5:91) was revealed. 'Umar said, "We have given up. We have given up." The caller of the Messenger of Allah ﷺ went around saying, "Wine has been forbidden."' This will be explained in *al-Mā'idah*, Allah willing.

At-Tirmidhī related that 'Alī ibn Abī Ṭālib said, "Abd ar-Raḥmān ibn 'Awf prepared some food for us and invited us and gave us wine to drink. The wine had an effect on us and then the time for the prayer came and they put me forward to lead it. I recited: "*Say: 'Unbelievers! I do not worship what you worship'*" (109:1) and then said "We worship what you worship." Then Allah revealed: "*You who believe! do not approach the prayer when you are drunk so that you will know what you are saying.*"' Abū 'Īsā said that it is a sound *ḥasan ḥadīth*.

The manner of the connection and order to what is before it is that Allah says: '*Worship Allah and do not associate anything with Him.*' (4:36) Then after faith, He mentions the prayer which is at the head of all acts of worship. That is why someone who abandons it is executed and its obligation is never cancelled. Then He mentions the preconditions without which it is not sound.

Most scholars and *fuqahā'* agree that what is meant by intoxication is the intoxication of wine, except for aḍ-Ḍaḥḥāk, who said that it is sleep since the Prophet ﷺ said, 'If one of you nods off while he is praying, he should go and lie down until he is no longer sleepy. If someone prays when he is drowsy, he may not know whether he is asking for forgiveness or asking for something bad for himself.' 'Abīdah as-Salmānī said that it means suppressing the urge to relieve oneself since the Prophet ﷺ said, 'None of you should pray holding his urine.' What aḍ-Ḍaḥḥāk and 'Abīdah said has a sound meaning because what is desired of the person praying is to face Allah with all his heart and not turn to anything else and to be free of anything that might pollute that – sleepiness, suppression of the urge to relieve oneself, hunger and anything else that distracts the mind and changes the state. The Prophet ﷺ said, 'When a meal is served and the prayer has been called, begin with the meal.' The Prophet ﷺ took note of the need to remove anything which could distract a person's thoughts so that they can turn to the worship of their Lord with a free heart and mind and be humble in the prayer. Concomitant with this *āyah* are Allah's words: *'It is the believers who are successful, those who are humble in their prayers.'* (23:1-2)

Ibn 'Abbās said that this *āyah* was abrogated by the one in *al-Mā'idah*. According to this, they were commanded not to pray when drunk and then commanded to pray in every instance. This was before the prohibition. Mujāhid said that it was abrogated by the prohibition of wine, as was also stated by 'Ikrimah and Qatādah. This is the sound view about this because of the *ḥadīth*s we have mentioned. It is related that 'Umar ibn al-Khaṭṭāb said, 'The *iqāmah* for the prayer was given and then the caller of the Messenger of Allah ﷺ called out, "No one who is drunk should come near the prayer."' An-Naḥḥās mentioned it. According to the position of aḍ-Ḍaḥḥāk and 'Abīdah, the *āyah* is one of judgment and is not abrogated.

This version of the verb *'approach'* (*taqrabu*) used here implies directly engaging in an action. If it were *taqrubu*, it would refer to physically approaching something. The *āyah* is addressed to the sober community. A drunk cannot distinguish since he is intoxicated, and so he is not the one addressed at this moment because he is witless. A person is instructed to perform what is mandatory for him and to expiate anything that was prescribed for him before he became intoxicated that he missed on account of his intoxication.

Scholars disagree about what is meant by *ṣalāt* here. One group said that it is the prayer itself, as Abū Ḥanīfah said. That is why Allah says: *'...so that you will know what you are saying.'* Another group said that it means places of prayer, which is what ash-Shāfi'ī says, and something is elided. Allah says elsewhere: *'...monasteries, churches, synagogues and mosques (*ṣalāwāt*) would have been pulled down and destroyed...'* (22:40) in which the word *ṣalawāt* is used to mean mosques. This is indicated by the rest of the *āyah* which commands people not to approach it while in a state of major impurity, which would give a traveller permission to pass through the mosque, but not to pray in it. Abū Ḥanīfah says that it means that a traveller who is in major impurity can do *tayammum* and pray. Another group says that it means both the places of the prayer and the prayer itself because the two are usually together.

'When you are drunk' is an inceptive and predicate, and the sentence is in the position of a *ḥāl* modifying approach'. *Sukarā* is the plural of *sukrān* (drunk), like *kaslān* and *kusālā*. An-Nakha'ī recited *'sakrā'* on the measure of *fa'lā*. It is a broken

plural of *sukrān*. It is based on '*sakrā*' because intoxication is a disaster which affects the intellect so a drunk is like someone who is knocked down. Al-A'mash recited '*sukrā*' like '*hublā*'. It is a single adjective modifying the group as they report about a group using the singular.

Intoxication is the opposite of sobriety and bars access to intelligence. *Sakira* is the verb for being intoxicated and it is also used for the eyes being bewildered as in 15:15: '*...they would only say, "Our eyesight is befuddled."*' *Sakkara* is used for blocking a split and so the intoxicated person is cut off from his senses. This *āyah* is evidence that drinking was allowed at the beginning of Islam up to the point of intoxication. Some people say that intoxication is logically forbidden and not allowed in any religion. They take intoxication here to mean sleep. Al-Qaffāl said that it is possible that they were allowed that amount of drinking which impels one to generosity, courage and zeal. This idea is found in poems, as Ḥassān said:

We drank it and it left us like kings.

This matter was dealt with in full in *al-Baqarah*. Al-Qaffāl said, 'As for what renders someone witless so that he is like someone insane or passes out, this is not permitted. If it happens without intention, then responsibility is removed from the person.' This is sound and will be discussed in more detail in *al-Mā'idah* in the story of Ḥamzah. When this was revealed the Muslims avoided drink at the times of the prayer. Then they drank after they had prayed '*Ishā*'. They continued to do that until its prohibition was revealed in *al-Mā'idah* (5:91).

The words '*so that you will know what you are saying*' mean that you know it and are certain of not making any mistake. The one who is intoxicated does not know what he is saying. That is why 'Uthmān ibn 'Affān said that the divorce of someone drunk is not binding. That is related from Ibn 'Abbās, Ṭāwūs, 'Aṭā', al-Qāsim and Rabī'ah. It is the position of al-Layth, Isḥāq, Abū Thawr and al-Muzanī. Aṭ-Ṭaḥāwī preferred it, saying, 'Scholars agree that a divorce by a lunatic is not accepted, and someone who is drunk is deranged by drink in the way that someone suffering from whispering is deranged by whispering.' They do not disagree that if someone drinks *banj* (henbane) and loses his rationality, his divorce is not accepted and they also apply that ruling to alcohol.

One group allows the divorce. 'Umar ibn al-Khaṭṭāb, Mu'āwiyah and a group of Tābi'ūn do so, and it is the position of Abū Ḥanīfah, ath-Thawrī and al-Awzā'ī, and the position of ash-Shāfi'ī varies. Mālik made people responsible for divorce, retaliation for injury and killing while drunk, but not marriage and sales. Abū Ḥanīfah said that all the actions and contracts of a drunk are ratified in the same way they would be if he were sober, except for apostasy. If he apostasises, his wife is not separated from him except as a recommendation. But Abū Yūsuf says that he is an apostate while drunk, which is also the position of ash-Shāfi'ī, but he is not executed while drunk nor asked to repent.

Imam Abū 'Abdullāh al-Māzinī said, 'There is an aberrant transmission we have that a divorce by someone drunk is not binding.' Muḥammad ibn 'Abd al-Ḥakam said that neither a divorce or emancipation are binding on a drunk person. Ibn Shās said that Shaykh Abu-l-Walīd said that the disagreement is about a person who is muddled but retains some sense. They cannot control themselves and are sometimes right and sometimes wrong. He said, 'As for a drunk who does not know heaven from earth or man from woman, there is no disagreement that he is like the insane in respect of all his states and states and dealings with other people and what is between him and Allah. However, if he misses prayers, they are not cancelled for him, which would be the case with the insane person, since causing himself to be drunk is like deliberately missing the prayer until its time has passed.' Sufyān ath-Thawrī said, 'Intoxication is defined as the muddling of the mind. When he is made to read and muddles his reading and says what is recognised as not right, then he is flogged.' Aḥmad said, 'When the mind is altered from sobriety, then he is intoxicated.' Something similar is related from Mālik. Ibn al-Mundhir said, 'When someone muddles his recitation, he is drunk as evidenced by His words: "*...so that you will know what you are saying.*" When he does not know what he is saying, he should avoid the mosque out of fear of sullying it. His prayer is not valid and if he prays, he must make it up. If he knows what he is saying and prays, his ruling is that of someone sober.'

nor in a state of major impurity

This is added to what preceded, in other words do not pray while in a state of *janābah*. '*Tajannabtum*', '*ajnabtum*' and '*janubtum*' all mean the same. The expression *junub* is not feminine, and has no feminine or plural because it has the measure of a verbal noun, like *bu'd* and *qurb*. Sometimes it is lightened and '*junb*' is said and some people have recited it like that. Al-Farrā' said that the verbs *januba* and *ajnaba* [and *jannaba* and *tajannaba*] are used for a man in *janābah*. It is said that the plural of *junub* in one dialect is *ajnāb*, like '*unuq* and *a'nāq*, and *ṭunub* and *aṭnāb*. The singular is *jānib*, and the plural of that is *junnāb*, like *rākib* and *rukkāb*. The root means distance. It is as if someone in *janābah* is far from the state of the prayer on account of the emission of sperm. [POEM ALREADY QUOTED ABOVE] A man who is *junub* is an exile. *Janābah* is a man mixing with a woman.

Most of the Community agree that the one in *janābah* is one rendered impure by ejaculation or the meeting of the private parts. Some Companions said that *ghusl* is only necessary in the case of ejaculation since the Prophet ﷺ said, 'Water is on account of water.' Muslim transmitted it. In al-Bukhārī, Ubayy ibn Ka'b said, 'Messenger of Allah, what about when a man has sexual intercourse with a woman and does not ejaculate?' He replied, 'He should wash what has touched the woman and then do *wuḍū'* and pray.' Al-Bukhārī said, 'Having a *ghusl* is safer and that was the final position. We have made their disagreement clear.' Muslim transmitted something similar in his collection. Abu-l-'Alā' ibn ash-Shikhkīr said that some *ḥadīth*s the Messenger of Allah ﷺ abrogate others in the same way that some parts of the Qur'an abrogate others. Abū Isḥāq said that this is abrogated. At-Tirmidhī said that it was the ruling at the beginning of Islam and then was abrogated.

According to the majority of scholars among the Companions and Tābi'ūn and the *fuqahā'* of the regions, *ghusl* is made mandatory by the contact of the private parts. There was a disagreement between the Companions and then they took the transmission of 'Ā'ishah from the Prophet ﷺ: 'When he sits between her limbs and the private parts touch, *ghusl* is obliged.' Muslim transmitted it. Abū Hurayrah transmitted something similar in the two *Ṣaḥīḥ* Collections. Muslim adds, 'Even if he does not ejaculate.' Ibn al-Qaṣṣār said that the Tābi'ūn and those after them (after some disagreement before them) agree to take the hadithof 'when the circumcised parts meet'. When there is consensus after disagreement, the disagreement is dropped.

Qāḍī 'Iyāḍ said, 'We do not know of anyone who says it after the disagreement of the Companions except for what was related from al-A'mash and Dāwūd al-Iṣbahānī after him. It is related that 'Umar made people abandon the *ḥadīth* stating, 'Water is on account of water,' when they disagreed. Ibn 'Abbās interpreted it as a wet dream, meaning that *ghusl* with water is obliged when a dream results in discharge of fluid. If there was no emission, even if he dreamed that he was having sex, there is no *ghusl* required. There is no disagreement between most scholars about this.

unless you are travelling

The literal meaning of this expression is traversing a path from one end to the other. The verb *'abara* is used for crossing a river. The *'abr* of a river is a ford. One also says *'ubr. Mi'bar* is what is used to cross it, whether that be a vessel or a bridge. Someone travelling on a path is *'ābir as-sabīl*. A camel which is *'ubru asfār* is one upon which journeys are continuously made and on which one travels through wasteland and in the middle of the day because of its swift gait. A poet said:

A she-camel swift in travel, quick-footed, agile.
crossing (*'ubr*) in the heat like a red-legged ostrich.

When people 'pass', they die. The poem goes:

Allah's Decree overcomes everything
and toys with both the anxious and the steadfast.

If we pass, there are others just like us.
If we live, we are still waiting for it.

One says, 'If we die, we have fellows. If we remain, death must come as if we had a vow in its coming.

Scholars disagree about the words: '*...unless you are travelling.*' 'Alī, Ibn 'Abbās, Ibn Jubayr, Mujāhid and al-Ḥakam said that it refers to travellers. It is not correct for anyone to approach the prayer in *janābah* without performing a *ghusl* except for a traveller who is permitted to do *tayammum*. This is the position of Abū Ḥanīfah because water is usually not lacking when someone is resident so someone in that situation can use water. A traveller performs *tayammum* if he cannot find water. Ibn al-Mundhir said that the People of Opinion say that if a traveller passes by a mosque which has a spring in it, he should do *tayammum* with earth, enter the mosque, draw water and then take the water out of the mosque and do *ghusl*. One group make an allowance for someone in *janābah* to enter the mosque in those circumstances. Some of them offer what the Prophet ﷺ said as evidence: 'The believer is not impure.' Ibn al-Mundhir remarked, 'That is what we say.'

Ibn 'Abbās, Ibn Mas'ūd, 'Ikrimah and an-Nakha'ī say that this is only applicable to someone who just passes through. It is the position of 'Amr ibn Dīnār, Mālik and ash-Shāfi'ī. One group say that someone in *janābah* may not enter the mosque unless he cannot find water, in which case he may do *tayammum* and pass through it. That is what ath-Thawrī and Isḥāq ibn Rāhawayh said. Aḥmad and Isḥāq said that if he does *wuḍu'*, he can sit in the mosque. Ibn al-Mundhir related that. Some of them report that the reason for this was that the doors of some of the houses of the Anṣār opened into the mosque and some of them would have to cross through the mosque while in *janābah*.

This is sound and is supported by what Abū Dāwūd reported from 'Ā'ishah: 'The Messenger of Allah ﷺ came when the doors of the rooms of his Companions opened into the mosque. He said, "Make these rooms face away from the mosque." Then the Prophet ﷺ went inside and people did not do anything, hoping that a dispensation would be made for them. He came out and repeated, "Make these rooms face away from the mosque. The mosque is not lawful for a menstruating woman or anyone in *janābah*."' We find in *Ṣaḥīḥ Muslim*: 'No opening should remain into the mosque except that of Abū Bakr.' So he ﷺ commanded the doors to be closed because that would lead to making the mosque a road used for crossing through. Abū Bakr's opening was excluded to honour him and was particular to him because the two of them were rarely apart.

It is related from the Prophet ﷺ that he did not give anyone permission to pass through the mosque or sit in it (in *janābah*) except for 'Alī ibn Abī Ṭālib. 'Aṭiyyah al-'Awfī related from Abū Sa'īd al-Khudrī that the Messenger of Allah ﷺ said, 'It is not proper or correct for any Muslim to be in the mosque while in *janābah* except for me and 'Alī.' Our scholars say that it is permitted for this to be the case because 'Alī's house was in the mosque as was the house of the Prophet ﷺ. Even if the two houses were not actually situated inside the mosque, they were directly connected to the mosque and their doors were inside the mosque and so the Messenger of Allah ﷺ made them part of the mosque and said, 'It is not proper for any Muslim…' Evidence for the fact that 'Alī's house was in the mosque is found in what Ibn Shihāb related from 'Abdullāh. He said, 'A man asked my father about 'Alī and 'Uthmān and which of them was better. 'Abdullāh ibn 'Umar told him, "This is the house of the Messenger of Allah ﷺ!" and he pointed to 'Alī's house beside it. There were only those two houses in the mosque.'

They were not in *janābah* in the mosque, but in their houses, and their houses were in the mosque since their doors opened onto it. They went through it in *janābah* when they left their houses. It is possible that that was particular to the two of them. The Prophet ﷺ had a special prerogative in respect of certain things, and this was one of them. Then the Prophet ﷺ singled out 'Alī and allowed him something that others were not allowed. In addition to the doors of the two of them, there were other doors which opened onto the mosque until the Prophet ﷺ ordered them to be blocked up except for 'Alī's door. 'Amr ibn Maymūn related that Ibn 'Abbās said that the Prophet ﷺ said, 'Block up these doors except for that of 'Alī.' So the Messenger of Allah ﷺ singled him out by leaving his door in the mosque. He would be in *janābah* in his house while his house was in the mosque.

As for his words ﷺ, 'No opening should remain in the mosque except that of Abū Bakr,' Allah knows best, but those doors which looked onto the mosque had openings in them while the doors of the houses were outside the mosque. So the Prophet ﷺ commanded those openings to be closed up but left that of Abū Bakr to honour him. An 'opening' (*khawkha*) is like a small window or niche. 'Alī's door was the door of a house by which one enters and leaves. Ibn 'Umar explained that by saying that they were the only two in the mosque.

Someone might say that it is confirmed that 'Aṭā' ibn Yasār said, 'Some of the Companions of the Prophet ﷺ were in *janābah* and they did *wuḍū'* and went to the mosque and conversed in it,' so this would indicate that it is permitted for someone in *janābah* to stay in the mosque if he does *wuḍū'*. That is the school of Aḥmad and Isḥāq. The reply to this is that *wuḍū'* does not remove *janābah*. Every place which is for worship and too noble for outward impurity should not be entered by someone who is not fit for that worship and cannot perform it. Most cases indicate that they did *ghusl* in their homes. If it is said that ability to worship is cancelled by breaking *wuḍū'*, [so it would not be lawful for him to perform the prayer and enter the mosque], we reply that because that happens frequently, it is difficult to do *wuḍū'* in that case. Allah's words: '*...unless you are travelling*' are sufficient. If someone is not permitted to remain in the mosque, then it is even more appropriate that he is not permitted to touch the Qur'an or recite it since it has even greater sanctity. Allah willing, this will be explained in the commentary on *Sūrat al-Wāqi'ah*.

Our scholars forbid someone in *janābah* to recite the Qur'an in general except for a few *āyah*s for protection. Mūsā ibn 'Uqbah related from Nāfi' from Ibn 'Umar that the Messenger of Allah ﷺ said, 'Someone in *janābah* and menstruating women should not recite any of the Qur'an.' Ibn Mājah transmitted it. Ad-Dāraquṭnī reported from Sufyān ibn Mis'ar and Shu'bah from 'Amr ibn Murrah from 'Abdullāh ibn Salamah that 'Alī said, 'Nothing stopped the Prophet ﷺ from reciting the Qur'an except being in *janābah*.' Sufyān said, 'Shu'bah said to me, "I have not related a *ḥadīth* better than it."' Ibn Mājah transmitted it from Muḥammad ibn Bashhār from Muḥammad ibn Ja'far from Shu'bah from 'Amr ibn Murrah, and he mentioned it with the same meaning and said that it is a sound *isnād*. Ibn 'Abbās related from 'Abdullāh ibn Rawāḥah that the Messenger of Allah ﷺ forbade anyone to recite the Qur'an while he was in *janābah*. Ad-Dāraquṭnī transmitted it.

'Ikrimah reported: 'Ibn Rawāḥah was lying down beside his wife and then went to a slave-girl of his who was in the corner of a room and had sex with her. His wife woke up and did not find him in the bed. She got up and went out and saw him on his slave-girl. She went back to the room, picked up a large knife and came out. He finished, got up and met her carrying the knife and asked, "What are you doing?" "What am I doing?" she replied, "If I had found you where you were, I would have plunged this knife between your shoulders!" He asked, "Where did you see me?" She replied, "I saw you on the slave-girl!" He said, "You did not see me. The Messenger of Allah ﷺ forbade that anyone recite the Qur'an while he is in *janābah*." "So recite it!" she retorted. He did not recite the Qur'an but recited:

"The Messenger of Allah came to us reciting His Book
as the star shining at dawn.

He brought us guidance after blindness,
and our hearts are certain that what it says will happen.

He spent the night with his side shunning his bed
when the idolaters are heavy in their beds."

She said, "I believe in Allah. My eyes have deceived me." Then he went to the Messenger of Allah ﷺ to inform him and he laughed until his molars showed.'

until you have washed yourselves completely.

Allah forbade the prayer except after a full washing. The term 'washing' is well-known, and it designates rubbing the hand with water over what is being washed. It is not fulfilled by sprinkling. After affirming this, scholars then disagree about when someone in *janābah* pours water on his body or immerses himself in water and does not rub. The well-known position in the school of Mālik is that that is not adequate without rubbing as well because Allah commands someone in *janābah* to wash in the same terms that He commands the person doing *wuḍū'* to wash their face and hands and the person doing *wuḍū'* has to pass his hands over his face and hands along with the water. Therefore, the same applies to his entire body and head. This is the position and choice of al-Muzanī. Abu-l-Faraj 'Amr ibn Muḥammad al-Mālikī said, 'This is understood from the expression "*ghusl*". If someone only pours water, he is not washing, but simply pouring it and immersing himself in it.' He added, 'This is what has come in the *ḥadīth*s of the Prophet ﷺ as in, "There is *janābah* under every hair, so wash the hair and clean the skin."' That is only by following it according to the limits we mentioned.

There is no definitive evidence in this *ḥadīth* for two reasons. One is that there is disagreement about its interpretation because Sufyān ibn 'Uyaynah said that it is an allusion to washing the private parts, and Ibn Wahb says, 'I have not seen anyone with more knowledge of the explanation of *ḥadīth*s than Ibn 'Uyaynah.'

The second is that this *hadīth* is transmitted by Abū Dāwūd in his *Sunan* and he stated that it is weak, as is the case of the transmission of Ibn Dāssāh. The transmission of al-Lu'lu'ī contains al-Ḥārith ibn Wajīh who is weak and whose hadiths are *munkar*. So evidence based on hadīth falls away and there just remains the linguistic interpretation which is supported by what is in the sound *hadīths* that the Prophet ﷺ was brought a child who urinated on him. He called for water and poured it on the urine but did not wash it. 'Ā'ishah transmitted that as did Umm Qays bint Miḥṣan. Muslim transmitted both of them.

The majority of scholars and *fuqahā'* say that it is permitted for someone in *janābah* to pour water or immerse himself provided it covers completely, even if he does not rub, as it is transmitted from Maymūnah and 'Ā'ishah that the Messenger of Allah ﷺ poured water over his body. Muḥammad ibn 'Abd al-Ḥakam said that, and Abu-l-Faraj related it from Mālik. He said, 'He is commanded to pour the water over [the body] in washing because someone who does not do that is not safe from the water missing part of his body which must be washed. Ibn al-'Arabī said, 'I am astonished at what Abu-l-Faraj related from the master of the School about washing less than this being accepted! Mālik absolutely did not state that either in a text or interpretation. It is merely one of his illusions!' But this is related from Mālik in a text. Marwān ibn Muḥammad at-Tāṭarī, who is a reliable Syrian, said, 'I asked Mālik ibn Anas about a man who immerses himself in water while in *janābah* and does not do *wuḍū'*.' He stated, 'His prayer is valid.' Abū 'Umar said, 'Neither rubbing nor *wudu'* are mentioned in this transmission, and it satisfies the requirement for Mālik. Nevertheless, the well-known position of his school that the requirement is not satisfied without rubbing.' This is based on an analogy with washing the face and hands.

The argument of the majority is that everything on which water is poured is washed. The Arabs say, 'The sky washed me.' 'Ā'ishah and Maymūnah described the *ghusl* of the Messenger of Allah ﷺ and did not mention rubbing. If it had been obligatory, he would not have omitted it because he was making clear what Allah meant. If he had done it, it would have been transmitted from him as it was transmitted that he made water reach the roots of his hair and cupped it onto his head and other points which are described in detail. Abū 'Umar said, 'It is not unknown that *ghusl* in Arabic sometimes means rubbing and sometimes pouring. Since this is the case, it is not impossible that Allah imposed on His slaves rubbing their hands over their faces with water in *wuḍū'* and pouring water on themselves in the washing for *ghusl* after *janābah* and menstruation. That is the washing which is in conformity with the *Sunnah* and included within the bounds of linguistic usage. Each of the two has a basis and so it is not necessary to compare one with the other because bases are not compared with one another in analogy. The scholars of the Community do not disagree about this. It is secondary rulings that are made to refer back to bases.' Success is by Allah.

The *ḥadīth* of Maymūnah and 'Ā'ishah refutes what is related from Ibn 'Abbās which states that when he did *ghusl* for *janābah,* he ﷺ washed his hands seven times and his genitals seven times. It is related that Ibn 'Umar said, 'The prayer was fifty and *ghusl* for *janābah* seven times and washing urine from clothes seven times. The Messenger of Allah ﷺ continued to ask until the prayer was made five and *ghusl* from *janābah* once and *ghusl* from urine once.' Ibn 'Abd al-Barr said that the *isnād* of this *ḥadīth* from Ibn 'Umar is weak and unclear, even though Abū Dāwūd transmitted it and the one before it from Shu'bah, the freedman of Ibn 'Abbās. This Shu'bah is not strong. They are both refuted by the hadith of Maymūnah and 'Ā'ishah. If someone cannot pass his hand over his body, Saḥnūn said that he should wipe what is near it or rub over it with a rag. According to *al-Wāḍiḥah*: 'He should pass his hand over every part of his body he can reach and pour water over any part of his body that his hands cannot reach.'

The position of Mālik about making water penetrate the beard varies. Ibn al-Qāsim related that he said that it is not mandatory to do that. Ashhab reported that it is. Ibn 'Abd al-Ḥakam said, 'I prefer that because the Messenger of Allah ﷺ used to make water penetrate his beard when doing *ghusl* for *janābah.* That is general, even if it is more evident for the hair of the head.' These are the two positions of scholars. In respect to the meaning, it is obligatory to wash all of the body and all of the skin under the beard. Therefore, it is mandatory to make the water reach the skin there and touch it with the hand. The obligation moves to the hair (rather than the skin under it) in *wuḍū'* because it is based on making things easier and replacing one part with another without that being due to necessity. That is why it is permitted to wipe over leather socks which is not permitted in *ghusl.* This is supported by the words of the Prophet ﷺ, 'There is *janābah* under every hair.'

Some people went further and made rinsing the mouth and snuffing water up the nose in *ghusl* mandatory by this *āyah,* Abū Ḥanīfah among them, because they are part of the face and covered by the ruling of the face like the cheeks and brow. If they are omitted in *ghusl*, the prayer must be repeated, but not if they are omitted in *wuḍū'*. Mālik said that neither is an obligatory element, either in *ghusl* for *janābah* or *wuḍū',* because they are inside the body. That is the position of Muḥammad ibn Jarīr aṭ-Ṭabarī, al-Layth ibn Sa'd, al-Awzā'ī and a group of Tābi'ūn. Ibn Abī

Laylā and Ḥammād ibn Abī Sulaymān said that they are mandatory in *wuḍū'* and *ghusl*, and that is the position of Isḥāq, Ibn Ḥanbal and some of the people of Dāwūd. That is also reported from az-Zuhrī and 'Aṭā'. It is also related from Aḥmad ibn Ḥanbal that rinsing is *sunnah* and snuffing is an obligation, and some Ẓāhirites say that.

The proof of those who say that they are not obligatory is that Allah did not mention them in His Book nor did His Messenger impose them and there is no consensus about them – and obligations are only established by these elements. Those who make them obligatory say that the proof is derived from the words: '*wash your faces*,' and the fact that it is not reported that the Prophet ﷺ ever omitted them in his *wuḍū'* or *ghusl*, and he clarified what Allah meant by both word and action. Those who make a distinction between them argue by the fact that the Prophet ﷺ rinsed his mouth, but did not order it to be done. His actions are recommended and not mandatory until there is evidence for that. He snuffed water up his nose and ordered it to be done and his command is always an obligation.

Our scholars say that there must be an intention in washing for *janābah* since Allah says: '*until you have washed yourselves*,' and that demands an intention. That is the position of Mālik, ash-Shāfi'ī, Aḥmad, Isḥāq and Abū Thawr. The same applies to *wuḍū'* and *tayammum*. They rely in this on the words of Allah: '*They were only ordered to worship Allah, making their* dīn *sincerely His.*' (98:5) Sincerity in intention is in drawing near to Allah and the aim of performing what He has obliged on His believing slaves. The Prophet ﷺ said, 'Actions are according to intentions.' This is an action. Al-Awzā'ī and al-Ḥasan said that *wuḍū'* and *tayammum* are permitted to be done without intention. Abū Ḥanīfah and his people say that every purification with water is allowed without intention but that *tayammum* is not allowed except with an intention, analogous to removing impurity from bodies and clothes. Al-Walīd ibn Muslim related it from Mālik.

As for the amount of water used for *ghusl*, Mālik related from Ibn Shihāb from 'Urwah ibn az-Zubayr from 'Ā'ishah that the Messenger of Allah ﷺ used to perform *ghusl* for *janābah* from a vessel which contained a *faraq* (approx. 10 litres). Ibn Wahb said that it is a measure made of wood. Ibn Shihāb used to say that it is enough for five *qisṭ*s of that measure used by the Banū Umayyah. Muḥammad ibn 'Īsā al-A'shā said that it is nine *ṣā'*s. He also said that it is five *qisṭ*s, and five *qisṭ*s contains twelve *mudd*s using the *mudd* of the Messenger of Allah ﷺ (approx.. 10 litres). We find in *Ṣaḥīḥ Muslim* that Sufyān said that a *faraq* is three ṣā's. Anas said, 'The Messenger of Allah ﷺ did *wuḍū'* with a *mudd* and *ghusl* with a *ṣā'* or up to five *mudds*.' The *ḥadīths* indicate the recommendation to use little water and that using a lot of water is blameworthy extravagance. The position of the school of the Ibāḍiyyah is to use a lot of water. That comes from Shayṭān.

If you are ill or on a journey

This is the *Āyah of Tayammum*. It was revealed about 'Abd ar-Raḥmān ibn 'Awf who was in *janābah* while he was wounded and was given a dispensation to do *tayammum*. Then the *āyah* became general for all people. It is said that it was revealed because the Companions lacked water in the al-Muraysi' expedition when 'Ā'ishah's necklace broke. Mālik transmits the *ḥadīth* from 'Abd ar-Raḥmān ibn al-Qāsim from his father from 'Ā'ishah. Al-Bukhārī has a chapter on this *āyah* in the Book of *Tafsīr*: Muḥammad reported from 'Abdah from Hishām ibn 'Urwah from his father that 'Ā'ishah said, 'A necklace belonging to Asmā' was lost and the Prophet ﷺ sent some men to look for it. The time for the prayer came and they were not in *wuḍū'* and could not find water. They prayed without being in *wuḍū'* and Allah sent down the *Āyah* of *Tayammum*.' This transmission does not mention the location and it mentions that the necklace belonged to Asmā' which differs from the *ḥadīth* of Mālik.

An-Nasā'ī mentioned from 'Alī ibn Mushar from Hishām ibn 'Urwah from his father that 'Ā'ishah said that she borrowed a necklace from Asmā' on a journey with the Messenger of Allah ﷺ and it slipped off her. The place where that happened was called aṣ-Ṣulṣul. This variant mentions that the necklace belonged to Asmā' and 'Ā'ishah had borrowed it from her. This clarifies Mālik's *ḥadīth* when he said, "Ā'ishah's necklace broke.' The *ḥadīth* in al-Bukhārī says, 'A necklace belonging to Asmā' was lost.' It mentions that the place was called aṣ-Ṣulṣul. At-Tirmidhī transmitted from al-Ḥumaydī from Sufyān from Hishām ibn 'Urwah from his father from 'Ā'ishah that her necklace fell off in the night of al-Abwā' and the Messenger of Allah ﷺ sent two men to look for it. This transmission from Hishām also attributes the necklace to her, but as something borrowed based on the evidence of the *ḥadīth* of an-Nasā'ī.

He said that the place was al-Abwā' as Mālik said, although it is without doubt. The *ḥadīth* of Mālik says: 'We roused the camel I had been on and found the necklace under it.' It says in al-Bukhārī that the Messenger of Allah ﷺ found it. All of this has a sound meaning. The transmitters do not disagree about the necklace nor the place where this took place and none of it is doubted because what is desired from the *ḥadīth* is the revelation of *tayammum*. The transmissions confirm the bųsiness of the necklace.

As for the words in the *ḥadīth* of at-Tirmidhī about sending two men, it is said that one of them was Usayd ibn Ḥuḍayr. Perhaps what is meant by 'men' in the *ḥadīth* of al-Bukhārī is two for which the plural is used since two is the minimum of a plural. It is also possible that other men went after them, and so it is a proper plural. Allah knows best. They were sent to look for it and looked, but did not find anything. When they returned, they stirred the camel and found the necklace under it. It is related that some Companions had suffered injuries and then became in *janābah* and complained about that to the Messenger of Allah ﷺ and this *āyah* was revealed. There is also no disagreement about what we mentioned. Perhaps they had received wounds in the expedition from which they were returning since there was fighting in it. Then the necklace was lost and the *āyah* revealed.

It is also said that the necklace was lost in the expedition against the Banū al-Muṣṭaliq. There is also no disagreement here because al-Muraysī' was the same expedition. The Prophet ﷺ raided the Banū al-Muṣṭaliq in 6 AH as is stated by Khalīfah ibn Khayyāṭ and Abū 'Umar ibn 'Abd al-Barr during which he put Abū Dharr al-Ghifārī in charge of Madīnah. It is also said that it was Numaylah ibn 'Abdullāh al-Laythī. The Messenger of Allah ﷺ raided the Banū al-Muṣṭaliq who had gone out and had halted at a watering place of theirs called al-Muraysī' in the direction of Qudayd towards the coast. He slew some of them and captured women and children. Their slogan on that day was 'Die! Die!' It is said that the Banū al-Muṣṭaliq had gathered to attack the Messenger of Allah ﷺ and when news of that reached him, he set out against them and met them at the watering place.

This is what has come about the beginning of *tayammum* and the reason for it. It is also said that the *Āyah* of *Tayammum* is found in *al-Mā'idah*, and it will be discussed there. Abū 'Umar said, 'Allah Almighty revealed the *Āyah* of *Tayammum*, which is the *Āyah* of *Wuḍū'* mentioned in *Sūrat al-Mā'idah* or the one in *Sūrat an-Nisā'*. *Tayammum* is not mentioned in these two *āyahs*. Both *āyah*s are Madinan.'

Illness denotes the body not being in balance and returning to twistedness and aberration. There are two types: major and minor. If it is major then it may be that death is feared if the person uses cold water or it may increase the illness or he may lose a limb. One does *tayammum* in these cases by consensus except what is reported from al-Ḥasan and 'Aṭā' that someone should purify themselves even if it causes their death. This is refuted by the words of Allah: *'He has not placed any constraint on you in the* dīn' (22:78) and: *'Do not kill yourselves.'* (4:29) Ad-Dāraquṭnī related that Ibn 'Abbās said about the words: *'If you are ill or on journey…'*, 'When a man had a wound or injury in the way of Allah and was in *janābah* and feared he would die if he washed, he did *tayammum*.' Sa'īd ibn Jubayr reported from Ibn 'Abbās that it is an allowance for a sick person to do *tayammum* with earth. 'Amr ibn al-'Āṣ did *tayammum* when he feared he would die from the intensity of the cold and the Prophet ﷺ did not command him to wash or to repeat the prayer. Even if the illness is minor, so that someone only fears illness or its increase or a delay in healing, they can do *tayammum* by the consensus of the School. Ibn 'Aṭiyyah said, 'As far as I recall.'

Al-Bājī mentioned the difference of opinion about it. Qāḍī Abu-l-Ḥasan said that an example is when a healthy person fears the onset of illness or fever or a sick person fears increased illness and the like, as Abū Ḥanīfah said. Ash-Shāfi'ī said, 'It is not permitted to do *tayammum*, if there is water, unless someone fears death.' Qāḍī Abu-l-Ḥasan related that from Mālik. Ibn al-'Arabī said, 'Ash-Shāfi'ī stated that the permission for a sick person to do *tayammum* if he fears death because of increased illness is not definite since it may or may not occur. It is not permitted to abandon a certain obligation for an uncertain fear.' We say that this is contradictory. If you say that if he fears death from the cold, he can do *tayammum*, then if it is permitted for fear of death, it is also permitted for fear of illness, because it is also something about which one is cautious. He said, 'It is extraordinary that ash-Shāfi'ī said, "If the price asked for water is a single grain more than its worth, in order to protect his property a person is not obliged to purchase it and must do *tayammum*." But not if he fears that he will become ill! There are no words equal to this.' What is sound in the position of ash-Shāfi'ī, according to al-Qushayrī, is: 'The illness for which *tayammum* is permitted is that from which death or loss of one of limbs is feared if someone uses water. If someone fears that their illness will be lengthened, the sound position of ash-Shāfi'ī is that *tayammum* is permitted.'

We find in Abū Dāwūd and ad-Dāraquṭnī from Yaḥyā ibn Ayyūb from Yazīd ibn Abī Ḥabīb from 'Imrān ibn Abī Anas from 'Abd ar-Raḥmān ibn Jubayr that 'Amr ibn al-'Āṣ said, 'I had a wet dream on a cold night during the expedition of Dhāt as-Salāsil and I feared death if I had a *ghusl*. I did *tayammum* and then led my companions in the *Ṣubḥ* prayer. They mentioned that to the Messenger of Allah ﷺ and he said, "'Amr, you led your companions in the prayer while in *janābah*?" I told him why I had not washed and added, "I heard Allah say: *'Do not kill yourselves. Allah is merciful to you.'* (4:29)" The Prophet of Allah ﷺ laughed and did not say anything.'

The *ḥadīth* indicates the permission to do *tayammum* on account of fear, not certainty of harm occurring. It also indicates the permission for someone doing *tayammum* to lead those who are in *wuḍū'* in the prayer. This is one of two positions with us. It is sound and it is what Mālik has in his *Muwaṭṭā'* and was read to him until the time he died. The second position is that such a man should not lead them because he lacks the virtue of the one in *wuḍū'* and the ruling of the imām is that he should be higher. Ad-Dāraquṭnī related from Jābir ibn 'Abdullāh that the Messenger of Allah ﷺ said, 'Someone doing *tayammum* should not lead those in *wuḍū'*.' Its *isnād* is weak.

Abū Dāwūd and ad-Dāraquṭnī also reported that Jābir said, 'We went out on a journey and one of us was hit by a stone and had an open head wound and then had a wet dream. He asked his companions, "Do you find any allowance for *tayammum*?" They replied, "We do not find any allowance when you can find water." He performed a *ghusl* and died. When we reached the Prophet ﷺ, we informed him about that and he exclaimed, "They killed him. May Allah kill them! Why did they not ask if they did not know? The rectification of the incompetent lies in asking. It would have been enough for him to do *tayammum* and bind his wound and then wipe over it and wash the rest of his body."'

Ad-Dāraquṭnī said, 'Abū Bakr said that only the people of Makkah have this sunnah and the people of the peninsula transmit it but do not relate it from 'Aṭā' from Jābir except via az-Zubayr ibn Khurayq who is not strong. He is opposed by al-Awzā'ī who related it from 'Aṭā' from Ibn 'Abbās, which is correct. There is disagreement from al-Awzā'ī and it is said that he had it from 'Aṭā' and he also said, 'It reached me from 'Aṭā'.' Al-Awzā'ī has another *mursal* from 'Aṭā' from the Prophet ﷺ. Ibn Abī Ḥātim said, 'I asked my father and Abū Zur'ah about it and they said that Ibn Abī-l-'Ashrīn from al-Awzā'ī from Ismā'īl ibn Muslim from 'Aṭā' from Ibn 'Abbās. He gives the *isnād* of the *ḥadīth*. Dāwūd said, 'It is permitted for anyone called "ill" to do *tayammum* since Allah says, "*If you are ill.*"' Ibn 'Aṭiyyah said, 'This position is disputed. According to scholars of the Community, it is for those who fear to use water or who are harmed by it, like those suffering from pox or measles or any other illness aggravated by water.' This is as was already mentioned from Ibn 'Abbās.

Tayammum is permitted on a journey, long or short, when there is no water. It is not a precondition that the journey be one on which the prayer is shortened. This is the position of Mālik and the majority of scholars. Some say that one can only do *tayammum* on a journey on which the prayer is shortened. Others say that the journey must be one of obedience to Allah. This is weak and Allah knows best. Scholars agree that it is permitted to do *tayammum* on a journey but they disagree about doing it when resident. Mālik and his people believe that it is permitted to do *tayammum* both while resident and on a journey. That is also the position of Abū Ḥanīfah and ash-Shaybānī. Ash-Shāfi'ī stated that it is not permitted for a healthy resident to do *tayammum* unless he fears death. This is the position of aṭ-Ṭabarī.

Ash-Shāfi'ī, al-Layth and aṭ-Ṭabarī also said, 'When there is no water available while someone is resident and they fear they will miss the time, both healthy and sick people should perform *tayammum* and pray and then repeat it.' Abū Yūsuf and Zafar said, '*Tayammum* is not permitted while resident either on account of an illness or for someone who fears to miss the time.' Al-Ḥasan and 'Aṭā' said that neither ill nor well people should do *tayammum* if there is water. The reason for the disagreement is what is understood from the *āyah*. Mālik and those who follow him say that Allah mentioned illness and travelling as preconditions for *tayammum*, explaining the most usual case of those who do not have water, whereas the most common situation of those who are resident is that they have water or are prevented from using it by an impediment or fear of missing the moment of the prayer. A traveller does *tayammum* by the text and a resident person by the meaning. The same applies to those who are ill who do it by the text and the healthy who do it by the meaning.

Those who forbid it for people who are resident say that Allah made *tayammum* a dispensation for the sick and travellers, just as He did breaking the fast and shortening the prayer, and *tayammum* is only allowed on those two conditions: illness and travelling, and a healthy resident is not included in that. As for the position of al-Ḥasan and 'Aṭā' which forbids it altogether when there is water, they say that Allah made it conditional on lack of water and so it is only permitted for someone to do *tayammum* when there is no water. Abū 'Umar said, 'Were it not for the position of the majority and traditions that are reported, the view of al-Ḥasan and 'Aṭā' would be sound. Allah knows best. Allah permitted 'Amr ibn al-'Āṣ to perform *tayammum* when he was travelling when he feared that he might die if he washed with water and so a sick person is more entitled to do that.'

There is evidence in the Book and *Sunnah* which allows *tayammum* while resident if someone fears they will miss the prayer if they go for water. As for the Book, it is in the words: '*...or any of you have come from the lavatory,*' clearly implying that if someone is resident when there is no water, they should do *tayammum*. 'Abd ar-Raḥīm al-Qushayrī has a text on it. He said, 'One does not look at the obligation of repeating it, because lack of water is a rare excuse when someone is resident. There are two positions about repeating it. Some of our people have a text about someone who does *tayammum* while resident and whether or not they repeat the prayer when they find water. The well-known position in the school of Mālik is that they do not repeat it and it is the sound position. Ibn Ḥabīb and Muḥammad ibn 'Abd al-Ḥakam say that they should always repeat it. Ibn al-Mundhir related that from Mālik. Al-Walīd said that he said, 'He washes, even if the sun has risen.'

In the *Sunnah* we have what al-Bukhārī reported from Abu-l-Juhaym ibn al-Ḥārith ibn aṣ-Ṣimmah al-Anṣārī who said, 'Once the Prophet ﷺ was coming from the direction of Bi'r Jamal. A man met him and greeted him but the Prophet ﷺ did not reply to him until he came to a wall. He wiped his face and hands and then returned his greeting.' Muslim related it but without the word 'Bi'r'. Ad-Dāraquṭnī transmitted it from Ibn 'Umar and added, 'Nothing kept me from returning the greeting to you but the fact that I was not in a state of purity.'

or any of you have come from the lavatory

The plural of *ghā'iṭ* is *ghīṭān* or *aghwāṭ*. The root of lavatory (*ghā'iṭ*) is a depression of the land. That is the source of the name the Ghouta (Ghūtu) of Damascus. It was in these low places that the Arabs would go for a call of nature because they would be concealed from people's eyes. Then it was made to refer to what emerges from the human being there. The verb *ghāṭa, yaghūṭu* is used for disappearing into the ground. Az-Zuhrī recited '*min al-ghayṭ*'. It possible that its root is *ghayyiṭ* and then it was lightened like *mayyit* and its like. It is possible that it is from *ghawṭ* as evidenced by *taghawwaṭa*, meaning to go the lavatory. The *wāw* of *ghawṭ* has been changed into a *yā'* as in the change of *ḥawl* to *ḥayl*.

Here '*aw*' (or) can mean 'and', meaning 'if you are ill or on a journey **and** one of you has come from the lavatory, you should do *tayammum*.' According to this, the reason for *tayammum* is the minor impurity, not the illness or the journey. So this indicates the permissibility of doing *tayammum* while resident as we already made clear. What is sound according to those who reflect, however, is that '*aw*' has its normal meaning here. Or '*aw*' has a meaning and *wāw* has a meaning. They believe that this is based on an elision and means: 'If you are so ill that you cannot touch water, or on a journey and do not find water and you need water.' Allah knows best.

The word lavatory (*ghā'iṭ*) includes in its meaning all things which break lesser purification. People disagree about their number. The most apt of what is said about that is that there are three categories of things that do that, about which there is no disagreement in our school: loss of consciousness, normal excretion, and intimate touching. In Abū Ḥanīfah's school, it is impurities which emerge from the body; he does not consider how and does not count touch. In the school of ash-Shāfi'ī and Muḥammad ibn 'Abd al-Hakam it is what issues from the two passages, and he does not consider the matter of normality, but does consider touching.

If this is affirmed then know that Muslims agree about loss of sanity by fainting, insanity or intoxication. There is *wuḍū'* on account of that. They disagree about sleep and whether it is breaks it or not. There are three positions. The first view is that of al-Muzanī, which is that sleep breaks *wuḍū'* and *wuḍū'* is obliged for it whether it is a little or a lot, just like other things which break *wuḍū'*. That is in accordance with the position of Mālik expressed in the *Muwaṭṭā'* in the words: 'You only have to do *wuḍū'* for impurities which issue from the genitals or the anus, or for sleep.' It is also demanded by the *ḥadīth* of Ṣafwān ibn 'Assāl which is transmitted by an-Nasa'ī, ad-Dāraquṭnī and at-Tirmidhī who considers it to be sound. They all relate it from 'Āṣim ibn Abī-n-Nujūd that Zirr ibn Ḥubaysh said, 'I went to Ṣafwān ibn 'Assāl al-Murādī to ask him about wiping over leather socks. He answered, "Yes, I was in the army which the Messenger of Allah ﷺ sent out and he commanded us to wipe over leather socks when we had put them on in a state of purity: for three days when we were travelling, and for a day and a night when we were resident. We did not remove them on account of urine, defecation or sleep. We only removed them on account of *janābah*."' This *ḥadīth* and the statement of Mālik make defecation, urine and sleep the same. They said that when there is a lot of sleep and the mind is overpowered by it, it breaks purity, and the same is true of a little. It is related that 'Alī ibn Abī Ṭālib said that the Messenger of Allah ﷺ said, 'The eyes are the string that binds the sphincter. So whoever sleeps should do *wuḍū'*.' This is general. Abū Dāwūd transmitted and ad-Dāraquṭnī transmitted it from Mu'āwiyah ibn Abī Sufyān from the Prophet ﷺ.

The second view is that which is reported from Abū Mūsā al-Ash'arī about his view that sleep does not break *wuḍū'* in any case unless someone actually does something in their sleep to break it. That is they assign someone to watch them while they sleep. If they do not do anything to break *wuḍū'*, then they rise from sleep and pray. It is related from 'Abīdah, Sa'īd ibn al-Musayyab and al-Awzā'ī in the transmission of Maḥmūd ibn Khālid. The majority take a position other than these two views. The position of Mālik is that every deep sleep breaks *wudu'*. However such a sleep occurs, *wudu'* is obliged on account of it. That is the position of az-Zuhrī, Rabī'ah and al-Awzā'ī in the transmission of al-Walīd ibn Muslim. Aḥmad ibn Ḥanbal said, 'If it is a light sleep in which the heart is not overcome, it does not impair [purity].' Abū Ḥanīfah and his people say that only someone who sleeps lying down or reclining (must do *wuḍū'*). Ash-Shāfi'ī said, 'If someone sleeps sitting down, he does not have to do *wudu'*. Ibn Wahb related that from Mālik.

What is sound of these positions is the well-known view of Mālik based on the *ḥadīth* of Ibn 'Umar: 'The Messenger of Allah was distracted from *'Ishā'* one night and delayed it until we dozed in the mosque and then woke up. Then we dozed off again and woke up. Then the Prophet ﷺ came out to us and said, "None of the people of earth are waiting for the prayer except you."' The imams related it and it is the soundest of what exists concerning this topic in respect of *isnād* and practice. The meaning of what Mālik said in the *Muwaṭṭā'* and Ṣafwān ibn 'Assāl in his *ḥadīth* is that *wudu'* is only broken by a deep sleep which overpowers a person as is evidenced by this *ḥadīth* and elsewhere. Ṣafwān's *ḥadīth* was also related by Wakī' from Mis'ar from 'Āṣim ibn Abī-n-Nujūd who said 'breaking wind' rather than 'sleep'. Ad-Dāraquṭnī said that only Wakī' from Mis'ar has 'breaking wind'.

Wakī' is a trustworthy imam from whom al-Bukhārī, Muslim and other imams transmit. The evidence in the *ḥadīth* of Ṣafwān about sleep breaking *wuḍū'* is dropped. What Abū Ḥanīfah believes is weak. Ad-Dāraquṭnī related from Ibn 'Abbās: 'The Messenger of Allah ﷺ was sleeping while in prostration until he snored or made a puffing noise. Then he got up and prayed. I said, 'Messenger of Allah, you slept!' He said, "*Wuḍū'* is only obliged for someone who sleeps lying down. When he lies down, his joints relax."' Abū Khālid has it from Qatādah and it is not sound. Ad-Dāraquṭnī said that. Abū Dāwūd transmitted it as '*Wuḍū'* is obliged for someone who sleeps lying down.' It is a *munkar ḥadīth* which is only related by Abū Khālid Yazīd ad-Ḍālānī from Qatādah. A group related the beginning of it from Ibn 'Abbās and did not mention any of that. Abū 'Umar ibn 'Abd al-Barr said, 'The *ḥadīth* is *munkar* and none of the trustworthy people of Qatādah related it. Only Abū Khālid ad-Dālānī has it and they object to him and he is not an authority according to what has been transmitted.'

As for the statement of ash-Shāfi'ī that every person who sleeps must do *wuḍū'* except for someone who is sitting, but anyone who is no longer sitting up and sleeps must do *wuḍū'*, that is the view of aṭ-Ṭabarī and Dāwūd. It is related from 'Alī, Ibn Mas'ūd and Ibn 'Umar because someone who is sitting down almost never sleeps deeply and so that is considered to be a light sleep. Ad-Dāraquṭnī related from 'Amr ibn Shu'ayb from his father from his grandfather that the Messenger of Allah ﷺ said, 'Someone who sleeps while sitting does not have to do *wuḍū'*, but someone who lies on his side must do *wuḍū'*.' As for what is outside the norm, we say what al-Bukhārī related from Qutaybah from Yazīd ibn Zuray' from Khālid from 'Ikrimah that 'Ā'ishah said, 'One of his wives did *i'tikāf* with the Messenger of Allah ﷺ and used to see blood and yellowness and put a dish under herself while she was praying.' This is outside the norm. It was an open vein and therefore an illness. We believe that there is no *wuḍū'* obliged for what is like this which emerges. This differs from ash-Shāfi'ī as we mentioned. Our success is with Allah. It gives an answer to the Ḥanafī who considers the abnormal to be impurity. It is sound and clarifies the school of Mālik ibn Anas.

or touched women,

This is read as *lāmastum* by Nāfi', Ibn Kathīr, Abū 'Amr, 'Āṣim and Ibn 'Āmir, and *lamastum* by Ḥamza and al-Kisā'ī. There are three positions about its meaning. One is that it means to have sexual intercourse, the second that it is about touching, and the third is that it is both. That is the meaning of *lāmastum* according to most people. It is, however, related that Muḥammad ibn Yazīd said, 'In language, *lāmastum* means "you kissed" or the like because each of them does it, and *lamastum* means "you had sex with and touched" where the action comes from the man rather than the woman.'

Scholars have five different positions about the ruling of the *āyah*. One group says that touching (*mulāsamah*) here is particular to the hand and *janābah* is only mentioned with water, and so this is not included in the meaning. What is meant by *'if you are ill'* means there is no way for him to do *tayammum*. The one in *janābah* has a *ghusl* or does not pray until he finds water. This is reported from 'Umar and Ibn Mas'ūd. Abū 'Umar says that none of the *fuqahā'* of the regions takes this position, either by opinion or transmission. Allah knows best, but it is based on a *ḥadīth* from 'Ammār and 'Imrān ibn Ḥuṣayn and one of Abū Dharr from the Prophet ﷺ about the *tayammum* of someone in *janābah*.

Abū Ḥanīfah takes the opposite view to this and says that touching means sexual intercourse. Someone in *janābah* does *tayammum*, and someone who touches with his hand is not mentioned, and so he does not break *wuḍū'* and if a man kisses his wife for pleasure, that does not break *wuḍū'*. They rely on the report of ad-Dāraquṭnī from 'Ā'ishah that the Prophet ﷺ kissed one of his wives and went to the prayer without doing *wuḍū'*. 'Urwah asked her, 'Was it you?' and she laughed. Mālik said that the one who touches by way of having sexual intercourse does *tayammum* and the one who touches with the hand only does *tayammum* if he has arousal. If he touches without sexual desire, there is no *wuḍū'*. Aḥmad and Isḥāq said that, and it is what the *āyah* demands. 'Alī ibn Ziyād said, 'If she is wearing a thick garment, he owes nothing. If it is light, he must do *wuḍū'*.' 'Abd al-Malik ibn al-Mājishūn said, 'If someone intentionally touches his wife with his hand to play, he must do *wuḍū'*, pleasure or not.'

In *al-Muntaqā*, Qāḍī Abu-l-Walīd al-Bājī stated, 'The precise position in the school of Mālik and his people is that *wuḍū'* is obliged for the intention of pleasure rather than its actual existence. If someone intends pleasure by touch, *wuḍū'* is obliged for him, whether he has pleasure or not.' This is the sense of what we find in the *'Utbiyyah* from 'Īsā from Ibn al-Qāsim. In the case of a simple erection, Ibn Nāfi' related from Mālik that it does not oblige *wuḍū'* nor washing the penis unless there is touch or prostatic fluid along with it. Abū Isḥāq said, 'An erection breaks *wuḍū'*. This is the position of Mālik in the *Mudawwanah*.' Ash-Shāfi'ī said, 'When some part of a man's body reaches a woman's body, whether it be a hand or some other limb, that breaks purity. This is the position of Ibn Mas'ūd, Ibn 'Umar, az-Zuhrī and Rabī'ah.' Al-Awzā'ī said that a touch with a hand breaks purity, but other than the hand does not based on Allah's words: *'touch it with their own hands'* (6:7).

Of these five positions, the most correct is that of Mālik. It is related from 'Umar and his son, 'Abdullāh. The position of 'Abdullāh ibn Mas'ūd is that touching implies what is less than sexual intercourse and *wuḍū'* is obliged for that. This is what is believed by most *fuqahā'*. Ibn al-'Arabī said, 'It is the literal meaning of the *āyah*. Allah's words in the beginning of the *āyah* about being in *janābah* conveys the idea of sexual intercourse. His words: *"have come from the lavatory"* conveys minor impurity. The words "*touched women*" convey the sense of touching and kissing. So there are three rulings. This is ultimate knowledge and information. If sexual intercourse had been meant by "touching", it would not have been repeated.'

As for the evidence which Abū Ḥanīfah deduces from the *ḥadīth* of 'Ā'ishah, the *ḥadīth* is *mursal*. Wakī' related it from Ḥabīb ibn Abī Thābit from 'Urwah from 'Ā'ishah. Yaḥyā ibn Sa'īd said that al-A'mash mentioned the *ḥadīth* from Ḥabīb from 'Amr. He said, 'Sufyān ath-Thawrī is the person with the best knowledge about it. He claimed that Ḥabīb did not listen to 'Urwah at all.' Ad-Dāraquṭnī said that. If it is said, 'You say that it is *mursal* and so you must accept it and act on it,' we reply that we left it in favour of the literal meaning of the *āyah* and the practice of the Companions.

If it is said that '*touching*' means sexual intercourse and that is related from Ibn 'Abbās, we reply that 'Umar and his son disagreed with him, and they were corroborated by 'Abdullāh ibn Mas'ūd who was a Kufan. Why then did they disagree with him? If it is said that touching (*mulāmasah*) is a reciprocal verb and it only happens between two. *Lams* with the hand is by one person and so it is confirmed that *mulamasah* is sexual intercourse. Another answer is that *mulāmasah* demands contact between two skins, whether that is from one or two because each of them is described as touching and touched. Another answer is that *mulāmasah* is from one person. That is why the Prophet ﷺ forbade the *mulāmasah* sale: the cloth is touched and it does not touch.

When Allah Almighty mentioned the cause of minor impurity, which is coming from the lavatory, He also mentioned the cause of *janābah*, which is touching. He made it clear what happens in both cases when there is lack of water as He had explained the ruling when there is water. We said that we do not forbid applying the term to sexual intercourse and touching, and the two rulings are as we made clear. It can also be recited in Form I as we mentioned. As for what ash-Shāfi'ī believed, that if a man touches a woman with any of his limbs without a barrier between him and her, for sexual desire or without, *wuḍū'* is obliged for him, that is also the literal meaning of the Qur'an. If she touches him, he is obliged to do *wuḍū'*, except for hair. *Wuḍū'* is not owed for someone who touches a woman's hair, with or without sexual desire. The same is true for teeth and nails which is different from skin. It is good if he is cautious and does *wuḍū'* on account of touching her hair. If he touches her with his hand and she touches him with her hand on top of a garment, there is nothing obliged for either of them, whether or not there is pleasure, unless it reaches the skin, and whether that is intentional or unintentional, and whether the woman is alive or dead when she is not a close relative.

His position varies about what the ruling is if someone touches a young girl or very old woman with their hand or one of his female relatives he is not permitted to marry. Sometimes he said that it breaks *wuḍū'* because Allah says: '*touched women*' and there is no difference (in that they are all women), and sometimes he said that it does not break it because there is no question of sexual desire in their case. Al-Marwazī said, 'Ash-Shāfi'ī's position reflects the literal text because Allah says: "*touched women,*" and does not say with or without sexual desire. That was the case with the Companions of the Messenger of Allah ﷺ who obliged *wuḍū'*: they did not stipulate sexual desire.' He said that it was the view of most of the Tābi'ūn.' He continued, 'As for what Mālik believed about the sexual desire and pleasure enjoyed through a garment making *wuḍū'* obligatory, al-Layth ibn Sa'd agreed with him regarding that. We do not know of anyone who said that except for those two.' He said, 'That is not sound because someone who does that does not touch his wife. He does not really touch her, He touches her garment.' They agree that if someone experiences pleasure without touching or desires to touch, *wuḍū'* is not obliged for him. That is also true of someone who touches the garment because he is not touching the woman.

As for what was mentioned about no one but al-Layth ibn Sa'd agreeing with Mālik, Abū 'Umar ibn 'Abd al-Barr mentioned that it was also the view of Isḥāq and Aḥmad. And it is related from ash-Sha'bī and an-Nakha'ī as well. They all said that if someone touches and experiences pleasure, he must do *wuḍū'*. As for his statement, 'That is not sound,' that statement itself is not sound. It has come in a sound report that 'Ā'ishah said, 'I used to sleep in front of the Messenger of Allah ﷺ and my feet were in his *qiblah*. When he prostrated, he nudged me and I pulled my feet up, and when he stood, I stretched them out again.' He added, 'The houses in that time did not have any lamps.' This is a text stating that the Prophet ﷺ touched and nudged 'Ā'ishah with his foot as we find in the transmission of al-Qāsim from 'Ā'ishah: 'When he wanted to prostrate, he nudged my foot and I pulled them up.' Al-Bukhārī transmitted it. This defines the words 'or touched'.

Thus although the literal wording of the *āyah* demands that any touching, no matter what it is, breaks *wuḍū'*, the Sunnah, which is the clarification of the Book of Allah, indicates that *wuḍū'* is obliged for some kinds of touching rather than others, [thus excluding] the one who does not experience pleasure or intend it. No one asks if there was a cloth over 'Ā'ishah's feet or if he hit her feet with his sleeve. The word 'nudge' (*ghamz*) always involves the hand. The verb is used for poking a ram to see whether or not it is plump. It is not touching with the sleeve. The foot of someone sleeping usually shows, especially when it is stretched out in a confined space. This was the case at that time. Do you not see that she said, 'When he stood, I stretched them out again' and 'The houses in that time did not have any lamps.' This is explicit. So it is clear that 'nudging' has its normal meaning of direct touching with the hand.

Another proof is also related from 'Ā'ishah. She said, 'One night I missed the Messenger of Allah ﷺ in the bed and searched for him. My hand touched the bottom of his feet. He was in the mosque and his feet were upright.' When she placed her hand on his foot while he was in prostration, he continued to prostrate. That is evidence that some touching does not break *wuḍū'*. If it is said that there was a barrier over his foot as al-Muzanī says, he is told, 'A foot is a foot without anything covering it unless some kind of cover is confirmed. The basic principle is to take the literal meaning. The agreement on what we mentioned it is like a text.'

It may be said that the Community agree that if a man tries to force a woman and the circumcised parts meet and she does not experience any pleasure in that, or she is asleep and does not experience pleasure or sexual desire, she is obliged to have a *ghusl*. That is also the ruling for kissing or touching with or without sexual desire: it breaks her purity and she must do *wuḍū'* because the meaning of feeling, touching and kissing is an action and not pleasure. We reply that we mentioned that al-A'mash and others differed from the consensus. This is evidence that using consensus as evidence when there is dispute is not binding. We have cited sound hadiths as evidence for the soundness of our position. You claim that ash-Shāfi'ī was not the first to take that position, but that Mālik took it before him as is well known by us: 'When the *ḥadīth* is sound, take it and leave what I said.' The *ḥadīth* confirms that, so why do you not take it? It is obliged in your school that if someone hits his wife and slaps her that breaks his *wuḍū'* since what is intended is the action. No one says this as far as I know. Allah knows best.

The imams, Mālik and others, related that the Prophet ﷺ used to pray with Umāmah bint Abī-l-'Āṣ, his granddaughter by Zaynab, on his shoulder. When he bowed, he put her down, and when he came up from prostration, he put her back. This refutes what ash-Shāfi'ī says in one of his two views: 'even if he touches a young girl, he breaks his purity,' holding to the word 'women'. This is weak: touching a young girl is like touching a wall. They disagree about his position regarding female relatives that he cannot marry because it does not take account of pleasure. We take pleasure into account. When pleasure is felt, the ruling exists and that obliges *wuḍū'*. As for the position of al-Awzā'ī about the hand in particular, that is based on the fact that touching usually is done with the hand and therefore he confined it to that rather than other limbs. So if he puts one of his feet under a woman's garment and touches her private parts or belly, that does not break *wuḍū'*. He said about a man who kisses his wife, 'If he came and asked me, I would tell him to do *wuḍū'*. If he does not do *wuḍū'*, I will not blame him.' Abū Thawr said that a man does not have to do *wuḍū'* for kissing or touching his wife. This is deduced from the school of Abū Ḥanīfah. Allah knows best.

and you cannot find any water,

The valid reasons for water being considered unavailable are: when there is no water at all or only a little; when there is fear of losing touch with your companions or camel because of looking for it; when there is fear of thieves or wild animals; when there is fear of missing the time of the prayer; when there is fear that using available water will cause you or others to suffer thirst. The same is true if the available water is needed for cooking. If any of these reasons exist, you should do *tayammum* and pray. Another instance is when a sick person cannot find anyone to give him the water that is there or fears it will harm him. Another instance, which applies to both the healthy and the sick person, is if the available water is too costly. That is also the case when someone is in prison or tied up [and their only access to water is buying it at a high price]. Al-Ḥasan said that a man should use all the money he has to buy water, even if that leaves him penniless. This is weak because the *Dīn* of Allah is ease. One group say that you should pay for water as long as it is not a third or more expensive than the normal price. Another group said that it is all right to buy a dirham's worth for two or three dirhams. All of this is found in the School of Mālik. Ashhab was asked, 'Is it permitted to buy a water-skin for ten dirhams?' He answered, 'I do not think that people have to do that.' Ash-Shāfi'ī said that there should be no increase in price at all.

Scholars disagree about whether the fact of having looked for water is a condition for the validity of *tayammum*. The apparent position of Mālik is that it is, and that is also the position of ash-Shāfi'ī. Qāḍī Abū Muḥammad ibn Naṣr says that its validity is not conditional on that and that is the position of Abū Ḥanīfah. It is related that Ibn 'Umar was on a journey and did not turn aside to look for water. Isḥāq said that it is not mandatory to look, except in your immediate surroundings, and he mentioned the *ḥadīth* of Ibn 'Umar. The first position is sounder and is the well-known position of Mālik in the *Muwaṭṭā'* because Allah says: '*...and you cannot find.*' This means that you must first look for water before doing *tayammum*. Also, on the basis of analogy, this is substituting for a normal obligation when one is unable to fulfil it, so you are only permitted to do it when there is certainty about the inability to accomplish what it is substituting as is the case with emancipation in *kaffārah* for fasting.

When lack of water is confirmed, there must either be despair of finding any, or a reasonable expectation of finding some, or an equal possibility of both. These are three cases. In the first, it is recommended to do *tayammum* at the beginning of the time because, although the excellence of water is forgone, it is still recommended to protect the excellence of the beginning of the time of the prayer. When the possibility of finding water or not finding it are equal *tayammum* should be resorted to at the middle of the time. Mālik's people related it from him. You should delay the prayer, hoping to obtain the excellence of water, as long as you do not miss the excellence of the beginning of the time. The excellence of the time is still obtained at the middle of the time, because it is close to it. When there is a real expectation of finding water the prayer should be delayed until the end of the time because the excellence of water is greater than the excellence of the beginning of the time. There is some disagreement about the excellence of the beginning of the time while there is no disagreement at all about the excellence of water. The excellence of the beginning of the time can be abandoned without that being due to necessity but it is only permitted to abandon the excellence of water out of necessity. The term 'time' in connection with the prayer here refers to the end of the preferred time as Ibn Ḥabīb said. If someone knows that they will find water at the end of time and prays, Ibn al-Qāsim says that it satisfies the requirement. If they find water, they repeat the prayer within the time only. 'Abd al-Malik ibn al-Māshijūn says, however, 'If he finds water afterwards, he must always repeat the prayer.'

The amount of water concerned here, when speaking of finding it, is what is sufficient for purification purposes. If there is less than what will be sufficient for purification purposes, you should do *tayammum* and not use the small amount. This is the position of Mālik and his people. It was stated by Abū Ḥanīfah and also ash-Shāfi'ī in one of his views. It is the position of the majority of scholars because Allah made the obligation dependent on one of two things: water or earth. If there is not enough water, then the water does not legally exist because what is desired is the existence of what is adequate to fulfil the obligation. In another statement, ash-Shāfi'ī said that you should use the water that is there and do *tayammum* as well, because as long as there is water there, the conditions for *tayammum* are not met. If someone uses it and it runs out, then they have to do *tayammum* because there is no water. The position of ash-Shāfi'ī also varies about someone who forgets they have water in their saddlebag and does *tayammum*. The sound position is that they should repeat the prayer because they had water with them and did not use it. The other view is that they do not need to repeat the prayer. That is the view of Mālik because they did not know about it at the time and so did not find it.

Abū Ḥanīfah permits using water which has been altered in some way because 'water' here is undefined and universal and so it includes the permission to do *wuḍū'* with both changed and unchanged water since both are called 'water'. We say that although it is general and undefined it is nevertheless about the genus itself and so only applies to all the kinds of water that come from the sky, to rivers and springs, both sweet or salty. Altered water, which contains other substances not considered part of the genus itself, such as vegetable water and rose water, is not included in it. Rulings concerning water will be dealt with in *al-Furqān*.

There is general agreement that *wuḍū'* and *ghusl* are not permitted with any drinks except *nabīdh* when there is no water. This *āyah* refutes doing even that. The *ḥadīth* which is mentioned from Ibn Mas'ūd about doing *wuḍū'* with *nabīdh* is not firm because it is related by Abū Zayd who is known, but it is not known that he accompanied Ibn Mas'ūd. Ibn al-Mundhir and others said that. That will also be explained in *al-Furqān*. The water whose absence allows *tayammum* must be pure and purifying and retain its normal qualities. One of those who wrote about the rulings of the Qur'an said about this *āyah* that *tayammum* is permitted in the absence of water in any form because 'water' is in the indefinite and includes every kind of water, whether it is mixed with something else or is on its own. No one is prevented from calling date *nabīdh* water and so *tayammum* is not permitted when it is available. This is the school of the Kufans, Abū Ḥanīfah and his people. For evidence of that they cited weak hadiths that will be mentioned in *al-Furqān* in the discussion on water.

then do tayammum with pure earth,

Tayammum is specified here for this Community as a dispensation for it. The Prophet ﷺ said, 'We were preferred over other people by three things: the entire earth was made a mosque for us and its earth is purification for us...' We have already mentioned that the reason for the revelation of the permission to do *tayammum* was the loss of the necklace as well as discussing when it is permitted to do it. Now we will discuss its linguistic and legal meaning as well as its description, how it should be done, what may be used for *tayammum*, who is permitted to do it and the conditions for it as well as other rulings concerning it.

Linguistically, the word *tayammum* means to aim for something, so the phrase: *'do tayammum with pure earth'* means 'aim for it'. You also aim for someone with a spear or arrow as al-Khalīl says:

I aimed (*yammamtuhu*) the spear at him, thrusting from the side, and told him,
'This is courage, not a game of slides.'

Al-Khalīl says, 'If someone says in this verse "*ammamtuhu*' he has erred because it says "thrusting" (*shazr*), which only comes from the side, and does not come from the front. 'Imru'u-l-Qays said:

I aimed (*tayammamtuhā*) for it at Adhri'āt while her people
were in Yathrib. The closest of her houses is far to see.

He also said:

She made (*tayammamat*) for the spring at Ḍārij,
the green algae shading it, rising up.

Another said:

I am like that. When a land is unlucky for me,
my camel's chest aims (*yammamat*) towards another land.

Al-A'shā Bāhilah said:

I made for (*tayammamtu*) Qays:
how many a harsh desert is before it!

Ḥumayd ibn Thawr said:

Ask the tribe where Umm Ṭāriq has gone (*yammamat*).
Is it the custom of the tribe to speak?

Ash-Shāfi'ī said:

My knowledge is with me. Wherever I aim (*yammamtu*), I carry it.
My belly is its vessel, not the inside of a trunk.

Ibn as-Sikkīt said that this *āyah* means 'aim for good earth' and then it is used so frequently that the term *tayammum* was used for wiping the face and hands with earth. Ibn al-Anbārī said that it means to wipe the face and hands with earth. This is legal meaning of *tayammum* since what is meant by it is an act of devotion. A sick person does *tayammum* for the prayer. A man who is *muyammam* obtains all he seeks. Ash-Shaybānī said:

We find that A'ṣur ibn Sa'd
is the successful man (*muyammam*) of the house, full of glory.

Another said:

Azhar was not born under a star of avarice. He is
the successful man (*muyammam*) of the house, generous in prosperity.

Allah mentioned *tayammum* in *al-Baqarah*, this *sūrah* and *al-Ma'idah.* The reference to it in this *sūrah* is the actual *Āyat* of *Tayammum*, and Allah knows best. Qāḍī Abū Bakr ibn al-'Arabī said, 'This is a problem for which no one has the solution. These two *āyahs* in *an-Nisā'* and *al-Mā'idah* mention *tayammum* and we do not know which of them 'Ā'ishah meant when she referred to the *Āyat* of *Tayammum.*' He said, 'Her *ḥadīth* indicates that *tayammum* was not known or done before that.' As for what he said about not knowing which of them 'Ā'ishah meant, it is in fact this *āyah,* as we mentioned. Allah knows best. He said, 'Her *ḥadīth* indicating that *tayammum* was not known or done before that, is sound and the people of *Sīrah* do not disagree about it because it was known that *ghusl* for *janābah* was not imposed before *wuḍū'*. It is also known among all the people of *Sīrah* that, from the time that the prayer was imposed in Makkah, it was only prayed doing *wuḍū'* in the same way that we do today. That indicates that the *Āyah* of *Wuḍū'* was revealed so that its previous implementation would be confirmed by Revelation. So at the time that the ruling of *tayammum* was revealed, the ruling of *wuḍū'* was already clear and undoubted.

Tayammum is obligatory for everyone who is responsible for doing the prayer when the time of the prayer comes and there is no water. Abū Ḥanīfah and al-Muzanī, the companion of ash-Shāfi'ī, allow it for *nāfilah* prayers since they do not mandate looking for it. Their evidence in the *sunnah* is that the Prophet ﷺ said to Abū Dharr, 'Good earth is the *wuḍū'* of the Muslim if he does not find water.' So he called it *wuḍū'* as he did water and so its ruling is the same as that of water, and Allah knows best. Our evidence is the words: *'if you cannot find...'* Allah did not say anything about looking for it. This has already been discussed. It is also a form of purification born of necessity such as that of a woman with constant bleeding because the Prophet ﷺ said, 'Wherever you are when the prayer catches you, do *tayammum* and pray.' That is the position of ash-Shāfi'ī and Aḥmad and it is related from 'Alī, Ibn 'Umar and Ibn 'Abbās.

Scholars agree that *tayammum* does not actually remove major or minor impurity, and if the one who did *tayammum* finds water, he is still in major or minor impurity because the Prophet ﷺ told Abū Dharr, 'When you find water, put it on your skin.' There is only something related from Abū Salamah ibn 'Abd ar-Raḥmān. Ibn Jurayj and 'Abd al-Ḥamīd ibn Jubayr ibn Shaybah from him. Ibn Abī Dhi'b related it from 'Abd ar-Raḥmān ibn Ḥarmalah. He said about someone in *janābah* who has done *tayammum* that, if he finds water, he does not have to have a *ghusl* or do *wuḍū'* until he breaks his purity. It is related from him that someone who does *tayammum* and prays and then finds water within the time should do *wuḍū'* and repeat the prayer. Ibn 'Abd al-Barr said, 'This is contradictory and has little transmission.' They did not consider Abū Salamah to have understanding equal to his companions, the Tābi'ūn, in Madīnah. There is general agreement that if someone does *tayammum* and then finds water before the time of the prayer has elapsed, the *tayammum* is invalid and he must use water.

Most say that if someone who has looked with effort for water and has none in his baggage does *tayammum* and prays and has finished his prayer, his prayer is complete because he performed the obligation as commanded. It is not permitted to then oblige him to repeat it without any authority. Some of them recommend that he should repeat it within the time if he does *wuḍū'* or has a *ghusl*. This is related from Ṭāwūs, 'Aṭā', al-Qāsim ibn Muḥammad, Makḥūl, Ibn Sīrin, az-Zuhrī and Rabī'ah. All of them say that the prayer should be repeated. Al-Awzā'ī recommended that but said that it is not mandatory based on what Abū Sa'īd al-Khudrī said, 'Two men set out on a journey without any water. They did *tayammum* with good earth and prayed. Then they found water within the time. One of them repeated the prayer and other did not. Then they went to the Messenger of Allah ﷺ and mentioned that to him. He told the one who did not repeat it, "You have observed the Sunnah and satisfied your prayer." He said to the one who did *wuḍū'* and repeated it, "You have a reward twice over."' Abū Dāwūd transmitted it and said that other than Ibn Nāfi' related it from al-Layth from 'Umayrah ibn Abī Nājiyyah from Bakr ibn Sawādah from 'Aṭā' from the Prophet ﷺ. The mention of Abū Sa'īd in this *isnād* is not preserved. Ad-Dāraquṭnī transmitted it and said, 'They later found water within the time.'

There is disagreement between scholars about what happens if someone finds water after they have begun the prayer. Mālik said that they do not have to stop the prayer. They should complete the prayer and do *wuḍū'* for future prayers. That is the view of ash-Shāfi'ī and Ibn al-Mundhir preferred it. Abū Ḥanīfah and a group including Aḥmad and al-Muzanī say that they should stop the prayer, do *wuḍū'* and re-start the prayer because of the availability of water. Their argument is that just as *tayammum* is invalid when there is water before the prayer takes place, so it is also invalid as long as any of the prayer remains. If part of it is invalid, all of it is invalid. That is based on the consensus of the Muslims that a woman doing *'iddah* based on months only has to do the minimum of it, but if she then menstruates, she deals with her *'iddah* on the basis of menstruation. They said, 'By analogy and reflection the same applies if someone comes upon water while they are praying. The proof is in the words of the Almighty: *'Do not make your actions of no worth.'* (47:33) All agree that it is permitted to start the prayer with *tayammum*, but disagree about stopping it when water is seen. Neither the Sunnah nor consensus confirm stopping. Part of their argument is also that if someone is obliged to fast for *ẓihār* or killing and fasts most of it and then finds a slave [to free], they do not cancel their fast and revert to emancipation. So similarly when someone starts the prayer with *tayammum*, they do not stop it and revert to *wuḍū'*.

They disagree about whether someone can pray more than one prayer with one *tayammum* or whether they have to do it for each prayer, both obligatory and *nāfilah*. Qāḍī Sharīk ibn 'Abdullāh said that *tayammum* must be done for each obligatory and *nāfilah* prayer. Mālik said that it must be done for each obligatory prayer because you are required to seek water for each prayer. Then if no water is found after looking for it, you do *tayammum*. Abū Ḥanīfah, ath-Thawrī, al-Layth, al-Ḥasan ibn Ḥayy and Dāwūd say that someone can pray whatever he wishes with one *tayammum* as long as he does not break it because he is pure as long as no water is found and it is not necessary to look for water when someone has despaired of finding it.

Malik's position is sounder because Allah has made it obligatory for everyone who stands for the prayer to look for water and, in its absence, He prescribed *tayammum* to make the prayer possible before the end of the time. Therefore, it is a form of purification made necessary by the circumstances but which is in itself deficient, as evidenced by the consensus of the Muslims that *tayammum* becomes invalid when water is discovered, even if you have not broken your purity, but that is not the case when purification was done with water.

Disagreement also exists about the permission to do *tayammum* before the time of the prayer arrives. Ash-Shāfi'ī and the people who hold the first position do not permit it because Allah says: *'and you cannot find water, then do* tayammum.*'* It is clear from that that the permission to do *tayammum* is connected to a particular circumstance, and and that circumstance cannot be said to exist before the time arrives. On this basis, no one should pray two obligatory prayers with only one *tayammum*. This is clear. Our scholars, however, disagree about what happens when someone does pray two obligatory prayers with one *tayammum*. Yaḥyā ibn Yaḥyā related from Ibn al-Qāsim that they must repeat the second prayer as long as it is still within the time. Abū Zayd ibn Abī al-Ghamr related that they must always repeat it. Similarly, it is related from Muṭarrif and Ibn al-Mājishūn that it must always be repeated. This is what our people argue about because the dispensation for it is conditional on seeking water. Ibn 'Abdūs mentioned that Ibn Nāfi' related from Mālik that even someone who joins prayers should do *tayammum* for each prayer. Abu-l-Faraj said that if someone makes up prayers with one *tayammum*, he owes nothing and is permitted to do that. This is on the basis that looking for water is not a precondition in that situation. The first is sounder, and Allah knows best.

Ṣa'īd (good earth) means the surface of the earth, whether there is soil on it or not. That is stated by al-Khalīl, Ibn al-A'rabī and az-Zajjāj. Az-Zajjāj said, 'I do not know of any disagreement about this among the people of language.' Allah says: *'We will certainly make everything on it a barren wasteland (ṣa'īd)'* (18:8), which means hard ground on which nothing grows. Allah also says: *'morning finds it a shifting heap of dust (ṣa'īd)'* (18:40). (Illustrative poetry) It is called *ṣa'īd* because it is the end point to which the earth rises (*yuṣa'ada*). The plural is *ṣu'adāt* as in the *ḥadīth*: 'Beware of sitting on roads (*ṣu'adāt).*'

Scholars disagree about its qualification with the word 'good'. One group says that *tayammum* can be done with every kind earth surface: soil, sand, stone, mineral or brine. This is the position of Mālik, Abū Ḥanīfah, ath-Thawrī and aṭ-Ṭabarī, and 'good' (*ṭayyib*) in this instance means pure. Another group said that 'good' means lawful. This is uncertain. Ash-Shāfi'ī and Abū Yūsuf said that it is the earth which produces growth which is good since Allah Almighty says: *'Good land yields up its plants by the permission of its Lord.'* (7:57) Hence it is not permitted according to them to do *tayammum* with anything else. Ash-Shāfi'ī says that *ṣa'īd* is only used for earth which produces dust. 'Abd ar-Razzāq mentioned that Ibn 'Abbās was asked which earth was best? He replied, 'Tillage soil.' Abū 'Umar said, 'What Ibn 'Abbās said indicates that *ṣa'īd* can be other than tilled soil.' 'Alī said, 'It is dust in particular.'

The book of al-Khalīl states that the words *'Do tayammum with good earth'* mean 'take some of its dust.' Ibn Fāris related it. It means that *tayammum* should be done with dust, and smooth stone has no dust on it. Aṭ-Ṭabarī said, 'Ash-Shāfi'ī stipulated that dust should be actually on the hands and *tayammum* with it entails moving it to the parts of the body subject to *tayammum* just as is the case with moving water in *wuḍū'*.' Aṭ-Ṭabarī said, 'There is no doubt that the word *ṣa'īd* is not a legally defined term, in spite of what ash-Shāfi'ī said, other than in the words of the Messenger of Allah ﷺ, "...its earth was made is purification for us." This is clear.' The people who take this position cite as evidence the words of the Prophet ﷺ, '...its earth was made is purification for us.' They said that this is part of the undefined and defined, but that is not the case. It is part of the text about certain specifics which are part of a generality. This can be seen in 55:68 and 2:98.

Linguists tell us that *ṣa'īd* is a noun meaning the surface of the earth as we mentioned, and it is the text of the Qur'an as we have made clear. There is no clarification after Allah's clarification. The Prophet ﷺ said, 'You must use earth. It will be enough for you.' So *ṣa'īd* describes the place, or it can simply mean 'earth'. 'Good' is its adjective. If someone makes '*ṭayyib*' mean 'lawful', then it is in the accusative for the *ḥāl* or by the verbal noun. If you confirm this, then know that the consensus regarding what we mentioned is that a man should do *tayammum* on pure fertile earth without it being moved or unlawfully taken. The consensus also is that it is forbidden to do *tayammum* on pure gold, silver, rubies, and emeralds or foods like bread, meat and other such things or impurities. There is disagreement on other substances, like minerals. Mālik and others allow it while ash-Shāfi'ī and others forbid it.

Ibn Khuwayzimandād says that Mālik permitted doing *tayammum* on grass when it is on the earth. There is disagreement about doing *tayammum* using snow. It is permitted in the *Mudawwanah* and *Mabsūṭ* but forbidden elsewhere. There is disagreement about doing *tayammum* on tree trunks and branches. Most forbid it.

The disagreement is about whether or not they are separate from the earth. Ath-Tha'labī mentioned from Mālik that if someone strikes a tree with their palms and wipes with it, that is allowed. Al-Awzā'ī and ath-Thawrī said that it is permitted on any surface of the earth and everything on it of trees and stones, and clods and the like, even ice and snow.

Ibn 'Aṭiyyah said, 'As for earth which has been moved, most of the school say that it is permitted to use it for *tayammum*. But it is also said in the school that that is forbidden. As for earth that has been baked like whitewash and plaster, there are two positions: permission and prohibition. There is disagreement about using walls.' The sound position is that using a wall is permitted because of the above-mentioned *ḥadīth* from Abū Juhaym ibn aṣ-Ṣimmah al-Anṣārī about the Prophet ﷺ not greeting him until he had struck his hands on the wall and wiped his face and hands. It is in al-Bukhārī and constitutes evidence for *tayammum* without dust as Mālik and those who agree with him say. It refutes ash-Shāfi'ī and those who support him about the only thing which is used for wiping being pure earth with dust that attaches to the hand.

An-Naqqāsh mentioned about Ibn 'Ulayyah and Ibn Kaysān allowing *tayammum* with musk and saffron. Ibn 'Aṭiyyah said, 'This is an error for various reasons.' Abū 'Umar said, 'Most scholars allow *tayammum* with salt mire – except Isḥāq ibn Rāhawayh. It is related that Ibn 'Abbās said about someone doing *tayammum* with mud: 'He should take some of the mud and smear it on part of his body and when it dries, then he can do *tayammum* with it.' Ath-Thawrī and Aḥmad said that it is permitted to do tayammum with the dust of felt. Ath-Tha'labī said, 'Abū Ḥanīfah permitted *tayammum* with kohl, arsenic, lime, gypsum, and ground jewels.' He said, 'When people do *tayammum* with filings of gold, silver, copper, brass, copper, and lead, it is not allowed because they are not a naturally occurring part of earth.'

wiping your faces and your hands.

'Wiping' (*mas-ḥ*) is a word with several meanings. It can mean sexual intercourse or swiping something with a sword and cutting it, and it is used of a camel travelling on its day. A woman who is *mas'ḥā'* has a flat bottom. A person is lacking (*mas'ḥah*) in beauty. Here it denotes passing the hand over what is wiped. If it is with an implement, it designates moving the tool to the hand and dragging it over what is wiped. That is what is meant by the words of the Almighty in the *āyah* in *al-Mā'idah*: '*...wipe your faces and hands*' (5:6) where '*minhu*' means transferring the dust to the place of *tayammum*. That is the position in ash-Shāfi'ī's school, but we do not share in that view because the Prophet ﷺ placed his hands on the ground, lifted them and blew on them. That indicates that the actual substance is not a condition as was further clarified by the *ḥadīth* about the wall. Ash-Shāfi'ī insists: 'Just as drops of water must be conveyed to the head, so wiping with dust must entail actually moving it.'

There is no disagreement that the ruling about the face in *tayammum* and *wuḍū'* is that it must be wiped fully, following its contours. Some permit not including things like wrinkles in leather socks and what lies between the fingers on the head. That is the position of Muḥammad ibn Maslamah in the School. Ibn 'Aṭiyyah related it. In this *āyah* Allah began with the face before the hands. That is the position of the majority. Al-Bukhārī has the *ḥadīth* of 'Ammār in the chapter on *tayammum* in which he mentioned wiping the hands before the face. Some the people of knowledge say that, based on analogy with the reversal of *wuḍū'*.

Scholars disagree about how far *tayammum* extends on the arms. Ibn Shihāb said up to the shoulders and that is related from Abū Bakr aṣ-Ṣiddīq. In the *Muṣannaf* of Abū Dāwūd al-A'mash reported that the Messenger of Allah ﷺ wiped up to the middle of his arms. Ibn 'Aṭiyyah said, 'No one says what this *ḥadīth* says as far as I recall.' It is said that it is up to the elbows, analogous with *wuḍū'*, which is the position of Abū Ḥanīfah, ash-Shāfi'ī and their people, ath-Thawrī, Ibn Abī Salama and al-Layth, all of whom related that reaching the elbows is a mandatory obligation. That is also stated by Muḥammad ibn 'Abdullāh ibn 'Abd al-Ḥakam and Ibn Nāfi' and is the position of Qāḍī Ismā'īl. Ibn Nāfi' said that anyone who wipes to the wrists must always repeat the prayer and Mālik said in the *Mudawwanah* that in that case it should be repeated within the time. Jābir ibn 'Abdullāh and Ibn 'Umar related from the Prophet ﷺ that wiping is up to the elbows. That was the position of Ibn 'Umar. Ad-Dāraquṭnī said, 'Qatādah was asked about doing *tayammum* on a journey and said, "Ibn 'Umar said that it was up to the elbows."' Al-Ḥasan and Ibrāhīm an-Nakha'ī also said that it is up to the elbows. He said that someone related from ash-Sha'bī from 'Abd ar-Raḥmān ibn Abzā from 'Ammār ibn Yāsir that the Messenger of Allah ﷺ said, 'To the elbows.' Abū Isḥāq said, 'I mentioned that to Aḥmad ibn Ḥanbal and he said, "How excellent!"'

Another group said that it is to the wrists. That is related from 'Alī ibn Abī Ṭālib, al-Awzā'ī, 'Aṭā' and in one transmission from ash-Sha'bī. It is stated by Aḥmad ibn Ḥanbal, Isḥāq ibn Rāhawayh, Dāwūd ibn 'Alī and aṭ-Ṭabarī. It is reported from Mālik and is the old position of ash-Shāfi'ī. Makḥūl said, 'I met with az-Zuhrī and we discussed *tayammum*. Az-Zuhrī said, "Wiping is to the armpits." I asked, "Where did you get this?" He answered, "From the Book of Allah Almighty. Allah says: '*wiping your faces and hands.*' It is all 'a hand'." I told him, "Allah Almighty says: '*As for thieves, male and female, cut off their hands.*' (5:38) Where is the hand cut off?" He said, "You have won the argument."' It is related from ad-Darāwardī that the wrists are the obligation and up to the armpits is meritorious. Ibn 'Aṭiyyah said, 'This position is not supported by analogy or evidence. People are making the term 'hand' undefined and making it extend to the shoulder. Other people use analogy and make it extend to the elbows. They are the majority of the people. Some people take the *ḥadīth* and stop at the wrists. That is also based on analogy by connecting it to cutting off of hands since that is a legal ruling and purification as this is purification. Some people stop at the *ḥadīth* of 'Ammār about palms.' That is the position of ash-Sha'bī.

Scholars also disagree about whether striking once with the hands is enough for the whole act of *tayammum*. In the *Mudawwanah* Mālik held that *tayammum* should be done with two strikes: once for the face and once for the hands. That is the position of al-Awzā'ī, ash-Shāfi'ī, Abū Ḥanīfah and his people, ath-Thawrī, al-Layth, and Ibn Abī Salamah. Jābir ibn 'Abdullāh and Ibn 'Umar related it from the Prophet ﷺ. Ibn Abī-l-Jahm says that it is done with one strike. This is related from al-Awzā'ī in the best known position from him. It is also the position of 'Aṭā' and ash-Sha'bī in one transmission. It was also stated by Aḥmad ibn Ḥanbal, Isḥāq, Dāwūd and aṭ-Ṭabarī. It is the firmest of what is related regarding that from the *ḥadīth* of 'Ammār. Mālik said in the book of Muḥammad, '*Tayammum* with a single strike is allowed.' Ibn Nāfi' said that it should always be repeated in that case.

Abū 'Umar, Ibn Abī Laylā and al-Ḥasan ibn Ḥayy said that two strikes are necessary, wiping the face with one of them and the forearms and elbows with the other. None of the people of knowledge other than them say that. Abū 'Umar said, 'When there is a disagreement between traditions as to how to perform *tayammum* and they are contradictory, the obligation is taken from the literal text of the Book and that indicates two strikes: one for the face and one for the hands up to the elbows based on it being analogous to *wuḍū'* and following what Ibn 'Umar did. He is someone whose knowledge of the Book of Allah is unrefuted. If anything is confirmed from the Prophet ﷺ about that, one must stop at that.' Success is by Allah.

Allah is Ever-Pardoning, Ever-Forgiving.

He continues to grant pardon which is ease and forgives wrong actions, meaning that He veils them and so the person is not punished for them.

أَلَمْ تَرَ إِلَى ٱلَّذِينَ أُوتُوا۟ نَصِيبًا مِّنَ ٱلْكِتَٰبِ يَشْتَرُونَ ٱلضَّلَٰلَةَ وَيُرِيدُونَ أَن تَضِلُّوا۟ ٱلسَّبِيلَ ۞ وَٱللَّهُ أَعْلَمُ بِأَعْدَآئِكُمْ ۚ وَكَفَىٰ بِٱللَّهِ وَلِيًّا وَكَفَىٰ بِٱللَّهِ نَصِيرًا ۞ مِّنَ ٱلَّذِينَ هَادُوا۟ يُحَرِّفُونَ ٱلْكَلِمَ عَن مَّوَاضِعِهِۦ وَيَقُولُونَ سَمِعْنَا وَعَصَيْنَا وَٱسْمَعْ غَيْرَ مُسْمَعٍ وَرَٰعِنَا لَيًّۢا بِأَلْسِنَتِهِمْ وَطَعْنًا فِى ٱلدِّينِ ۚ وَلَوْ أَنَّهُمْ قَالُوا۟ سَمِعْنَا وَأَطَعْنَا وَٱسْمَعْ وَٱنظُرْنَا لَكَانَ خَيْرًا لَّهُمْ وَأَقْوَمَ وَلَٰكِن لَّعَنَهُمُ ٱللَّهُ بِكُفْرِهِمْ فَلَا يُؤْمِنُونَ إِلَّا قَلِيلًا ۞ يَٰٓأَيُّهَا ٱلَّذِينَ أُوتُوا۟ ٱلْكِتَٰبَ ءَامِنُوا۟ بِمَا نَزَّلْنَا مُصَدِّقًا لِّمَا مَعَكُم مِّن قَبْلِ أَن نَّطْمِسَ وُجُوهًا فَنَرُدَّهَا عَلَىٰٓ أَدْبَارِهَآ أَوْ نَلْعَنَهُمْ كَمَا لَعَنَّآ أَصْحَٰبَ ٱلسَّبْتِ ۚ وَكَانَ أَمْرُ ٱللَّهِ مَفْعُولًا ۞ إِنَّ ٱللَّهَ لَا يَغْفِرُ أَن يُشْرَكَ بِهِۦ وَيَغْفِرُ مَا دُونَ ذَٰلِكَ لِمَن يَشَآءُ ۚ وَمَن يُشْرِكْ بِٱللَّهِ فَقَدِ ٱفْتَرَىٰٓ إِثْمًا عَظِيمًا ۞

44 Do you not see those who were given a portion of the Book trading in misguidance and wanting you to be misguided from the way? 45 Allah knows best who your enemies are. Allah suffices as a Protector; Allah suffices as a Helper. 46 Some of the Jews distort the true meaning of words, saying,' We hear and disobey,' and 'Listen without listening,' and *'Rā'inā!'* twisting them with their tongues, disparaging the *dīn*. If they had said, 'We hear and we obey,' and 'Listen,' and, *'Undhurnā!'* that would have been better for them and more upright. But Allah has cursed them for their unbelief. Very few of them believe. 47 You who have been given the Book! believe in what We have sent down confirming what is with you, before We obliterate faces, turning them inside out, or We curse you as We cursed the Companions of the Sabbath. Allah's command is always carried out. 48 Allah does not forgive anything being associated with Him but He forgives whoever He wills for anything other than that. Anyone who associates something with Allah has committed a terrible crime.

وَمَن يُشْرِكْ بِٱللَّهِ فَقَدِ ٱفْتَرَىٰٓ إِثْمًا عَظِيمًا ﴿٤٨﴾ أَلَمْ تَرَ إِلَى ٱلَّذِينَ يُزَكُّونَ
أَنفُسَهُم ۚ بَلِ ٱللَّهُ يُزَكِّى مَن يَشَآءُ وَلَا يُظْلَمُونَ فَتِيلًا ﴿٤٩﴾ ٱنظُرْ كَيْفَ
يَفْتَرُونَ عَلَى ٱللَّهِ ٱلْكَذِبَ ۖ وَكَفَىٰ بِهِۦٓ إِثْمًا مُّبِينًا ﴿٥٠﴾ أَلَمْ تَرَ إِلَى ٱلَّذِينَ
أُوتُوا۟ نَصِيبًا مِّنَ ٱلْكِتَٰبِ يُؤْمِنُونَ بِٱلْجِبْتِ وَٱلطَّٰغُوتِ وَيَقُولُونَ
لِلَّذِينَ كَفَرُوا۟ هَٰٓؤُلَآءِ أَهْدَىٰ مِنَ ٱلَّذِينَ ءَامَنُوا۟ سَبِيلًا ﴿٥١﴾
أُو۟لَٰٓئِكَ ٱلَّذِينَ لَعَنَهُمُ ٱللَّهُ ۖ وَمَن يَلْعَنِ ٱللَّهُ فَلَن تَجِدَ لَهُۥ نَصِيرًا ﴿٥٢﴾ أَمْ لَهُمْ
نَصِيبٌ مِّنَ ٱلْمُلْكِ فَإِذًا لَّا يُؤْتُونَ ٱلنَّاسَ نَقِيرًا ﴿٥٣﴾

49 Do you not see those who claim to be purified? No, Allah purifies whoever He wills. They will not be wronged by so much as the smallest speck. 50 Look how they invent lies against Allah. That suffices as an outright felony. 51 Do you not see those who were given a portion of the Book believing in idols and false gods and saying of those who disbelieve, 'These people are better guided on their path than those who believe?' 52 Those are the ones Allah has cursed. And if someone is cursed by Allah you will not find anyone to help him. 53 Or do they indeed really own a portion of Allah's kingdom? In that case they do not give so much as a scrap to other people!

This was revealed about the Jews of Madīnah. Ibn Isḥāq said, 'Rifā'ah ibn Zayd was one of the important Jews. When he spoke to the Prophet ﷺ, he twisted his tongue and attacked Islam and criticised it. Allah revealed: *"Do you not see those who were given a portion of the Book..."*' *'Trading'* means to exchange, and it is in the position of the accusative for the *ḥāl*. There is some elision in the words which implies that they buy misguidance in exchange for guidance as Allah says in His words: '*Those are the people who have sold guidance for misguidance.*' (2:16) Al-Qutabī and others said that.

wanting you to be misguided from the way

This is added to it. They desire to mislay and depreciate the path of the truth. Al-Ḥasan recited '*tuḍallū*': desiring you to be misguided.

Allah knows best who your enemies are.

He knows better than you do. Do not keep their company for they are your enemies. *'Knows best'* (*a'lam*) can simply mean 'know' (*'alim*) as in 30:27 where the word *ahwan* simply means *hayyin*.

Allah suffices as a Protector.

The *bā'* is redundant because it means: 'Be content with Allah. He will protect you against your enemies.' *'Walī'* and *'naṣīr'* are in the accusative for clarification or, if you wish, for the *ḥāl*.

Some of the Jews distort the true meaning of words...

Az-Zajjāj said that 'some' can either be connected to what was before it, and so there is no stop at *'Helper'*, or it is separate and then one can stop there. It implies: 'Among the Jews are some people who distort,' and then there is elision. This is the school of Sībawayh. [ILLUSTRATIVE POEM] Al-Farrā' said that *'min'* is elided and it means, 'There are some Jews who distort. This is as we see in 37:164. [ILLUSTRATIVE POEM] Al-Mubarrad and az-Zajjāj deny it because the elision of something connected is like eliding part of the word.

Abū 'Abd ar-Raḥmān as-Sulamī and Ibrāhīm an-Nakha'ī recited *'al-kalāma'*. An-Naḥḥās said that *'al-kalim'* is more fitting because they used to distort the words of the Prophet ﷺ or what they have of the Torah. They did not distort all words. *'Distort'* means to give words an interpretation other than their true interpretation. Allah censured them for that because they did it intentionally. It is said that it refers to the description of the Prophet ﷺ.

The words *'We hear and disobey'* mean: 'We hear what you say and disobey your command.' Regarding *'Listen without listening'* Ibn 'Abbās said, 'They used to say to the Prophet ﷺ, "Hear and let us not hear you." This is what they meant – may Allah curse them! and by this they showed that they meant 'Listen without hearing something disliked or insult.' Al-Ḥasan and Mujāhid said that. It means 'not listening to you,' in other words not responding or accepting what you say. An-Naḥḥās said, 'If that had been the case, it would be "*masmū'*". The meaning of *'rā'inā'* was discussed in *al-Baqarah*.

twisting them with their tongues,

This means to twist them away from the Truth, inclining to what is in their hearts. The root is *layy*, which means twisting together. It is in the accusative by the verbal noun or, if you wish, it can be a direct object and its root is *'lawyan'* and the *wāw* is assimilated into the *yā'*.

disparaging the *dīn*.

This is added to it. This is attacking the *dīn*. It means that they say to their companions, 'If he had been a Prophet, he would have known that we are abusing him.' So Allah showed that to His Prophet. It was one of the signs of his Prophethood and He forbade them to say this.

that would have been better for them and more upright.

'More upright' means that it would have been more correct for them.

Very few of them believe.

They have very little belief and so they do not deserve to be called believers. It is said that it means only a few of them believe. This is unlikely because Allah reported that He cursed them because of their disbelief.

You who have been given the Book, believe in what We have sent down

Ibn Isḥāq said that the Messenger of Allah ﷺ spoke to the leaders of the Jews, including 'Abdullāh ibn Ṣūriyā al-A'war and Ka'b ibn Asad, and told them, 'Company of Jews! Fear Allah and submit. By Allah, you know that what I have brought you is the truth.' They said, 'We do not recognise that, Muḥammad.' They denied what they knew and persisted in disbelief and so Allah revealed this about them. *'Muṣaddiq'* (believe) is in the accusative for the *ḥāl*.

before We obliterate faces,

Obliteration is to wipe out the trace of a thing and efface it completely as the Almighty says: *'When the stars are extinguished* (ṭumisat).' (77:8) The verb is *naṭmisu and naṭmusu*, two dialectical possibilities for the future tense. One also says *ṭasama, yaṭsimu* and *yaṭsumu*, meaning to obliterate. For obliterating tracks, one says *ṭamasa* or *ṭasama*, in two dialectical usages. Allah says: '*Our Lord, obliterate* (aṭmis) *their wealth*' (10:88), meaning to destroy it, as Ibn 'Arafah said. One says *'ṭamastuhu fa-ṭamasa'* (I obliterated it and it was obliterated). It is transitive. You can say *'ṭamasa'llāhu baṣarahu'* (Allah obliterated his sight) and his sight was obliterated when the traces of the eye was gone. It can also be used to mean 'blind' as in Allah's words: *'If We wished, We could put out their eyes.'* (36:44)

Scholars disagree about what is meant by this *āyah*. Is it actual, so that the face becomes like the back of the head without nose, mouth and eyes, or does it just designate misguidance in their hearts and success being stripped away from them? It is related that Ubayy ibn Ka'b said that it means: 'Before We misguide them completely after which they will not be guided.' He believes that it is a metaphor, and if they do not believe, Allah will do that to do them as a punishment. Qatādah said that it means before We make their faces blank, in other words remove their features, meaning their noses, lips, eyes and eyebrows. This is what the people of language say. It is reported from Ibn 'Abbās and 'Aṭiyyah al-'Awfī said that *ṭams* means to remove the eyes in particular. It is also used for turning back and walking backwards.

Mālik said, 'At the beginning of Islam Ka'b al-Aḥbar passed by a man reciting this in the night. He covered his face with his palms and went backwards to his house and became Muslim on the spot. He said, "By Allah, I feared that I would not reach my house before my face was obliterated!"' The same was done by 'Abdullāh ibn Salām when this *āyah* was revealed. He heard it and went to the Messenger of Allah ﷺ before he went to his family and became Muslim. He said, 'Messenger of Allah, I did not know whether I would reach you before my face turned around.'

If it is asked how they could be threatened with the obliteration of their faces if they did not believe, and then, when they did not believe, this did not happen to them, the answer is that when those people and those who followed them believed, the threat was removed from the rest. Al-Mubarrad said, 'The threat still remains and is anticipated.' He added, 'There must be that obliteration and transmogrification among the Jews before the Day of Rising.'

or We curse you as We cursed the Companions of the Sabbath.

This refers to the people with those faces. The curse of the Companions of the Sabbath was when Allah transformed them into apes and pigs, as al-Ḥasan and Qatādah reported.

Allah's command is always carried out.

When it changes from the first person plural to the third, that indicates that the the matter is certain. *'Amr'* (command) is a verbal noun in the position of an object. It means that Allah brings into existence whatever He wishes. It is said that it means that all that He reports will be will be as He reported.

Allah does not forgive anything being associated with Him...

It is related that the Prophet ﷺ recited: *'Allah forgives all wrong actions'* (39:53) and a man said to him, 'Messenger of Allah! *Shirk*!' and this was revealed. This is one of the *muḥkam* verses on which there is absolute agreement in the Community. The phrase: *'but He forgives whoever He wills for anything other than that'* is the *mutashābih* about which scholars speak. Muḥammad ibn Jarīr aṭ-Ṭabarī said, 'This *āyah* makes it clear that every one with a major wrong action is subject to the will of Allah. If He wishes, He will pardon his wrong action, and if He wishes, He will punish him for it as long as it is not *shirk* in Allah.' One of them said, 'Allah explained that by His words: *"If you avoid the serious wrong actions you have been forbidden, We will erase your bad actions from you."* (4:31) Know that if He wishes, He will forgive the minor wrong actions of someone who avoids major wrong actions but does not forgive those of the one who does major wrong actions.'

Some of the people of *ta'wīl* believe that this abrogates the *āyah* at the end of *al-Furqān.* Zayd ibn Thābit said, '*Sūrat an-Nisā'* was revealed six months after *Sūrat al-Furqān.*' The sound position is that there is no abrogation because abrogation in statements is impossible. The two must be combined as will be mentioned in *al-Furqān.* We find in at-Tirmidhī that 'Alī ibn Abī Ṭālib said, 'There is no *āyah* in the Qur'an which I love more than this *āyah.*' This is a *gharīb ḥasan ḥadīth.*

Do you not see those who claim to be purified?

There are three points in this. Firstly, although this is apparently a general expression, none of the interpreters disagree that it is about the Jews. They disagree about the meaning of *'claim to be purified.'* Qatādah and al-Ḥasan said that it refers to their words: *'We are Allah's children and His loved ones'* (5:18) and their words: *'No one will enter the Garden except for Jews or Christians.'* (2:111) Aḍ-Ḍaḥḥāk and as-Suddī said that it is about their saying, 'We have no wrong actions. What we do in the day is forgiven at night and what we do at night is forgiven in the day and we are like sinless children.' Mujāhid, Abū Mālik and 'Ikrimah said, 'They put the children in front in the prayer because they have no wrong actions,' but this is very far from what the *āyah* means. Ibn 'Abbās said, 'It is about their words: "Our fathers who died will intercede for us and purify us."' 'Abdullāh ibn Mas'ūd said that it refers to their mutual praise. This is the best of what is said. It is the literal meaning of the *āyah. Tazkīyah* is to purify and free oneself of wrong actions.

Secondly, this *āyah* and the *āyah*: *'Do not declare yourselves pure'* (53:22) require one to disregard those who attribute purity to themselves. Allah purifies people who do good actions and there is no consideration of anyone's declaration of their own purity. What is important is Allah's purification of them. It is reported in *Ṣaḥīḥ Muslim* that Muḥammad ibn 'Amr ibn 'Aṭā' said, 'I named my daughter Barrah and Zaynab bin Abī Salamah told me, "The Messenger of Allah ﷺ forbade this name (Barrah). I was called Barrah. The Messenger of Allah ﷺ said, 'Do not declare yourselves pure. Allah knows better than you who the people of piety (*birr*) are.' They asked, 'What should we call her?' He replied, 'Call her Zaynab.''" The Book and the *Sunnah* indicate that it is forbidden for anyone to declare their own purity and integrity. This frequently happens in Egyptian families when they describe themselves with terms which indicate purification, like Zakī ad-dīn, Muḥyi ad-dīn and the like, but there are many ugly Muslims with these names whose qualities totally contradict their names.

Thirdly, as for someone else declaring someone else's purity and praising them, al-Bukhārī reports from Abū Bakr that a man was mentioned in the presence of the Prophet ﷺ and a man praised him and the Prophet ﷺ said, 'Woe to You! You have severed the neck of your companion!' several times. He continued, 'If one of you must praise, then he should say, "I reckon such-and-such" if he sees that he is like that, and Allah is his Reckoner. Do not declare anyone pure to Allah.' He forbade excessive praise of qualities someone does not possess because that might bring about vanity and pride and they will think that they actually have that position. That will lead them to stop acting and not to seek increased excellence. That is why the Prophet ﷺ said what he said. Another *ḥadīth* says, 'You have broken the back of your brother' when someone was described with a quality he did not have.

This is how scholars interpret his words ﷺ, 'Throw dust in the faces of the praisers.' It means those who falsely praise someone for a quality they do not possess in order to lead them on. As for praising a person for qualities they do have and for their praiseworthy actions, that will encourage them to continue and encourage people to imitate them in that. When someone praises people for what they do have, they are not false praisers. It has to do with intentions. *'Allah knows a squanderer from a good manager.'* (2:220)

The Prophet ﷺ praised poetry and oratory and did not encourage throwing dust in the faces of the speakers, nor did he command others to do so. As when Abū Ṭālib said:

> White, the clouds are asked for rain by his face,
> the supporter of orphans and protection of widows.

It is like when al-'Abbās and Ḥasan expressed praise in poetry. When Ka'b ibn Zuhayr eulogised him and he himself ﷺ praised his Companions: 'You are few in greed and many in alarm.'

As for his words ﷺ in the sound *ḥadīth*: 'Do not exaggerate praise of me as the Christians did with 'Īsā, the son of Mary. Say: "The slave of Allah and His

Messenger."' It means: do not describe me with qualities I do not possess by which you seek to praise me as the Christians describe 'Īsā with what he did not possess when they call him the son of God and disbelieve and are misguided by that. This is about putting something beyond its limits. Exceeding the merit of something by attributing a quality to it it does not possess is perpetrating a wrong action. Certainly if anyone had been entitled to such an attribution, it would have been the Messenger of Allah ﷺ.

They will not be wronged by so much as the smallest speck.

'They' refers to both those mentioned who declare their own purity and those whom Allah declares pure. Allah will not wrong anyone at all. According to Ibn 'Abbās, 'Aṭā' and Mujāhid the 'speck' (*fatīl*) referred to is the little thread you find on a date stone. It is also said that it is the skin around the date stone, as reported also by Ibn 'Abbās, Abū Mālik and as-Suddī. It is said that it is the skin that comes between your fingers and your palms when they are twisted together. It is in all these cases an allusion to the smallness and insignificance of a thing. Allah will not wrong anyone in any way at all. Something very similar can be seen in His words: *'They will not be wronged by so much as the tiniest speck.'* (4:124) That is the tiny dot on the pack of the date pit from which the palm grows. This will be discussed later. Censuring one of the kings, a poet said:

He gathers the army of thousands and attacks
and then does not deprive the enemy of a speck (*fatīl*).'

Look how they invent lies against Allah

Then the Prophet ﷺ was astonished at that. He said: *'Look how they invent lies against Allah'* when they said: *'We are the sons of Allah and those His loved ones.'* (5:18) It refers to the Jews. It is said that it is them declaring their own purity, as Ibn Jurayj said. It is related that they said, 'We have no sins except the sins of our children on the day they were born.'

Iftirā' is inventing. The words which follow: *'That suffices as an outright felony'* is in the accusative for clarification. It makes the sin great and censures it. The Arabs use this sort of expression both for censure and praise.

Do you not see those who were given a portion of the Book believing in idols and false gods.

This is a reference to the Jews. There is disagreement about the interpretation of *jibt* (idols) and *ṭāghūt* (false gods). Ibn 'Abbās, Ibn Jubayr and Abu-l-'Āliyah said that *jibt* means 'sorcerer' in Abyssinian and *ṭāghūt* means soothsayer. 'Umar ibn al-Khaṭṭāb said that *jibt* is sorcery and *ṭāghūt* is shayṭān. Ibn Mas'ūd said that the words *jibt* and *ṭāghūt* refer to Ka'b ibn al-Ashraf and Ḥuyayy ibn Akhṭab. 'Ikrimah said that *jibt* is Ḥuyayy ibn Akhṭab and *ṭāghūt* is Ka'b ibn al-Ashraf, citing evidence in the words of Allah: *'still desiring to turn to a shaytanic source for judgment.'* (4:60) Qatādah said that *jibt* is shayṭān and *ṭāghūt* is the soothsayer. Ibn Wahb related from Mālik ibn Anas: '*Ṭāghūt* is what is worshipped other than Allah.' He said, 'I heard those who say that *jibt* is shayṭān.' An-Naḥḥās mentioned that.

It is said that they are both what is worshipped other than Allah or obeyed in disobedience to Allah. This is good. The root of *jibt* is *jibs*, which means something in which there is no good, and the *tā'* has replaced the *sīn*, according to Quṭrub. It is said that *jibt* is Iblīs and *ṭāghūt* are his friends. What Mālik said regarding this is good, and is indicated by the words of Allah: '*Worship Allah and keep clear of false gods* (*ṭāghūt*)' (16:36) and: '*Those who shun the worship of false gods* (*ṭāghūt*)' (39:17). Qaṭan ibn al-Mukhāriq related from his father that the Messenger of Allah ﷺ said, 'Divining by pebbles and birds and auguring from lines are part of *jibt*.' Abū Dāwūd transmitted it in the *Sunan*. It is said that *jibt* is that all that Allah has forbidden and *ṭāghūt* is all of a person's wrondoing. Allah knows best.

and saying of those who disbelieve,

The Jews say to the unbelievers of Quraysh, 'You are better guided than those who believe in Muḥammad.' That was that Ka'b ibn al-Ashraf who went out with seventy riders from among the Jews to Makkah after the Battle of Uḥud to make an alliance with Quraysh to fight the Messenger of Allah ﷺ. Ka'b stayed with Abū Sufyān who gave him good lodgings. The Jews stayed in the houses of Quraysh and made a contract with them to fight Muḥammad. Abū Sufyān said, 'You are a man who reads the Book and teaches. We are illiterate and so do not know. Which of us is better guided and closer to the truth? Us or Muḥammad?' Ka'b replied, 'By Allah, you are better guided than Muḥammad.'

Or do they indeed really own a portion of Allah's kingdom?

'Am lahum' is *'a lam'* and the *mīm* is connective. This is denial, meaning that they do not have any of the kingdom. If they had any of it, they would not give anyone any of it because of their miserliness and envy. It is said that it means: 'Do they have a portion which exists?' So the 'or' severs and is separate from what is before it and begins a new sentence. It is said that it is added to something elided because they refused to follow Muḥammad ﷺ. It implies: 'Are

they more entitled to Prophethood than the one I sent or do they have a portion of the kingdom?'

In that case they do not give so much as a scrap to other people!

They would deny people their rights. Allah is telling us what He knows about them. According to Ibn 'Abbās, Qatādah and others *naqīr* is the spot on the back of a date-stone. Ibn 'Abbās also said that *naqīr* is an indentation that a man makes with his finger, as he does in the earth. Abu-l-'Āliyah said, 'I asked ibn 'Abbās about *naqīr* and he put the end of his thumb on the inside of his index finger and raised them. Then he said, "This is the *naqīr*."' The root of *naqīr* is a piece of wood that is hollowed out and then *nabīdh* is made in it. It was prohibited and then that was abrogated. A person with a noble *naqīr* has a noble origin. '*Idhan*' here has no effect because the conjunctive *fā'* is added to it. It would be permitted for it to be in the accusative. Sībawayh said, 'In the regents of verbs, "*idhan*" is in the position of "I suppose". It means that it has no effect when the words do not rely on it. If it is at the beginning of a phrase and what follows it it is in the future, it is in the accusative as when you say, "I will visit you" and the answer is "Then (*idhan*) I will honour you."' 'Abdullāh ibn 'Atamah aḍ-Ḍabbī said:

> Stop your donkey so that it does not graze in our meadow,
> then (*idhan*) it will be stopped and the wild ass will be sad.

It is in the accusative because what is before '*idhan*' is complete and the words start anew. It is between two things. When the conjunctive *fā'* or the conjunctive *wāw* is added, then it can act as a regent and be ineffective. As for acting as regent, it is because what follows the *wāw* starts anew by way of adding one sentence to another. It is permitted outside the Qu'ran and we also see it in 17:76 and in the Qur'an of Ubayy. As for being ineffective, it is because what follows the *wāw* is only after words added to it. According to Sībawayh, the accusative is for the verb with *idhan* because it is imperfect by *an*, and al-Khalīl says that *an* is implied after *idhan*.

Al-Farrā' claimed that *idhan* is written with *alif* (*idhān*) because it is like *mithl*, *lan* and *an*, and *tanwīn* is not added to particles.

أَمْ يَحْسُدُونَ ٱلنَّاسَ عَلَىٰ مَآ ءَاتَىٰهُمُ ٱللَّهُ مِن فَضْلِهِۦ ۖ فَقَدْ ءَاتَيْنَآ ءَالَ إِبْرَٰهِيمَ
ٱلْكِتَٰبَ وَٱلْحِكْمَةَ وَءَاتَيْنَٰهُم مُّلْكًا عَظِيمًا ﴿٥٤﴾ فَمِنْهُم مَّنْ ءَامَنَ بِهِۦ وَمِنْهُم مَّن
صَدَّ عَنْهُ ۚ وَكَفَىٰ بِجَهَنَّمَ سَعِيرًا ﴿٥٥﴾

54 Or do they in fact envy other people for the bounty Allah has granted them? We gave the family of Ibrāhīm the Book and Wisdom, and We gave them an immense kingdom. 55 Some of them believe in him, and some bar access to him. Hell will suffice as a Searing Blaze!

Or do they in fact envy other people for the bounty Allah has granted them?

'*They*' means the Jews again. The '*people*' referred to means the Prophet ﷺ in particular, according to Ibn 'Abbās, Mujāhid and others. They envied him for Prophethood and his Companions for believing in it. Qatādah said that '*people*' means the Arabs. The Jews envied them for the Prophethood that had emerged among them. Aḍ-Ḍaḥḥāk said that the Jews envied Quraysh for that Prophethood.

Envy is blameworthy and the person with it will be afflicted by sorrow and it eats up good actions as fire eats up wood, as Anas transmitted from the Prophet ﷺ. Al-Ḥasan said, 'I have not seen any wrongdoer more like someone who is wronged than someone with envy: constant desire, abiding sorrow and a lesson which does not end.' 'Abdullāh ibn Mas'ūd said, 'Do not infringe Allah's blessings.' He was asked, 'Who infringes Allah's blessings?' He replied, 'Those who envy people for the favour Allah has bestowed on them.' Allah says in one of the Scriptures: 'The envier is the enemy of blessing. He is angry at My Decree and not receiving blessing with My allotting.' Manṣūr the faqīh says:

Tell the one who envies me:
"Do you know the one to whom you show poor manners?

You show bad banners to Allah in respect of His judgment
When you are not pleased about what He has given me.'

It is said envy was the first wrong action by which Allah was disobeyed in heaven and the first by which He was disobeyed in earth. Iblīs envied Ādam in heaven, and Qābīl envied Hābīl on the earth. Abu-l-'Atāhīyah said about people:

O Lord! People are not fair to me.
How can it be that when I am fair to them, they wrong me?

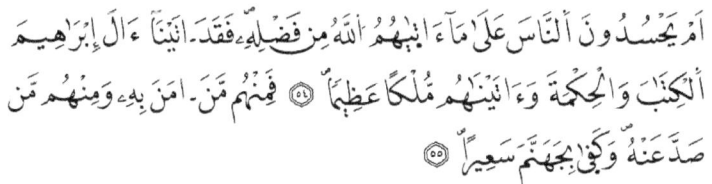

If I have something, they confront me to take it,
If I want to strive for something, they stop me.

If they receive something I spend on them, they are not grateful.
If I do not spend on them they abuse me.

If a misfortune befalls me, they are happy about it.
If I have a blessing they envy me.

So my heart refuses to be kind towards them,
and my eyes and lids are closed to them.

It is said that if you are happy to be safe from enviers, your business is grievous for them. A man of Quraysh said:

They envy blessing when it appears
and attack it with false words.

When Allah bestows His blessing,
the words of the enemies of blessings do not harm it.

And how excellent are the following words:

Be patient in the face of the envy of an envier.
Your patience will kill him.

Fire consumes itself
when it does not find anything to consume.

Some of the people of commentary have said about Allah's words: *'Our Lord, show us those jinn and men who misguided us and we will place them beneath our feet so that they will be among the lowest of the low'* (41:29) that by 'jinn' He means Iblīs and by 'men' He means Qābīl. Iblīs was the first to make unbelief a custom and Qābīl was the first to make murder a custom. The root of all of that is envy. A poet said:

The crow walks with a gait
about what has happened in the past,

Envying the sand-grouse, wanting to walk like it,
and then a leg cramp afflicts it.

We gave the family of Ibrāhīm the Book and Wisdom and We gave them an immense kingdom.

Allah tells us that He gave Ibrāhīm the Book and Wisdom and gave his family an immense kingdom. Hammām ibn al-Ḥārith said, 'They were supported by angels.' It is said that it it is a reference to the kingdom of Sulaymān as Ibn 'Abbās stated. It is also said that it means that they envied Muḥammad for the wives Allah allowed him and so the immense kingdom in this is that He allowed Dāwūd ninety-nine wives and Sulaymān more than that.

Aṭ-Ṭabarī prefers that what is meant is the great kingdom Sulaymān was given and women being made lawful for him. What is meant is the denial of the Jews and refuting their assertion that, 'If he had been a Prophet, he would not want a lot of wives and Prophethood would have distracted him from that.' Allah reported that Dāwūd and Sulaymān used to rebuke them and the Jews admitted that Sulaymān had a thousand wives. 'A thousand wives?' the Prophet ﷺ asked them. 'Yes,' they replied, '300 with dowries and 600 concubines, and Dāwūd had a hundred wives.' The Prophet ﷺ said to them, 'Is not a thousand with one man and a hundred with one man more than nine wives?' They were silent. At that time he had nine wives. It is said that Sulaymān had the greatest number of wives among the Prophets. The point of his great number of wives is that he had the strength of forty Prophets. Whoever is stronger can have more wives. It is said that what is meant by marriage is a greater number of tribes because every woman has two tribes, one on her father's side and one on her mother's side. Whenever someone marries a woman, the faces of the tribe turn towards him and help him against his enemies.

It is also said that if someone's *taqwā* is greater, his appetite is greater because someone who is not godfearing enjoys looking and touching. Do you not see what is related in the report? 'The two eyes commit fornication and the two hands commit fornication.' So when looking and touching are a sort of gratification, there is less sexual intercourse. Someone who is godfearing does not look or touch and so his appetite is concentrated in himself and he is capable of more sex. Abū Bakr al-Warrāq said, 'Every appetite strengthens the self except for sexual intercourse. It purifies the heart. That is why the Prophet used to do it.'

Some of them believe in him, and some bar access to him.

Some believe in the Prophet ﷺ, who was mentioned, and some turn aside and do not believe in him. It is said that the pronoun 'him' refers to Ibrāhīm. It means: some of the family of Ibrāhīm believed in him and some barred access to him. It is said that it refers to the Book of Allah. Allah knows best.

إِنَّ ٱلَّذِينَ كَفَرُوا۟ بِـَٔايَٰتِنَا سَوْفَ نُصْلِيهِمْ نَارًا كُلَّمَا نَضِجَتْ جُلُودُهُم بَدَّلْنَٰهُمْ جُلُودًا
غَيْرَهَا لِيَذُوقُوا۟ ٱلْعَذَابَ إِنَّ ٱللَّهَ كَانَ عَزِيزًا حَكِيمًا ﴿٥٦﴾ وَٱلَّذِينَ ءَامَنُوا۟ وَعَمِلُوا۟
ٱلصَّٰلِحَٰتِ سَنُدْخِلُهُمْ جَنَّٰتٍ تَجْرِى مِن تَحْتِهَا ٱلْأَنْهَٰرُ خَٰلِدِينَ فِيهَآ أَبَدًا
لَّهُمْ فِيهَآ أَزْوَٰجٌ مُّطَهَّرَةٌ وَنُدْخِلُهُمْ ظِلًّا ظَلِيلًا ﴿٥٧﴾

56 As for those who reject Our Signs, We will roast them in a Fire. Every time their skins are burned off, We will replace them with new skins so that they can taste the punishment. Allah is Almighty, All-Wise. 57 But as for those who believe and do right actions, We will admit them into Gardens with rivers flowing under them, remaining in them timelessly, for ever and ever. In them they will have spouses of perfect purity and We will admit them into cool, refreshing shade.

The meaning of '*roast*' in this context was discussed in *al-Baqarah*. Ḥumayd ibn Qays recited '*naṣlīhim*', i.e. 'We roast them'. A sheep that is *maṣlīyah*' is roasted. '*Fire*' is in the accusative, according to this reading, by the removal of the genitive which implies 'with a Fire'. '*Every time their skins are burned off*' means that they receive new skins. The verb is *naḍija* with the verbal nouns *nuḍj* and *naḍj*. A person whose opinion is *naḍīj* has a sound opinion. Those who attack the Qur'an among the *zindīq*s say, 'How is it permitted to punish skin which did not disobey Allah?' The answer is: 'It is not the skin which is being punished or tortured. The pain occurs to the soul because it is that which feels and recognises. So the replacing of skin is in addition to the punishment of the souls as indicated by His words here and His words: *"Whenever the Blaze dies down, We will increase it for them"* (17:97). What is meant in this is both the punishment to bodies and causing pain to spirits. If He had meant the skins, He would have said "*yudhqinna*".'

Muqātil said that the fire consumes them seven times a day, and al-Ḥasan said that is seventy thousand times a day. Every time they are consumed, they are told, 'Return!' and they return as they were. Ibn 'Umar said, 'When they are burned, their skins are replaced with skins white like parchment.' It is said that 'skins' means 'shirts' as Allah says: '*…you will see the evildoers yoked together in chains, wearing shirts of tar.*' (14:49-50) They are called skins because they cling close to their skins as is said of a thing particular to a person that it is 'a skin between his eyes.' Ibn 'Umar said:

They blame me for [love of] Sālim and I blame them.
The skin between the eye and the nose is sound (*sālim*).

When the shirts are burned, they are replaced. A poet says:

Blame clothes Taym in their green skins.
Woe to Taym on account of their green shirts!

'Shirts' means skins. It is said that it means: 'We will replace the first skins with new as a craftsman is told, "Make me another ring from this ring," and he breaks it and fashions a ring for you from it.' The ring that is fashioned is the first although it has changed; the silver is the same. That is how it is with the self when it becomes dust and becomes nothing and then Allah Almighty brings it to life. It is like the case of a brother of yours who is healthy and then you see him after that when he is seriously ill and you ask him, 'How are you?' He replies, 'I am not the same person you know,' yet he is, but his circumstances have changed. So his words, 'I am not the same person you know' are metaphorical as are His words: '*...with new skins*'. It is like Allah's words: *'On the Day the earth is changed to other than the earth.'* (14:48) It is that very same earth but its hills, mountains, rivers and trees have changed. It has become wider and everything on it levelled as will be explained in *Sūrat Ibrāhīm*. Expressing this idea, a poet said:

People are not people as they used to be,
and the abode is not the abode I used to know.

Ash-Sha'bī said, 'A man went to Ibn 'Abbās and said, "Do you see what 'Ā'ishah has done! She censures the time she lives in and recites the verses of Labīd:

'Those who lived in their shelters have departed
and I remain afterwards like a skin with scabies.

They enjoyed joking and abasement
and their speaker is censured even if he does not make trouble.'

She said, 'May Allah have mercy on Labīd. How would it have been if he had reached this time of ours!'" Ibn 'Abbās said, "If 'Ā'ishah censures the time she lives in, even 'Ād censured their time because a long time after they were destroyed a long spear like the the spears of their time was found in Khuzā'ah, on which was written: 'A land where we were and we were with its people when people were people and the land was the land.'"' The land remains as it is although its circumstances and those of people have changed and are not recognised."'

Allah is Almighty, All-Wise.

Allah is Almighty and nothing can resist Him or He misses nothing. He is Wise in what He promises His slaves.

We will admit them into cool, refreshing shade.

Then Allah describes the people of the Garden. There is a deep shade which no sun penetrates and which has no heat in it. Al-Ḥasan said that it is described as cool shade because no heat, hot wind or the like enters it, as happens with the shade of this world. Aḍ-Ḍaḥḥāk said that it is the shade of the trees and of their palaces. Al-Kalbī says that it means an eternal shade.

إِنَّ ٱللَّهَ يَأْمُرُكُمْ أَن تُؤَدُّوا۟ ٱلْأَمَـٰنَـٰتِ إِلَىٰٓ أَهْلِهَا وَإِذَا حَكَمْتُم بَيْنَ ٱلنَّاسِ أَن
تَحْكُمُوا۟ بِٱلْعَدْلِ ۚ إِنَّ ٱللَّهَ نِعِمَّا يَعِظُكُم بِهِۦٓ ۗ إِنَّ ٱللَّهَ كَانَ سَمِيعًۢا بَصِيرًا ﴿٥٨﴾

58 Allah commands you to return to their owners the things you hold on trust and, when you judge between people, to judge with justice. How excellent is what Allah exhorts you to do! Allah is All-Hearing, All-Seeing.

Allah commands you to return to their owners the things you hold on trust

This *āyah* is one of the matrices of rulings which contain all the *dīn* and the Sharī'ah. There is disagreement about who is addressed by it. 'Alī ibn Abī Ṭālib, Zayd ibn Aslam, Shahr ibn Ḥawshab and Ibn Zayd say that it is addressed to the rulers of the Muslims in particular. It is for the Prophet ﷺ and his commanders and then extends to those after them.

Ibn Jurayj and others said that it is addressed particularly to the Prophet ﷺ about the key to the Ka'bah when he took it from 'Uthmān ibn Abī Ṭalḥah al-Hajabī al-'Abdarī and his nephew Shaybah ibn 'Uthmān. They were unbelievers at the time of the conquest of Makkaḥ. Al-'Abbās asked for it so that he could add care of the Ka'bah to the right of drawing water. The Messenger of Allah ﷺ entered the Ka'bah and smashed the idols inside it. He pushed back the Maqām of Ibrāhīm and Jibrīl brought down this *āyah* to him. 'Umar ibn al-Khaṭṭāb said, 'The Messenger of Allah ﷺ emerged reciting this *āyah* and I had never heard it before.' He summoned 'Uthmān and Shaybah and said, 'Take it eternally forever. Only a wrongdoer will take it from you.' Makkī reported that Shaybah did not want to hand over the key. When he handed it over, he said to the Prophet ﷺ: 'Take it as the trust of Allah.'

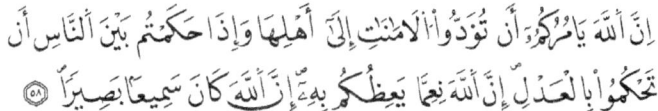

Ibn 'Abbās said that the *āyah* is addressed to guardians in particular, to admonish women about disobedience and the like and returning them to their husbands. The most evident position is that is general to all people. So it is about the rulers and what is entrusted to them with respect to the division of property, restoring injustices and being fair in rulings. This is what aṭ-Ṭabarī prefers. It then applies to people preserving deposits and being careful in testimony and other things, as a man judges in an incident and the like. The prayer, zakāt and all acts of worship are trusts from Allah.

It is related in a *marfū'* form with this meaning from Ibn Mas'ūd from the Prophet ﷺ: 'Being killed in the Way of Allah expiates all wrong actions – or everything – except trusts. The trust is in the prayer. The trust is in fasting. The trust is in speaking, and stronger than that are deposits.' Abū Nu'aym mentioned it in *al-Ḥilyah*. Among those who said that the *āyah* is general to all were al-Barā' ibn 'Āzib, Ibn Mas'ūd, Ibn 'Abbās, and Ubayy ibn Ka'b. They said that trusts include everything: *wuḍū'*, the prayer, zakāt, *janābah*, fasting, measures, weights and deposits. Ibn 'Abbās said, 'Allah did not allow anyone with straitened means nor the wealthy to hold on to a trust.'

This is the consensus. They agree that trusts should be returned to their owners, whether they are pious or impious. Ibn al-Mundhir said that. *Amānah* is a verbal noun which has the meaning of an object which is why it has a plural. The meaning of the structure is that Allah reports about how the People of the Book concealed the description of Muḥammad ﷺ and said that the idolaters were better guided. That was treachery on their part. Then the discussion moves on to all trusts. So the structure of the *āyah* includes every trust, and they are numerous, as we mentioned. The bases in rulings are deposits, finds, pledges and the *'āriyyah* loan.

Ubayy ibn Ka'b said that he heard the Messenger of Allah ﷺ say, 'Return the trust to the one who entrusted it to you and do not betray the one who betrays you.' Ad-Dāraquṭnī transmitted it. Anas and Abū Hurayrah reported something similar from the Prophet ﷺ. It was already mentioned in *al-Baqarah*. Abū Umamah said, 'I heard the Messenger of Allah ﷺ say in his *khuṭbah* in the Farewell *Ḥajj*: "An *'āriyyah* must be returned and the loan of a milk animal returned. A debt must be paid and the claimant is a creditor."' It is sound and transmitted by at-Tirmidhī and others. Ad-Dāraquṭnī added, 'A man said, "And the contract of Allah?" He said, "It is even more right to fulfil the contract of Allah."'

He said that this *āyah* and the *ḥadīth* require deposits to be returned. They are guaranteed to be in their original state, whether or not they are concealed and whether or not they have been misused. That is the view of 'Aṭā', ash-Shāfi'ī,

Aḥmad and Ashhab. It is related that Ibn 'Abbās and Abū Hurayrah guaranteed deposits. Ibn al-Qāsim related from Mālik that if someone borrows an animal, or something else which is not concealed, and it is destroyed while in his possession, and he is telling the truth about its destruction, he is only liable if some kind of misusage was involved. This is the position of al-Ḥasan al-Baṣrī and an-Nakha'ī. It is the position of the Kufans and al-Awzā'ī. They said the meaning of the words of the Prophet ﷺ, 'The *'āriyyah* (deposit) must be returned' corresponds to Allah's words: *'Allah commands you to return to their owners the things you hold on trust.'*

If a trust is destroyed, the one entrusted is not liable for it as long as he is telling the truth. The same is the case with an *'āriyyah* when it is destroyed without misusage because the holder did not take it on the basis of liability. When it is destroyed on account of his misusage, then he must pay its value because of his misuse of it. It is related from 'Alī, 'Umar and Ibn Mas'ūd that there is no liability in respect of an *'āriyyah*. Ad-Dāraquṭnī related from 'Amr ibn Shu'ayb from his father from his grandfather that the Messenger of Allah ﷺ said, 'The trustee is not liable.' Ash-Shāfi'ī argued by what Safwān said to the Prophet ﷺ when he borrowed his armour, 'Is it a guaranteed loan or one that will be returned?' He said, 'One that will be returned.'

When you judge between people, to judge with justice.

Aḍ-Ḍaḥḥāk said that the claimant provides evidence and an oath is taken by the person who disputes it. This is addressed to rulers, governors and judges, but the meaning includes all people as we mentioned in connection with trusts. The Prophet ﷺ said, 'On the Day of Rising those who are just will be on minbars of light at the right hand of the All-Merciful. Both of His hands are right hands. They are those who are just in respect of their judgments, their families and what they are put in charge of.' The Prophet ﷺ said, 'All of you are shepherds. Each of you is responsible for his flock. An amir is a shepherd. A man is a shepherd in respect of his family. A woman is a shepherd in respect of her husband's house and children. All of you are shepherds and each of you is responsible for his flock.' These sound hadiths include all of those people as shepherds and judges in their various ranks. The same holds true of a scholar with judgment because when he gives a fatwa, rules, judges, distinguishes between the lawful and unlawful, obligatory and recommended, sound and false, all of that is a trust to be returned and a ruling to be judged.

How excellent is what Allah exhorts you to do.

The meaning of *'ni'immā'* was discussed in *al-Baqarah*.

Allah is All-Hearing, All-Seeing

Allah describes Himself as being All-Hearing, All-Seeing and He sees as He says: *'I will be with you, Hearing and Seeing.'* (20:46) This is the course of hearing which is logically indicated. Hearing and sight also indicate their opposites: being deaf and blind. In the case of opposites, it must be one or the other. The Almighty is pure of imperfections. It is impossible for perfect actions to issue from one described with imperfections, such as someone without hearing or sight creating hearing and sight. The community agree that the Almighty is free of any imperfections. It is also an adequate proof when accompanied with the text of the Qur'an in the debate of those gathered under the word of Islam. The Lord is exalted above what those with illusions imagine and lying falsifiers forge. *'Glory be to your Lord, the Lord of Might, beyond anything they describe.'* (37:180)

يَـٰٓأَيُّهَا ٱلَّذِينَ ءَامَنُوٓا۟ أَطِيعُوا۟ ٱللَّهَ وَأَطِيعُوا۟ ٱلرَّسُولَ وَأُو۟لِى ٱلْأَمْرِ مِنكُمْ
فَإِن تَنَـٰزَعْتُمْ فِى شَىْءٍ فَرُدُّوهُ إِلَى ٱللَّهِ وَٱلرَّسُولِ إِن كُنتُمْ تُؤْمِنُونَ
بِٱللَّهِ وَٱلْيَوْمِ ٱلْـَٔاخِرِ ذَٰلِكَ خَيْرٌ وَأَحْسَنُ تَأْوِيلًا ﴿٥٩﴾

59 You who believe, obey Allah and obey the Messenger and those in command among you. If you have a dispute about something, refer it back to Allah and the Messenger, if you believe in Allah and the Last Day. That is the best thing to do and gives the best result.

As there was a direction to rulers in previous *āyah*, Allah beginning with them and commanding them to return trusts and to judge between people with justice, in this *āyah*, He moves on to the ruled and commands them firstly to obey Him, which entails obeying His commands and avoiding His prohibitions, then secondly to obey His Messenger in what he commands and forbids, and thirdly, according to the position of the majority, including Abū Hurayrah, Ibn 'Abbās and others, to obey their rulers. Sahl ibn 'Abdullāh at-Tustarī said, 'Obey the ruler in seven things: minting dirhams and dinars, weights and measures, judgments, ḥajj, *Jumu'ah*, the two *'īd*s and *jihād*.' Sahl said, 'When a ruler forbids a scholar to give a fatwa, he should not give it. If he does so, he disobeys, even if the ruler is tyrannical.'

Ibn Khuwayzimandād said, 'It is mandatory to obey the ruler in respect of that which comprises Allah's obedience. It is not mandatory in respect of anything which entails disobedience to Allah. This is why we say that it is not permitted to obey the rulers of our time nor assist them nor esteem them, but it is mandatory to go on expeditions with them, and they are responsible for judgment, the appointment of the imamate and *ḥisbah.* The establishment of that is part of the Sharī'ah. If they lead us in the prayer and are impious in that they perform acts of disobedience, it is permitted to pray behind them. If they are innovators, it is not permitted to pray behind them unless there is fear of them, in which case you should pray behind them out of *taqiyyah* (dissembling) and then repeat the prayer.' It is related that 'Alī ibn Abī Ṭālib said, 'It is a duty of the ruler to judge with justice and to discharge trusts faithfully. When he does that, the Muslims are obliged to obey Him because Allah commanded us to return trusts and be just and then He commanded obedience.'

Jābir ibn 'Abdullāh and Mujāhiḍ said that *'those in command'* are the people of Qur'an and knowledge. That is the choice of Mālik, and aḍ-Ḍaḥḥāk says the same. He said that it means the *fuqahā'* and scholars of the *dīn.* Mujāhid related that it is the Companions of Muḥammad ﷺ. 'Ikrimah reported that it refers to Abū Bakr and 'Umar. Sufyān ibn 'Uyaynah related that 'Ikrimah was asked about *umm walad*s. He said, 'They are free.' He was asked. 'On what grounds?' He replied, 'By the Qur'an.' He said it was by this *āyah* since 'Umar was the one in command and he said, 'She is free, even if she has a miscarriage.' This will be discussed in *al-Ḥashr* (59:7). Ibn Kaysān said, 'They are those of intelligence and opinion who manage people's affairs.'

The soundest of these positions is the second. The first is because they have command and judgment. The two *Ṣaḥīḥ* Collections report from Ibn 'Abbās that this *āyah* was revealed about 'Abdullāh ibn Ḥudhāfah ibn Qays ibn 'Adī as-Sahmī when the Prophet ﷺ sent him out in charge of an expedition. Abū 'Umar said that 'Abdullāh ibn Ḥudhāfah was known to be a joker and one of his jokes was that he commanded them to collect firewood and light it. When it was lit, he commanded them to throw themselves into it. He said to them, 'Did not the Messenger of Allah ﷺ command you to obey me! He said, "Whoever obeys my amīr has obeyed me."' They said, 'We believe in Allah and follow His Messenger, but we are not going to jump into the Fire!' The Messenger of Allah ﷺ said that their action was correct and said, 'There is no obedience to a creature in disobedience to the Creator. Allah Almighty says: *"Do not kill yourselves."* (4:29)' It is a sound *ḥadīth* with a well known *isnād.* Muḥammad ibn 'Amr ibn 'Alqamah related from 'Umar ibn al-Ḥakam ibn Thawbān that Abū Sa'īd al-Khudrī said, "Abdullāh ibn Ḥudhāfah ibn Qays as-Sahmī was one of the people of Badr. He was a joker.' Az-Zubayr mentioned from 'Abd al-Jabbār ibn Sa'īd from 'Abdullāh ibn Wahb that al-Layth ibn Sa'd said, 'I heard that he released the strap of the camel of the Messenger of Allah ﷺ on one of his journeys so that the Messenger of Allah ﷺ almost fell off.' Ibn Wahb said, 'I asked al-Layth, "To make him laugh?" "Yes," he answered, "he was a joker."' Maymūn ibn Mahrān, Muqātil and al-Kalbī said that '*those in command*' are the people in charge of military expeditions.

The soundness of the second position is indicated by Allah's words: '*If you have a dispute about something, refer it back to Allah and the Messenger.*' So the command is to refer it back to the Book of Allah and the *Sunnah* of His Prophet ﷺ, and that is to none other than the scholars who know how to refer things back to the Book and the *Sunnah*. This indicates that it is mandatory to ask scholars and obey their fatwas. Sahl ibn 'Abdullāh said, 'People will remain in a good state as long as they esteem their ruler and their scholars. When they esteem these two, Allah will put both this world and the Next World right for them. When they make light of them, He will ruin things for them in this world and the Next World.'

The third position is specific and the fourth is even more so. The fifth is refuted by the literal words of the *āyah*, even if the meaning is sound. The intellect gives every virtue a basis and every *adab* an originating spring. It is that which Allah made a basis for the *dīn* and support for this world. So Allah obliged responsibility in its totality and made this world managed by His rulings. An intelligent person is closer to his Lord than all those who strive without intelligence. This is reported from Ibn 'Abbās. Some people claim that it refers to 'Alī and the protected imāms. If that had been the case, what would be the point of the words: '*refer it back to Allah and the Messenger*'? It would tell people to refer to the imām and those in command. This is imposing something over the Book and *Sunnah*. This abandoned position differs from the view of the majority.

The reality of obedience is obeying a command just as disobedience is its opposite, opposing a command. Obedience (*ṭā'ah*) is derived from *aṭā'a*, to comply. Disobedience (*ma'ṣiyah*) is derived from '*aṣā*', to oppose. *Ūlū* is the plural of *dhū*, not analogous to other words, like *nisā'* (women), *ibl* (camels) and *khayl* (horses). They are plural nouns with no singular.

If you have a dispute about something

This means if you argue and disagree and each has his own argument and evidence. The noun '*naz'*' means attraction. *Munāza'ah* is a struggle between arguments. An example of it is found in the *ḥadīth*: 'Do not contend with me about the Qur'an.' Al-A'shā said:

> Reclining, I contended with them for a sprig of basil
> and a sweet wine from a constant jug.

The word '*something*' here refers to a matter of the *dīn*. So you should refer judgment to the Book of Allah or to His Messenger by asking directly while he was alive or examining his *Sunnah* after his death. This is the position of Mujāhid, al-Al-A'mash and Qatādah, and it is sound. Whoever does not think this is lacking in faith since Allah says: *'If you believe in Allah and the Last Day.'* It is said that it means you should say, 'Allah and His Messenger know best.' This is a refutation. It is as 'Umar ibn al-Khaṭṭāb said, 'Returning to the truth is better than quarrelling about falsehood.'

However, the first view is sounder because 'Alī said, 'What we have is only in the Book of Allah and this page or an understanding given to a Muslim man.' If it had been as the speaker said, that would invalidate the *ijtihād,* for which this community is singled out, as well as the deduction which it gives. Other examples are made and it is so that one can find what is correct. Abu-l-'Āliyah said, 'It is explained by Allah's words: *"If they had only referred it to the Messenger and those in command among them, those among them able to discern the truth about it would have had proper knowledge of it…"* (4:83) as long as it is not something about which only Allah has knowledge and none of His creatures do. That is the thing about which you should say, "Allah knows best".' 'Alī, for instance, deduced the minimum period of pregnancy, which is six months, from Allah's words: *'His bearing and weaning take thirty months'* (46:15) and His words: *'Mothers should nurse their children for two full years – those who wish to complete the full term of nursing.'* (2:233). Subtracting two years from thirty months leaves six months. There are many examples of this.

refer it to Allah and His Messenger,

This is proof that you should act by his *Sunnah* ﷺ and that it is a model to follow. The Prophet ﷺ said, 'Abandon doing what I have forbidden you to do and do what I have commanded you to do as much as you can. Those before you were destroyed by the great number of their questions and their disagreement with their Prophets.' Muslim transmitted it. Abū Dāwūd reported from Abū Rāfi' that the Prophet ﷺ said, 'I should not find any of you lying on their beds who hear one of the things I myself have commanded or forbidden and who then says, "We do not know. We follow what we find in the Book of Allah."' Al-'Irbāḍ ibn Sāriyyah said that he was present when the Messenger of Allah ﷺ was addressing the people with the words: 'Does one of you reclining on his bed suppose that Allah has not forbidden anything except what is in this Qur'an? By Allah, I have commanded, warned and forbidden things. They are like the Qur'an or even more mandatory.' At-Tirmidhī transmitted it from al-Miqdām ibn Ma'dīkarib and said that it is a *gharīb ḥasan ḥadīth.* The words of Allah about that are definitive: *'Those who oppose his command should beware of a testing trial coming to them.'* (24:63)

That is the best thing to do and gives the best result.

This means that referring your disagreement to the Book and the *Sunnah* is better than arguing. *'The best result'* means the best origin or that to which a thing returns. The verb *āla, ya'ūlu* means to go to something, and it is said that it is to gather something and put it right, and the term *ta'wīl* includes several meanings which make it problematic even though the word itself is not problematic. One says, *'Awwala-llāhu 'alayka amrak'* and it means 'bring it together.' It can mean; 'better than your interpretation'.

أَلَمْ تَرَ إِلَى الَّذِينَ يَزْعُمُونَ أَنَّهُمْ ءَامَنُوا بِمَا أُنزِلَ إِلَيْكَ وَمَا أُنزِلَ مِن
قَبْلِكَ يُرِيدُونَ أَن يَتَحَاكَمُوا إِلَى الطَّاغُوتِ وَقَدْ أُمِرُوا أَن
يَكْفُرُوا بِهِ وَيُرِيدُ الشَّيْطَانُ أَن يُضِلَّهُمْ ضَلَالًا بَعِيدًا ﴿٦٠﴾ وَإِذَا قِيلَ
لَهُمْ تَعَالَوْا إِلَىٰ مَا أَنزَلَ اللَّهُ وَإِلَى الرَّسُولِ رَأَيْتَ الْمُنَافِقِينَ
يَصُدُّونَ عَنكَ صُدُودًا ﴿٦١﴾

60 Do you not see those who claim that they believe in what has been sent down to you and what was sent down before you, still desiring to turn to a satanic source for judgment in spite of being ordered to reject it? Shayṭān wants to misguide them far away. 61 When they are told, 'Come to what Allah has sent down and to the Messenger,' you see the hypocrites turning away from you completely.

Yazīd ibn Zuray' related from Dāwūd ibn Abī Hind that ash-Sha'bī reported, 'There was a quarrel between one of the hypocrites and one of the Jews and the Jew summoned the hypocrite to the Prophet ﷺ since he knew that he did not accept bribes and the hypocrite summoned the Jew to their judges since he knew that they took bribes for judgments. When they disagreed, they agreed in the end to take it to a soothsayer in Juhaynah and Allah revealed about that: *"Do you not see those who claim that they believe in what has been sent down to you,"* which refers to the hypocrite, *"and what was sent down before you,"* which refers to the Jew.' Aḍ-Ḍaḥḥāk said, 'The Jew summoned the hypocrite to the Prophet ﷺ and the hypocrite summoned him to Ka'b ibn al-Ashraf, who is the *ṭāghūt* (satanic source) referred to.'

Abū Ṣāliḥ related that Ibn 'Abbās said, 'There was a quarrel between one of the hypocrites, called Bishr, and a Jew. The Jew said, "Let us go to Muḥammad." The hypocrite said, "Rather to Ka'b ibn al-Ashraf," who was the one Allah called *ṭāghūt*. The Jew refused to take it to anyone except the Messenger of Allah ﷺ. When the hypocrite saw that, he went with him to the Messenger of Allah ﷺ who judged in favour of the Jew. When they left, the hypocrite said, "I am not satisfied. Let us go to Abū Bakr." He also judged in favour of the Jew, but the man was still not satisfied and said, "Let us go to 'Umar." They went to 'Umar and the Jew said, "We went to the Messenger of Allah ﷺ and then to Abū Bakr, but he is still not satisfied." 'Umar asked the hypocrite, "Is that true?" "Yes," he replied. He said, "Wait until I come out to you." He went inside, picked up his sword and then struck the hypocrite until he was cold. He said, "That is my judgment on the one who is not pleased with the decision of Allah and the decision of His Messenger." The Jew fled and the *āyah* was revealed. The Messenger of Allah ﷺ said, "You are Fārūq." Jibrīl descended and said, "'Umar distinguished between the truth and falsehood," and so he is called Fārūq (one who differentiates).'

All of the *āyah*s were revealed about that up to the end of *āyah* 65.

Shayṭān wants to misguide them far away.

The participle '*dalāl*' is in the accusative, meaning that he wants to completely misguide them. Allah uses the verbal noun together with the verb for emphasis. Another example is the words: '*Allah causes you to grow from the earth*' (71:18) where he also uses the verbal noun in this way. This matter has already been mentioned in full.

you see the hypocrites turning away from you completely.

The word *ṣudūd* is a verbal noun according to al-Khalīl. The usual verbal noun is *ṣadd*. The Kufans say that both are verbal nouns.

فَكَيْفَ إِذَآ أَصَٰبَتْهُم مُّصِيبَةٌۢ بِمَا قَدَّمَتْ أَيْدِيهِمْ ثُمَّ جَآءُوكَ
يَحْلِفُونَ بِٱللَّهِ إِنْ أَرَدْنَآ إِلَّآ إِحْسَٰنًا وَتَوْفِيقًا ﴿٦٢﴾ أُو۟لَٰٓئِكَ ٱلَّذِينَ
يَعْلَمُ ٱللَّهُ مَا فِى قُلُوبِهِمْ فَأَعْرِضْ عَنْهُمْ وَعِظْهُمْ وَقُل لَّهُمْ
فِىٓ أَنفُسِهِمْ قَوْلًۢا بَلِيغًا ﴿٦٣﴾

62 How will it be when a disaster strikes them because of what they have done, and then they come to you swearing by Allah: 'We desired nothing but good and reconciliation'? 63 Allah knows what is in such people's hearts so turn away from them and warn them and speak to them with words that take effect.

The word '*kayf*' is asking about their state or what they will do. Because of their failure to help, humiliation will afflict them as illustrated by the words: *'You will never go out with me, nor will you ever fight an enemy with me'* (9:83). It is also said that it a reference to the killing of their companion. The sentence ends with the words: *'because of what they have done'*, and then Allah reports about their actions. That was after 'Umar killed their companion, his people came to demand his blood money and swore this oath. It is said that their words meant, 'We only wanted justice in arbitration from you and settling things between litigants and good in reconciling.' Ibn Kaysān said that it means justice and the right. A similar example is found in Allah's words concerning them: *'They will swear, "We only desired the best."'* (9:107) Allah tells us that they were lying when He says: *'Allah knows what is in such people's hearts.'* Az-Zajjāj said that the words: *'Allah knows what is in such people's hearts'* mean that Allah knows that they are hypocrites, and for us, it means 'Know that they are hypocrites.'

so turn away from them and warn them and speak to them with words that take effect.

The instruction to *'turn away'* from them can either mean 'from punishing them' or 'from accepting their excuses.' To *'warn them'* is to alarm them. And to *'speak to them with words that take effect'* means to rebuke them strongly both privately and publicly. Al-Ḥasan said, 'Tell them, "If you display what is in your hearts, I will kill you."' *'Words that take effect'* are eloquent and a man can be eloquent with his tongue while concealing what is in his heart. The Arabs say, *'Aḥmaq bilgh* (or *balgh*)', which means 'Someone stupid may still obtain his desire.'

It is said that the words: *'How will it be when a disaster strikes them…'* were revealed about those who built the Mosque of Harm. When Allah revealed their hypocrisy and ordered the mosque to be destroyed, they made oaths to the Messenger of Allah ﷺ in order to defend themselves, saying they had only done that out of a desire to obey Allah and conform to the Book of Allah.

وَمَآ أَرۡسَلۡنَا مِن رَّسُولٍ إِلَّا لِيُطَاعَ بِإِذۡنِ ٱللَّهِۚ وَلَوۡ أَنَّهُمۡ إِذ ظَّلَمُوٓاْ
أَنفُسَهُمۡ جَآءُوكَ فَٱسۡتَغۡفَرُواْ ٱللَّهَ وَٱسۡتَغۡفَرَ لَهُمُ ٱلرَّسُولُ
لَوَجَدُواْ ٱللَّهَ تَوَّابٗا رَّحِيمٗا ﴿٦٤﴾

64 We sent no Messenger except to be obeyed by Allah's permission. If only when they wronged themselves they had come to you and asked Allah's forgiveness and the Messenger had asked forgiveness for them they would have found Allah Ever-Returning, Most Merciful.

We sent no Messenger except to be obeyed by Allah's permission.

The use of the extra particle *'min'* before Messenger is used for stress. He is *'to be obeyed'* in respect of what he commands and forbids. The expression *'by Allah's permission'* can mean according to Allah's knowledge or by Allah's granting success.

If only when they wronged themselves they had come to you and asked Allah's forgiveness

Abū Ṣādiq related that 'Alī said, 'A bedouin came to us three days after the burial of the Messenger of Allah ﷺ. He threw himself on the grave of the Messenger of Allah ﷺ and poured dust on his head. He said, "Messenger of Allah, we heard your words and you retained from Allah and so we retained from you. Part of what Allah revealed to you is: *'If only when they wronged themselves they had come to you…'* I have wronged myself and I have come to you so that you could ask forgiveness for me." There was a call from the grave, "He has forgiven you."' *'They would have found Allah Ever-Returning'* means that He would accept their repentance.

فَلَا وَرَبِّكَ لَا يُؤۡمِنُونَ حَتَّىٰ يُحَكِّمُوكَ فِيمَا شَجَرَ بَيۡنَهُمۡ ثُمَّ لَا
يَجِدُواْ فِيٓ أَنفُسِهِمۡ حَرَجٗا مِّمَّا قَضَيۡتَ وَيُسَلِّمُواْ تَسۡلِيمٗا ﴿٦٥﴾

65 No, by your Lord, they are not believers until they make you their judge in the disputes that break out between them, and

then find no resistance within themselves to what you decide and submit themselves completely.

Mujāhid and others said that what is meant by this *āyah* are the people already mentioned who took their arbitration to the satanic source. It was revealed about them. Aṭ-Ṭabarī said, the word '*No*,' refutes what was mentioned, implying: 'The business is not as they claim about believing in what was revealed to you.' Then a new sentence starts with: '*By Your Lord*.' It is also said that '*No*' is an oath of negation, and it becomes one '*No*,' rather than repeating it twice. The verb *shajara* means to disagree and to be muddled. The noun 'tree' (*shajar*) is called that because of the diversity of its branches. The branches of a howdah are '*shijār*' because they interpenetrate. A poet said:

May my life your ransom! The spears thrust against each other (*shawājir*)
and the people are timid in the encounter.

Ṭarafah said:

They are the judges, the masters of guidance,
and the inspectors of people in disputes (*shajir*).

One group said that this was revealed about az-Zubayr and an Anṣārī who had a dispute about the watering of a garden. The Prophet ﷺ told az-Zubayr, 'Water your land and then let the water pass through to your neighbour.' The opponent said, 'I see you give to your cousin!' The face of the Messenger of Allah ﷺ changed colour and he told az-Zubayr, 'Water, Zubayr, and then retain the water until it reaches the wall.' Then this was revealed. It is a firm sound *ḥadīth* that al-Bukhārī related from 'Alī ibn 'Abdullāh from Muḥammad ibn Ja'far from Ma'mar. Muslim related it from Qutaybah from al-Layth. Both have it from az-Zuhrī. There is disagreement about who the Anṣārī man is. Some people said that he was one of the Anṣār who was one of the people of Badr. Makkī and others said that he was Ḥāṭib ibn Abī Balta'ah. Ath-Tha'labī and al-Mahdawī said that it was Ḥāṭib. It is said that his name was Tha'labah ibn Ḥāṭib.

Others said that the first view is the sound one because he is neither specified nor named. Both al-Bukhārī and Muslim said 'a man of the Anṣār'. Aṭ-Ṭabarī preferred the opinion that the *āyah* was revealed about a hypocrite and a Jew. Mujāhid said that and then its generality can also include the story about az-Zubayr. Ibn al-'Arabī said, 'That is sound. Anyone who doubts a ruling given by the Messenger of Allah ﷺ is an unbeliever, but the Anṣārī man made an error and the Prophet ﷺ ignored it and ignored his slip since he knew that he had certainty.

It was a slip and is for no one after the Prophet ﷺ. Anyone who is not pleased with the ruling of a judge and attacks him and rejects him is asked to repent. If he attacks the judge himself and not the ruling, then he can be disciplined or excused.' This will be explained at the end of *al-A'rāf.*

If the reason for the revelation is what we mentioned about the *ḥadīth,* then its *fiqh* is that the Prophet ﷺ followed the course of reconciliation between az-Zubayr and his opponent. Az-Zubayr was nearest the water source. He ﷺ told him to take water first, as was his right, but not take it in full and then release the water to his neighbour. The Prophet ﷺ encouraged him to be magnanimous and make things easy. When the Anṣārī heard this, he was not happy with it and became angry because he did not want him to hold back the water at all. That is when he uttered this bold, destructive statement, 'Is it because he is your aunt's son?' thereby impugning the judgment. Then the Prophet ﷺ became angry and judged in favour az-Zubayr that he should take his full right.

If it is asked, 'How could he give judgment when he was angry when he said, "A *qāḍī* should not give judgment when he is angry"?' We say, 'That is because he is protected from error in conveying and in judgments by the logic of his absolute truthfulness in everything he conveyed from Allah. So there is no one else like him among judges.' This *ḥadīth* also guides judges to make things easy between litigants, even when the right of one of the parties is clear. Mālik forbade that and ash-Shāfi'ī's position varies. This *ḥadīth* is clear evidence of the permissibility if they are reconciled. Otherwise, the one with the right takes his right and the ruling is confirmed.

The people of Mālik disagree about how the water should be released from the higher to the lower. Ibn Ḥabīb said, 'The higher person admits the water into his garden and irrigates with it until the water reaches between the level of the walls to the height of the two ankles of the one standing to block the admission of the water and thenthe should divert the rest of the water until it reaches the height of the ankles of the one next to him who, in turn, does the same until it reaches the furthest garden. That is how Muṭarrif and Ibn al-Mājishūn explained it, and Ibn Wahb stated that.' Ibn al-Qāsim said, 'When the water reaches the height of the ankles, he releases it all to those lower than him and he does not keep any of it in his garden. Ibn Ḥabīb said, 'I prefer the position of Muṭarrif and Ibn al-Mājishūn, and they had better knowledge of it because they lived in Madīnah and the judgment was made there and that was the normative practice there.

Mālik related from 'Abdullāh ibn Abī Bakr that he heard that the Messenger of Allah ﷺ said about the water-course of Mahrūz and Mudhaynib: 'Keep the water until it reaches the ankles and then release it from the higher to the lower.' Abū 'Umar said, 'I do not know that this *ḥadīth* is connected back to the Prophet ﷺ by any path. The highest aspect of its *isnād* is what Muḥammad ibn Isḥāq mentioned from Abū Mālik ibn Tha'labah from his father that the people of Mahrūz came to the Prophet ﷺ and he ruled that when the water reaches the ankles, the upper person does not keep it back.' 'Abd ar-Razzāq mentioned from Abū Ḥāzim al-Qurṭubī from his father from his grandfather that the Messenger of Allah ﷺ gave a ruling on the water-course of Mahrūz that each garden should hold the water back until it reaches the ankles and then release it. The same is true of any other water-course. Abū Bakr al-Bazzār was asked about hadiths on this topic and said, 'I do not recall any firm *ḥadīth* from the Prophet ﷺ regarding it.' Abū 'Umar said, 'Confirming this, even if it does not have this exact wording, there is a definite *ḥadīth* whose soundness is agreed upon.'

Ibn Wahb related it from al-Layth ibn Sa'd and Yūnus ibn Yazīd both from Ibn Shihāb that 'Urwah ibn az-Zubayr related that 'Abdullāh ibn az-Zubayr related from az-Zubayr that he had a dispute with a man of the Anṣār who had been present at Badr with the Messenger of Allah ﷺ about the ditches of al-Ḥarrah from which they both used to get water for their palm-trees. The Anṣārī said, 'Release the water,' and he refused. They took their dispute to the Prophet ﷺ. Abū 'Umar said that the *ḥadīth* is *mursal* and said that there is evidence for the other – 'When the water reaches the level of the ankles, the higher does not keep it back,' – in the position of Ibn al-Qāsim. In respect of reflection, if the higher person only released the water when it was above the ankles, that water would not be stopped in the minimum period and would not stop until it ended if it was all released. Releasing all of it after the higher person has taken what reaches the ankles has a more universal benefit and greater use in that in which people share. So the position of Ibn al-Qāsim is more fitting in every case. This is when its source is not owned by the lower person in particular. That is what one is entitled to by work, sound ownership, or longstanding entitlement and confirmed ownership. So each has his right according to what he owns and according to the basis of the issue. Success is by Allah.

then find no resistance within themselves to what you decide

There is no constriction and doubt. The word 'resistance (*ḥaraj* and *ḥarajah*)' is used for a dense tree. The plural is *ḥirāj*. Aḍ-Ḍaḥḥāk says, 'The sin is by denying what you decide.'

and submit themselves completely

This means that they obey what you command regarding your decision. Az-Zajjāj said that *'taslīman'* is a verbal noun of emphasis. This means that they submit to your ruling completely without harbouring any doubts whatsoever.

وَلَوْ أَنَّا كَتَبْنَا عَلَيْهِمْ أَنِ اقْتُلُوٓا أَنفُسَكُمْ أَوِ اخْرُجُوا مِن دِيَٰرِكُم
مَّا فَعَلُوهُ إِلَّا قَلِيلٌ مِّنْهُمْ وَلَوْ أَنَّهُمْ فَعَلُوا مَا يُوعَظُونَ بِهِۦ لَكَانَ خَيْرًا
لَّهُمْ وَأَشَدَّ تَثْبِيتًا ﴿٦٦﴾ وَإِذًا لَّءَاتَيْنَٰهُم مِّن لَّدُنَّآ أَجْرًا عَظِيمًا ﴿٦٧﴾ وَلَهَدَيْنَٰهُمْ
صِرَٰطًا مُّسْتَقِيمًا ﴿٦٨﴾

66 If We had directed them to kill themselves or leave their homes, they would not have done so, except for a very few. But if they had done what they were urged to do, it would have been better for them and far more strengthening. 67 In that case We would have given them an immense reward from Us 68 and We would have guided them on a straight path.

If We had directed them to kill themselves or leave their homes,

The reason for revelation of this *āyah* is that Thābit ibn Qays ibn Shammās and a Jew were boasting to one another. The Jew said, 'By Allah, it was prescribed for us to kill ourselves and so we killed ourselves. The number of dead reached seventy thousand.' Thābit said, 'By Allah, if it were written for us to kill ourselves, we would do so!' Abū Isḥāq as-Sabī'ī said the words: "*'If We had directed them...*" were revealed and a man said, "If he had commanded us, we would have done it. Praise be to Allah who protected us." That reached the Messenger of Allah ﷺ and he said, "There are men in my community in whom faith is stronger than firm mountains."' Ibn Wahb reported that Mālik said that the speaker was Abū Bakr aṣ-Ṣiddīq. Makkī also said that. An-Naqqāsh said that it was 'Umar ibn al-Khaṭṭāb. It is reported that Abū Bakr said, 'If it were written for us, I would begin with myself and the people of my house.' Abu-l-Layth as-Samarqandī said that the speakers were 'Ammār ibn Yāsir, Ibn Mas'ūd and Thābit ibn Qays. They said, 'If Allah had commanded us to kill ourselves or leave our homes, we would have done it.' The Prophet ﷺ then said, 'Faith is stronger in some men of my community than in firm mountains.'

'Law' is a particle which indicates the impossibility of one thing through the impossibility of another. Allah reported that He did not prescribe that for us out of

compassion for us, so that our disobedience is not publicly displayed. How many a command we fall short of while it is easy, so how much more would that be the case with this matter when it is so difficult! But, by Allah, the Muhājirūn left their homes empty and went out to seek a life pleasing to Allah.

they would not have done so, except for a very few.

This refers to killing themselves and leaving their homes. *'A very few'* is an appositive of the *wāw*. It implies: 'None but a very few would have done it.' The Kufans say that it is for repetition and it means: 'Only a few of them would have done it.'

'Abdullāh ibn 'Āmir and 'Īsā ibn 'Umar recite it exceptionally as *'illā qalīlan'*. That is how it is in the copies of the Qur'an of Syria. The rest have it as *'qalīlun'*. All grammarians consider that to be better. It is said that it is in the accusative based on an implied verb which implies: 'except for a very few of them.' The nominative is better because the expression is more fitting for the meaning and it does, in fact, contain the meaning. The very few were Abū Bakr, 'Umar, and Thābit ibn Qays as we mentioned. Al-Ḥasan and Muqātil add 'Ammār and Ibn Mas'ūd.

It would have been better for them and far more strengthening.

In this world and the Next. It would have been more strengthening in respect of the Truth.

An immense reward from Us.

That is in the Next World. It is said that *lām* is the *lām* of the apodosis and *'idhan'* indicates the apodosis. The meaning is: 'If they had done that, We would have given them what they were promised.

وَمَن يُطِعِ ٱللَّهَ وَٱلرَّسُولَ فَأُوْلَٰٓئِكَ مَعَ ٱلَّذِينَ أَنْعَمَ ٱللَّهُ عَلَيْهِم مِّنَ ٱلنَّبِيِّـۧنَ
وَٱلصِّدِّيقِينَ وَٱلشُّهَدَآءِ وَٱلصَّٰلِحِينَۚ وَحَسُنَ أُوْلَٰٓئِكَ رَفِيقًا ﴿٦٩﴾ ذَٰلِكَ
ٱلْفَضْلُ مِنَ ٱللَّهِۚ وَكَفَىٰ بِٱللَّهِ عَلِيمًا ﴿٧٠﴾

69 Whoever obeys Allah and the Messenger will be with those whom Allah has blessed: the Prophets and the truly sincere, the martyrs and the righteous. What excellent company such people are! 70 That is favour from Allah. Allah suffices as a Knower.

Whoever obeys Allah and the Messenger will be with those whom Allah has blessed: Allah is referring back to what was commanded. If the hypocrites had done it when they were admonished, it would have been better for them. Then Allah mentions the reward of the one who does it. This *āyah* elucidates the words of Allah: *'Guide us to the straight path, the path of those You have blessed'* in the *Fāṭihah.* It is what is meant by the Prophet's words when he died ﷺ: 'O Allah, with the Highest Companion.' We find in al-Bukhārī that 'Ā'ishah reported that she heard the Messenger of Allah ﷺ say, 'No Prophet dies until he is given a choice between this world and the Next.' She said, 'I heard him say in the illness in which he died, while his voice was becoming hoarse: *"With those whom Allah has blessed: the Prophets and the truly sincere, the martyrs and the righteous."* So I thought that he had been given a choice.'

One group says that this *āyah* was revealed when 'Abdullāh ibn Zayd ibn 'Abd Rabbih al-Anṣārī – whose idea the *adhān* was – said, 'Messenger of Allah, when you die and we die, you will be in 'Illiyūn and we will not meet with you.' He mentioned his sorrow about that and the *āyah* was revealed. Makkī related that when the Prophet ﷺ died, 'Abdullāh said, 'O Allah, make me blind so that I do not see anything after him,' and he became blind on the spot. Al-Qushayrī also related it with the words: 'O Allah, make me blind so that I do not see anything after my beloved until I meet my beloved!' and he went blind on the spot.

Ath-Tha'labī reported that it was revealed about Thawbān, the freedman of the Messenger of Allah ﷺ. He had great love for him and little patience without him. He went to him one day and his colour was pale and his body emaciated. Sorrow could be seen in his face. The Prophet ﷺ said to him, 'Thawbān, what has changed your colour?' He said, 'Messenger of Allah, I have neither harm nor pain, but when I do not see you, I yearn for you and am very distressed until I meet you. Then I remembered the Next World and feared that I would not see you there because I understood that you will he elevated with the Prophets, and if I enter the Garden, my station will be below your station. If I do not enter, then I will never see you!' Then Allah revealed this *āyah.* Al-Wāḥidī mentioned it from al-Kalbī.

It is reported from Masrūq: 'The Companions of the Messenger of Allah ﷺ said, "We do not want to part from you in this world. When you leave us, you will be raised above us!" Then Allah revealed this.' Obedience to Allah goes with obedience to His Messenger, but He mentioned it to honour his worth and that of his family. The words: *'with those Allah has pleased'* mean in the same abode and bliss, enjoying the vision of them and their presence. They are not equal in degree. They vary, but they visit one another following what they did in this world. Each of them are provided with Allah's pleasure in it according to their state. They have no feeling of being less excellent. Allah says: *'We will strip away any rancor in their hearts.'* (7:43)

the Prophets and the truly sincere, the martyrs and the righteous.

The noun *ṣiddīq* (truly sincere) is an intensive form from *ṣidq* (truthfulness) or *taṣdīq* (confirmation). The *ṣiddīq* is the one who realises in his actions what he says on his tongue. It is said that they are the best of the followers of the Prophets who preceded them in confirmation, like Abū Bakr aṣ-Ṣiddīq. The meaning of *ṣidq* and *shahīd* were explained in *al-Baqarah*. What is meant by the martyrs are 'Umar, 'Uthmān and 'Alī. The righteous are the rest of the Companions, may Allah be pleased with all of them. It is said that the martyrs are those killed in the way of Allah and the righteous are the righteous of the Community of Muḥammad, the Messenger of Allah ﷺ. The expression includes every righteous person and martyr. Allah knows best.

What excellent company such people are!

The noun *'rifq'* means tenderness. A companion is called *rafīq* because one relies on his company and a group (*rifqah*) rely on one another, and that is a possible meaning of the words: *'What excellent company such people are!'*: each of them is good as a companion. The Prophet ﷺ said, 'The best companions are four,' and Allah only mentioned four here, so reflect on it.

Al-Akhfash said that *'rafīq'* is in the accusative for the *ḥāl*. It implies the plural. The Kufans said that it is in the accusative for distinction and that is why it is in the singular. It is as if it means: each one of them is excellent as a companion. It is as Allah says: '*...then We bring you out as children*' (22:5) where *ṭifl* is in the singular, meaning, 'We bring each of you out as a child.' The same usage is seen in 42:45. The meaning of this *āyah* is seen in the words of the Prophet ﷺ: 'The best companions are four.' Allah only mentioned four here, so again reflect on that.

This *āyah* is evidence for the rightness of the caliphate of Abū Bakr. That is because when Allah mentions the ranks of His *awliyā'* in His Book, He begins with the highest, who are the Prophets, and then praises the *ṣiddīqūn* and put nothing between them. The Muslims agree that Abū Bakr is the *Ṣiddīq* as they agree that Muhammad ﷺ is a Messenger. So just as it is confirmed and sound that he was the *Ṣiddīq* and he was the second with the Messenger of Allah ﷺ, it is not permitted to put anyone ahead of him. Allah knows best.

That is favour from Allah.

Allah states that no one obtains their degree by their obedience, but rather only by the favour and generosity of Allah. This differs from the Mu'tazilites who claim that you obtain it by your actions. Allah is gracious to His friends purely by His favour to them. It is not permitted for anyone to praise himself for something he has not himself done. That indicates the invalidity of their position. Allah knows best.

يَٰٓأَيُّهَا ٱلَّذِينَ ءَامَنُوا۟ خُذُوا۟ حِذْرَكُمْ فَٱنفِرُوا۟ ثُبَاتٍ أَوِ ٱنفِرُوا۟ جَمِيعًا ﴿٧١﴾

71 You who believe, take all necessary precautions, then go out to fight in separate groups or go out as one body.

You who believe, take all necessary precautions,

This is addressed to the sincere believers among the community of Muḥammad ﷺ and commands them to do *jihād* against the unbelievers and to go out in the Way of Allah and in defence of the Sharī'ah. The aspect of its composition and connection to what is before it is that after Allah mentions obeying Allah and obeying His Messenger, He commands those who obey to work for the revival of His *dīn* and to prioritise the call to Him. He instructs them not to attack their enemy until they have sought out information about them and know how to repel them. He confirms that to them and says: *'Take all necessary precautions…'* teaching them how to act in a war situation. This does not negate reliance on Allah. It is the station which is reliance itself as was mentioned in *Āli 'Imrān.*

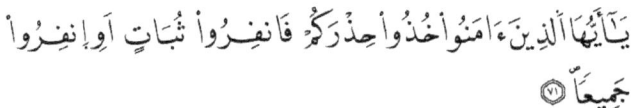

The word used for 'precaution' is *ḥidhr* or *ḥadahr* like *mithl* and *mathal*. They are two dialectical possibilities. Al-Farrā' said that *ḥadhar* is the most frequently used although *ḥidhr* is also heard. You say, '*khudh ḥidhraka*,' meaning 'take care'. You say, 'Take your weapons as a cautionary measure,' because being on guard is achieved by doing that. Caution does not avert the decree. This is different from the Qadariyyah position which is that caution actually averts danger and prevents the tricks of the enemy and that, if that were not the case, there would be no point in commanding us to take precautions. They are told, 'The *āyah* does not adduce any evidence that precaution is of any use against the decree, but we are commanded not to cast ourselves to destruction. It is exemplified by the *ḥadīth*, "Hobble the camel and trust (in Allah)." The Decree will occur as decreed and Allah does whatever He wills. Acting in that way is in order to put the soul at peace, not an attempt to escape from the decree; it is merely about being cautious.' The evidence of that is that Allah Almighty praises the Companions of His Prophet ﷺ when He says: *'Say: "Nothing can happen to us except what Allah has ordained for us."'* (9:51) If anything other than what is decreed for them had happened to them, then these words would be meaningless.

then go out to fight in separate groups

Nafara is a verb used for a camel bolting. It means to rise to fight the enemy. The ruler calls on the people to turn out to fight the enemy (*istinfara*). *Nafīr* is the name of the troop who go out (*nafara*). Its root is *nifār* and *nufūr* which is the alarm that causes the bolting. An example of its use is found in Allah's words: *'they turn their backs and run away* (nufūr).' (17:56) The verb *nafara* is also used of leather when it swells. It also means to protrude. Abū 'Ubayd said, 'It is used when something runs away from something else.' Ibn Fāris said, '*Nafar* is a number of men from three to ten. *Nafīr* means the same as do *nafr* and *nafrah.*' Al-Farrā' relates it as *nafrah.* The Day of *Nafr* is the day when people hasten from Minā.

Thubāt means separate groups and alludes to sorties. It is said that *thubīna* is the sound plural in the feminine and masculine. 'Amr ibn Kulthūm said:

But on the day we feared for them, in the morning
our cavalry spread out in groups and companies (*thubīn*).

So '*thubāt*' alludes to squadrons. One is a *thubah.* It is a group of people. The root is *thubayyah.* An army is comprised of different companies, each a *thubbah. Thubbah* is also the middle of a watering-basin to which the water returns. An-Naḥḥās said, 'Someone weak in Arabic might imagine that they are the same and that one is part of the other, but there is a difference between them. The diminutive of a *thubbah* of a basin is *thuwaybah* because it comes from verb *thāba, yathūbu,* and that of *thubbah,* meaning a company, is *thubayyah.*' Someone else said that the *thubbah* of a basin has the *wāw* of the verb itself elided and that *thubbah,* meaning a company, is defective from *thabā, yathbū.* It is also possible that *thubbah,* meaning a company, comes from the *thubbah* of a basin because when the water returns, it collects. According to this, the diminutive of a company is *thuwaybah,* and one of the two is included in the other. It is said that *thubbah* of the group is derived from the verb which means to praise someone in his lifetime and collects together his excellent renown. Therefore it refers to gathering.

or go out as one body.

This means as a large army with the Messenger ﷺ, as Ibn 'Abbās and others said. The squadrons only go out with the permission of the ruler so that they have information and support from behind them if they require reinforcement. The rules about expectations, booty and rules of armies and obligation of going out will be dealt with in *al-Anfāl* and *at-Tawbah*, Allah willing.

Ibn Khuwayzimandād reported that it is said that this *āyah* was abrogated by the words of Allah: *'Go out to fight, whatever your circumstances or desires'* (9:41) and the *āyah*: *'If you do not go out to fight, He will punish you with a painful punishment.'* (9:39) is abrogated by His words: *'then go out to fight in separate groups or go out as one body'* and: *'It is not necessary for the believers to go out all together.'* (9:122) This is because the obligation of *jihād* is a *kifāyah* one [not individual but communal]. When the borders are guarded by some of the Muslims, then the obligation is cancelled for the rest. The truth is that both *āyahs* are judgment *āyahs*, one at the moment when the need becomes incumbent on everyone and the other when a few fulfil it.

وَإِنَّ مِنكُمْ لَمَن لَّيُبَطِّئَنَّ فَإِنْ أَصَٰبَتْكُم مُّصِيبَةٌ قَالَ قَدْ أَنْعَمَ ٱللَّهُ عَلَىَّ
إِذْ لَمْ أَكُن مَّعَهُمْ شَهِيدًا ﴿٧٢﴾ وَلَئِنْ أَصَٰبَكُمْ فَضْلٌ مِّنَ ٱللَّهِ لَيَقُولَنَّ كَأَن
لَّمْ يَكُنۢ بَيْنَكُمْ وَبَيْنَهُۥ مَوَدَّةٌ يَٰلَيْتَنِى كُنتُ مَعَهُمْ فَأَفُوزَ فَوْزًا
عَظِيمًا ﴿٧٣﴾

72 Among you there are people who hang back and if you encounter a setback then they say, 'Allah has blessed me in that I was not there with them.' 73 But if you meet with favour from Allah they say – as if there were no friendship between you and them – 'Oh! If only I had been with them so that I too might have won a great victory.'

Among you there are people who hang back

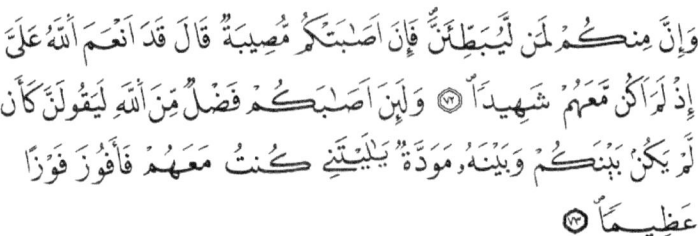

This is a reference to the hypocrites. Hanging back is delaying. There are various meanings possible here. One is that they fail to go on expeditions and make others do the same. Another is that among those who visit you there are some who make a display of faith. The hypocrites seem to be Muslims since they submit to their rulings. The *lām* in '*liman*' is for stress and the second is the lam of the oath. '*Man*' is in the position of the accusative and it is connected to '*hang back*' because it has the meaning of the oath whose predicate is '*minkum*'. Mujāhid, an-Nakha'ī and al-Kalbī recited, *'la-yubṭi'anna'* which has the same meaning as *'la-yubaṭṭi'anna'*. They mean the same.

It is also said that what is meant here are certain believers because Allah usually differentiates between the believers and hypocrites and here says: *'among you'* whereas He says in *at-Tawbah*: *'They are not of your number.'* (9:56) This is not in keeping with the apparent meaning and context. The plural here is used for the type and lineage as we explained, not faith. This is what the majority say and it is the sound view, Allah willing. Allah knows best.

'If you encounter a setback' means in respect of some being killed and defeated. They refer to hanging back as a blessing. Only a hypocrite would consider this a blessing, especially at that time. It is unlikely that a believer would say this. Look also at the *ḥadīth* transmitted from Abū Hurayrah from the Prophet ﷺ about the hypocrites: 'The hardest prayers for them are *'Ishā'* and *Fajr*. If they had known what was in them, they would have come to them crawling.' One version says, 'If one of them knew that he would find a fatty bone, then he would attend it.'

'But if you meet with favour' refers to gaining booty and victory. If this happens, the hypocrite is envious and regretful about the booty while doubting the reward from Allah and that is why he said this. There is a change in the normal order of words. It is said that the words: *'as if there were no friendship between you and them'* mean 'as if there was no contract between you to do jihad.' It is said that it is in the accusative for the *ḥāl*.

'They say' is recited by al-Ḥasan as *'la-yaqūlunna'* with the meaning of 'who' since it is not specific. Reading it as *'la-yaqūlanna'* is repeating it and it is singular. Ibn Kathir and Ḥafṣ from 'Āṣim recite *'lam takun'* referring to 'friendship'. If it is recited as *'lam yakun'*, it makes *mawaddah* (friendship) mean *'wudd'*.

The statement of the hypocrite: *'If only I had been with them…'* stems from their envy or sorrow at missing the booty while still having doubt about the repayment from Allah. The word *'won'* is the apodosis of the wish. That is why it is in the accusative. Al-Ḥasan recited *'afūzu'* with *ḍammah* as wishing for victory. It is as if it is saying, 'Would that I could win a great victory.' It is with a *fatḥah* for the apodosis and means: 'I could win with them,' and that would imply an *'an'* because it is based on the interpretation of the verbal noun. It implies, 'Would that I could have been present and victorious.'

فَلْيُقَٰتِلْ فِي سَبِيلِ ٱللَّهِ ٱلَّذِينَ يَشْرُونَ ٱلْحَيَوٰةَ ٱلدُّنْيَا بِٱلْءَاخِرَةِ ۚ وَمَن
يُقَٰتِلْ فِي سَبِيلِ ٱللَّهِ فَيُقْتَلْ أَوْ يَغْلِبْ فَسَوْفَ نُؤْتِيهِ أَجْرًا
عَظِيمًا ﴿٧٤﴾

74 So let those who sell the life of this world for the Next World fight in the Way of Allah. If someone fights in the Way of Allah, whether he is killed or is victorious, We will pay him an immense reward.

So let those who sell the life of this world for the Next World fight in the Way of Allah.

This is addressed to the believers, meaning that they fight the unbelievers in the Way of Allah. They expend their lives and property for the sake of Allah. *'For the Next World'* means to gain the reward of the Next World.

If someone fights in the Way of Allah, whether he is killed or is victorious,

'If someone fights' is the precondition, the words: *'whether he is killed or victorious'* are added, and the apodosis is: *'We will pay him an immense wage.'* The verb *'is killed'* refer to someone being martyred and *'victorious'* to someone gaining booty. One group recite *'fa-l-yuqātil'* with a *sukūn* on the *lām* while another recite *'fa-li-yuqātil'* with a *kasrah* on the *lām* for the imperative.

Allah speaks of the two possible outcomes for those who fight, which spare the need of mentioning anything between them. Ibn 'Aṭiyyah mentioned that. The literal meaning of the *āyah* would demand that the one who is killed as a martyr is the equal of someone who returns with booty. We find in *Ṣaḥīḥ Muslim* that Abū Hurayrah reported that the Messenger of Allah ﷺ said, 'Allah gives a guarantee to anyone who goes out in the way of Allah: "I will repay anyone who goes out for no other reason than doing *jihād* in My Way and belief in Me and affirmation of My Messengers either by admitting him into the Garden or returning him to his home from which he left with the reward he has obtained or booty."' 'Abdullāh ibn 'Amr reported that the Messenger of Allah ﷺ said, 'There is no raid or expedition in the Way of Allah in which people take booty without them sending ahead two-thirds of their reward from the Next World and a third remaining for them. If no booty is taken, then they have the full reward.'

The words 'with the reward he has obtained or booty' appear to mean that the one who is martyred has one of two things: the reward without booty or the booty and no reward. This differs from the *ḥadīth* of 'Abdullāh ibn 'Amr.

Some people discard his *ḥadīth* because the *isnād* contains Ḥumayd ibn Hāni' who is not known. The first *ḥadīth* is preferred because of its fame. Others have said that there is no contradiction between them and no disagreement and that 'or' in the *ḥadīth* of Abū Hurayrah means 'and' as the Kufans say. It is indicated by the transmission of Abū Dāwūd who said, 'reward **and** booty.' Some of the transmitters of Muslim also related it with 'and'. Ḥumayd ibn Hāni' Miṣrī listened to Abū 'Abd ar-Raḥmān al-Ḥublā and 'Amr ibn Mālik. Ḥaywah ibn Shurayḥ and Ibn Wahb related from him. The first *ḥadīth* applies to pure intention and sincerity in jihad. It is for that that Allah guarantees for him either martyrdom or returning to his family rewarded with booty. The second *ḥadīth* applies to the intention to do jihad, but with obtaining booty. When his intention is divided, then his reward is lessened. The Sunnah indicates that the one who gets booty has a reward just as the Book indicates that. So there is no contradiction.

Then it is said that the diminishment of the reward of the person who gets booty is based on the fact that the one who gets booty by what Allah lets him have of this world enjoys it and removes the hardships of life from him. Those who strive and do not obtain anything and remain with the hardships of life and are steadfast in their state are given their reward in full which is not the case with the first group. It is like the words in the *ḥadīth*, 'Some of us have died without consuming any of their reward, including Muṣ'ab ibn 'Umayr, and some of us have had their fruits ripen and have been given them.'

وَمَا لَكُمْ لَا تُقَاتِلُونَ فِي سَبِيلِ ٱللَّهِ وَٱلْمُسْتَضْعَفِينَ مِنَ ٱلرِّجَالِ وَٱلنِّسَآءِ
وَٱلْوِلْدَٰنِ ٱلَّذِينَ يَقُولُونَ رَبَّنَآ أَخْرِجْنَا مِنْ هَٰذِهِ ٱلْقَرْيَةِ ٱلظَّالِمِ أَهْلُهَا وَٱجْعَل
لَّنَا مِن لَّدُنكَ وَلِيًّا وَٱجْعَل لَّنَا مِن لَّدُنكَ نَصِيرًا ﴿٧٥﴾

75 What reason could you have for not fighting in the Way of Allah – for those men, women and children who are oppressed and say, 'Our Lord, take us out of this city whose inhabitants are wrongdoers! Give us a protector from You! Give us a helper from You!'?

What reason could you have for not fighting in the Way of Allah?

This is encouraging *jihād*. It includes delivering the oppressed from the hands of the idolatrous unbelievers who were inflicting an evil punishment on them and seducing them from the *dīn*. So Allah obliged *jihād* to elevate His word and to give victory to His *dīn* and to rescue the weak believers, even if that entails loss of lives. Rescuing captives is obligatory for Muslims, either by fighting or ransom. It is mandatory because property is less important than people's lives. Mālik said, 'It is mandatory for people to ransom captives even if that entails all their property.' There is no disagreement about that since the Prophet ﷺ said, 'Relieve the one in distress.' This matter was dealt with in *al-Baqarah*. Similarly they said that they must support them because charity is easier than ransoming. If the captive is wealthy, should the person who pays the ransom seek repayment from him? Scholars take two positions, the soundest of which is that he should.

for those men, women and children who are oppressed

The words *'who are oppressed'* continue on from *'Allah'*, meaning, 'in the Way of Allah and for the cause of those who are oppressed.' Thus rescuing the oppressed is an integral part of the Way of Allah. This is what is preferred by az-Zajjāj and az-Zuhrī stated it. Muḥammad ibn Yazīd said, 'I prefer that "*oppressed*" follows on from "*Way*", meaning to rescue the oppressed. So there are two different ways.' The oppressed refers to those believers in Makkah who were being demeaned and harmed by Quraysh. They are the ones meant by the words of the Prophet ﷺ, 'O Allah, save al-Walīd ibn al-Walīd, Salamah ibn Hishām, 'Ayyāsh ibn Abī Rabī'ah and those of the believers who are oppressed.' Ibn 'Abbās said, 'My mother and I were among the oppressed.' In al-Bukhārī in the chapter on this *āyah* he said, 'I and my mother were among those excused. I was one of the children and she was one of the women.'

Our Lord, take us out of this city whose inhabitants are wrongdoers!

The city referred to is Makkah by the consensus of interpreters. It is described as wrongdoing, even though it is the people who were actually that by the attachment of the pronoun. It is as you say, 'I passed by a man with a vast house, noble father or beautiful slavegirl.' The man is described with that because of the linguistic attachment between them: the pronoun. If you were to say, 'I passed by the noble man, 'Amr,' there is no question because nobility belongs to 'Amr.' An attribute can only be assigned to a man by attachment, which is the pronoun *hā'*. This attribute is neither dual nor plural because it takes the place of the verb. It means: 'whose people were wrongdoing'. This is why He does not say *'ẓālimīn'* (wrongdoers). You say, 'I passed by two men whose parents were noble (*karīm*, masculine singular), whose slavegirls were beautiful (*ḥasanah*), and men whose fathers were noble (*karīm*) and slave-girls were beautiful (*ḥasanah*).

Give us a protector from You! Give us a helper from You!'?

'*Ladunka*' has the meaning of 'directly from You'. A Protector will deliver us and a Helper will help us against them.

ٱلَّذِينَ ءَامَنُوا۟ يُقَـٰتِلُونَ فِى سَبِيلِ ٱللَّهِ ۖ وَٱلَّذِينَ كَفَرُوا۟ يُقَـٰتِلُونَ فِى سَبِيلِ
ٱلطَّـٰغُوتِ فَقَـٰتِلُوٓا۟ أَوْلِيَآءَ ٱلشَّيْطَـٰنِ ۖ إِنَّ كَيْدَ ٱلشَّيْطَـٰنِ كَانَ ضَعِيفًا ﴿٧٦﴾

76 Those who believe fight in the Way of Allah. Those who disbelieve fight in the way of false gods. So fight the friends of Shayṭān! Shayṭān's scheming is always feeble.

Those who fight in the Way of Allah do so in obedience to Allah. Abū 'Ubaydah and al-Kisā'ī said that the word *ṭāghūt* (false gods) can be masculine or feminine. Soothsayers, both male and female, were called *ṭāghūt.* Ḥajjāj related from Ibn Jurayj that Abū az-Zubayr heard that when Jābir ibn 'Abdullāh was asked about the *ṭāghūt* to whom they used to go for arbitration, he said that there was one in Juhaynah and one in Aslam. Every area had one.

Abū Isḥāq said, 'The evidence that it is about Shayṭān are the words in the rest of the *āyah.* It means his scheming and the scheming of those who follow him.' It is also said that what is meant is the Battle of Badr when Shayṭān told the idolaters that they would be victorious. This will be dealt with in *al-Anfāl* (8:48).

أَلَمْ تَرَ إِلَى ٱلَّذِينَ قِيلَ لَهُمْ كُفُّوٓا۟ أَيْدِيَكُمْ وَأَقِيمُوا۟ ٱلصَّلَوٰةَ وَءَاتُوا۟ ٱلزَّكَوٰةَ فَلَمَّا كُتِبَ
عَلَيْهِمُ ٱلْقِتَالُ إِذَا فَرِيقٌ مِّنْهُمْ يَخْشَوْنَ ٱلنَّاسَ كَخَشْيَةِ ٱللَّهِ أَوْ أَشَدَّ خَشْيَةً ۚ وَقَالُوا۟
رَبَّنَا لِمَ كَتَبْتَ عَلَيْنَا ٱلْقِتَالَ لَوْلَآ أَخَّرْتَنَآ إِلَىٰٓ أَجَلٍ قَرِيبٍ ۗ قُلْ مَتَـٰعُ ٱلدُّنْيَا قَلِيلٌ
وَٱلْـَٔاخِرَةُ خَيْرٌ لِّمَنِ ٱتَّقَىٰ وَلَا تُظْلَمُونَ فَتِيلًا ﴿٧٧﴾

77 Do you not see those who were told: 'Hold back from fighting but establish the prayer and pay *zakāt*'? Then when fighting is prescribed for them, a group of them fear people as Allah should be feared, or even more than that. They say, 'Our Lord, why have you prescribed fighting for us? If only You would give us just a little more time!' Say, 'The enjoyment of this world is very brief. The Next World is better for those who are godfearing. You will not be wronged by so much as the smallest speck.'

'Amr ibn Dīnār related from 'Ikrimah from Ibn 'Abbās that 'Abd ar-Raḥmān ibn 'Awf and some of his companions came to the Prophet ﷺ in Makkah and said, 'Prophet of Allah, we were mighty when we were idolaters. When we believed, we became abased.' He said, 'I was commanded to pardon. Do not fight the people.' When Allah moved him to Madīnah, He commanded him to fight and they refrained and so the *āyah* was revealed, as an-Nasā'ī transmits in his *Sunan*. Al-Kalbī said that. Mujāhid said that it is the Jews that are meant. Al-Ḥasan said that it is about the believers since '*fear people*' refers to fearing the idolaters of Makkah. What they felt was fear rather than opposition. As-Suddī said, 'They were people who became Muslim before the obligation to fight. When it was made obligatory, they disliked that.'

It is said that it describes the hypocrites and means that they fear death at the hand of the idolaters as they fear death from Allah. The words *'even more than that'* is a sign of the weakness of their belief. This is most in keeping with the context of the *āyah*. We seek refuge with Allah from the suggestion that such a statement would come from one of the noble Companions who knew that the time of death is decreed and provision allotted. They obeyed the commands of Allah without reservation. They knew that attaining the Next Abode is better than remaining in this immediate abode as is known from their biographies, may Allah be pleased with all of them. The only possibility was that it was someone whose feet were not yet planted firmly in their faith yet and whose breast had not yet opened completely to Islam. The people of faith have different degrees. The faith of some is perfect and of others imperfect. Imperfect faith is that of someone whose self was averse to doing what he was commanded to do when hardship was involved. Allah knows best.

Say, 'The enjoyment of this life is brief.' The Next World is for the godfearing.

The godfearing are those who fear acting in any way that expresses disobedience to Allah as was already discussed in *al-Baqarah*. The '*enjoyment of this life*' is experiencing its benefits and its pleasures. It is called '*brief*' because it does not endure. The Prophet ﷺ said, 'The metaphor of my relationship to this world is that of a rider who rests under a tree and then travels on and leaves it behind.' This topic was discussed at length in *al-Baqarah*.

أَيْنَمَا تَكُونُوا يُدْرِككُّمُ الْمَوْتُ وَلَوْ كُنتُمْ فِي بُرُوجٍ مُّشَيَّدَةٍ وَإِن تُصِبْهُمْ حَسَنَةٌ
يَقُولُوا هَٰذِهِ مِنْ عِندِ اللَّهِ وَإِن تُصِبْهُمْ سَيِّئَةٌ يَقُولُوا هَٰذِهِ مِنْ عِندِكَ قُلْ كُلٌّ
مِّنْ عِندِ اللَّهِ فَمَالِ هَٰؤُلَاءِ الْقَوْمِ لَا يَكَادُونَ يَفْقَهُونَ حَدِيثًا ﴿٧٨﴾

78 Wherever you are, death will catch up with you, even if you are in impregnable fortresses. If a good thing happens to them, they say, 'This has come from Allah.' But if a bad thing happens to them, they say, 'This has come from you.' Say, 'Everything comes from Allah.' What is the matter with these people that they scarcely understand a single word?

Wherever you are, death will catch up with you,

The '*mā*' is redundant. This is addressed generally, even if those referred to in this particular context are the hypocrites or the weak believers who asked for '*a little more time*', meaning until our time of death. It is more likely to be the hypocrites since they said when affliction occurred at Uḥud: '*If they had only been with us, they would not have died or been killed.*' (3:156) Allah refutes them here by saying: '*Wherever you are, death will catch up with you, even if you are in impregnable fortresses.*' Ibn 'Abbās said that according to what Abū Ṣāliḥ related from him.

even if you are in impregnable fortresses.

The singular of *burūj* (fortresses) is *burj*. It is a tall building and great castle. When describing a she-camel, Ṭarafah said:

As if there was a Roman fortress guarding it,
built with gypsum, baked bricks and stones.

Ṭalḥah ibn Sulaymān recited '*yudrikukum*' which is rare and only comes in poetry. [POEM]

Scholars disagree about what is meant by *burūj* (fortresses). Most, and it is the sound position, say that what is meant are fortresses located on elevated land because they are the most effective in terms of defence and impregnability, which is why Allah used it as a metaphor here. Qatādah said that they are fortified castles. Ibn Jurayj and most say that. Corroborating that are the words of 'Āmir ibn aṭ-Ṭufayl to the Prophet ﷺ, 'Do you have any strong impregnable fortress?' Mujāhid says that it means castles. Ibn 'Abbās says that it means fortresses, strongholds and citadels. The word '*impregnable*' (*mushayyadah*) is said to mean 'tall', according to az-Zajjāj and al-Qutabī. 'Ikrimah says that it means being covered with gypsum.

Qatādah said it means fortified. *Mushayyad* and *mashīd* mean the same. Another example of its use is: *'stuccoed palaces'* (22:45). Form II implies intensification. It is said that *mushayyad* means 'tall' and *mashīd* is 'stuccoed with plaster'. The verb *shāda* and *ashāda* are used for applying plaster to buildings.

As-Suddī said that what is meant by *burūj* are the constellations of the zodiac. Makkī reported this from Mālik, pointing out that the term is used for the constellations in several other *āyahs*: *'By Heaven and the Houses (burūj) of the Zodiac'* (85:1), *'He placed constellations (burūj) in the sky'* (25:61) and *'We have placed constellations (burūj) in heaven.'* (15:16) Ibn al-'Arabī also related it from Ibn al-Qāsim from Mālik. An-Naqqāsh related from Ibn 'Abbās that it is about iron castles. Ibn 'Aṭiyyah said, 'The literal words do not give this sense.'

This *āyah* is a refutal of the Qadariyyah position about lifespans. This tells us that the time of death is decreed. The *rūḥ* must depart from the body when the time of its death is reached, whether by being killed, dying or whatever means Allah has decreed for it. The Mu'tazilites claim that if someone had not been killed, he would have gone on living. This was refuted in *Āli 'Imrān*. The unbelievers and hypocrites, however, agree with this hypothesis.

Using land and building to preserve property and lives in some way is a common practice. It is the *sunnah* of Allah in respect of His slaves. That is a refutation of those who say that reliance on Allah entails abandoning all secondary means. Making use of land is one of the greatest means to fulfil what we are commanded to do in this respect and the Prophets made use of it in the form of ditches and other defensive measures. Al-Aḥnaf was asked, 'What is the wisdom of walls?' He replied, 'To repel fools until the wise come and protect it.'

If we accept the statement of Mālik and as-Suddī that what is meant is the constellations of the heaven, they are twelve and are immense celestial bodies. They are called *burūj* because of their prominence. The verb *baraja* means to appear openly and be elevated. Illustrating that are Allah's words: '*...and do not display your beauty as it was previously displayed (*tabarruj*) in the Time of Ignorance.*' (33:33) Allah Almighty created the constellations as stations for the sun and moon and decreed a time for them. He made some of them southern and some northern to indicate benefits and as a sign of the qiblah as well as a means to calculate the ends of the night and ends of the days so that we would know the times for *tahajjud* and other things for our daily life.

If a good thing happens to them, they say, 'This has come from Allah.'

This is what the hypocrites say when a time of fertility comes to them. If something bad happens, such as a drought, they attribute it to the bad luck of the Prophet ﷺ and his Companions. It is said that *'good'* here is health and security and *'bad'* is illness and fear. It is said that good is wealth and bad is poverty. It is said is that good is blessing, conquest and the booty acquired on the Day of Badr, and evil is affliction, hardship and being killed on the Day of Uḥud. It is said that the good is ease and the bad is harm. These are the statements of the commentators, Ibn 'Abbās and others, on this *āyah*.

But if a bad thing happens to them, they say, 'This has come from you.'

This was revealed about the Jews and hypocrites. That is because when the Messenger of Allah ﷺ came to Madīnah, they said, 'We have seen decrease in our prices and crops since the time this man and his Companions came to us.' Ibn 'Abbās said that *'from you'* means 'on account of your poor management'. It is also said that it is 'because of your bad luck' as we mentioned. It means: 'Bad luck has afflicted us because of you.' They said this from the point of view of believing in bad omens and luck.

Say, 'Everything comes from Allah.'

They are told that everything – hardship and ease, victory and defeat – is from Allah, by His decree.

What is the matter with these people that they scarcely understand a single word?

'These people' are the hypocrites. It means: 'What is wrong with them that they do not understand that everything is from Allah?'

مَّآ أَصَابَكَ مِنۡ حَسَنَةٖ فَمِنَ ٱللَّهِۖ وَمَآ أَصَابَكَ مِن سَيِّئَةٖ فَمِن نَّفۡسِكَۚ وَأَرۡسَلۡنَٰكَ
لِلنَّاسِ رَسُولٗاۚ وَكَفَىٰ بِٱللَّهِ شَهِيدٗا ٧٩

79 Any good thing that happens to you comes from Allah. Any bad thing that happens to you comes from yourself. We have sent you to mankind as a Messenger. Allah suffices as a Witness.

Any good thing that happens to you comes from Allah.

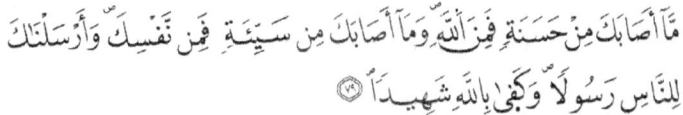

Whatever good comes to you, Muḥammad, in terms of fertility, ease, health and safety, is by the favour of Allah and His goodness to you. Whatever drought and hardship is because of a wrong action for which you are being punished. While it is addressed to the Prophet ﷺ, it is his community which is meant. It means: 'O people, whatever prosperity and expansion come to you, that is Allah's favour to you, and any drought and constriction of provision is because of your actions.' It is because of your wrong actions that it has happened to you. Al-Ḥasan, as-Suddī and others said that. This sort of address is seen elsewhere in the Qur'an as in 65:1.

It is said that it is addressed to human beings as a whole and means the entire species as when Allah says: *'By the Late Afternoon, truly man is in loss.'* (103:1) It means mankind as a whole is in loss. You can see this from the exception: *'except for those who believe.'* The exception is only made from a comprehensive group. According to this interpretation, *'Any bad thing'* begins a new sentence. It is also said that there is some elision in the words and it means: 'What is the matter with these people that they scarcely understand a single word so that they say, "Any good thing that happens to you comes from Allah."'

It is said that the interrogative *alif* is implied, meaning 'Does it come from yourself?' Examples of this elision are seen in 26:22 and 6:77 where the question is implied. Abū Khirāsh al-Hudhalī said:

They calmed me and said, 'Little Khālid, do not be alarmed.'
I said, 'I did not recognise the faces. [Is it] them? Them!'

It means 'Is it them?' and the interrogative *alif* is implied. This is a common usage. Al-Akhfash said that *'mā'* means 'which'. It is also said that it is a precondition. An-Naḥḥās said that what is correct is what al-Akhfash said because it was revealed about something particular in the form of a drought. This is not about disobedience at all. If it had been it would be *'mā aṣabta'*.

'Abd al-Wahhāb ibn Mujāhid related from his father from Ibn 'Abbās, Ubayy and Ibn Mas'ūd that they recited, after the words *'from yourself'*, 'and I have written it down against you.' This reading in fact is a commentary. Some people, who are deviant, confirm this as part of the Qur'an, and the *ḥadīth* about that from Ibn Mas'ūd and Ubayy is broken because Mujāhid did not see Ibn Mas'ūd or Ubayy.

According to those who say that the *'good'* here was Badr and the *'bad'* Uḥud, what happened was a punishment for the disobedience of the archers whom the Prophet ﷺ had commanded to guard their backs and not leave their positions, but who then left when they thought that Quraysh were defeated and the Muslims were taking booty. Khālid ibn al-Walīd, who was with the unbelievers that day, saw that the rear of the army of the Messenger of Allah ﷺ was exposed because of what the archers had done and he took a group of horsemen and circled around until he was behind the Muslims and then attacked. The archers had all abandoned their position except for the banner-bearer who followed the instructions of the Messenger of Allah ﷺ and stood firm until he was martyred where he stood as was dealt with in *Āli 'Imrān*. Allah revealed this *āyah* which is similar to His words in *Āli 'Imrān*: '*...when a calamity happens to you...*', meaning the Battle of Uḥud, '*... when you have already inflicted twice as much...*', in the Battle of Badr, '*...you say, "How could this possibly happen?" Say, "It has come from your own selves."*' (3:165)

It is not possible for the '*good*' here to be obedience and the '*bad*' disobedience, as the Qadariyyah say, since if that had been the case, it would be '*mā aṣabta*' (rather than *mā aṣābaka*) as has been mentioned. They say that it means [initiating] the action and we say that it is acquisition. Good can [in certain circumstances] mean obedience and bad disobedience as in Allah's words: '*Those who produce a good action will receive ten like it. But those who produce a bad action will only be repaid with its equivalent.*' (6:160)

In this *āyah*, as we explained, 'good' is fertility and 'bad' drought, and 'good' ease and 'bad' hardship as we find in the *āyah* of *al-A'rāf*: '*We seized Pharaoh's people with years of drought and scarcity of fruits so that hopefully they would pay heed.*' (7:130) In it '*sinīn*' is drought year after year during which they were denied rain and so there was little produce and prices were high. '*Whenever a good thing came to them, they said, "This is our due." But if anything bad happened to them, they would blame their ill fortune on Mūsā and those with them.*'" They would think that their ill fortune came from them and would say, 'This is because of our following and obeying you.' So Allah refuted them: '*No indeed! Their ill fortune will be with Allah.*' (7:131)

It means that that both the omen of blessing and the omen of ill luck, good and evil, benefit and harm, all come from Allah Almighty. None of it is the action of the creature, as evinced by the words of Allah when He reported that they ascribed their ill-fortune to the Prophet ﷺ: '*But if a bad thing happens to them, they say, "This has come from you"*' and His words: '*Your evil omen is with Allah*' (27:47) and again: '*What assailed you on the day the two armies met was by Allah's permission.*' (3:166) So everything is by the Decree and decision of Allah and His knowledge. The *āyahs* of the Book bear witness on behalf of one another.

Our scholars say that when someone believes in Allah and the Last Day, they do not doubt that everything is by the Decree of Allah and by His will and volition. It is as Allah says: '*We will test you with both good and evil as a trial*' (21:35) and: '*When Allah desires evil for a people, there is no averting it. They have no protector apart from Him.*' (13:11) Some people of the *Sunnah*, who lack knowledge, are also attracted to this *āyah* and use it as evidence as the Qadariyyah use it as evidence. As we said, the Qadariyyah say that good here is obedience and bad is disobedience and they claim that Allah attributes disobedience to man when He says: *'Any bad thing that happens to you is from yourself.'* This is how they are connected to it. The argument of the others is: *'Everything comes from Allah,'* and they ascribe both good and evil to Allah rather than to creation. The ignorant in both parties attach themselves to it because they base that on the bad being disobedience, and that is not the case, as we made clear. Allah knows best.

If the Qadariyyah say that the 'good thing' is obedience, meaning that obedience is from Allah, this is not actually their belief because, in their school, they believe that the doing of the good action and bad action are directly attributable to the person doing them. If they really had an argument in it, Allah would have had to have said, 'What you do (*aṣabta*) of good and what you do of evil' since the doer of good and bad is the same and the good and bad are only related to him by his action, not by the action of someone else. Imām Abu-l-Ḥasan Shīth ibn Ibrāhīm ibn Muḥammad ibn Ḥaydarah states this in his book, *Juz' al-Ghalaṣim fī ifḥām al-mukhāṣim.*

We have sent you to mankind as a Messenger.

This can be using a verbal noun for stress or it means 'someone with a Message.'

Allah suffices as a Witness.

Allah is sufficient as a Witness to the truthfulness of the Message of His Prophet ﷺ and that he is speaking the truth. It is in the accusative for clarification and the *bā'* is redundant.

مَّن يُطِعِ ٱلرَّسُولَ فَقَدۡ أَطَاعَ ٱللَّهَۖ وَمَن تَوَلَّىٰ فَمَآ أَرۡسَلۡنَٰكَ عَلَيۡهِمۡ حَفِيظٗا ٨٠

80 Whoever obeys the Messenger has obeyed Allah. If anyone turns away, we did not send you to them as their keeper.

Allah has informed us that to obey His Messenger is to obey Him. We read in *Ṣaḥīḥ Muslim* from Abū Hurayrah that the Prophet ﷺ said, 'Whoever obeys me has obeyed Allah. Whoever disobeys me has disobeyed Allah. Whoever obeys the ruler has obeyed me and whoever disobeys the ruler has disobeyed Allah.'

'Their keeper' is their watcher and the one who observes their actions. The job of the Prophet ﷺ is only to convey the Message. Al-Qutabī says that it means 'reckoner' and so Allah abrogated this by the *Āyah* of the Sword and commanded him to fight those who oppose Allah and His Messenger.

وَيَقُولُونَ طَاعَةٌ فَإِذَا بَرَزُوا مِنْ عِندِكَ بَيَّتَ طَآئِفَةٌ مِّنْهُمْ غَيْرَ ٱلَّذِى
تَقُولُ وَٱللَّهُ يَكْتُبُ مَا يُبَيِّتُونَ فَأَعْرِضْ عَنْهُمْ وَتَوَكَّلْ عَلَى ٱللَّهِ وَكَفَىٰ
بِٱللَّهِ وَكِيلًا ﴿٨١﴾ أَفَلَا يَتَدَبَّرُونَ ٱلْقُرْءَانَ وَلَوْ كَانَ مِنْ عِندِ غَيْرِ ٱللَّهِ
لَوَجَدُوا فِيهِ ٱخْتِلَٰفًا كَثِيرًا ﴿٨٢﴾

81 They have the word, 'Obedience!' on their tongues but when they leave your presence, a group of them spend the night plotting to do other than what you say. Allah is recording their nocturnal plotting. So let them be and put your trust in Allah. Allah suffices as a Guardian. 82 Will they not ponder the Qur'an? If it had been from other than Allah, they would have found many inconsistencies in it.

They have the word, 'Obedience!' on their tongues but when they leave your presence, a group of them spend the night plotting to do other than what you say. Allah is recording their nocturnal plotting.

They say, 'We are commanded to obey.' It is possible that 'obedience' is in the accusative rather than the nominative and so it means: 'We obey completely.' This is the reading of Naṣr ibn 'Āṣim, al-Ḥasan and al-Jaḥdarī. This is about the hypocrites, according to most commentators, in other words, 'When they are with you, they say, "We obey."' However, their words are of no use because it is not true obedience if it is not based on belief. Allah says that the obedience they display is not real. If obedience without belief had been real, it would have been judged for them. It is confirmed that obedience must be accompanied by belief.

The verb *barazū* means 'they went out'. The verb, *bayyata*, used with 'a group' is in the masculine because the group was composed of men. The Kufans assimilate the *tā'* into the *ṭā'* because they are pronounced from the same source. Al-Kisā'ī considers that ugly with the verb, but the Basrans do not consider it ugly.

The verb *bayyata* means to lie and adulterate. It is also said that it means to change and alter, referring to the Prophet's words regarding what he entrusted to them and commanded them to do. *Tabyīt* means alteration. An example of that meaning is seen in the words of the poet:

They came to me and I was not pleased with what they changed (*bayyatū*)
They used to bring me something objectionable:

That I marry Mundhir to their widow.
Does a free man marry a slave to someone free?

It also means plotting at night. When people spend the night reflecting on what to do as in Allah's words: *'He is with them when they spend the night saying things which are not pleasing to Him.'* (4:108) The Arabs say, 'It is a matter reflected on at night' because night is a time when people can devote themselves to that. A poet says:

They agreed on their business at night.
Then in the morning they were in tumult.

Another usage of this is making the decision at night (*bayyata*) to fast. *Bayyūt* is water that has become cool over night. The same word denotes a business over which someone spends the night in anxiety. Al-Hudhalī says:

I make its preparation an object of distress
when I fear spending a night worrying over a perplexing matter.

Taybīt and *bayāt* both describe coming on the enemy at night. It is also used for doing something at night. It also said that it is to decide something.

If it is asked what the wisdom is in first mentioning the group and then spending the night, it is answered that by that Allah is pointing out His knowledge of those who remain in their unbelief and hypocrisy and overlooking those He knew would revert from that. It is said that it designates the state of those who are present, but confused in their affair. Those who listen and are silent are not mentioned. Allah knows best.

Allah is recording their nocturnal plotting.

Allah clearly records what they do in the pages of their actions and they will be repaid for what they did. Az-Zajjāj said that it means that He sends it down to you in the Book. This *āyah* is evidence that words alone are of no account as we mentioned. They say, 'Obedience' and articulate it, but Allah does not give reality to their obedience and judge it as being valid on their account because they do not actually have belief. So it is confirmed that someone obedient is only obedient when he believes.

So let them be and put your trust in Allah. Allah suffices as a Guardian.

This means, according to aḍ-Ḍaḥḥāk, do not mention their names, referring to the hypocrites. It is also said that it means: 'Do not punish them.' Then Allah commanded them to trust in Him and rely on Him for help against their enemy.

It is said that it is abrogated by the words of Allah: *'O Prophet! Do jihād against the unbelievers and the hypocrites.'* (9:83)

Will they not ponder the Qur'an?

Then Allah censures the hypocrites for turning away from pondering the Qur'an and reflecting on its meanings. The verb *'ponder'* means to reflect on the consequence of something. A *ḥadīth* says: 'Do not plot together.' This refers to carrying things through to their end. *Tadbīr* is a person managing his business as if he were looking to the end of it.

That is indicated by this *āyah* and by Allah's words in *Sūrat Muḥammad*: *'Will they not then ponder the Qur'an or are there locks upon their hearts?'* (47:24) It is mandatory to ponder the Qur'an in order to truly know its meaning. This refutes the false position of those who say, 'Only take the *tafsīr* which is confirmed to have been given by the Prophet ﷺ and it is forbidden to interpret it based on what the Arabic language will allow.' It is evidence for the command to investigate it and deduce from it and not merely follow precedent and it is also evidence for the validity of analogy (*qiyās*).

If it had been from other than Allah, they would have found many inconsistencies in it.

This means disparities and contradictions, as Ibn 'Abbās, Qatādah and Ibn Zayd said. Not included in this are the different expressions of the readings and the expressions of the metaphors, evidence, and the numbering of *sūrah*s and *āyah*s. What is meant is real inconsistency and contradiction. It is said that it means: 'If what you are told had been from other than Allah, it would have had inconsistencies in it.' It is said that inconsistency is found in anyone who speaks many words, either in respect of description and wording or regarding the excellence of the meaning, or with regard to contradiction or lies. Allah Almighty revealed the Qur'an and commanded them to ponder it because no one will find in it any differences with regard to description or confutation of a meaning or contradiction or lie in respect what is said about the Unseen and what people conceal.

وَإِذَا جَآءَهُمْ أَمْرٌ مِّنَ ٱلْأَمْنِ أَوِ ٱلْخَوْفِ أَذَاعُوا بِهِۦ وَلَوْ رَدُّوهُ إِلَى ٱلرَّسُولِ
وَإِلَىٰٓ أُولِى ٱلْأَمْرِ مِنْهُمْ لَعَلِمَهُ ٱلَّذِينَ يَسْتَنۢبِطُونَهُۥ مِنْهُمْ وَلَوْلَا فَضْلُ ٱللَّهِ
عَلَيْكُمْ وَرَحْمَتُهُۥ لَٱتَّبَعْتُمُ ٱلشَّيْطَٰنَ إِلَّا قَلِيلًا ﴿٨٣﴾

83 When news of any matter reaches them they spread it about, whether it is of a reassuring or disquieting nature. If they had only referred it to the Messenger and those in command among them, those among them able to discern the truth about it would have had proper knowledge of it. If it were not for Allah's favour to you and His mercy, all but a very few of you would have followed Shayṭān.

When news of any matter reaches them they spread it about,

'Idhā' has the sense of a precondition without an apodosis, even if a *mā* were to be added to it. It is rarely used. This was mentioned at the beginning of *al-Baqarah.*

When they hear of any matter which involves security, such as the victory of the Muslims and their killing of their enemies, or which involves fear, which is the opposite, they spread it about and talk about it before ascertaining its truth. It is said that this was done by the weak Muslims, as al-Ḥasan said, because they gossipped about the affairs of the Prophet ﷺ, thinking they were doing nothing wrong. Aḍ-Ḍaḥḥāk and Ibn Zayd said that it is about the hypocrites, and they were forbidden to do that since they would be propagating false rumours.

If they had only referred it to the Messenger and those in command among them,

If only they had not spoken about it until it was announced by the Prophet ﷺ or those in command, who are the people of knowledge and *fiqh*, as al-Ḥasan, Qatādah and others said. As-Suddī and Ibn Zayd and said they are the rulers. It is said that they are the commanders of expeditions.

those among them able to discern the truth about it would have had proper knowledge of it.

The words *'proper knowledge of it'* mean that they would have known what to disclose of it and what to conceal. The word *istinbāṭ* (*able to discern*) is derived from 'extracting water'. *Nabṭ* is the water brought out when water first comes from a well which is dug. *Nabaṭ* (Nabateans) are called that because they extract what is in the ground (as farmers). *Istinbāṭ* linguistically means extraction. It indicates *ijtihād* in the absence of a text on which there is consensus.

If it were not for Allah's favour to you and His mercy, all but a very few of you would have followed Shayṭān.

It is in the nominative by the inceptive according to Sibawayh, and he believes that it is not permitted to have an explicit predicate. The Kufans say that it is in the nominative by '*lawlā*'.

There are three positions regarding the meaning of this. Ibn 'Abbās and others said that it means: 'They would have announced it except for a few who did not divulge it.' A group of grammarians, al-Kisā'ī, al-Akhfash, Abū 'Ubayd, Abū Ḥātim and aṭ-Ṭabarī said that. It is said that it means: 'He knows that only a few of them would discern it.' Al-Ḥasan and others said that, and az-Zajjāj preferred that. He said, 'This is the deduction which most recognise because inquiry is a report.' Al-Farrā' preferred the first because expeditions are known when the telltale and others make them known, and the news passes from one person to another. Al-Kalbī said, 'That is why I prefer that the disclosure is meant by the exception.' An-Naḥḥās said that these two views are based on the metaphor and a reversal of the normal sentence order.

The third position is that it is not a metaphor: 'If it had not been for Allah's favour and mercy to you by sending a Messenger among you to establish the evidence for you, you would have rejected and been idolaters except for a few of you.' There is a fourth view by aḍ-Ḍaḥḥāk: it means 'you would have followed Shayṭān except for a few,' i.e. the Companions of the Messenger of Allah ﷺ. It means those whose hearts are tested for *taqwā*. According to this view, the exception is '*a very few*'. Al-Mahdawī said that most scholars reject this view since, if it were it not for Allah's favour and mercy, all of them would have followed Shayṭān.

فَقَٰتِلْ فِى سَبِيلِ ٱللَّهِ لَا تُكَلَّفُ إِلَّا نَفْسَكَ وَحَرِّضِ ٱلْمُؤْمِنِينَ عَسَى ٱللَّهُ أَن
يَكُفَّ بَأْسَ ٱلَّذِينَ كَفَرُوا۟ وَٱللَّهُ أَشَدُّ بَأْسًا وَأَشَدُّ تَنكِيلًا ﴿٨٤﴾

84 So fight in the way of Allah – you are only answerable for yourself – and spur on the believers. It may well be that Allah will curb the force of the unbelievers. Allah has greater force and greater power to punish.

So fight in the way of Allah

'*So fight*' is connected by the *fā'* to the words: '*If someone fights in the Way of Allah, whether he is killed or is victorious, We will pay him an immense reward.*' (4:73). 'For this reason, fight in the way of Allah.' It is also said that it is connected to the words:

'What reason could you have for not fighting in the Way of Allah?' (4:75) It is as if Allah is saying: 'Do not fail to fight against the enemy and help the persecuted believers, even if you are on your own, because Allah has promised victory.' Az-Zajjāj said, 'Allah commands His Messenger ﷺ to do *jihād*, even if he has to fight alone, because he is guaranteed victory.'

Ibn 'Aṭiyyah said, 'This is the literal meaning, but there is no report that fighting was obliged for him alone, rather than the community, at any time. So it means, and Allah knows best, that it is addressed to him, and is an example of what is to be said to each one personally. In other words: "This is said to you, Muḥammad, and to each member of your community: *'Fight in the way of Allah and you are only answerable for yourself.'*"' So it is obliged for every believer to struggle, even if they are on their own. Exemplifying that are the words of the Prophet ﷺ, 'By Allah, I will fight them until I am killed.' And the same was articulated by Abū Bakr in the *Riddah*: 'If my right hand opposes me, I will strive against it with my left.'

It is said that this was revealed on the day of Lesser Badr. When Abū Sufyan left Uḥud, he promised to meet the Messenger of Allah ﷺ on the anniversary of Badr. When the time came, the Messenger of Allah ﷺ went out with seventy men but Abū Sufyān did not come and there was no fighting. This is according to the meaning of what Mujāhid said in *Āli 'Imrān*. The connection of this to what came before it is that Allah describes the hypocrites with mixing things up and spreading false rumours and then commands His Prophet ﷺ to turn away from them and be serious in fighting in the Way of Allah, even if no one helped him in that.

you are only answerable for yourself

'You are answerable' ends in a *ḍammah* because it is the future tense. It is not in the jussive because it is not the reason for the first. Al-Akhfash claims that it is permitted for it to be in the jussive. *'Yourself'* is a predicate whose subject is not named. This means: you will not be punished for what others do.

spur on the believers.

This means that you should encourage them to do *jihād* and fight. You encourage someone to do something when you command them to do it. *Ḥāraḍa 'alā*, *akabba 'alā*, and *wāẓaba 'alā* mean the same.

It may well be that Allah will curb the force of the unbelievers.

This is an aspiration, and aspiration, where Allah is concerned, is something that is bound to happen, so that the verb 'may be' in Arabic here becomes something mandatory. Another example of that is found in the words: *'He Who I sincerely hope will forgive my mistakes on the Day of Reckoning.'* (26:82)

Allah has greater force and greater power to punish.

This means striking power and authority and power to do what He wills. Al-Ḥasan and others said that *tankīl* means to punish. Ibn Durayd said, 'Allah struck him with a *nuklah*, meaning a punishment which will deter him. *Nakāl* is an exemplary punishment and *mankal* is an implement of punishment. He said:

He imposed on their backs an instrument of punishment (*mankal*).'

If someone says, 'We see that the unbelievers are more powerful and stronger, and you say that "perhaps" means "certainty", so where is that promise?' he is told, 'This promise exists, even if it is not mandatory that it remain constant and continue. Even if it only exists for an instant, the promise is true. Allah restrained the force of the idolaters at Lesser Badr and the unbelievers failed to live up to their promise to fight. He says: *"Allah spared the believers fighting."* (33:25) This was also true at Ḥudaybīyah when the idolaters wanted to commit treachery and take the opportunity to do so. The Muslims became aware of them and went out and took them as hostages. That was when the emissaries were going between them [negotiating] the truce. It is what is meant by His words: *"It is He Who held their hands back from you."* (45:24) Allah put terror into the hearts of the parties of the Confederates and they left without fighting, just as He expelled the Jews without fighting, as He says: *"Allah spared the believers fighting."* The Jews left their homes and property without fighting the believers. All of this is violence which Allah spared the believers. The Jews and Christians, in spite of their great numbers, submitted with humility to be subject to the *jizyah* and did not fight. So Allah spared the believers their force.' Praise be to Allah, the Lord of the Worlds.

مَّن يَشْفَعْ شَفَٰعَةً حَسَنَةً يَكُن لَّهُۥ نَصِيبٌ مِّنْهَا ۖ وَمَن يَشْفَعْ
شَفَٰعَةً سَيِّئَةً يَكُن لَّهُۥ كِفْلٌ مِّنْهَا ۗ وَكَانَ ٱللَّهُ عَلَىٰ كُلِّ شَىْءٍ
مُّقِيتًا ﴿٨٥﴾

85 Those who join forces for good will receive a reward for it. Those who join forces for evil will be answerable for it. Allah gives all things what they deserve.

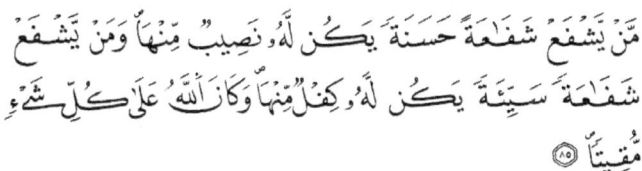

The root of *shafāʿah* (intercession) and *shufʿah* (property pre-emption) and the like comes from the word *shafʿ*, which means one of a pair. *Shāfiʿ* (intercessor) is taken from it because he joins with the person who has a need. A camel is called *shufūʿ* when it has two loads on one frame. The root means to add one to another, and pre-emption means to add the property of the owner to one's own property. Intercession (*shafāʿah*) is when you join someone to your rank and mediation. It is actually to display the position of the intercessor with the one for whom there is intercession and giving a benefit to the one interceded for.

Commentators disagree about meaning of this *āyah*. Mujāhid, al-Ḥasan, and Ibn Zayd and others said that this is people joining together for their needs. Whoever joins forces to help others has a reward. Whoever joins forces to harm them is answerable. It is also said that the good *shafaʿah* is for obedience and piety, and the bad is for disobedience. The reward is mandatory for anyone who joins forces for good to put things right between two people. Anyone who strives to spread slander and calumny sins. This is close to the first. It is said that good *shafāʿah* means supplication for the Muslims and the bad is praying against them. We find in a sound tradition: 'A supplication which a Muslim man makes secretly for his brother is answered. At his head is a guardian angel. Whenever he makes supplication for good for his brother, the angel who guards him says, "Amen, and for you the same."' This is a reward. The same applies to evil. It will rebound on him. The Jews used to pray against the Muslims. It is said that it means that whoever joins with his companion in *jihād* will have a portion of the reward. Whoever joins with another in falsehood will have a portion of the sin. Al-Ḥasan also said that the good is what is permitted in the *dīn* and the evil is what is not permitted. This statement seems to be universal.

Kifl means burden and sin, as al-Ḥasan and Qatādah said. As-Suddī and Ibn Zayd said that it means a portion. It is derived from camel-cloth (*kisāʾ*) which the rider puts on the camel's hump so that he does not fall. The verb *iktifala* is used for putting a riding-cloth on the camel because it does not use all of the back. It is to use a portion of the back as one uses a portion of good and evil. We find in the Book of Allah: *'He will give you a double portion (*kiflayn*) of His mercy.'* (57:37) The intercessor will be repaid with what is permitted, even if the intercession is not granted because of His words here. We find in *Ṣaḥīḥ Muslim*: 'Intercede with me and you will be rewarded, and Allah will decree whatever He wishes on the tongue of His Prophet."

Allah gives all things what they deserve.

Muqīt means powerful. Part of that is the words of az-Zubayr ibn 'Abd al-Muṭṭalib:

I restrain myself from the one with rancor,
when I am fully able (*muqīt*) to do him ill.

So it means: 'Allah gives every man his food.' An example of that is the words of the Prophet ﷺ, 'It is enough of a wrong action for a man that those he provides (*yuqītu*) for should perish.' This means family and others who are in his care. Ibn 'Aṭiyyah mentioned it. You say, '*quttuhu, aqūtuhu, qawt,* and *aqattuhu, uqītuhu iqātah.* The person is *qā'it* and *muqīt.* Al-Kisā'ī related '*aqāta, yuqītu'*. As for the words of the poet,

I have the power (*muqīt*) to reckon...

Aṭ-Ṭabarī said about it that it does not have the prior meaning, but means 'stopped'.

Abū 'Ubaydah said that *muqīt* means the preserver. Al-Kisā'ī says it means the powerful. An-Naḥḥās prefers the first because *muqīt* is derived from *qūt* (nourishment). Al-Farrā' said that it is the One Who gives every man his food. We find in a *ḥadīth*: 'It is enough sin that a man causes to perish [by neglect] those he feeds.' Ath-Tha'labī mentioned it. Allah knows best. Ibn Fāris related in *al-Mujmal* that *muqīt* means the one with power and it is also the protector and the witness. Food is *qīt* or *qūt.* Allah knows best.

وَإِذَا حُيِّيتُم بِتَحِيَّةٍ فَحَيُّوا بِأَحْسَنَ مِنْهَا أَوْ رُدُّوهَا إِنَّ اللَّهَ كَانَ عَلَىٰ كُلِّ
شَيْءٍ حَسِيبًا ﴿٨٦﴾

86 When you are greeted with a greeting, return the greeting or improve on it. Allah takes account of everything.

When you are greeted with a greeting,

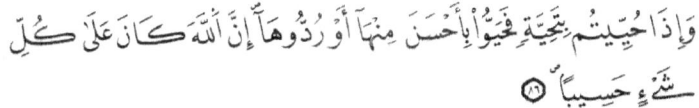

Taḥīyah is in the measure of *taf'ilah* from the word *ḥayyā.* The root is *taḥīyah,* like *tarḍiyyah* and *tasmīyah,* and the *yā'* is assimilated into the *yā'. Taḥiyyah* is a greeting. It is the *salām.* It means 'to pray for life'. '*Taḥiyyātu lillāh*' means safety from disasters. It is said that it is the kingdom. 'Abdullāh ibn Ṣāliḥ al-'Ijlī said, 'I asked al-Kīsā'ī about the meaning of "*taḥiyyātu lillāh*" and he said that it is like *barakāt.* I asked, "And what is the meaning of *barakāt*?" He answered, "I have not heard anything regarding it." I asked Muḥammad ibn al-Ḥasan and he said, "It is something by which Allah's slaves worship Him." I went to Kufa and met 'Abdullāh ibn Idrīs and said, "I asked al-Kīsā'ī and Muḥammad about the words: *'taḥiyyātu lillāh'* and their answer was such-and-such." 'Abdullāh ibn Idrīs said, "They have no knowledge of poetry and these things! *Taḥiyyah* is kingdom." He recited:

"I led it to Abū Qābūs until I made it kneel over his kingdom with my army.'"

Ibn Khuwaymandād said,

I travelled with him to an-Nu'mān
until I made it kneel over his kingdom with my army.

[ANOTHER SIMILAR POEM]

Al-Qutabī said, 'He said "*taḥiyyātu lillāh*" in the plural because there were kings in the earth who are greeted with different forms of greetings and therefore we are told to say, "*taḥiyyātu lillāh*" because the expressions indicate kingdom and allude to Allah Almighty.'

The way it is connected to what comes before it is: 'When you go out for jihad as was commanded, then give the greeting of Islam in your journey. Do not say to those who give you the greeting of *salām*, "You are not a believer." Rather reply with *salām*. The rulings of Islam apply to them.'

Scholars disagree about the meaning and interpretation of this *āyah*. Ibn Wahb and Ibn al-Qāsim report from Mālik that this *āyah* is about blessing the sneezer and replying to the one who blesses him. This is weak since nothing in the words that indicate this. The reply to the one who blesses the sneezer is included in the idea of returning the greeting by analogy. It is what Mālik meant if he said that. Allah knows best.

Ibn Khuwayzimandād says that the *āyah* can be applied to a gift since it is for the reward. If someone gives a person a gift in expectation of a recompense, they have a choice: they can either return it or accept it and give something back of the same value. Abū Ḥanīfah said something like this. 'Greeting' here is the gift because of his words, 'return it', since it is not possible to return the greeting itself. Taken literally, the words would imply returning the same, which is the gift. So He commanded recompense if he accepts it or to return the gift itself. This is not possible with a greeting. The ruling about the gift for a reward and a pure gift will be dealt with in *Sūrat ar-Rūm* (30:39) What is sound here is that *taḥīyah* is a greeting since Allah says: *'When they come to you, they greet you with words Allah has never used in greeting you.'* (58:8)

An-Nābighah adh-Dhubyānī said:

The princesses greet them among them
while the red gowns hang on the trestles.

It means that they are greeted.

This is the position of most commentators who say that it refers to the greeting. That being the case, the *fiqh* of the *āyah* is that scholars agree that initiating the greeting is a desirable *sunnah* and to reply is obligatory by the words here in the *āyah*. They disagree about whether one individual answering for a whole group satisfies the requirement or not. Mālik and ash-Shāfi'ī believe that it does while the Kufans believe that it is an individual requirement. They said that the greeting is not the same as the reply because initiating it is a voluntary act but returning it is obligatory. If a non-Muslim greets them, that does not cancel their duty of returning it. That indicates that returning the greeting is an individual obligation, and so Qatādah and al-Ḥasan said, 'If someone praying returns the greeting verbally, it does not break his prayer because he is doing what he was commanded to do.' Other people take a different position.

The evidence of the first group is what Abū Dāwūd reports from 'Alī ibn Abī Ṭālib that the Prophet ﷺ said, 'When a group pass, it is enough that one of them greets.' This is an actual text on the subject of the dispute. Abū 'Umar said, 'It is a *ḥasan ḥadīth* without any contradiction. The *isnād* contains Sa'īd ibn Khālid, who is Sa'īd ibn Khālid al-Khuzā'ī. He was a Madinan and some say that there was nothing wrong with him while others, including Abū Zur'ah, Abū Ḥātim, and Ya'qūb ibn Shaybah, say that he is weak. They make this *ḥadīth* of his *munkar* because he alone has this *isnād* on the basis that 'Abdullāh ibn al-Faḍl did not listen to 'Ubaydullāh ibn Abī Rāfi'. Al-A'raj was between them in other than this *ḥadīth*.' Allah knows best.

They also cited the words of the Prophet ﷺ, 'A small group greets a large group.' When they agree that one greets a group and there is no need for the members of the group to repeat it, so one can reply to a group and represent the rest as is the case with a *farḍ kifāyah*. Mālik related from Zayd ibn Aslam that the Messenger of Allah ﷺ said, 'A rider greets someone walking. When one of the people gives the greeting, that is enough for them.' Our scholars said that this indicates that the response of one is enough because he only said that it is satisfies the requirement for them in what is mandatory. Allah knows best. That is how our scholars interpret this *ḥadīth* and make it an argument for one person answering. This is unsettled.

Return the greeting or improve on it.

Improving on it is to add to it and so one says, 'Peace be upon you and the mercy of Allah' to someone who said, 'Peace be upon you,' and if someone says, 'Peace be upon you and the mercy of Allah,' one adds, 'and His blessings.' This is the end and there is no further increase. Allah Almighty says when speaking about his noble house: *'May Allah's mercy and His blessings be upon you.'* (11:73)

If he reaches the end of the greeting, you add 'and' (*wāw*) at the beginning of your words and say, 'And peace be upon you and the mercy of Allah.' A simple return of the greeting is also to say, 'And upon you be Peace' to the one who said 'Peace be upon you' to you. All of the greeting should be in the plural, even if you are only greeting a single person. Al-A'mash related that Ibrāhīm an-Nakha'ī said, 'When you greet one person, say, "Peace be upon you" in the plural. There are angels with him.' The answer is also given in the plural. Ibn Abī Zayd said, 'A Muslim says, "Peace be upon you," and the response is "And upon you be Peace" or "Peace be upon you" as was said to him. That is the meaning of His words, "*return it.*"'

It is preferred when giving the greeting, and it is correct behaviour, to put the name of Allah Almighty before that of the creature. Allah says, *'Peace be upon the family of Yāsīn'* (37:130); in the story of Ibrāhīm: *'May Allah's mercy and His blessings be upon you'* (11:73); and reporting about Ibrāhīm: *'Peace be upon you.'* (19:47) We find in the *Ṣaḥīḥ* collections of al-Bukhārī and Muslim from Abū Hurayrah that the Messenger of Allah ﷺ said, 'Allah Almighty created Ādam sixty cubits in height. When He created him, he said, "Go and greet that group," who were a group of angels who were seated. "Listen to how they greet you. It is your greeting and the greeting of your descendants." He went and said, "Peace be upon you." They said, "And Peace be upon you and the mercy of Allah." So they added "and the mercy of Allah." All of those who enter the Garden will have the form of Ādam and his height of sixty cubits. Creatures have become smaller and smaller until the present time.'

As well as being sound, this *ḥadīth* contains seven points. First, it describes Ādam's creation. Second, we will enter the Garden in his form by Allah's grace. Third, a few greet many. Fourth, the name of Allah is put first. Fifth, the answer is similar. Sixth, one can add to the greeting. Seventh, all give the answer, as the Kufans said. Allah knows best. Putting the name of the person greeted first is not forbidden or disliked since it is confirmed that the Prophet ﷺ said to a man who had not prayed properly, 'On you be Peace. Go back and pray. You have not prayed.' 'Ā'ishah said in response to Jibrīl's greeting, 'And upon you be Peace.' Al-Bukhārī transmitted it.

'Ā'ishah's *ḥadīth* contains the *fiqh* that when a man sends a greeting to someone else, he must return it as he would do if it was spoken directly to him. A man came to the Prophet ﷺ and said, 'My father gives you the greeting.' He answered, 'And Peace be upon you and your father.' An-Nasā'ī and Abū Dāwūd related that Jābir ibn Sulaym said, 'I met the Messenger of Allah ﷺ and said, "On you be Peace, Messenger of Allah." He said, "Do not say, 'On you be Peace.' 'On you be Peace' is the greeting the dead. Rather say, 'Peace be upon you.'"' This *ḥadīth* is not confirmed other than the fact that it was an Arab custom to put first the name of someone against whom one prayed for evil as when one says, 'On him be the curse of Allah and His anger.' Allah Almighty says: *'On you is My curse until the Day of Rising.'* (38:78) That was also the custom and habit of poets in greeting the dead. It is like their words:

On you be Peace, Qays ibn 'Āṣim,
    and His mercy as long as He wishes to show mercy.

Another, ash-Shammākh, said:

On you be Peace from a prince, and blessed is the
    Hand of Allah in that divided earth.

He forbade that. It was not because it is a prescribed expression for the dead, because it is confirmed that he ﷺ greeted the dead as he greeted the living and said, 'Peace be upon you, abode of a believing people and, Allah willing, we will join you.' 'Ā'ishah said, 'I said, "Messenger of Allah, what should I say when I go to the graves?" He answered, "Say: 'Peace be upon you, people of the abodes of the believers.'"' This will be discussed in at-*Takāthur*, Allah willing. It is probable that the *ḥadīth* of 'Ā'ishah and others is about greeting all the people of the graves when visiting them and overlooking them, and the *ḥadīth* of Jābir ibn Sulaym is specific to greeting when passing with the intention of visiting. Allah knows best.

The *sunnah* is that a rider greets a walker, someone standing greets someone sitting and a few greet many. This is reported in *Ṣaḥīḥ Muslim* from the *ḥadīth* of Abū Hurayrah. He said that the Messenger of Allah ﷺ said, 'A rider greets...' He began with the rider because of his high position and because that is further from vanity. That is like what he said about someone walking. It is said that when some is sitting in a state of gravity firmness and stillness, he has the prerogative to do that rather than the person walking because his state is the opposite of that. As for a small group greeting a large group, it is to preserve the honour of the large number of Muslims. Al-Bukhārī added in this *ḥadīth*: 'A small group greets a large group.'

As for an adult greeting a child, Ash'ath related that al-Ḥasan used to think that one does not greet children. He said, 'That is because the reply is an obligation and a child is not obliged to reply. That is why one should not greet them.' It is related that Ibn Sīrīn used to greet children, but did not listen to them. Most scholars say that it is better to greet them than not to do so. It is reported in the two *Ṣaḥīḥ* collections that Sayyār said, 'I was walking with Thābit and he passed by some children and greeted them. He mentioned that he was walking with Anas who passed by some children and greeted them. He, in turn, related that he was walking with the Messenger of Allah ﷺ when he passed by some children and greeted them.' This was part of his great character ﷺ. Part of it is teaching children and encouraging them to learn the sunnahs and teach them the proper manner of the *Sharī'ah* in it.

It is permitted to greet women unless one fears being tempted by young women through an impulse from Shayṭān or treacherous eyes. As for women who are removed from that and old women, it is good to greet them because one is safe from what we mentioned. This is the position of 'Aṭā' and Qatādah. Mālik and a group of scholars said that. The Kufans rejected it when none of them are close relatives (*maḥram*). They said, 'Since the adhan, *iqāmah*, and reciting aloud in the prayer are cancelled for women, so responding to the greeting is also cancelled for them, and therefore they are not greeted.'

The first is the sound position based on al-Bukhārī's transmission that Sahl ibn Sa'd said, 'We used to be happy on the day of *Jumu'ah*.' He was asked, 'Why?' He said, 'There was an old woman among us who used to go to Buḍa'ah (Ibn Maslamah said that was palm-grove in Madīnah) and pull up by the roots the garden-beet (*silq*) and put them in a pot. Then she would grind some barley. When we had prayed *Jumu'ah*, we would visit her and she would bring it to us. We used to be happy because of that. We did not have lunch or an afternoon nap except after *Jumu'ahs*.'

The *sunnah* of the greeting and the response is that they should be out loud. It is not enough to indicate them by gesture with the finger or palm according to ash-Shāfi'ī. We say that it is enough if it is at a distance. Ibn Wahb related from Ibn Mas'ūd: '*As-Salām* is one of the Names of Allah which Allah put on the earth, so spread it among you. When a man greets people and they return the greeting to him, he has a degree over them because he reminded them. If they do not reply, those who are better than them reply to him.'

Al-A'mash related from 'Amr ibn Murrah that 'Abdullāh ibn al-Ḥārith said, 'When a man greets people, he has a higher degree. If they do not return it to him, the angels reply to him and curse them. When the one greeted returns it, he should make his answer heard because if the greeter does not hear, then he has not answered him. Do you not see that when the one greeted says the *salām*, and the greeter does not hear it, that it is a greeting from him. So when he gives a response that is not heard, it is not really a response. It is related that the Prophet ﷺ said, 'When you greet, make it audible. When you return it, make it audible. When you sit, sit with security and none of you should raise his voice over that of another.'

Ibn Wahb said that Usāmah ibn Zayd said that Nāfi' said, 'I was travelling with a man of the *fuqahā'* of Syria called 'Abdullāh ibn [Abī] Zakariyyā and my mount held me back. Then I caught up with him and did not greet him. He asked, "Why did you not greet me?" I answered, "I was just with you."' He said, 'It is sound. When the Companions of the Messenger of Allah ﷺ were travelling and a tree parted them and then they met again, they would greet one another.'

When an unbeliever greets you, the ruling about the reply to him is to say 'And on you.' Ibn 'Abbās and others said that what is meant by the *āyah* is: 'When you are greeted by a believer, then improve on it, and if it is from an unbeliever, then return it as the Messenger of Allah ﷺ said, "And on you."' 'Aṭā' said, 'The *āyah* is specifically about the believers. If someone other than them greets you, then say to them, "And on you."'

Using 'and' or omitting it are both found in *Ṣaḥīḥ Muslim*. There is a clear transmission without 'and'. There is some problem with keeping 'and' because it demands sharing and so he must enter with them into whatever they have asked for: of death or death of the *dīn*. Commentators have different views about that. The first is that 'and' has its normal meaning of joining, although we answer against them and they are not answered against us as the Prophet ﷺ said. It is also said that it is redundant. It is said that it marks a new sentence. The first is more likely. The elision of 'and' is better in meaning and sounder and better known in transmission. Most scholars take that view.

They disagree about returning the greeting of people of the *dhimmah* and whether or not it is obligatory in the way that it is obligatory to respond to Muslims. It was the position of Ibn 'Abbās, ash-Sha'bī and Qatādah that it was, holding to the general meaning of the *āyah* and the command in the sound *Sunnah* to return it. Mālik, according to Ashhab, and Ibn Wahb believed that it is not mandatory. If you reply, you say, 'And on you.' Ibn Ṭāwūs preferred that one say in reply to them, '*alāka-s-salām*,' meaning 'Peace is above you.' Some of our scholars prefer '*as-silām*', meaning 'stones'. The position of Mālik and others regarding that is enough as comes in *ḥadīth*. In *Sūrat Maryam*, we will deal with initiating the greeting in 19:47. We find in *Ṣaḥīḥ Muslim* from Abū Hurayrah that the Prophet ﷺ said, 'You will not enter the Garden and will not believe until you love one another. Shall I direct to something which, if you do it, will make you love one another? Spread the greeting of Peace among you.' This implies spreading it among Muslims rather than idolaters. Allah knows best.

One does not greet someone who is praying. If he is greeted, he has a choice. He can return it by a gesture with his finger or wait until he finishes the prayer to return it. One should not greet someone in the lavatory. He is not obliged to return it. A man came to the Prophet ﷺ in such a situation and he told him, 'If you find or see me in this situation, do not greet me. If you do greet me, I will not return it.' One does not greet someone reciting the Qur'an so as to break his recitation. He also has a choice: to stop and return it or wait until he finishes. One does not greet someone in the bath-house when his private parts are uncovered or when he is busy with what is done inside the bath-house. If someone is not like that, he can be greeted.

Allah takes account of everything.

He preserves it. It is said that He is enough for it. Form IV of the verb (*aḥsaba*) means to satisfy. It is like the expression *'ḥasbuka-llāh' (*Allah is enough for you). Qatādah said that it means to take account as in measuring out. It is said that it is the form *fa'īl* from 'reckoning' (*ḥisāb*), and this is good here because of the quantitative sense of the *āyah*: a person has more or less or has a full amount of what comes to him. An-Nasā'ī reported that 'Imrān ibn Ḥusayn said, 'A man came to the Prophet ﷺ and said, "Peace be upon you." He responded to him [with the same] and then the man sat down. The Prophet ﷺ said, "Ten." Then another man came and said, "Peace be upon you and the mercy of Allah," and he responded to him and the man sat down. He said, "Twenty." Then yet another man came and said, "Peace be upon you and the mercy of Allah and His blessings," and he responded to him and that man sat down. He said, "Thirty."'

This report contains an explanation: when he says, 'Peace be upon you' to his Muslim brother, ten good deeds are written for him. When he says, 'Peace be upon you and the mercy of Allah,' twenty good deeds are written for him. When he says, 'Peace be upon you and the mercy of Allah and His blessings,' thirty good deeds are written for you. The same is true with the reward for the reply. Allah knows best.

ٱللَّهُ لَآ إِلَٰهَ إِلَّا هُوَ لَيَجْمَعَنَّكُمْ إِلَىٰ يَوْمِ ٱلْقِيَٰمَةِ لَا رَيْبَ فِيهِ وَمَنْ أَصْدَقُ
مِنَ ٱللَّهِ حَدِيثًا ﴿٨٧﴾

87 Allah, there is no god but Him. He will gather you to the Day of Rising about which there is no doubt. And whose speech could be truer than Allah's?

The *lām* attached to *'He will gather'* is the *lām* of the oath. This was revealed about those who doubt the Resurrection and Allah is swearing by Himself. Every *lām* after which there is a doubled *nūn* is reinforcement and it is the *lām* of the oath. It means that this will occur after death and from under the earth. It is called 'the Day of Rising' because people will rise to the Lord of the Worlds on it. It is also said that people will rise from their graves for it. The Almighty says: *'Do such people not realise that they will be raised up on a Terrible Day, the Day mankind will stand before the Lord of all the worlds.'* (83:4-6) It is called the Day of Rising because people will rise from the graves for it. Allah says: *'The Day they will swiftly emerge from their graves.'* (71:42) The root of *qiyāmah* has a *wāw*.

And whose speech could be truer than Allah's?

'Speech' is in the accusative case for clarification. It means 'No one is more truthful than Allah.' Ḥamzah and al-Kisā'ī recite *'azdaq'* with *zāyy* while the rest have *'aṣdaq'*.

فَمَا لَكُمْ فِى ٱلْمُنَٰفِقِينَ فِئَتَيْنِ وَٱللَّهُ أَرْكَسَهُم بِمَا كَسَبُوٓا۟ أَتُرِيدُونَ أَن
تَهْدُوا۟ مَنْ أَضَلَّ ٱللَّهُ وَمَن يُضْلِلِ ٱللَّهُ فَلَن تَجِدَ لَهُۥ سَبِيلًا ﴿٨٨﴾

88 How is it that you have become two parties regarding the hypocrites, when Allah has returned them to unbelief for what they did? When Allah misguides someone, you will find no way for him.

How is it that you have become two parties regarding the hypocrites,

This means two differing parties. Muslim reported from Zayd ibn Thābit that the Prophet ﷺ went out to Uḥud and some of the people with him returned to the city. So the Companions of the Prophet ﷺ fell into two groups about them. Some said that they should be killed and some said not. Then this was revealed. At-Tirmidhī transmitted it and added that he said ﷺ, 'It [Madīnah] is good.' And he said ﷺ, 'It will expel the foul as fire expels the dross of iron.' He said that it is a sound *ḥasan ḥadīth*. Al-Bukhārī said, 'It is good and will expel the foul as fire expels the dross of silver.'

The hypocrites referred to here were 'Abdullāh ibn Abī Ubayy and his people who failed the Messenger of Allah ﷺ at Uḥud and returned with their fighters after they had set out, as was mentioned in *Āli 'Imrān*. Ibn 'Abbās said that those referred to were some people in Makkah who believed but did not emigrate. Aḍ-Ḍaḥḥāk said, 'They said, "If Muḥammad is victorious, He will acknowledge us. If our people are victorious, we prefer that." The Muslims were in two parties: those who befriended them and those who declared themselves free of them and so Allah revealed this.'

Abū Salamah ibn 'Abd ar-Raḥmān reported from his father that it was revealed about some people who came to Madīnah and made a show of Islam. They fell ill with the fever of Madīnah and turned back and left Madīnah. Some of the Companions of the Prophet ﷺ met them and asked, 'Why did you return?' They replied, 'The fever of Madīnah struck us and we fell ill with it.' They said, 'Do you not have a model in the Messenger of Allah ﷺ?' Some said that they were hypocrites and some said that they were Muslims, not hypocrites, and Allah revealed this. They came to Madīnah, claiming to have emigrated, and then reverted and asked the Messenger of Allah ﷺ for permission to go back to Makka to collect some of their goods with which they traded. The believers disagreed about them. Some said that they were hypocrites and some said that they were believers. Allah made their hypocrisy clear and revealed this *āyah* and ordered that they be killed. These two views are mutually supported by the end of the following *āyah*, '*...until they have made hijrah...*'. The first is the soundest and it is preferred by al-Bukhārī, Muslim and at-Tirmidhī.

'Two parties' is in the accusative for the *ḥāl*. As you say, 'Is Mālik standing (*qā'iman*)?' Al-Akhfash said this. The Kufans said that it is the predicate of '*mā lakum*' like the predicate of *kāna*' and '*ẓanantu*'. The definite article can be added to it. Al-Farrā' related '*arkasahim*' and '*rakazahim*,' indicating their reversion to unbelief. An-Naḍr ibn Shumayl and al-Kisā'ī said *nakasahim*. *Naks* and *raks* is to turn something on its head or return its beginning to its end. *Markūs* means *mankūs*. We find in the reading of 'Abdullah and Ubayy '*rakasahum*'. Ibn Rawāḥah said:

They have reverted to dark sedition,
like the darkness of the night, followed by two groups.

Irtikasa means to fall back into something from which someone has been saved. The Rukūsiyyah are a sub-sect of people between the Christians and Sabaeans. *Rākis* is an ox in the place where grain is trodden on, and the oxen go around that place.

Do you desire to guide people Allah has misguided?

Do you desire to guide them to the reward by making their ruling that of being believers? If Allah misguides someone, you will find no way to guide him and produce an argument on their behalf. This refutes the Qadariyyah and others who say that their guidance is created. This was already mentioned.

وَدُّوا۟ لَوْ تَكْفُرُونَ كَمَا كَفَرُوا۟ فَتَكُونُونَ سَوَآءً فَلَا تَتَّخِذُوا۟ مِنْهُمْ أَوْلِيَآءَ حَتَّىٰ
يُهَاجِرُوا۟ فِى سَبِيلِ ٱللَّهِ فَإِن تَوَلَّوْا۟ فَخُذُوهُمْ وَٱقْتُلُوهُمْ حَيْثُ وَجَدتُّمُوهُمْ
وَلَا تَتَّخِذُوا۟ مِنْهُمْ وَلِيًّا وَلَا نَصِيرًا ﴿٨٩﴾ إِلَّا ٱلَّذِينَ يَصِلُونَ إِلَىٰ قَوْمٍۭ بَيْنَكُمْ وَبَيْنَهُم
مِّيثَٰقٌ أَوْ جَآءُوكُمْ حَصِرَتْ صُدُورُهُمْ أَن يُقَٰتِلُوكُمْ أَوْ يُقَٰتِلُوا۟ قَوْمَهُمْ
وَلَوْ شَآءَ ٱللَّهُ لَسَلَّطَهُمْ عَلَيْكُمْ فَلَقَٰتَلُوكُمْ فَإِنِ ٱعْتَزَلُوكُمْ فَلَمْ يُقَٰتِلُوكُمْ وَأَلْقَوْا۟
إِلَيْكُمُ ٱلسَّلَمَ فَمَا جَعَلَ ٱللَّهُ لَكُمْ عَلَيْهِمْ سَبِيلًا ﴿٩٠﴾

89 They would like you to disbelieve as they disbelieve so that you will all be the same. Do not take any of them as friends until they have made hijrah in the Way of Allah. But if they run away then seize them and kill them wherever you find them. Do not take any of them as either a friend or helper – 90 except for those who seek shelter with people with whom you have a treaty, or who come to you greatly perturbed at the prospect of fighting either you or their own people. If Allah had willed, He could have given them the upper hand over you and then they would have fought you. If they keep away from you and do not fight you and submit to you, Allah has not given you any way against such people.

They would like you to disbelieve as they disbelieve so that you will all be the same.

They want you to be unbelievers and hypocrites like them. Allah commanded that we be free of them.

Do not take any of them as friends until they have made hijrah in the Way of Allah.

It is as Allah says elsewhere: *'...you are not responsible for their protection until they make hijrah.'* (8:72) There are various types of *hijrah*. One was *hijrah* to Madīnah to help the Prophet ﷺ and it was mandatory at the beginning of Islam until he said, 'There is no emigration after the Conquest [of Makkah].' It was the same with the emigration of the hypocrites with the Prophet ﷺ on expeditions and the emigration of those who became Muslim in the Abode of War. It is mandatory. There is the *hijrah* (avoidance) by the Muslims from what Allah has forbidden as the Prophet ﷺ said, 'The emigrant is the one who avoids what Allah has forbidden.' These two kinds of emigration are still in force today. There is also *hijrah* from the people of disobedience until they revert, in order to discipline them. One does not speak with them nor mix with them until they repent, following the way the Prophet ﷺ acted with Ka'b and his companions [when they stayed back from the Tabuk expedition].

But if they run away then seize them and kill them wherever you find them.

'If they run away' from *tawḥīd* and emigration, *'then seize them and kill them.'* This is general to all places, and Allah knows best. Then He moves to the exception:

except for those who seek shelter with people with whom you have a treaty,

This means that they join them and enter with them into protection and alliance. It means: 'Do not kill a people with whom you have a treaty.' They keep their contracts. Then the contracts were nullified and so this was nullified. This is the position of Mujāhid, Ibn Zayd and others, and it is the soundest of what is said about the *āyah*. Abū 'Ubayd said that it means they are connected by lineage. An example of that usage is found in the words of al-A'shā:

When she connected, she said, 'Is it Bakr ibn Wā'il?'
Bakr insulted her, but noses are spited.

He means: when she gave her lineage. Al-Mahdawī said that scholars deny this because lineage does not preclude fighting and killing the unbelievers. An-Naḥḥās said, 'This is a grave error because it propounds the view that Allah would forbid fighting anyone related to the Muslims by kinship. Kinship existed between the idolaters and the first Muslims. An even greater demonstration of ignorance is to believe that it existed and was then abrogated, because the people of interpretation agree that what abrogated it was in *at-Tawbah,* which was revealed after the Conquest of Makkah and after the warring had ended.' Aṭ-Ṭabarī said something along those lines.

Some scholars believe that it refers to those who have safe conduct, not to those with kinship. So someone related to a people by safe conduct is secure since all of them are secure. There is disagreement about which of those who had a treaty with the Prophet ﷺ is meant here. It is said that it is the Banū Mudlij. Al-Ḥasan said that there was a treaty between them and Quraysh and there was a treaty between Quraysh and the Messenger of Allah ﷺ. 'Ikrimah said that it was revealed about Hilāl ibn 'Uwaymir, Surāqah ibn Ju'shum and Khuzaymah ibn 'Āmir ibn 'Abd Manāf who all had a treaty with the Messenger of Allah ﷺ. It is said that it was Khuzā'ah. Aḍ-Ḍaḥḥāk said that Ibn 'Abbās said that it means the people with whom you have a treaty: the Banū Bakr ibn Zayd ibn Manāh. They had a truce and a treaty.

This *āyah* contains evidence for the confirmation of truces between the people of war and the people of Islam if that is beneficial to the Muslims, as will be dealt with elsewhere in *al-Anfāl* and *at-Tawbah*, Allah willing,

or who come to you greatly perturbed at the prospect of fighting either you or your own people.

The adjective '*greatly perturbed*' means that their hearts are constricted. The noun *ḥaṣr* means the difficulty of a speaker to speak and *ḥaṣar* means to conceal a secret. Jarīr said:

The critics searched for my error and discovered,
Umāmah, you were stingy, concealing your secret.

In the *āyah*, it is in the past tense and the particle '*qad*' is implied, according to al-Farrā'. It is a *ḥāl* modifying something nominative implied in 'come to you,' as you say, 'So-and-so has come who has lost his mind.' Az-Zajjāj says that it means: 'They come to you,' and then he reports as an appositive to that, 'they are greatly perturbed'. It is said that it is in the genitive as an adjective of 'people'. The recension of Ubayy has: '*mīthāqun ḥaṣirat ṣudūruhum*.' It does not have 'come to you'. It is said that it implies: 'Or they come to you as men or people whose hearts are constricted.' So it is an adjective in the accusative for the *ḥāl*. Al-Ḥasan recited '*ḥaṣiratan*'. It is in the accusative for the *ḥāl*. It can also be in the nominative for the inceptive and predicate. It is related '*ḥaṣiratin ṣudūruhum*' and the nominative is permitted.

Muḥammad ibn Yazīd said that it is a supplication against them as you say, 'May Allah curse the unbeliever.' Al-Mubarrad said that. Some commentators consider this to be weak and say, 'This demands [a supplication against them] not to fight their people. This is unsound because they were unbelievers and their people were unbelievers.' The answer is that its meaning is sound and so lack of fighting in the case of the Muslims is to weaken them and in the case of their people, it is to demand them.

'Or' means 'and', meaning, 'a people who have an alliance with you and they come to you with their hearts constricted about fighting with you and so they disliked to fight either of the two parties.' It is possible that they are contracted to that and so it is a kind of contract, or they said, 'We submit and will not fight.' So it is possible that that was accepted from them at the beginning of Islam until Allah opened their hearts to *taqwā* and expanded them to Islam. The first is more evident, and Allah knows best.

If Allah had willed, He could have given them the upper hand over you

Allah could have given the idolaters power over the believers and strengthened the unbelievers, which could be either by the punishment of seeing the spread of objectionable and acts of disobedience, as Allah says: *'We will test you until We know the true fighters among you and those who are steadfast and test what is reported of you'* (47:31)', or by testing and trial in order to to purify the believers of wrong actions, as Allah says: *'so that Allah can purge those who believe.'* (3:141) Allah does whatever he wishes and gives power to whomever He wishes.

The order and connection to what came before is: 'Kill the hypocrites about whom you disagreed unless they make *hijrah*. Otherwise, they are connected with people with whom you have a treaty and so they enter into it and come under the judgment of it. Otherwise they are those who come to you with their breasts constricted about fighting you or fighting their people and so they enter among you and you do not fight them.'

سَتَجِدُونَ ءَاخَرِينَ يُرِيدُونَ أَن يَأْمَنُوكُمْ وَيَأْمَنُوا۟ قَوْمَهُمْ كُلَّ مَا
رُدُّوٓا۟ إِلَى ٱلْفِتْنَةِ أُرْكِسُوا۟ فِيهَا ۚ فَإِن لَّمْ يَعْتَزِلُوكُمْ وَيُلْقُوٓا۟ إِلَيْكُمُ ٱلسَّلَمَ
وَيَكُفُّوٓا۟ أَيْدِيَهُمْ فَخُذُوهُمْ وَٱقْتُلُوهُمْ حَيْثُ ثَقِفْتُمُوهُمْ ۚ وَأُو۟لَٰٓئِكُمْ
جَعَلْنَا لَكُمْ عَلَيْهِمْ سُلْطَٰنًا مُّبِينًا ﴿٩١﴾

91 You will find others who desire to be safe from you and safe from their own people. Each time they are returned to fitnah they are overwhelmed by it. If they do not keep away from you or submit to you or refrain from fighting, seize them and kill them wherever you find them. Over such people We have given you clear authority.

You will find others who desire to be safe from you and safe from their own people.

This is similar to the meaning of the previous *āyah*. Qatādah said, 'It was revealed about some people from Tihāmah who asked for safe-conduct from the Prophet ﷺ in order to to be safe with both him and their own people.' Mujāhid said that it was revealed about some people from Makkah. As-Suddī said that it was revealed about Nu'aym ibn Mas'ūd who asked for security from both the Muslims and the idolaters. Al-Ḥasan said that it was about some of the hypocrites. It is also said that it was revealed about the tribes of Asad and Ghaṭafān who came to Madīnah and became Muslim and then returned to their homes and reverted to disbelief.

Each time they are returned to fitnah they are overwhelmed by it.

Yaḥyā ibn Waththāb and al-A'mash recited '*riddū*' [instead of '*ruddū*') because the root is '*rudidū*' and there is assimilation and the *rā'* given a *kasrah*. *Fitnah* here means disbelief. It is said that it means: 'There will be those who offer you peace so that you grant them security. But when unbelief presents itself to them again, they are with their people in it.' '*They are overwhelmed by it*' means revert from the contract which they made. It is said: 'When they are called to *shirk*, they respond and revert to it.'

وَمَا كَانَ لِمُومِنٍ اَنْ يَّقْتُلَ مُومِنًا اِلَّا خَطَئًا وَمَن قَتَلَ مُومِنًا
خَطَئًا فَتَحْرِيرُ رَقَبَةٍ مُّومِنَةٍ وَدِيَةٌ مُّسَلَّمَةٌ اِلَىٰٓ أَهْلِهِۦٓ إِلَّآ أَن
يَصَّدَّقُوا فَإِن كَانَ مِن قَوْمٍ عَدُوٍّ لَّكُمْ وَهُوَ مُومِنٌ فَتَحْرِيرُ
رَقَبَةٍ مُّومِنَةٍ وَإِن كَانَ مِن قَوْمٍ بَيْنَكُمْ وَبَيْنَهُم مِّيثَٰقٌ
فَدِيَةٌ مُّسَلَّمَةٌ اِلَىٰٓ أَهْلِهِۦ وَتَحْرِيرُ رَقَبَةٍ مُّومِنَةٍ ۝ فَمَن لَّمْ يَجِدْ
فَصِيَامُ شَهْرَيْنِ مُتَتَابِعَيْنِ تَوْبَةً مِّنَ اللَّهِ وَكَانَ اللَّهُ عَلِيمًا
حَكِيمًا ﴿٩٢﴾

92 A believer should never kill another believer unless it is by mistake. Anyone who kills a believer by mistake should free a believing slave and pay blood-money to his family unless they forgo it as a *ṣadaqah*. If he is from a people who are your enemies and is a believer, you should free a believing slave. If he is from a people you have a treaty with, blood money should be paid to his family and you should free a believing slave. Anyone who cannot find the means should fast two consecutive months. This is a concession from Allah. Allah is All-Knowing, All-Wise.

A believer should never kill another believer unless it is by mistake.

This *āyah* is one of the matrices of judgment. It means that it is not acceptable for any believer to kill another one except by mistake. *'Mā kāna'* is not negative, but a prohibition. If it had been a negative, then there would not have been any believer who killed another believer at all because that which is denied by Allah cannot exist as in His statement: *'you could never make their trees grow.'* (27:60)

Qatādah said, 'It means that he cannot do this within the covenant of Allah.' It is said that it is about what happened in the past, as that may not be done now in any manner. Then there is a separate exception which is not connected to the first one. It is that in which '*illā*' means 'but'. The implication is: he should not kill him at all, but if he does do so by mistake, then there are consequences stemming from that. This is the position of Sībawayh and az-Zajjāj. Another example of the separate exception are Allah's words: *'They have no real knowledge of it, only conjecture.'* (4:157) [POEMS WITH EXAMPLES] There are many instances of this usage.

The *āyah* was revealed because 'Ayyāsh ibn Abī Rabī'ah killed al-Ḥārith ibn Yazīd. When al-Ḥārith emigrated as a Muslim, 'Ayyāsh met him and killed him, not aware of the fact that he had become Muslim. When he was told, he went to the Prophet ﷺ and said, 'Messenger of Allah, you know what happened to me with al-Ḥārith. I did not know he was Muslim and killed him.' The *āyah* was then revealed.

It is said that it is an exception connected to what precedes it, in other words, it is not for a believer to kill a believer nor take retaliation from him unless it is by mistake. Then there is no retaliation taken from him, but instead it is such-and-such. Another view is that it means, 'If it is decreed.' So '*kāna*' means it occurs and exists. It is as if Allah is saying, 'It does not exist, is not confirmed or allowed for a believer to kill a believer except by mistake since he is overcome at times.' So in these two interpretations, the exception is not separate.

The *āyah* points out the vileness of doing it intentionally, as when you say, 'You! It can only be that you have said this out of forgetfulness!' Intention and deliberation are greater even though the prohibition to say it is absolute.

It is said that it means 'nor by mistake.' An-Naḥḥās said, 'It is not permitted for "*illā*" to mean "and". That is not known in the Arabic language and is not sound in meaning because errors are not forbidden and it is not to be understood from these words that they constitute evidence that it is permitted for an unbeliever to kill a Muslim. The blood of a Muslim is inviolable. "Believer" rather than "Muslim" is mentioned to stress his tenderness, brotherhood, compassion and belief.'

There are many kinds of accidental killing. There are innumerable cases of a mistake to which lack of intention is connected. For instance, you might shoot at the ranks of idolaters and hit a Muslim, or someone runs in front of you who deserves to be killed, such as an adulterer, *muḥārib* or apostate, and you attempt to kill him but kill someone else thinking that it was him, killing him by mistake, or you shoot at a target and it hits someone, or similar things. There is no disagreement about this.

'Mistake' (*khaṭa'*) is a noun from *akhṭa'a, khaṭa'* and *ikhṭā'*, describing what someone does unintentionally. So *khaṭa'* is a noun that takes the place of *ikhṭā'*. It is said when you intend to do something and do something else, that is a mistake. If you do other than what you intended, it is a mistake. Al-A'mash recited '*khaṭā'in*' with *maddah* in the three places.

Ibn al-Mundhir said that these words of Allah constitute the judgment of Allah that blood-money should be paid for a believer who is killed unintentionally. The firm Sunnah is reported from the Messenger of Allah ﷺ about that and it is the consensus of the people of knowledge.

Dāwūd believed that there is retaliation between free people and slaves for a life and for all injuries for which retaliation is possible, holding to the words of Allah: '*We have prescribed for them in it: a life for a life…*' (5:45) and the words of the Prophet ﷺ, 'The blood of the Muslims is the same without any difference between free people and slaves.' That is the position of Ibn Abī Laylā. Abū Ḥanīfah and his people said that there is no retaliation between free people and slaves except for a life, but not where injuries are concerned. Scholars agree that this *āyah* does not include slaves, but means free people as the Prophet ﷺ said, 'The blood of the Muslims is the same,' meaning free Muslims. That is the majority position. Since there is no retaliation between slaves and free people in respect of what is less than life, it is more fitting that that also applies to a life. This was discussed in *al-Baqarah*.

should free a believing slave

This is the expiation which Allah obliges for killing and *ẓihār*. Scholars disagree about what redeems it. Ibn 'Abbās, al-Ḥasan, ash-Shāfi'ī, an-Nakha'ī, Qatādah and others said that it must be a slave who prays and understands faith. A child is not sufficient to redeem it, which is the sound view, although 'Aṭā' ibn Abī Rabāḥ says that a child born among the Muslims does redeem it. A group, including Mālik and ash-Shāfi'ī, said that it is redeemed by anyone over whom the prayer is said when they die and who are buried as Muslims. Mālik said, 'I prefer someone who prays and fasts.'

According to most scholars, someone blind, disabled, who has his hands or feet amputated or palsied does not redeem it. Most allow someone lame or one-eyed. Mālik said, 'If he is not very lame.' According to Mālik, ash-Shāfiʿī, and most scholars, someone with an amputated hand or foot does not redeem it, but they do according to Abū Ḥanīfah and his people. According to most of them, someone insane does not redeem it and, according to Mālik, someone suffering from intermittent jinn possession does not either. According to ash-Shāfiʿī, they do. According to Mālik the conditions of it are not met unless the person freed has reached the age of two, but ash-Shāfiʿī allows that. According to Mālik, al-Awzāʿī and the People of Opinion, a *mudabbar* does not satisfy it, but they do according to ash-Shāfiʿī and Abū Thawr. Ibn al-Mundhir preferred it. Mālik said that it is not valid to free part of a person since Allah uses the term '*raqabah*'. If someone frees part of someone, he is not said to have freed a '*raqabah*', but only part of him.

They also disagree about what the purpose of this is. It is said that it is for the rectification and purification of the wrong action of the killer. His wrong action was not having due care and attention so that a person whose blood was protected died at his hands. It is said that it is about providing a replacement for voiding Allah's due in the life of the person killed. He had a right to enjoy life and this is disposing of what it was lawful for him to dispose of while alive. Allah also has a right that He is owed, which is that the deceased was one of His slaves, young or old, free or slave, Muslim or *dhimmī*, that distinguished him from beasts and animals. In addition, it was hoped that he would have offspring who would worship and obey Allah. So his killer must repay the name mentioned and the meaning described. That is why he is obliged to pay this *kaffārah*. Whichever of these ideas exist, it is clear that it applies to any person who kills another by mistake. The one who kills deliberately is like him, but even more obliged to expiate for his action. Allah knows best.

and pay blood-money to his family

This is the payment to the victim's relative which is in compensation for his blood. 'Pay': *musallamah* is paid and settled. In His Book, Allah does not specify what should be paid as blood money. It is a general command and does not make responsibility for its payment fall on either the paternal relatives (*ʿāqilah*) or on the killer. That is derived from the *Sunnah*. There is no doubt that support is made mandatory on the paternal relatives, which is not analogous to basic principles in respect of fines and responsibility. What is obliged on paternal relatives does not oblige increased harshness or add to the burden of the killer. It is pure assistance.

Abū Ḥanīfah believed that in respect of support, it is mandatory on the people of the *dīwān* register to help.

Reports are confirmed from the Messenger of Allah ﷺ that blood money is a hundred camels and the Prophet ﷺ paid them to Ḥuwayyiṣah, Muḥayyiṣah and 'Abd ar-Raḥmān for 'Abdullāh ibn Sahl who was killed at Khaybar. The people of knowledge agree that it is a hundred camels for the people of camels. They disagree about what it is for other people. One group say that it is a 1000 dinars in gold for people who use gold like the people of Syria, Egypt and the Maghrib. This is the position of Mālik, Aḥmad, Isḥāq, the People of Opinion, and one of the positions of ash-Shāfi'ī in the Old School. It is also related from 'Umar, 'Urwah ibn az-Zubayr and Qatādah. For the people of silver, who are the people of Iraq, Persia and Khorasan, it is 12,000 dirhams. Al-Muzanī said, 'Ash-Shāfi'ī said that blood money should be paid in camels. If that is impossible, then it is their value in dirhams and dinars according to the estimation of 'Umar: 1000 dinars for the people of gold and 12,000 dirhams for the people of silver.'

Abū Ḥanīfah and his people and ath-Thawrī said that the blood money in silver is 12,000 dirhams. Ash-Sha'bī related from 'Ubaydah that 'Umar made the blood money of the people of gold 1000 dinars, the people of silver 12,000 dirhams, the people of cattle 200 cows, the people of sheep a hundred sheep, the people of camels a hundred camels, and the people of robes 200 robes. Abū 'Umar said, 'This *ḥadīth* indicates that dinars and dirhams are one of the forms that blood money can take, and that is not based on substitution or value. It is the literal meaning of the *ḥadīth* reported from 'Uthmān, 'Alī and Ibn 'Abbās.'

Abū Ḥanīfah disagreed with what is related from 'Umar about cattle, sheep and robes. It was stated by 'Aṭā', Ṭāwūs and a group of the Tābi'ūn. It is the position of the seven *fuqahā'* of Madīnah. Ibn al-Mundhir said that a group said that the blood money for a free Muslim is a hundred camels and that that is the only blood money stipulated by the Messenger of Allah ﷺ. This is the position of ash-Shāfi'ī and it was stated by Ṭāwūs. Ibn al-Mundhir said, 'The blood money for a free Muslim is a hundred camels at every time as the Messenger of Allah ﷺ stipulated.' Transmissions from 'Umar vary about the number of dirhams and none of them reach the level of being considered sound because they are *mursal*. I have informed you of the school of ash-Shāfi'ī and he and I take that position.

Fuqahā' disagree about the age of the camels with which blood money may be paid. Abū Dāwūd related from 'Amr ibn Shu'ayb from his father from his grandfather that the Messenger of Allah ﷺ judged that the blood money for accidental killing was a hundred camels which should consist of thirty two-year-old she camels (*bint makhāḍ*), thirty three-year-old she-camels (*bint labūn*), thirty four-year-old she-camels (*ḥiqqah*), and ten male three-year-old camels (*ibn labūn*).

Al-Khaṭṭābī said, 'I do not know of any of the *fuqahā'* who take this *ḥadīth*. Most scholars believe that the blood money for accidental killing consists of five [categories].' That is what the People of Opinion and ath-Thawrī say. That is also what Mālik, Ibn Sīrīn and Aḥmad ibn Ḥanbal say, although they disagree about the categories. The People of Opinion and Aḥmad ibn Ḥanbal said that a fifth are two-year-old male camels (*ibn makhāḍ*), a fifth are two-year-old she camels, a fifth are three-year-old she-camels, a fifth are four-year-old she-camels, and a fifth are five-year-old she-camels (*jadha'ah*). This position is related from Ibn Mas'ūd. Mālik and ash-Shāfi'ī said that a fifth are four-year-old she-camels, a fifth are five-year-old she-camels, a fifth are three-year-old she-camels, a fifth are two-year-old she camels, and a fifth are three-year-old male camels. This position is related from 'Umar ibn 'Abd al-'Azīz, Sulayman ibn Yasār, az-Zuhrī, Rabī'ah, and al-Layth ibn Sa'd.

Al-Khaṭṭābī said, 'The People of Opinion have a tradition about it, although it is transmitted by 'Abdullāh from Khishf ibn Mālik, who is unknown and is only known by this *ḥadīth*.' Ash-Shāfi'ī turned from this position because of what we mentioned regarding the defect in its transmitter, and because it contains male three-year-old camels when male three-year-old camels have no place in the ages of *zakāt* camels. In the story of the *qasāmah*, it is related that blood money was paid for the one killed at Khaybar which consisted of a hundred of the *zakāt* camels, and a male three-year-old camel was not one of the ages for *zakāt* camels.

Abū 'Umar said, 'Zayd ibn Jubayr related from Khishf ibn Mālik from 'Abdullāh ibn Mas'ūd that the Messenger of Allah ﷺ divided the blood money for accidental killing into five parts. This is only *marfū'* through Khishf ibn Mālik al-Kūfī aṭ-Ṭā'ī who is unknown because he is only related from by Zayd ibn Jubayr ibn Ḥarmal aṭ-Ṭā'ī of the Banū Jusham ibn Mu'āwiyah, one of the reliable men among the Kufans. In the *Sunan*, ad-Dāraquṭnī mentioned the *ḥadīth* of Khishf ibn Mālik from Ḥajjāj ibn Arṭāh from Zayd ibn Jubayr from Khishf ibn Mālik from 'Abdullāh ibn Mas'ūd who said, 'The Messenger of Allah ﷺ judged that the blood money for accidental killing was a hundred camels: twenty four-year-old she-camels, twenty five-year-old she-camels, twenty three-year-old she-camels, twenty two-year-old she camels, and twenty male two-year-old camels.'

Ad-Dāraquṭnī said that it is a weak *ḥadīth*, and not established among those with knowledge of *ḥadīth* for several reasons. One is that it differs from what Abū 'Ubaydah related from 'Abdullāh ibn Mas'ūd from his father with a sound *isnād* which is not criticised and cannot be interpreted. Abū 'Ubaydah had better knowledge of his father's *ḥadīth*, his position and his fatwa than Khishf ibn Mālik and his like. 'Abdullāh ibn Mas'ūd was too godfearing and zealous of his *dīn* to relate that the Messenger of Allah ﷺ gave a judgment and then give a fatwa different to it. Such a thing cannot be conceived of in the case of 'Abdullāh ibn Mas'ūd. When he was speaking of an issue brought to him, about which he had not heard anything from the Messenger of Allah ﷺ and about which he had not heard a position, he would say, 'I will speak of it by my opinion and if it is correct, it is from Allah and His Messenger. If it is an error, it is from me.' When he had given a fatwa and later found that it coincided with the judgment of the Messenger of Allah ﷺ about something similar, he was very happy, and no one had seen him happier, because of his fatwa agreeing with the judgment of the Messenger of Allah ﷺ. How could someone who is like this relate something from the Messenger of Allah ﷺ and then oppose it?

Another reason is that we only know the *marfū'* report which mentions male two-year-old camels from Khishf ibn Mālik from 'Abdullāh ibn Mas'ūd, an unknown man who is only related from by Zayd ibn Jubayr ibn Ḥarmal al-Jushamī. The people who have knowledge of *ḥadīth* do not take as authoritative a single report transmitted by an unknown man. They believe that knowledge is established by a report which is transmitted by someone well-known and reputable, or a man who becomes no longer unknown. He becomes no longer unknown when two men or more relate from him. If that happens, then the term unknown is removed from him and he becomes known. As for that which is only related by a single man who alone has the report, one must stop and hesitate about that report of his until something else corroborates it. Allah knows best.

Another reason is that we do not know of anyone who related the *ḥadīth* of Khishf ibn Mālik from Zayd ibn Jubayr except al-Ḥajjāj ibn Arṭāh, who is a man known for *tadlīs* (forgery) and who related from those he had not met or listened to. Transmission from him was abandoned by Sufyān ibn 'Uyaynah, Yaḥyā ibn Sa'īd al-Qaṭṭān and 'Īsā ibn Yūnus after they had sat with him and reported from him. They are enough for knowledge of a man. Yaḥyā ibn Ma'īn said that the hadiths of al-Ḥajjāj ibn Arṭāh are not authoritative. 'Abdullāh ibn Idrīs said, 'I heard al-Ḥajjāj say that a man is not attacked until he abandons the group prayer.' 'Īsā ibn Yūnus said, 'I heard al-Ḥajjāj say, "I went out to the prayer jostled by porters and vegetable sellers."' Jarīr said, 'I heard al-Ḥajjāj say, "Love of wealth and reputation has destroyed me."'

Other points are mentioned. One of them is the fact that a group of trustworthy men related this *ḥadīth* from al-Ḥajjāj ibn Arṭāh and they disagreed about him regarding it. There are too many points to mention. What we have mentioned is enough evidence of the weakness of what the Kufans believe about blood money even though Ibn al-Mundhir, in spite of his great esteem, preferred it as will be dealt with.

Ḥammād ibn Salamah related from Sulaymān at-Taymī from Abū Mijlaz from Abū 'Ubaydah that Ibn Masūd said, 'The blood money for accidental homicide is divided into five parts: twenty four-year-old she-camels, twenty five-year-old she-camels, twenty two-year-old she-camels, twenty three-year old she-camels, and twenty three-year-old male camels.' Ad-Dāraquṭnī said, 'This is a good *isnād* and its transmitters are trustworthy. The same is related from 'Alqamah from 'Abdullāh.' This is the school of Mālik and ash-Shāfi'ī: that blood money is divided into five categories.

Al-Khaṭṭābī said, 'It is related that a group of scholars said that blood money for accidental homicide is divided into four categories. They are ash-Sha'bī, an-Nakha'ī, and al-Ḥasan al-Baṣrī. That was also the position of Isḥāq ibn Rāhawayh. They said: twenty-five five-year-old she-camels, twenty-five four-year-old she-camels, twenty-five three-year old she-camels, and twenty-five two-year-old she-camels.' That is related from 'Alī ibn Abī Ṭālib.

Abū 'Umar said, 'The position of Mālik and ash-Shāfi'ī is related from Sulaymān ibn Yasār. There is nothing about it from a Companion, but it was the practice of the people of Madīnah.' That is what Ibn Jurayj related from Ibn Shihāb. What we mentioned from Ibn Mas'ūd agrees with the position of Mālik and ash-Shāfi'ī.

Abū 'Umar said, 'The ages of the camels in respect of blood money is not based on analogy or reflection. It is taken by following and speculation. In the case of what is taken from a tradition, there is no place for speculation. All espouse what is believed to be sound from the early generations, may Allah be pleased with all of them.'

As for what al-Khaṭṭābī related about not knowing who took the *ḥadīth* of 'Amr ibn Shu'ayb, Ibn al-Mundhir related it from Ṭāwūs and Mujāhid, although Mujāhid put thirty five-year-old she-camels in place of the two-year-old she-camels. Ibn al-Mundhir said, 'I take the first view.' He meant the position of 'Abdullāh and the People of Opinion, which ad-Dāraquṭnī and al-Khaṭṭābī considered to be weak. Ibn 'Abd al-Barr said, 'Because it is the minimum of what is said, and we related a *marfū'* *ḥadīth* from the Prophet ﷺ which agrees with this view. It is extraordinary that in spite of his critical faculty and efforts, Ibn al-Mundhir took a *ḥadīth* that the people of criticism do not agree is sound! But confusion and forgetfulness can affect a person. Perfection belongs to the Master of Majesty alone.'

Traditions from the Prophet ﷺ confirm that the blood money for accidental homicide is paid by the paternal relatives, and the people of knowledge agree on that. The consensus of the people of knowledge that blood money for accidental homicide is paid by the paternal relatives is evidence that what is meant by the words of the Prophet ﷺ to Abū Rimthah when he and his son visited him, 'He should not inflict something on you nor you on him' is about intentional rather than accidental homicide. They agree that any amount owed, which is more than a third of the blood money, should be paid by the paternal relatives, but they disagree about when the amount owed is a third or less. The position of most scholars is that the paternal relatives are not liable for an intentional killing, nor when there is a confession, nor when there is an agreement with the plaintiff. They are only liable for what is more than a third in the case of the blood money for accidental homicide. What is less than a third comes from the property of the perpetrator. One group said that blood money for accidental homicide is paid by the paternal relatives of the perpetrator, whether great or small, because the liability of the maximum is the liability of the minimum, and the blood money for intentional killing comes from the property of the perpetrator, great or small. This is the position of ash-Shāfi'ī.

The ruling is that paternal relatives pay the blood money in instalments. The paternal relatives (*'āqilah*) are the *'aṣabah* (paternal relations) and do not include a woman's child nor the brothers of the mothers. Similarly, the *Dīwān* are not paternal relatives according to the position of most of the people of the Hijaz. The Kufans say that the paternal relatives are part of the people of the *D*īwān. The paternal relatives pay the blood money in instalments over three years according to the ruling of 'Umar and 'Alī because the camels may be pregnant and that might harm them. The Prophet ﷺ used to pay it all at once to achieve certain things. One of them was to give it in order to achieve reconciliation and defrayment. Another was to quickly bring back harmony. Once Islam had prepared the ground, the Companions enabled it to be paid in this manner. Ibn al-'Arabī said that. Abū 'Umar said, 'Scholars, both old and modern, agree that blood money paid by the paternal relatives is paid over three years and not less than that. They agree that it is owed by adult males.

The historians and scholars agree that in Jāhiliyyah times, blood money was paid by paternal relatives and the Messenger of Allah ﷺ confirmed that practice in Islam, and they used to seek help in paying it. So when Islam came that continued in the same manner until the *Dīwān* was established. The *fuqahā'* concur on the transmission of that and take that position. They agree that there was no *Dīwān* in the time of the Messenger of Allah ﷺ or the time of Abū Bakr and that it was established by 'Umar and brought people together. He assigned authority to the people of every region and assigned them the duty of fighting the enemy near them.

Another area included in this is the killing of unborn foetuses. That can happen when someone strikes the mother's belly and she miscarries and the child dies. All scholars said that full blood money is owed whether it was by accident or deliberate after *qasāmah* (and it is also said without *qasāmah*). They disagree about what indicates that a child is born alive. There is agreement that when it cries, suckles or takes a definite breath, it is alive and full blood money is owed. Abū Ḥanīfah and ash-Shāfi'ī said that a movement indicates life. Mālik said that it does not unless that movement continues for a long period. Male and female are the same in this respect. If the foetus is born dead, the person who caused the injury owes a high-value slave or slave-girl. If the woman does not miscarry but the child dies in the womb without emerging, no blood money is owed. There is an undisputed consensus on all this.

Al-Layth ibn Sa'd and Dāwūd said that if the woman dies from the blow to her abdomen and then a foetus emerges dead after her death, a high-value slave is owed for it. It is the same whether she delivers it before or after her death. Aṭ-Ṭaḥāwī took the argument of the majority of *fuqahā'* and said, 'They agreed, al-Layth included, that if a blow is dealt to her abdomen while she is alive and she dies while a foetus is inside of her without miscarrying, nothing is owed for it, and the same is true if it miscarries after her death.' A high-value slave (*ghurrah*) can only be white. Abū 'Amr ibn al-'Alā' said about the words of the Prophet ﷺ, 'An expensive slave or slave-girl is owed for a foetus', 'If it had not been that *ghurrah* has a meaning he would only have said, 'slave or slave-girl', but he meant white slaves. Only a white slave or slave-girl is accepted as blood money. A black slave or slave-girl is not accepted.'

Scholars disagree about the value. Mālik said that the value should be fifty dinars or 600 dirhams, a twentieth of the blood money of a free Muslim and a tenth of the blood money of his free mother. This is the position of Ibn Shihāb, Rabī'ah and all the people of Madīnah. The People of Opinion say that the value is 500 dirhams. Ash-Shāfi'ī said, 'The age of a *ghurrah* is seven or eight years old. It does not have to be accepted if the slave has a defect.' The school of Mālik insists that there is a choice between giving a *ghurrah* or a tenth of the blood money of the mother: twenty dinars in gold if they are people who use gold or 600 dirhams if they are people who use silver, or five camels of zakatable age.

Mālik and his people say that it should come from the property of the perpetrator. That is the position of al-Ḥasan ibn Ḥayy. Abū Ḥanīfah, ash-Shāfi'ī and his people said that the paternal relatives should pay it. That is sounder based on the *ḥadīth* of al-Mughīrah ibn Shu'bah that two women were married to two Anṣārī men. One variant says that they haggled with one another and one of them struck the other with a post and killed her. The two men took the case to the Prophet ﷺ and said, 'Should we pay blood money for what has not eaten, drunk or cried? Is something like this eyed?' He remarked, 'Rhymed prose like that of the Arabs!' He judged that a *ghurrah* should be paid for it and gave it to the paternal relatives of the woman. It is a sound confirmed *ḥadīth*. It is a text about a matter of disagreement regarding which there must be a ruling. When the paternal kin must pay the blood money for woman who was struck, then that also applies to the foetus by analogy and reflection.

Our scholars argue by the words of the one against whom the ruling was given, 'How should I pay?' They said, 'This indicates that one against whom the ruling was made was specified: it is the perpetrator. If the blood money for the foetus had been against the paternal relatives, he would have used the plural rather than the singular pronoun.'

By analogy, the crime of every perpetrator is held against the perpetrator unless there is an unopposed proof which establishes something different, such as consensus which cannot be opposed or a text in the Sunnah transmitted by single reputable transmitters which cannot be opposed. Then ruling must be made accordingly. Allah says: *'What each self earns is for itself alone. No burden-bearer can bear another's burden.'* (6:164)

There is no disagreement between scholars that when a foetus emerges alive, there is expiation (*kaffārah*) for it as well as blood money. They disagree about expiation when it emerges dead. Mālik said, 'There is both a *ghurrah* and expiation for it.' Abū Ḥanīfah and ash-Shāfi'ī said that there is a *ghurrah* but not expiation for it.

They disagree about the inheritance of a foetus. Mālik and ash-Shāfi'ī and their people said, 'There is a *ghurrah* for a foetus and there is inheritance from a foetus according to the Book of Allah because it is blood money. Abū Ḥanīfah and his people said that there is a *ghurrah* only for the mother because it is an injury to her by removing part of her and it is not blood money.' Part of the evidence for that is that it is not considered male or female as is necessary where blood money is concerned. So it indicates that it is like a limb. Ibn Hurmuz said, 'Its blood money goes to its parents: the father receives two-thirds and the mother a third since it had life from both of them. If one of them has died, then all of it goes to the remaining parent, father or mother, and the brothers do not inherit anything.'

unless they forgo it as a *ṣadaqah*.

Its basis is '*yataṣaddaqū*' and the *tā'* is elided into the *ṣād*. *Taṣaddaq* is giving. It means: unless the relatives who are the heirs of the victim absolve the killers from paying the mandatory blood money. It is an exception from the first. Abū 'Abd ar-Raḥmān and Nubayḥ recited '*taṣaddaqū*' as did Abū 'Amr although he has a double *ṣād*. According to this reading, it is permitted to elide the second *tā'*. If it is read in the third person with *yā'*, then it is not permitted to elide it. The mode (*ḥarf*) of Ubayy and Ibn Mas'ūd is '*yataṣaddaqū*'.

As for the expiation, which is due to Allah Almighty, it is not cancelled by their forgoing it because the perpetrator has killed a person who worshipped Allah and so he must deliver another to worship Allah. The blood money which was their right is cancelled and the expiation is obliged from the wealth of the perpetrator and is not set aside.

If he is from a people who are your enemies and is a believer,

This is when a believer is killed in the land of the unbelievers or in their wars, thinking that he is one of the unbelievers. This is the meaning according to Ibn 'Abbās, Qatādah, as-Suddī, 'Ikrimah, Mujāhid and an-Nakha'ī: if this victim is a believer who remained among his people who are unbelievers, '*your enemies*', no blood money is owed for him. The expiation is to free a slave. That is the well-known position according to Mālik, and Abū Ḥanīfah also said that.

The blood money is cancelled for two reasons: one is that the relatives of the victim are unbelievers and it is not valid to give it to them to strengthen them, and the second is that there is less inviolability for this person who believed but did not emigrate, as Allah says: '*But as for those who believe but have not emigrated, you are not in any way responsible for their protection until they emigrate.*' (8:72)

One group said that the reason for cancelling blood money is that the relatives are unbelievers. So it is the same whether or not he is killed among the Muslims or among his people, or did not emigrate, or emigrated and then returned to his people: the expiation for his death is freeing a slave and not blood money, since it is not valid to give it to the unbelievers. If blood money were mandatory, then it would be mandatory for the treasury to pay it to the treasury. So blood money is not mandatory in this situation, even if it occurs in the territory of Islam. This is the position of ash-Shāfi'ī and it is the position taken by al-Awzā'ī, ath-Thawrī and Abū Thawr. According to the first view, if a believer is killed in the land of the Muslims while his people are at war, then blood money is paid to the treasury and expiation is also necessary.

Concerning this topic we find in *Ṣaḥīḥ Muslim* that Usāmah said: 'The Messenger of Allah ﷺ sent us on an expedition and in the morning we arrived at al-Ḥuraqāt in the tribe of Juhaynah. I caught up to a man and he said, "There is no god but Allah." I stabbed him and felt uneasy about that. I mentioned it to the Messenger of Allah ﷺ and he said, "He said, 'There is no god but Allah" and then you killed him!'" I answered, "Messenger of Allah, he only said it out of fear of the weapons!" He demanded, "Did you split open his heart so as to know whether he said it truly or not?"' He ﷺ did not order retaliation or blood money. It is related from Usāmah that the Messenger of Allah ﷺ asked forgiveness for him three times and told him to free a slave. He did not order retaliation or blood money for him.

Our scholars say that the cancellation of retaliation is clear because it was not done out of simple aggression. There are three reasons for the cancellation of blood money. The first is because he had permission to fight and so the taking of a life which is forbidden is a mistake. The second is that the man was one of the enemy and not one of the friends of the Muslims which would entitle him to blood money. The third is that Usāmah admitted the killing and there was no evidence and no relatives of the deceased. It may have been that Usāmah had no wealth with which to pay blood money. Allah knows best.

If he is from a people you have a treaty with,

This is about *dhimmīs* and someone, with whom there is a treaty, who is killed accidentally. Blood money and expiation are obliged. Ibn 'Abbās, ash-Shāfi'ī, an-Nakha'ī, and ash-Shāfi'ī said that. Aṭ-Ṭabarī chose it. He said, 'Allah left it undefined, and did not say "believer", as he said about a believer being killed, and from the people of war. When something undefined is preceded by something defined it indicates that it is different.' Al-Ḥasan, Jābir and Ibrāhīm also said that the meaning is: 'If the victim is a believer from a people with a treaty, their treaty obliges that they are entitled to his blood money and so the expiation for his accidental killing is freeing a slave and paying blood money.' Al-Hasan recited it and said, 'If he is from a people with whom you have a treaty and is a believer.'

Al-Hasan said that if a Muslim kills a *dhimmī*, there is no expiation. Abū 'Umar said, 'According to the people of the Hijaz, the meaning of the *āyah* refers to Allah's words: *'A believer should never kill another believer unless it is by mistake.'* Then He says: *'If he is from a people,'* referring to that believer. Allah knows best. Ibn al-'Arabī said, 'What I believe is that the sentence bases the undefined on the defined.' This is the idea of what al-Ḥasan said and Abū 'Umar related from the people of the Hijaz.

The phrase *'blood money should be paid'* is in the indefinite and does not demand blood money specifically. It is said that this is about the idolaters of the Arabs who had a treaty for a certain period with the Prophet ﷺ that they would become Muslim or war would be announced. There was blood money and expiation owed for any of them who were killed. Then it was abrogated by: *'An announcement to those idolaters you have a treaty with'* (9:1).

Scholars agree that the blood money of a woman is half that of a man. Abū 'Umar said that her blood money is half because her inheritance is half that of a man and her testimony is half that of a man. This is for accidental killing. If it is murder, there is retaliation between men and women as Allah has said: *'A life for a life'* (5:45) as was mentioned in *al-Baqarah.*

Ad-Dāraquṭnī related from Mūsā ibn 'Alī ibn Rabāḥ al-Lakhmī that he heard that a blind man used to recite verses in the 'Īd festival in the caliphate of 'Umar ibn al-Khaṭṭāb, saying:

People! I have encountered something objectionable!
Should a blind man pay blood money to a sound sighted man?
They both fall together and both of them are broken!

That was when a blind man was led by a sighted man and they fell into a well. The blind man fell on the sighted man who died. 'Umar judged that the blind man owed blood money for the sighted man. Scholars disagree about when a man falls on another and one of them dies. It is related from Ibn az-Zubayr that the upper person is liable for the lower, but not the lower for the higher. This is the position of Shurayḥ, an-Nakha'ī, Aḥmad, and Isḥāq. Mālik said that when a man pulls another man so that they both fall and die, that blood money is owed by the paternal kin of the one who pulled. Abū 'Umar said, 'I think that there is disagreement about this, and Allah knows best. Some of the later scholars among our people and the people of ash-Shāfi'ī make him liable for half the blood money because the one who did it died from the one who fell on him.' Al-Ḥakam and Ibn Shubrumah said, 'If one man falls on another man from the top of a house and one of them dies, the one who survived is liable.'

Ash-Shāfi'ī said that when one man collides with another and they both die, the blood money of the one who was run into is owed by the paternal relatives of the one who collided with him, and there is no blood money for the one who collided. He said about when two horsemen collide and both die that each of them owes half of the blood money of the other because each of them died on account of his own action and the action of his fellow. 'Uthmān al-Battī and Zafar said that. Mālik, al-Awzā'ī, al-Ḥasan ibn Ḥayy, and Abū Ḥanīfah and his people said that when two horsemen collide and they both die, the paternal kin of each of them owes the blood money of the other. Ibn Khuwayzimandād said, 'That is also the case with two ships that collide when the skipper did not divert the ship nor the horseman the horse.' It is related from Mālik about two ships and two horsemen that each of them is liable for the full value of what he destroyed.

Scholars disagree about the details of the blood money of the People of the Book. Mālik and his people say that it is half that of a Muslim. The blood money of a Magian is 800 dirhams and that of their women is half of that. This position is related from 'Umar ibn 'Abd al-'Azīz, 'Urwah ibn az-Zubayr and 'Amr ibn Shu'ayb. That is also what Aḥmad ibn Ḥanbal said. It was related by Sulaymān ibn Bilāl from 'Abd ar-Raḥmān ibn al-Ḥārith ibn 'Ayyāsh ibn Abī Rabī'ah from 'Amr ibn Shu'ayb from his father from his grandfather that the Prophet ﷺ made the blood money of a Jew or Christian half of that of a Muslim. Ath-Thawrī also related from this 'Abd ar-Raḥmān.

Ibn 'Abbās, ash-Sha'bī and an-Nakha'ī said that if someone from a people there is treaty with is killed by mistake, it is of no concern whether they are a Muslim or unbeliever. Their blood money is the same as that of a Muslim. That is the position of Abū Ḥanīfah, ath-Thawrī, 'Uthmān al-Battī and al-Ḥasan ibn Ḥayy. They made all blood money the same, be it a Muslim, Jew, Christian, Magian, someone with a treaty or *dhimmī*. That is also the position of 'Aṭā', az-Zuhrī and Sa'īd ibn al-Musayyab. Their argument is Allah's word, '*fidyah*'. That demands that their blood money is equal to that of a Muslim. In that they relied on what Muḥammad ibn Isḥāq took from Dāwūd ibn al-Ḥuṣayn from 'Ikrimah from Ibn 'Abbās in the story of the Banū Qurayẓah and an-Naḍīr, in which the Messenger of Allah ﷺ made their blood money the full blood money. Abū 'Umar said, 'This is a *ḥadīth* with some softness. Something like it is not authoritative.'

Ash-Shāfi'ī said that the blood money of a Jew or Christian is a third of that of a Muslim and that of a Magian is 800 dirhams. His argument is that that is the minimum of what is said about that. The *dhimmi* is innocent except where there is certainty or proof. This position is related from 'Umar and 'Uthmān. That was stated by Ibn al-Musayyab, 'Aṭā', al-Ḥasan, 'Ikrimah, 'Amr ibn Dīnār, Abū Thawr and Isḥāq.

Anyone who cannot find the means should fast two consecutive months.

The means referred to is either a slave or enough money to buy one. The person must fast two consecutive months. If he breaks it, he has to start again. This is the position of the majority. Makkī said that ash-Sha'bī said, 'Fasting two months satisfies the requirement of blood money and freeing a slave if someone cannot find it.' Ibn 'Aṭiyyah said, 'This statement is weak because blood money is owed by the paternal kin, not the killer.' Aṭ-Ṭabarī related this position from Masrūq.

There is no disagreement that menstruation does not constitute breaking the expiation fast. The woman just purifies herself and begins fasting again immediately without delay and continues the fast based on what she has already done. She does not owe anything other than that unless she becomes pure before dawn and fails to fast that day, knowing that she is pure. If she does that, then most scholars say that she must start anew. Abū 'Umar said that.

There is disagreement about a sick person who has fasted part of the two consecutive months. There are two views. Mālik said that no one who has to fast two consecutive months by the Book of Allah should break it except for an excuse: either menstruation or illness. They should not break it because of travelling. Those who said that a sick person continues where he stopped were Sa'īd ibn al-Musayyab, Sulaymān ibn Yasār, al-Ḥasan, ash-Sha'bī, 'Aṭā', Mujāhid, Qatādah and Ṭāwūs. Sa'īd ibn Jubayr, an-Nakha'ī, al-Ḥakam ibn 'Uyaynah, and 'Aṭā' al-Khurāsānī said a sick person must start anew, and that is what Abū Ḥanīfah and his people and al-Ḥasan ibn Ḥayy said, and is one of the positions of ash-Shāfi'ī. His other position is like that of Mālik who says that he should continue from where he stopped. Ibn Shubrumah said, 'He makes up that day alone if he has an overwhelming excuse like the fast of Ramadan.'

Abū 'Umar said, 'The evidence of those who say that a sick person should build on what he has done is because, in illness, he has an excuse for breaking the consecutiveness which was not deliberate. Allah pardons that which is not deliberate. The evidence for those who say that he must start anew is that consecutiveness is an obligation and is not cancelled except for a valid excuse. The sin is cancelled based on analogy with the prayer because it consists of consecutive *rak'ahs* and when someone breaks them with an excuse, they start anew and do not build on what they have done.

This is a concession from Allah.

It is in the accusative for the verbal noun. *Tawbah* here means return. It touches on the need of someone who errs for repentance because he was not careful as he should have been. It is said that it means: 'He should fast as a dispensation from Allah by accepting fasting instead of freeing a slave. That comes from His words: *'Allah knows that you have been betraying yourselves and He has turned towards you'* (2:187) by lightening, *and 'He knows that you will not keep count of it, so He has turned towards you.'* (73:20)

Allah is All-Knowing, All-Wise.

Allah, before and after time, knows all known things and is Wise in what He judges and carries out.

وَمَن يَقْتُلْ مُؤْمِنًا مُّتَعَمِّدًا فَجَزَآؤُهُۥ جَهَنَّمُ خَـٰلِدًا فِيهَا وَغَضِبَ
ٱللَّهُ عَلَيْهِ وَلَعَنَهُۥ وَأَعَدَّ لَهُۥ عَذَابًا عَظِيمًا ﴿٩٣﴾

93 As for anyone who kills a believer deliberately, his repayment is Hell, remaining in it timelessly, for ever. Allah is angry with him and has cursed him, and has prepared for him a terrible punishment. As for anyone who kills a believer deliberately, his repayment is Hell.

Scholars disagree about what constitutes deliberate killing. 'Aṭā', an-Nakha'ī and others said that it is when the one who kills does so with metal such as a sword, dagger, spear and the like which is sharpened for cutting or with something that he knows will entail death in the form of heavy stones and the like. One group said that it is anyone who kills with metal, stones or the like of that. That is the position of the majority.

In His Book, Allah mentions the deliberate and the mistake, but not the semi-deliberate. Scholars disagree about what is said about that. Ibn al-Mundhir said that Mālik did not recognise it, saying that the Book of Allah only talks of the deliberate and the mistake. Al-Khaṭṭābī also mentioned that from Mālik and added, 'We do not recognise the semi-deliberate.' Abū 'Umar also adds that Mālik and al-Layth ibn Sa'd did not recognise the semi-deliberate. In their view, if anyone is killed by what does not normally kill, such as a bite, slap, whip, stick and the like, that is considered deliberate and there is retaliation. Abū 'Umar said, 'That is the position of a group of Companions and Followers.' The majority of the *fuqahā'* believe that this is all semi-deliberate. It is mentioned from Mālik and Ibn Wahb and a group of Companions and Followers said that.

Ibn al-Mundhir said, 'The semi-deliberate is acted on in our view.' Those who affirmed the semi-deliberate include ash-Sha'bī, al-Ḥakam, Ḥammād, an-Nakha'ī, Qatādah, Sufyān ath-Thawrī, the people of Iraq, and ash-Shāfi'ī. We related that from 'Umar ibn al-Khaṭṭāb and 'Alī ibn Abī Ṭālib. This is sound. It is more correct to preserve life since the basic position is that it should be protected. It is not made lawful except by a clear matter regarding which there is no confusion. There is confusion here because it is somewhere in between being deliberate and a mistake and has the judgment of being semi-deliberate. The blow was intended, but killing was not intended. Killing occurred without being intended and so retaliation is cancelled and the blood money made severe.

The like of this is sound in respect of the Sunnah. Abū Dāwūd related from 'Abdullāh ibn 'Amr that the Messenger of Allah ﷺ said, 'The blood money for accidental killing which is semi-deliberate, which is with a whip or a stick, is a hundred camels, forty of which are pregnant with foetuses intact.' Ad-Dāraquṭnī related from Ibn 'Abbās that the Messenger of Allah ﷺ said, 'Deliberate killing has retaliation by the hand. In the case of accidental killing, there is no retaliation, but blood money. If someone is killed in ignorance by a stone, stick or whip, there is severe blood money in respect of the age of the camels.' It is also related from Sulaymān ibn Mūsā from 'Amr ibn Shu'ayb from his father from his grandfather that the Messenger of Allah ﷺ said, 'The blood money for semi-deliberate killing is made more severe, as in the case of deliberate killing, but the person who did it is not killed in retaliation.' This is a text.

Ṭāwūs said about someone killed while still in a battle, in which there is a fighting exchange using sticks or whips or stones thrown, that blood money is paid for him and no one is killed for him because it is not known who killed him. Aḥmad ibn Ḥanbal said that the expression 'in ignorance' indicates a case which is obscure due to the turmoil and the situation is not clear. Isḥāq said, 'This is when there is mutual wounding and killing of one another. It is as if it was from blindness which is confusion.' Ad-Dāraquṭnī mentioned it.

Those who say that there is a category of semi-deliberate killing disagree about what the severe blood money should be. 'Aṭā' and ash-Shāfi'ī said that it is thirty four-year-old she-camels, thirty five-year-old she-camels, and forty *khalīfah*s (pregnant camels). This position is related from 'Umar, Zayd ibn Thābit, al-Mughīrah ibn Shu'bah, and Abū Mūsā al-Ash'arī. It is the position of Mālik in his view which permits the existence of semi-deliberate killing. The well-known position of his school is that he only stated that in the story of the Mudlijī who hit his son with a sword.

It is said that it constitutes of categories: a quarter three-year-old she-camels, a quarter four-year-old camels, a quarter five-year-old camels and a quarter two-year-old camels. This is the position of an-Nu'mān and Ya'qūb. Abū Dāwūd mentioned it from Sufyān from Abū Isḥāq from 'Āṣim ibn Ḍamrah from 'Alī. It is said that it consists of five parts: twenty two-year-old she-camels, twenty three-year-old she-camels, twenty three-year-old male camels, twenty four-year-old she-camels, and twenty five-year-old she-camels. This is the position of Abū Thawr. It is said that it is forty five-year-old she-camels which have completed their year, thirty four-year-old she-camels, and thirty three-year-old she-camels. This is related from 'Uthmān ibn 'Affān, and it is the position of al-Ḥasan al-Baṣrī, Ṭāwūs and az-Zuhrī. It is also said that it is thirty-four pregnant camels which have completed their year, thirty-three four-year-old she-camels, and thirty-three five-year-old she-camels. That is the position of ash-Sha'bī and an-Nakha'ī. Abū Dāwūd mentioned it from Abu-l-Aḥwaṣ from Abū Isḥāq from 'Āṣim ibn Ḍamrah from 'Alī.

They disagree about who is obliged to pay the blood money for the semi-deliberate killing. Al-Ḥārith al-'Uklī, Ibn Abī Laylā, Ibn Shubrumah, Qatādah and Abū Thawr said that the killer must pay it from his own money. Ash-Sha'bī, an-Nakha'ī, al-Ḥakam, ash-Shāfi'ī, ath-Thawrī, Aḥmad, Isḥaq and the People of Opinion said that it is owed by the paternal relatives. Ibn al-Mundhir said that the view of ash-Shāfi'ī is sounder based on the *ḥadīth* of Abū Hurayrah that the Prophet ﷺ made the paternal relatives of the one who dealt the blow pay the blood money of a foetus. Scholars agree that the paternal relatives do not have to pay the blood money for deliberate killing and that it comes from the property of the perpetrator. This was discussed in *al-Baqarah*.

They all agree that the killer owes expiation in the case of accidental killing. They disagree about it when the killing was deliberate. Mālik and ash-Shāfi'ī thought that expiation was owed in the case of deliberate killing in the same way as when someone was killed by accident. Ash-Shāfi'ī said, 'If expiation is obliged for the accidental, it is more proper for it to be obliged for the deliberate.' He said, 'If it is prescribed to prostrate for forgetfulness in the prayer, it is more proper that it should be obliged for a deliberate error. What Allah Almighty mentioned about the expiation of the deliberate does not cancel what is obliged for the accidental.'

It is said that a deliberate killer must do expiation when he is pardoned and not killed. If he is killed in retaliation, no expiation is taken for him from his property.

It is also said that it should be taken. If someone kills himself, expiation is taken from his property. Ath-Thawrī, Abū Thawr and the People of Opinion say that expiation is only obliged where Allah obliged it. Ibn al-Mundhir said, 'That is what we say, because expiation is a form of worship and it is not permitted to base a punishment on it. It is not permitted for anyone to impose an obligation binding on Allah's servants except by the Book, Sunnah or consensus. There is no proof in any of what we have mentioned for someone who imposes an expiation on someone who kills deliberately.'

They disagree about what happens when a group kills a man by mistake. One group say that expiation is due from each of them, as is stated by al-Ḥasan, 'Ikrimah, an-Nakha'ī, al-Ḥārith al-'Uklī, Mālik, ath-Thawrī, ash-Shāfi'ī, Aḥmad, Isḥāq, Abū Thawr and the People of Opinion. Another group say that one *kaffārah* covers all of them. Abū Thawr said that and it is related from al-Awzā'ī. Az-Zuhrī made a distinction between emancipation and fasting in expiation. He said about a group who shoot a catapult and kill a man that they all must free a slave and if they cannot do it, then each of them must fast two consecutive months.

An-Nasā'ī reported from al-Ḥasan ibn Isḥāq al-Marwazī, who is trustworthy, from Khālid ibn Khidāsh from Ḥātim ibn Ismā'īl from Bushayr ibn al-Muhājir from 'Abdullāh ibn Buraydah from his father that the Messenger of Allah ﷺ said, 'In the sight of Allah, killing a believer is worse than the disappearance of this world.' 'Abdullāh reported that the Messenger of Allah ﷺ said, 'The first thing for which a person will be called to account is the prayer, and the first judgment between people will be about loss of life.'

Ismā'īl ibn Isḥāq related from Nāfi' ibn Jubayr ibn Muṭ'im that 'Abdullāh ibn 'Abbās was asked whether repentance was possible for a murderer. Ibn 'Abbās replied as if he was astonished at the question and said two or three times, 'What do you say?' Then he said, 'Woe to you! How can he repent? I heard our Prophet ﷺ say, "The victim will come holding his head in one of his hands, with the collar of his killer in the other hand, his veins full of blood, until they stop. The victim will say to Allah Almighty, 'Lord, this one killed me!' Allah will say to the killer, 'You are wretched,' and he will be taken to the Fire."' Al-Ḥasan reported that the Messenger of Allah ﷺ said, 'I did not argue with my Lord about anything as I argued with him regarding the killing of a believer but He did not answer me.'

Scholars disagree about whether someone who murders can repent. Al-Bukhārī reported that Sa'īd ibn Jubayr said, 'The people of Kufa disagreed about it, so I travelled to Ibn 'Abbās and asked him about it. He said "This *āyah* was revealed: '*As for anyone who kills … his repayment…*' and it was the last to be revealed about it and nothing abrogated it."' An-Nasā'ī reported from him, 'I asked Ibn 'Abbās whether there is any repentance for someone who kills a believer. "No," he answered, and I recited to him the *āyah* in *al-Furqān*, "*Those who do not call on any other god together with Allah...*" (25:68) and he said, "This is a Makkan *āyah* which was abrogated by a Madinan *āyah*: *'As for anyone who kills a believer deliberately...*'"' Something similar is related from Zayd ibn Thābit. The *āyah* of *an-Nisā'* was revealed six months after the *āyah* of *al-Furqān*, or eight months, both of which an-Nasā'ī reported from Zayd ibn Thābit.

The Mu'tazilites believed that this *āyah*, along with these reports of Zayd and Ibn 'Abbās, is undefined and said that it refines His words: *'He forgives whomever He wills for anything other than that.'* (2:48) They thought that the threat will be definitely carried out on every killer. So they combine the two *āyah*s and say that it implies: 'He forgives whomever He wills for anything other than that except someone who kills deliberately.'

A group of scholars, including 'Abdullāh ibn 'Umar, Zayd and Ibn 'Abbās believed that the killer can repent. Yazīd ibn Hārūn related from Abū Mālik al-Ashja'ī that Sa'd ibn 'Ubaydah said, 'A man came to Ibn 'Abbās and said, "Is there repentance for someone who deliberately kills a believer?" "No," he replied. When the man left, his companions said to him, "Is that the *fatwā* which you give us? You used to give us a *fatwā* that the repentance of someone who kills is accepted." He said, "I think that he is an angry man who wants to kill a believer." They went after him and found that to be the case.'

This is the position of the people of the *Sunnah*, and it is sound. This *āyah* is specific. The evidence of the specification is found in *āyah*s and reports. They agree that the *āyah* was revealed about Miqyas ibn Ṣubābah (or Ḍubābah). He and his brother Hishām became Muslim. He found Hishām murdered among the Banū an-Najjār and told the Prophet ﷺ about that. He wrote telling them to hand over the killer of his brother and sent a man of the Banū Fihr with him. The Banū an-Najjār said, 'By Allah, we do not know who killed him, but we will pay the blood money.' They gave him a hundred camels. The two left and returned to Madīnah. Miqyas attacked the Fihrī man and killed him and left for Makkah as an apostate. He composed:

'I killed Fihr for him and imposed
his blood money on the masters of the Banū an-Najjār, the lords of Fāri'.

I unleashed my vengeance and got my revenge.
I was the first to return to the idols.'

The Prophet ﷺ said, 'I will not give him security in or outside of sanctuary.' He commanded that he be killed on the day Makkah was conquered while he was clinging to the Ka'bah.

This is confirmed by the transmission of commentators and scholars of the *dīn*; one must not attack the Muslims. Then taking the literal meaning of the *āyah* is not more proper than taking the literal meaning of the words: *'Good actions eradicate bad actions'* (11:114) and: *'It is He who accepts repentance from His slaves'* (42:25) and: *'He forgives whoever He wills for anything apart from that.'* (4:48) Taking the literal meaning of the two is contradictory and so there must be specification and then it is possible to combine the *āyat* of *al-Furqān* with this *āyah* and there is no abrogation or contradiction. That is by the general wording of the *āyah* of *an-Nisā'* making the *āyah* of *al-Furqān* specific, and so it means that his repayment will be that unless he repents, especially when the factor of the killing is combined with the factor of the threat of punishment.

Reports about this are numerous, like the *ḥadīth* of 'Ubādah ibn aṣ-Ṣāmit to whom he said ﷺ, 'Give me allegiance on the basis that you not associate anything with Allah or fornicate or steal or take a life which Allah has made inviolable except for a right. If any of you fulfils that, his wage is up to Allah. If someone does any of that and is punished for it, that it is its expiation. If someone does something of that and Allah veils him, his business is up to Allah. If He wishes, He will pardon him. If He wishes, He will punish him.' The imams related it and the two *Ṣaḥīḥ* collections transmitted it. There is also the *ḥadīth* of Abū Hurayra from the Prophet ﷺ about the man who killed a hundred people which Muslim, Ibn Mājah and others transmitted as well as other confirmed reports.

Then they agree with us about a man against whom there is testimony that he killed and he confirms that he killed deliberately. The relatives go to the ruler and the *ḥadd* punishment is carried out on him and he is killed in retaliation. This person is not pursued in the Next World and the threat is not carried out on him. There is a consensus on what is demanded by the *ḥadīth* of 'Ubādah. They are proved wrong in their holding to the apparent meaning of the words: *'As for anyone who kills a believer deliberately, his repayment is Hell.'* It includes the specification that we mentioned. If it is like that, the meaning is that this *āyah* is specific as we mentioned or it is applied to what was related from Ibn 'Abbās who said that '*deliberately*' means that he thought it lawful to kill him. There is consensus that this leads to unbelief.

One group said that the one who kills is subject to the will of Allah, whether he repents or not. Abū Ḥanīfah and his people said that. If someone says that Allah's words here indicate that he is an unbeliever because He is only angry with an unbeliever outside of faith, we believe that this is a threat and that not carrying out a threat is nobility as is said:

When I threaten or promise him,
I do not carry out my threat but I fulfil my promise.

A second response is that the killer merits that and deserves it because of his terrible wrong action. This was stated by Abū Miljaz Lāḥiq ibn Ḥumayd, Abū Ṣāliḥ and others. Anas ibn Mālik reported that the Prophet ﷺ said, 'When Allah promises a reward to His slave, He fulfils it. If He threatens him with a punishment, it is up to His will. If He wishes, He will punish him, and if He wishes, He will pardon him.'

There is some doubt regarding these two reports. As for the first, al-Qushayrī said, 'This is debatable because the words of the Lord cannot differ unless it is meant to define the undefined. This is permitted in respect of words. As for the second, if it is related that it is *marfū'*, an-Naḥḥās said, 'This is a clear error. Allah said: *"That is their repayment – Hell – because they disbelieved."* (18:109). No one said, "He repaid them." This is an error in Arabic because He says after it, *"...his repayment is Hell."* It is applied to the means that He repays them with.' The third is that their repayment is Hell if they do not repent and persist in wrong action until they meet their Lord in unbelief because of the misfortune of disobedience.

In his book, *The Abrogating and Abrogated*, Hibatullāh mentions that this *āyah* is abrogated by the words: *'He forgives whomever He wills for anything apart from that.'* (4:48) He said that this is the consensus of the people except for Ibn 'Abbās and Ibn 'Umar, who stated that it is an *āyah* of judgment. What he says is somewhat questionable because it concerns the general and the specific rather than abrogation. Ibn 'Aṭiyyah said that. This is good, because abrogation does not enter into reports. The meaning allows it.

An-Naḥḥās said in *Ma'ānī al-Qur'ān*, 'The scholars of the people of investigation say that it is an *āyah* of judgment and that he will be punished if he does not repent. If he repents, his business is clear since Allah says: *"I am Ever-Forgiving to anyone who repents."* (20:82) This is not outside of it. *Khulūd* does not demand perpetuity. Allah says: *"We did not give any human being before you immortality"* (21:35) and: *"He thinks that his wealth will make him live forever."* (104:3).' Zuhayr said:

Nothing lasts forever (*khālid*) except the firm mountains.

This all indicates that the word *khuld* can be used with other than the meaning of actual eternity. This can depart when this world departs. It is as the Arabs say, 'I will make so-and-so imprisoned forever,' but the prison comes to an end and vanishes as does the one in prison. That is also like their words in supplication, 'May Allah make his kingdom last forever.'

يَـٰٓأَيُّهَا ٱلَّذِينَ ءَامَنُوٓاْ إِذَا ضَرَبْتُمْ فِى سَبِيلِ ٱللَّهِ فَتَبَيَّنُواْ وَلَا تَقُولُواْ لِمَنْ أَلْقَىٰٓ إِلَيْكُمُ ٱلسَّلَـٰمَ لَسْتَ مُؤْمِنًا تَبْتَغُونَ عَرَضَ ٱلْحَيَوٰةِ ٱلدُّنْيَا فَعِندَ ٱللَّهِ مَغَانِمُ كَثِيرَةٌ كَذَٰلِكَ كُنتُم مِّن قَبْلُ فَمَنَّ ٱللَّهُ عَلَيْكُمْ فَتَبَيَّنُوٓاْ إِنَّ ٱللَّهَ كَانَ بِمَا تَعْمَلُونَ خَبِيرًا ﴿٩٤﴾

94 You who believe, when you go out to fight in the Way of Allah verify things carefully. Do not say, 'You are not a believer, to someone who greets you as a Muslim, simply out of desire for the goods of this world. With Allah there is booty in abundance. That is the way you were before but Allah has been kind to you. So verify things carefully. Allah is aware of what you do. You who believe! when you go out to fight in the Way of Allah verify things carefully.

This is connected to killing and *jihād*. *Ḍarb* is travelling in the land for whatever reason, when one travels for trade, on an expedition or something else and is connected to booty. This *āyah* was revealed about a group of Muslims who passed a man on their journey with camels and sheep which he was selling. He greeted the people and said, 'There is no god but Allah. Muḥammad is the Messenger of Allah.' One of them attacked him and killed him. When that was mentioned to the Prophet ﷺ, it was hard on him and the *āyah* was revealed.

It was related by al-Bukhārī from Ibn 'Abbās: 'A man was with some sheep of his and the Muslims met him and he said, "Peace be upon you," and they killed him and took his sheep. So Allah revealed this *āyah* about that to His words: "... *simply out of desire for the goods of this world.*" Those were the sheep.' Elsewhere it is stated that the Prophet ﷺ paid blood money for him to his family and returned his sheep. There is disagreement about who the killer and the victim were. Most say that the killer was Muḥallim ibn Jaththāmah and the victim was 'Āmir ibn al-Aḍbaṭ. He ﷺ prayed against Muḥallim who only lived for seven days after that and then was buried but the earth would not accept him. This happened three times. When they saw that the earth would not accept him, they threw him into a ravine. The Prophet ﷺ said, 'The earth accepts worse than him.' Al-Ḥasan said, 'It keeps those who are worse than him, but that was a warning to the people not to do what he did.'

In the *Sunan* of Ibn Mājah, 'Imrān ibn Ḥusayn said, 'The Messenger of Allah ﷺ sent an army of the Muslims against the idolaters and they fought them in a fierce fight and turned their backs on them, and a man who was one of my kin attacked one of the idolaters with a spear. When he was standing over him, he said, "I testify that there is no god but Allah. I am a Muslim." He stabbed him and killed him. He went to the Messenger of Allah ﷺ and said, "Messenger of Allah, I am destroyed!" "What have you done?" he asked two or three times. He told him what he had done and the Prophet ﷺ said, "Did you split open his belly to see what was in his heart?" He said, "Messenger of Allah, if I opened his belly, would I have known what is in his heart?" "No," he replied, "you did not accept what he said nor did you know what was in his heart." The Messenger of Allah ﷺ was silent about him and he died a short time later. We buried him and found him on the surface of the earth in the morning. We said, "Perhaps an enemy has disinterred him." We buried him again and commanded our lads to guard him. In the morning he was again on the surface of the earth. We said, "Perhaps the lads dozed off." We buried him and then guarded him ourselves. In the morning he was on the surface of the earth once more. So we threw him into a ravine.'

It is also said that the killer was Usāmah ibn Zayd and the victim was Mirdās ibn Nuhayk al-Ghatafānī al-Fazārī from the Banū Murrah, part of the people of Fadak. Ibn al-Qāsim mentioned that from Mālik. It is said that Mirdās became Muslim in the night and told his family. When the Prophet ﷺ told Usāmah that the matter was terrible, he swore that he would never fight a man who said, 'There is no god but Allah'. This has been mentioned previously. It is also said that the killer was Abū Qatādah or Abū ad-Dardā'.

There is no disagreement about the one the earth threw up after his death. That was Muḥallim whom we mentioned. Perhaps these things happened close to the same time and the *āyah* was revealed about all of them. It is related that the Messenger of Allah ﷺ returned the sheep and camels and paid his blood money to achieve reconciliation. Allah knows best. Ath-Tha'labī mentioned that the commander of that expedition was a man called Ghālib ibn Faḍālah al-Laythī. It is also said that it was al-Miqdād, as as-Suhaylī said.

'Verify things carefully' means 'Reflect'. Most recite *fa-tabayyanū* and this is preferred by Abū 'Ubaydah and Abū Ḥātim. They said that it is a command to make things

clear. One says, 'I verified the matter and the matter became clear.' So it can be transitive and intransitive. Ḥamzah recited *tathabbatū,* meaning to confirm. The first is more emphatic because one might confirm something while it still is not verified.

'Idhā' points to the precondition and that is why the *fā'* is added to the 'verify' and acts as its apodosis. [POEM] It is also good for it not to have an apodosis. [POEM] It is confirmed that one must verify the situation in respect of killing, whether resident or on a journey. There is no disagreement about that. A journey is singled out for mention because the event about which the *āyah* was revealed occurred during a journey.

Do not say, 'You are not a believer', to someone who greets you as a Muslim.

It can be read with *silm* or *salam* (submission) instead of *salām* (peace). Al-Bukhārī said that. It is read in all these forms. Abū 'Ubayd al-Qāsim ibn Sallām recited *'as-salām'*. The people of investigation disagreed with him and said that *'salam'* is more fitting here because it means submission as Allah says: *'They will offer their submission (*salam*): "We will not do any evil."'* (16:28) *Salam* is submission. In that case, it would mean, 'Do not say that to someone who comes and submits to you.' It is said that it is the words, 'Peace be upon you.' That refers to the first because his giving the greeting of Islam announces that he obeys and submits. It is possible that it means isolation and abandonment. Al-Akhfash said that someone says, 'So-and-so is *salām'* when he does not mix with anyone. *Silm* is a truce. *'You are not a believer'* is related from Abū Ja'far as *'mu'man'*. When you grant someone safe conduct, he is *'mu'man'*.

If a Muslim meets an unbeliever with whom he has no treaty he is permitted to kill him. If he says, 'There is no god but Allah,' he is not permitted to kill him because he is protected by the protection of Islam which defends his life, property and family. If he is killed after that, the killer is killed in retaliation for him. That did not happen at the beginning of Islam when they thought that the other person did it out of fear of weapons and the one who was protected was the one who said it merely did so to seek safety. The Prophet ﷺ informed them that he was protected whenever he said it. That is why he asked Usāmah, 'Did you split open his heart so that you would not know whether he said it or not.' Muslim transmitted it. It means: 'Did you look to see whether he was telling the truth or lying?' That is not possible and there only remained what was on the tongue. There is an immense amount of *fiqh* concerning this matter, which is that judgments are based on probabilities and on the outward, not on one being aware of secrets.

If someone says, 'Peace be upon you,' he must not be killed until it is known what is behind it because there is uncertainty. Mālik said about an unbeliever who is found and says, 'I have come seeking safe-conduct,' 'These are unclear matters and I think that he should be returned to his place of safety and not be judged to be Muslim, because disbelief was confirmed for him and he must display what indicates what he says. It is not enough to say, "I am a Muslim," or "I am a believer" or, indeed, that he prays unless he utters the *shahādah* about which the Prophet ﷺ said "I was commanded to fight people until they said, 'There is no god but Allah.'"'

If someone prays or performs a specific act of Islam, our scholars disagree about them. Ibn al-'Arabī said, 'We think that he is not a Muslim simply by virtue of that. If he is asked, "What is behind this prayer?" and he answers, "It is the prayer of a Muslim," he is told to say, "There is no god but Allah." If he says it, his truthfulness is verified. If he refuses, then we know that he is playing games. Some think that his claim to Islam is apostasy, but what is sound is that he is a disbeliever who prays and it is not apostasy. That is also the case with someone who says, "Peace be upon you." He is asked to say the *shahādah*. If he says it, his guidance is verified. If he refuses, his obstinacy is clear and he is killed.' '*Verify*' refers to the unclear matter, or means 'establish the truth' and do not be hasty. If someone kills him, they have done something forbidden. If it is said that the Prophet ﷺ was harsh to Muḥallim and he was cast from his grave. What was his outcome? We said that because he knew his intention, he did not care about his Islam and he killed him deliberately because of the bad-feeling that had existed between them in the Jāhilyyah.

simply out of desire for the goods of this world.

This means seeking to take his property. The things of this world are called 'goods' (*'urūḍ*) because they are passing and ephemeral (*'āriḍ*) and not firm. Abu-Ubaydah said, 'All of the goods of the life of this world are *'araḍ*.' An illustration of that can be seen in the *ḥadīth*: 'This world consists of immediate goods which both pious and impious consume.' *'Arḍ* means all goods except for dirhams and dinars.

We find in *Ṣaḥīḥ Muslim* that the Prophet ﷺ said, 'Wealth is not an abundance of goods. Wealth is self-sufficiency.' One of the scholars composed about this:

Be satisfied with what will be sufficient for you and be content.
    You do not know whether you will see the morning or evening.

Wealth is not having much property.
    Wealth and poverty have to do with the self.

This verifies the words of Abū 'Ubaydah: 'Wealth includes everything that makes a person wealthy.'

We find in *Kitāb al-'Ayn*: '*'Araḍ* is what is obtained of this world. It includes: *"You desire the goods ('araḍ) of this world."* (8:67) Its plural is *'urūḍ*.' We find in *al-Mujmal* by Ibn Fāris: '*'Araḍ* is what occurs to a person in the form of illness or the like, and the *'araḍ* of this world is what it contains of wealth, be that a little or a lot.' *'Arḍ* are goods other than money. The verb *a'raḍa* is to present something. *'Arḍ* is also the breadth of a thing.'

With Allah there is booty in abundance

This is a promise from Allah for the one who obtains it correctly and lawfully without committing the unlawful. It means: do not fall over one another to get it.

That is the way you were before

This means that is how you were concealing your faith from your people out of fear of them until Allah gave you might in the *dīn* and defeat of the idolaters. Now they are like that, each on guard against his people. When he reaches you, it is not proper for you to kill him until you verify his position. Ibn Zayd said that the meaning is: 'You were unbelievers like that and *"Allah has been kind to you"* by making you become Muslim, and so they may also be like that. If someone becomes Muslim immediately upon meeting you, you must clarify his position.'

This *āyah* is evidence that faith is by this statement since Allah says: *'Do not say, "You are not a believer," to someone who greets you as a Muslim.'* They said that since it is forbidden to say, 'You are not a believer' to someone who says, 'There is no god but Allah' it is forbidden to kill him based on his simple statement. He simply has to say, 'There is no god but Allah. I am a believer.' Were it not that faith consisted of this statement, then their statement would not have been doubted.

The people were uncertain about whether or not this statement was just their effort to seek protection and so they killed him. Allah only assigned judgment to His servants according to outward appearance. The Prophet ﷺ said, 'I was commanded to fight people until they say, "There is no god but Allah."' That does not mean that faith is mere words. Do you not see that the hypocrites used to say this and they were not believers as we explained in *al-Baqarah*? The clarification is found in the words of the Prophet ﷺ, 'Did you split open his heart?' That establishes that faith consists of affirmation and more and that its reality is verification by the heart. We can only act on what we hear.

This is also used as evidence by those who say that the repentance of a *zindīq* is accepted when he displays Islam. They said, 'That is because Allah Almighty did not distinguish between *zindīqs* and others who display Islam.' This was discussed at the beginning of *al-Baqarah*. It refutes the Qadariyyah. Allah reported that He was gracious to the believers from among all creatures by singling them out for success. The Qadariyyah say that He created all of them for faith. If it had been as they claim, then there is no sense in the believers being singled out for grace among people. '*Verify*" is then repeated for stress.

Allah is aware of what you do.

This is a warning about differing from what Allah has commanded. It means: 'Guard yourselves and avoid errors which will destroy you.'

لَّا يَسْتَوِي الْقَاعِدُونَ مِنَ الْمُؤْمِنِينَ غَيْرُ أُولِي الضَّرَرِ وَالْمُجَاهِدُونَ فِي سَبِيلِ اللَّهِ
بِأَمْوَالِهِمْ وَأَنفُسِهِمْ فَضَّلَ اللَّهُ الْمُجَاهِدِينَ بِأَمْوَالِهِمْ وَأَنفُسِهِمْ عَلَى الْقَاعِدِينَ دَرَجَةً
وَكُلًّا وَعَدَ اللَّهُ الْحُسْنَىٰ وَفَضَّلَ اللَّهُ الْمُجَاهِدِينَ عَلَى الْقَاعِدِينَ أَجْرًا عَظِيمًا ﴿٩٥﴾
دَرَجَاتٍ مِّنْهُ وَمَغْفِرَةً وَرَحْمَةً وَكَانَ اللَّهُ غَفُورًا رَّحِيمًا ﴿٩٦﴾

95 Those believers who stay behind – other than those forced to by necessity – are not the same as those who do jihad in the Way of Allah, sacrificing their wealth and themselves. Allah has given those who do jihad with their wealth and themselves a higher rank than those who stay behind. Allah has promised the Best to both, but Allah has preferred those who do jihad over those who stay behind by an immense reward: 96 high ranks conferred by Him as well as forgiveness and mercy. Allah is Ever-Forgiving, Most Merciful.

Those believers who stay behind are not the same

Ibn 'Abbās said, 'Those who stayed behind from Badr and those who went out to it are not the same.' Then Allah says: '*other than those forced to by necessity*'. Necessity implies chronic illness. The Imāms report that Zayd ibn Thābit said, 'I was beside the Messenger of Allah ﷺ when the Revelation overcame him and the thigh of the Messenger of Allah ﷺ fell on my thigh and I have never felt anything heavier than his thigh. Then it left him and he said, "Write." So I wrote on a shoulder-blade: "*Those believers who stay behind are not the same as those who do jihād* ..." to the end of the *āyah*. Ibn Umm Maktūm, who was blind, stood up when he heard the excellence of those who do *jihād.* He asked, "Messenger of Allah, what about the believers who cannot do *jihād*?" When he finished speaking, the Revelation overcame the Messenger of Allah ﷺ and his thigh fell on mine and it was heavier the second time than it had been the first time. Then it left him and he said, "Recite, Zayd." I recited: *"Those believers who stay behind are not the same as those who do jihād."* The Messenger of Allah ﷺ said: *"other than those forced to by necessity."*'" Zayd said, 'So Allah revealed it alone and then connected it to it. By the One Who has my soul in His hand, it is as if I could see where it joined at a crack on the shoulder-blade.'

In al-Bukhārī, Miqsam, the freedman of 'Abdullāh ibn al-Ḥārith, reported that he heard Ibn 'Abbās say, '"*Those believers who stay behind are not the same...*" refers to those who stayed behind and did not go to Badr and those who went to Badr.'

Scholars say that the 'people of necessity' are those who had excuses which prevented them from going out on *jihād.* It is a sound confirmed report that the Prophet ﷺ said when he returned from one of his expeditions, 'There are men in Madīnah who have not crossed a valley nor travelled any distance but they are with you. They are those kept back by an excuse.' That means that the one who is kept back by an excuse has the reward of those who go on *jihād.* It is said that it is possible that their reward is the same. There is scope within Allah's grace. His reward is grace without actual entitlement. He rewards a sincere intention with a different reward than the one for the action. It is said that such a person is given his reward without it being multiplied while the one who went on the expedition has it multiplied. Allah knows best. The first view is sounder, Allah willing, based on the sound *ḥadīth* about that: 'There are men in Madīnah...' and by the *ḥadīth* of Abū Kabshah al-Anmārī: 'This world is for four people...' which was mentioned in *Āli 'Imrān.* It is also the sense of the *ḥadīth*: 'When someone is ill, Allah says, "Write for My slave what he would have done while healthy until he recovers or I take him to Me."'

Some scholars take this *āyah* to mean that the people in the *Dīwān* have a greater reward than those who go out voluntarily, because the people of the *Dīwān* receive the stipend, act in hardships, and endure fright in respect of expeditions and commands. They are greater than those who do it voluntarily since they are calm and in a good state in large rows and the like. Ibn Muḥaywīz said, 'Those with stipends are better than volunteers because of the fear that they experience. Makḥūl said, 'The terrors of expeditions cancel out the terrors of the Rising.'

Connected to this is the opinion that wealth is better than poverty since Allah mentioned wealth which enables righteous actions. People disagree about this while they agree that need on account of poverty is disliked and that someone who is arrogant because of wealth is blameworthy. Some believe that the wealthy are better because they can use their wealth, and capacity is better than lack of capacity. Al-Māwardī said, 'This is the school of those who are overpowered by love of high rank.' Others believe that poverty is better because it is better to abandon this world. Al-Māwardī said, 'This is the school of those who are overpowered by love of security.'

Others believe that it is better to be in between the two matters by ceasing to be poor and having the lowest level of wealth, in order to obtain the excellence of both and to be safe from the blame of both situations. Al-Māwardī said, 'This is the school of those who think that balance is better and that the best of matters is the middlemost.' Excellent are the words of the wise poet:

You who seek refuge with Allah from lack of wealth
and from desire one day to what is not desired.

other than those forced to by necessity

The Kufans and Abū 'Amr read 'other' as *'ghayru'* and al-Akhfash says that it describes those who stay behind because it does not mean particular individuals and so it is like an indefinite noun. So it is permitted to described them with 'other'. It means: 'They are not the same as those who stay behind who were forced by necessity.' It means: healthy people who stay behind are not the same. Az-Zajjāj said that.

Abū Ḥawyah recited *'ghayri'* as an adjective modifying 'believers', meaning 'the believers who are not forced to by necessity are not the same as healthy believers'. The people of Makkah and Madīnah read it *'ghayra'* as an exception from those who stay behind or the believers, meaning 'except for those who are forced to by necessity. They are the same as those who do jihad.' If you wish, it is a *ḥāl* modifying those who stay behind, and it means, 'Healthy people who stay behind are not the same,' meaning while they are healthy. It is also permitted for the *ḥāl* to modify them because the word for them is definite. It is as you say, 'Zayd came [and he was] not sick.' We mentioned that the reason for the revelation indicates the idea of the accusative. Allah knows best.

high ranks conferred by Him as well as forgiveness and mercy

Some people say that the preference is first by a *'rank'* and then *'ranks'*. This is for stress and clarification. It is said that the excellence of those who do *jihād* over those who stay behind out of necessity is one rank, and their excellence over those who stay behind without excuse is several ranks. Ibn Jurayj, as-Suddī and others said that. It is said that *'rank'* is elevation, meaning that their renown is elevated and they are raised by praise. This is what *'rank'* means. *'Ranks'* means in the Garden. Ibn Muḥayrīz said, 'There are seventy ranks and the distance between each two ranks is that which a swift steed can travel in seventy years.' It can mean 'He preferred them with ranks' or can stress *'an immense reward'*. The *'immense reward'* consists of ranks, forgiveness and mercy. It can be in the nominative, i.e. 'Those are ranks'.

The noun *'reward'* is in the accusative by *'preferred'*. If you wish, it is a verbal noun, and that is better: it is not then in the accusative by *'preferred'* because it has its two objects, which are *'over those who stay behind'* and *'rank'*. *'Ranks'* are stages one on top of the other. We find in the *Ṣaḥīḥ* that the Prophet ﷺ said, 'There are a hundred ranks in the Garden that Allah has prepared for those who strive in His Way. Between every two ranks is what is between the heaven and earth.'

Allah has promised the Best to both.

'The Best' is the Garden, in other words Allah has promised the Garden to both of them. It is also said that it is specific to those who do *jihād*, or to those who do *jihād* and those physically unable to do so. Allah knows best.

إِنَّ ٱلَّذِينَ تَوَفَّىٰهُمُ ٱلْمَلَٰٓئِكَةُ ظَالِمِىٓ أَنفُسِهِمْ قَالُواْ فِيمَ كُنتُمْ قَالُواْ كُنَّا مُسْتَضْعَفِينَ
فِى ٱلْأَرْضِ قَالُوٓاْ أَلَمْ تَكُنْ أَرْضُ ٱللَّهِ وَٰسِعَةً فَتُهَاجِرُواْ فِيهَا فَأُوْلَٰٓئِكَ مَأْوَىٰهُمْ جَهَنَّمُ
وَسَآءَتْ مَصِيرًا ﴿٩٧﴾ إِلَّا ٱلْمُسْتَضْعَفِينَ مِنَ ٱلرِّجَالِ وَٱلنِّسَآءِ وَٱلْوِلْدَٰنِ لَا
يَسْتَطِيعُونَ حِيلَةً وَلَا يَهْتَدُونَ سَبِيلًا ﴿٩٨﴾ فَأُوْلَٰٓئِكَ عَسَى ٱللَّهُ أَن يَعْفُوَ عَنْهُمْ
وَكَانَ ٱللَّهُ عَفُوًّا غَفُورًا ﴿٩٩﴾

97 The angels ask those they take while they are wronging themselves, 'What were your circumstances?' They reply, 'We were oppressed on earth.' They say, 'Was Allah's earth not wide enough for you to have made hijrah elsewhere in it?' The shelter of such people will be Hell. What an evil destination! 98 Except for those men, women and children who really are oppressed and do not have any other possibility and are not guided to any way. 99 It may well be that Allah will pardon them. Allah is Ever-Pardoning, Ever-Forgiving.

What is being referred to here is a group of the people of Makkah who became Muslim and displayed faith in the Prophet ﷺ and then, when the Prophet ﷺ emigrated, they remained with their people and a group of them were influenced by them. When the Battle of Badr took place, they went out with the unbelievers and this *āyah* was revealed. It is said that when they looked down on the number of the Muslims, they had doubts about their *dīn* and apostasised and were killed in their apostasy. The Muslims said, 'These companions of ours were Muslims and were forced to go out, so ask forgiveness for them,' and the *āyah* was revealed. The first is sounder.

Al-Bukhārī reported that Muḥammad ibn 'Abd ar-Raḥmān said, 'Conscription for an expedition was forced on the people of Madīnah [by Ibn az-Zubayr] and I was one of those conscripted. I met 'Ikrimah, the client of Ibn 'Abbās, and told him. He forbade me to go on it in the strongest possible terms. Then he said that Ibn 'Abbās had said that, in the time of the Messenger of Allah ﷺ, some of the Muslims were drafted in with the idolaters to bring up their numbers. They would be given their shares and then throw them away. An arrow would be shot and hit one of them and kill him, or he would be struck a blow and killed. Then Allah revealed: *'The angels ask those they take while they are wronging themselves.'*

The angels ask those they take while they are wronging themselves,

It is possible that the verb is in the past tense without the feminine marker since the word for angels, *'malā'ikah'*, is not a real feminine. It is also possible that it is a verb, based on the idea 'will take them' and one of the two *tā*'s is elided. Ibn Fūrak reported from al-Ḥasan that it means that they take them to the Fire. It is said that they take their souls, and that is the most apparent meaning. It is said that what is meant is the Angel of Death since Allah says: *'Say: "The Angel of Death, who has been given charge of you."'* (32:11)

'Wronging themselves' is in the accusative for the *ḥāl*, meaning while they are doing wrong to themselves. The *nūn* of *ẓālimīn* is elided for lightening and because of the *iḍāfah*, as in seen in 5:95. The words of the angels: *'What were your circumstances?'* is a rebuke, meaning, 'Were you among the Companions of the Messenger of Allah ﷺ or were you idolaters?'

They reply, 'We were oppressed on earth.'

'On earth' here means in Makkah. Their excuse is not sound since they were able to employ devices and were guided to the path. The angels acquainted them with their *dīn*, saying: *'Was Allah's earth not wide enough?'* These questions and answers

mean that they died as Muslims who wronged themselves by not emigrating. If they had died as unbelievers, none of this would be said. Allah did not mention them among the Companions because of the seriousness of what they did and none of them are specified as being believers and it is possible that they apostasised. Allah knows best. Then Allah excluded some people from them, referring to those who were truly weak, like 'Ayyāsh ibn Abī Rabī'ah, Salamah ibn Hishām and others for whom the Messenger of Allah ﷺ prayed.

Ibn 'Abbās said, 'My mother and I were among those Allah was referring to in this *āyah*.' He was a child at that time. His mother was Umm al-Faḍl Lubābah bint al-Ḥārith, the sister of Maymūnah. Her other sister was Lubābah the younger. She was one of nine sisters about whom the Prophet ﷺ said, 'The sisters are believers.' They included Salmā, al-'Uṣmā' and Ḥafīdah who is called Umm Ḥafīd and her name was Huzaylah. They consisted of six full sisters and three maternal sisters, who were Salmā, Salāmah, and Asmā' bint 'Umays al-Khath'amiyyah, the wife of Ja'far ibn Abī Ṭālib, then Abū Bakr aṣ-Ṣiddīq and then 'Alī, may Allah be pleased with all of them.

The question *'What were your circumstances?'* is a question of rebuke. *'What'* has the *alif* omitted – *fīma* instead of *fīmā* – to differentiate between the question and report, and there is a stop at it so that both the *alif* and the vowel are not elided. The question *'Was Allah's earth not wide enough for you?'* is a reference to Madīnah, implying, 'Were you not able to emigrate and distance yourselves from those who oppressed you?' This *āyah* contains evidence for emigrating from a land in which Allah is disobeyed. Sa'īd ibn Jubayr said, 'When disobedience to Allah is committed in a land, then leave it.' He recited this. It is related that the Prophet ﷺ said, 'If anyone flees with his *dīn* from one land to another, even by a span, the Garden becomes mandatory for him, and he is the companion of Ibrāhīm and Muḥammad ﷺ.'

The phrase: *'The shelter of such people will be Hell'* shows that their destination will be the Fire. Emigration is mandatory for everyone who becomes Muslim and the accompanying *'What an evil destination'* is in the accusative for explanation. The words: *'...do not have any other possibility'* means no other device. It is a general expression for the various means of escape. The *'possibility'* is that of reaching Madīnah, according to Mujāhid, as-Suddī and others. The correct view is that it is general to all means of escape.

It may well be that Allah will pardon them.

This refers to those who have no possibility to emigrate. They incur no wrong action which needs to be pardoned, but it means that they see that they will have to endure extreme hardship if they emigrate and if they are not able to bear that hardship, they think will be punished. Allah removed that doubt since He does not impose extreme hardship. If someone has no provision or mount, they are permitted to not emigrate. So the *āyah* means that they will not be required to answer for not emigrating at the Reckoning.

Allah is Ever-Pardoning, Ever-Forgiving.

The past and present tense are the same in respect of Allah.

وَمَن يُهَاجِرْ فِي سَبِيلِ اللَّهِ يَجِدْ فِي الْأَرْضِ مُرَاغَمًا كَثِيرًا وَسَعَةً ۚ وَمَن
يَخْرُجْ مِن بَيْتِهِ مُهَاجِرًا إِلَى اللَّهِ وَرَسُولِهِ ثُمَّ يُدْرِكْهُ الْمَوْتُ فَقَدْ وَقَعَ أَجْرُهُ عَلَى
اللَّهِ ۗ وَكَانَ اللَّهُ غَفُورًا رَّحِيمًا ﴿١٠٠﴾

100 Those who make hijrah in the Way of Allah will find many places of refuge on the earth and ample sustenance. If someone leaves his home, making hijrah to Allah and His Messenger, and death catches up with him, it is Allah Who will reward him. Allah is Ever-Forgiving, Most Merciful.

Those who make hijrah in the Way of Allah will find many places of refuge on the earth

There is disagreement about the interpretation of '*murāgham*' (places of refuge). Mujāhid said that it is 'a way by which one goes away'. Ibn 'Abbās, aḍ-Ḍaḥḥāk, ar-Rabī' and others say that it is the road by which one departs and moves. Ibn Zayd says that it is a place to which one emigrates. Abū 'Ubaydah said that. An-Naḥḥās said that all these statements have similar meanings. It is the way by which one departs and moves in the state of emigration, and it is also a name for the place to which one goes. It is derived from *raghām* (dust) and the verb which means 'to make someone's nose cling to the dust,' in other words humble him. Form III means that you shun and oppose someone. It is said that someone is called *muhājir* and *murāgham* because when a man became Muslim, he opposed his people and left them, and so leaving is called *murāgham* and his going to the Prophet ﷺ is called *hijrah*.

As-Suddī said that *murāgham* means someone seeking livelihood. Ibn al-Qāsim said, 'I heard Mālik say, "*Murāgham* is travelling in the land."' All of these explain the meaning and are very similar. The special sense of the expression is that it is the places to which people go, as we mentioned. Each of two opponents 'throws dust on the other's nose' by forcing him to do what he wants. The unbelievers of Quraysh put dust on the noses of those kept back in Makkah. If some of them had emigrated, they would have put dust on the noses of Quraysh by gaining refuge from them. That protection is the place called *murāgham*. An example of that is the words of an-Nābighah:

Like a mountain in whose corners one seeks refuge,
an impregnable place of protection and place to which to flee.

ample sustenance.

This means provision. Ibn 'Abbās, ar-Rabī' and aḍ-Ḍaḥḥāk said that. Qatādah said that it means expansion from misguidance to guidance and from poverty to wealth. Mālik says that it means spaciousness in the lands. This is an example of the eloquence of the Arabs. The expansiveness of the land and number of strongholds is ampleness in sustenance and the expansion of the breast to its cares and thought and other sorts of relief. A poet expressed this:

When my dear friend wanted to cut me off,
I felt a wide expanse before me.

Another said:

But I have widespread commotion
in the land's length and breadth.

Mālik said that this *āyah* indicates that no one should remain in a land where the early Muslims are cursed and in which actions are done without legal justification, because there are many places of refuge and ample sustenance in the world. Some scholars also use this *āyah* as evidence for the fact that when the *ghāzī* leaves to go on an expedition, and then dies before fighting, he receives a share of the booty, even if he did not take part in the actual fighting. Ibn Lahī'ah reported that from Yazīd ibn Ḥabīb from the people of Madīnah and it is also reported from Ibn Mubārak.

If someone leaves his home, making hijrah to Allah and His Messenger,

'Ikrimah, the freedman of Ibn 'Abbās, said, 'I searched for fourteen years for the name of person referred to here until I found it.' 'Ikrimah's words indicate that the honour of this knowledge is long-lasting and that concern for it is a virtue. It is like what Ibn 'Abbās said: 'I spent years wanting to ask 'Umar about the two women who helped each other against the Messenger of Allah ﷺ and only awe of him restrained me from doing so.' 'Ikrimah said that the man referred to was Ḍamrah ibn al-'Īṣ or al-'Īṣ ibn Ḍamrah ibn Zinbā'. Aṭ-Ṭabarī related it from Sa'īd ibn Jubayr. It is said that it was Ḍumayrah, as well as Junda' ibn Ḍamrah of the Banū al-Layth. He was one of those persecuted in Makkah and was ill. When he heard what Allah revealed about *hijrah*, he said, 'Take me out!' A litter was prepared for him and he was taken out but died on the road at Tan'īm, and Allah revealed this about him.

Abū 'Umar mentioned that it was said to be Khālid ibn Ḥizām ibn Khuwaylid, the nephew of Khadījah, and that he emigrated to Abyssinia but a snake bit him on the road and he died before reaching it and then the *āyah* was revealed about him. Allah knows best. Abu-l-Faraj al-Jawzī says that it was Ḥabīb ibn Ḍamrah. As-Suddī said that it was Ḍamrah ibn Jundub aḍ-Ḍamarī. It is reported from 'Ikrimah that it was Jundub ibn Ḍamrah al-Junda'ī. Ibn Jābir said that it was Ḍamrah ibn Baghīḍ of the Banū 'l-Layth. Al-Mahdawī related that it was Ḍamrah ibn Ḍamrah ibn Nu'aym. It is said that it was Ḍamrah ibn Khuzā'ah. Allah knows best.

Ma'mar related that Qatādah said, 'When the words: *"The angels ask those they take while wronging themselves,"* were revealed one of the Muslims who was ill said, "By Allah, I have no excuse! I have a guide for the road and I am wealthy. Carry me!" They carried him and he died on the road. The Companions of the Prophet ﷺ said, "If only he had reached us, he would have had a full reward!" He died at Tan'īm. His sons went to the Prophet ﷺ and told him the story and: *"If anyone leaves his house, making hijrah..."* was revealed. His name was Ḍamrah ibn Jundub or Jundub ibn Ḍamrah. Allah was Forgiving about his prior *shirk* and Merciful when He accepted his repentance.'

Ibn al-'Arabī said that scholars divide travelling in the land into two types: flight and seeking. The first has six categories.

1. Emigration, which is leaving the Abode of War for the Abode of Islam. It was an obligation in the time of the Prophet ﷺ and this obligation will remain until the Day of Rising. What ended with the Conquest was going to the Prophet ﷺ wherever he was. Whoever remains in the Abode of War is a rebel whose state varies.

2. Leaving a land of innovation. Ibn al-Qāsim said, 'I heard Mālik say, "It is not lawful for anyone to remain in a land in which the early Muslims are cursed."' Ibn al-'Arabī said, 'This is sound. If you are unable to change that, leave it. Allah says:

"When you see people engrossed in mockery of Our Signs, turn from them..." (6:68)'

3. Leaving a land in which the *ḥarām* predominates. It is obligatory for every Muslim to seek the lawful.

4. Fleeing to avoid harm to the body. That is allowed by Allah. If someone fears for himself, Allah has given permission for him to leave and flee to save himself. The first to do this was Ibrāhīm. When he feared for himself from his people, he said: *'I am emigrating to Allah'* (29:26) and: *'I am going towards my Lord. He will be my guide.'* (37:99) The same is true of Mūsā: *'He left there fearful and on his guard.'* (28:21)

5. Fear of illness when there is an unhealthy climate in a land and one leaves it for a purer one. The herdsmen were allowed to do this by the Prophet ﷺ when they were affected by the fever of Madīnah and went out until they recovered. An exception to that is the plague. Allah forbade fleeing from it in a sound *ḥadīth* from His Prophet ﷺ as explained in *al-Baqarah*. Our scholars said that it is disliked.

6. Fleeing out of fear of harm to property. The sanctity of a Muslim's property is like that of his blood, and his family is the same.

As for seeking, it has two broad categories: seeking the *dīn* and seeking this world. As for seeking the *dīn*, its many types fall into nine categories.

1. Travel for reflection, as Allah says: *'Have they not travelled in the land and seen the final fate of those before them?'* (30:90) That is frequent. It is said that Dhu-l-Qarnayn travelled in the lands to see their marvels. It is said that it is to implement what is right in them.

2. Travelling to *ḥajj*. This is obligatory while the first is recommended.

3. Travelling for *jihād*, which has certain rules.

4. Travelling to seek basic provision. If a man finds it difficult to find while resident, he must travel to seek it through hunting, wood-gathering or finding water. It is obligatory for him.

5. Travelling for trade and earning beyond mere sustenance. That is permitted by the bounty of Allah since Allah says: *'There is nothing wrong in seeking bounty from your Lord.'* (2:198) This is a reference to trade and it is a blessing from Allah which Allah bestowed in the journey to hajj, let alone when it is on its own.

6. Travelling in search of knowledge, which is well-known.

7. Seeking to visit certain places. The Prophet ﷺ said, 'Steeds are only driven to three mosques.'

8. Going to the frontiers for *ribāṭ* and to increase the numbers to defend them.

9. Visiting brothers in Allah. The Messenger of Allah ﷺ said, 'A man visited a brother of his in another town and Allah appointed an angel to guard him on his way. When he came to him, the angel asked, "Where are you going?" He said,

"I am going to a brother of mine in this town." He asked, "Do you have some property with him that you want to check on?" He answered, "No, it is only that I love him for the sake of Allah Almighty." He said, "I am the messenger of Allah to you to tell you that Allah loves you as you love this man for His sake."' Muslim and others transmitted it.

وَإِذَا ضَرَبْتُمْ فِي الْأَرْضِ فَلَيْسَ عَلَيْكُمْ جُنَاحٌ أَن تَقْصُرُوا مِنَ الصَّلَوٰةِ
إِنْ خِفْتُمْ أَن يَفْتِنَكُمُ الَّذِينَ كَفَرُوا إِنَّ الْكَافِرِينَ كَانُوا لَكُمْ عَدُوًّا مُّبِينًا ﴿١٠١﴾

101 When you are travelling in the land, there is nothing wrong in your shortening your prayer if you fear that those who disbelieve may harass you. The unbelievers are your clear-cut enemies.

When you are travelling in the land, there is nothing wrong in your shortening your prayer

Scholars disagree about the legal status of shortening prayers on a journey. It is related from a group that it is obligatory. That is the position of 'Umar ibn 'Abd al-'Azīz, the Kufans, Qāḍī Ismā'īl and Ḥammād ibn Abī Sulaymān. Their evidence is found in the *hadīth* of 'Ā'ishah: 'The prayers were prescribed as two *rak'ah*s each.' Those who oppose it have no proof. It is complete on the journey. That weakens [their view]. The consensus of the *fuqahā'* is that it is not a fundamental ruling of the prayer of a traveller contrasting it to the prayer of someone who is resident. Other Companions, like 'Umar, Ibn 'Abbās, and Jubayr ibn Muṭ'im said, 'The prayer was prescribed as four while resident and two on a journey and one in the case of fear.' Muslim related it from Ibn 'Abbās. The *ḥadīth* of 'Ā'ishah was related by Ibn 'Ajlān from Ṣāliḥ ibn Kaysān from 'Urwah: 'The Messenger of Allah ﷺ prescribed the prayers as two *rak'ah*s each.' Al-Awzā'ī said from Ibn Shihāb from 'Urwah that 'Ā'ishah said, 'Allah prescribed the prayer for the Messenger of Allah ﷺ as two *rak'ah*s each,' noted the confusion here and added that 'prescribed' cannot be taken literally because *Maghrib* is three *rak'ah*s and *Ṣubḥ* is never shortened. Both are neither increased nor decreased. All of this weakens the text but not the *isnād*.

Ibn al-Jahm said that Ashhab reported from Mālik that it is obligatory to shorten the prayer. The well-known position of his school and that of most of his people and most of the scholars of the Salaf and modern scholars is that it is *sunnah* to shorten it. That is also the position of ash-Shāfi'ī and it is sound. Allah willing. The school of most Baghdādī Mālikīs is that there is a choice where the obligatory prayer is concerned. This is the position of the people of ash-Shāfi'ī. They disagree about which is better. Some, like al-Abharī and others, say that it is better to shorten, but it is also said that performing it in full is better. That is related from ash-Shāfi'ī. Abū Sa'īd al-Farawī al-Mālikī related that the sound position in the school of Mālik is that the traveller has a choice regarding this.

The words of Allah are clear: '*...there is nothing wrong in your shortening your prayer*' and Mālik recommended shortening the prayer on journeys. He also thought that the prayer should be repeated within the time if someone has prayed it in full. Abū Muṣ'ab reported in his *Mukhtaṣar* from Mālik and the people of Madīnah, 'Shortening the prayer on a journey is *sunnah* for men and women.' Abū 'Umar said, 'This is enough for you concerning the position of the school of Mālik, although there is no disagreement that he said that someone who does it in full should repeat it within the time. That is recommended for the one with understanding but is not mandatory.'

Ash-Shāfi'ī says that the shortening outside of fear is *sunnah*. When there is fear on a journey, it is based on the Book and the *Sunnah*. If someone prays four in that situation, he owes nothing, but it is not liked for someone to abandon the *sunnah* by praying it in full. Abū Bakr al-Athram said, 'I asked Aḥmad ibn Ḥanbal, "Can a man pray four *rak'ahs* on a journey?" "No!" he answered, "I do not like it. The *Sunnah* is two *rak'ahs*."' We find in the *Muwaṭṭā'* of Mālik from Ibn Shihab that a man of the family of Khālid ibn Asīd said to 'Abdullah ibn 'Umar, 'Abū 'Abd ar-Raḥmān, we find the fear prayer and the prayer when resident mentioned in the Qur'an, but we do not find any mention of the travelling prayer in it.' Ibn 'Umar responded, 'Son of my brother! Allah Almighty sent us Muhammad ﷺ when we knew nothing. We only do as we saw him doing.' This tells us that shortening the prayer on a journey when there is no fear is *sunnah*, not obligatory because it is not mentioned in the Qur'an. The shortening which is mentioned in the Qur'an is conditional on travelling, joining prayers and also fear. It is only permitted in His Book with these two conditions. Something similar in the Qur'an is: '*If any of you do not have the means to marry...*' (4:25)

Allah says: '*When you are safe again perform the prayer in the normal way*' (4:102), meaning perform it in full. The Messenger of Allah ﷺ shortened the prayers except for *Maghrib* from four *rak'ahs* to two on journeys. He was safe in all of them and only feared Allah Almighty. So that is the *sunnah* established by the Prophet ﷺ in addition to the rulings of Allah like all that he made *sunnah* and elucidated which was not mentioned in the Qur'an. That is made clear by the words 'as we saw him doing,' coupled with the *ḥadīth* of 'Umar when he asked the Messenger of Allah ﷺ about shortening the prayer when travelling when there is no fear. The words, 'This is *ṣadaqah* which Allah has given you, so accept His *ṣadaqah*,' are evidence that Allah has allowed something in His Book with a stipulation and then allowed it on the tongue of His Messenger without the stipulation.

Ḥanẓalah ibn 'Umar was asked about the travelling prayer and said that it was two *rak'ahs*. The questioner continued, 'So where is *"if you fear that those who disbelieve may harass you"* when we are safe?' He said, 'It is the *Sunnah* of the Messenger of Allah ﷺ.' This is Ibn 'Umar who called it *sunnah*. Ibn 'Abbās said, 'How then do we leave them?' Abū 'Umar said, 'Mālik did not think that the *isnād* of this *ḥadīth* was straight because the man who asked Ibn 'Umar is not named. He dropped a man from the *isnād*. The man who was not named was Umayyah ibn 'Abdullāh ibn Khālid ibn Usayd ibn Abī al-'Īṣ ibn Umayyah ibn 'Abd Shams ibn 'Abd Manāf. Allah knows best.'

Scholars disagree about the distance beyond which the prayer may be shortened. Dāwūd said that it is a long or short journey, even three miles, with respect to attending *Jumu'ah*, holding to what Muslim related from Anas ibn Mālik: 'When the Messenger of Allah ﷺ went on a journey of three miles (or three parasangs), he would pray two *rak'ahs*.' There is no authoritative proof in that because there is uncertainty. According to what is implied by one of them, it could be the definition of the distance where one begins to shorten, and the journey was longer than that. Allah knows best.

Ibn al-'Arabī says, 'Some people toyed with the *dīn* and said that when someone leaves his town, he can shorten the prayer and break the fast. The one who said that is not an Arab and does not understand the meaning of 'journey' with the Arabs or is making light of the *dīn*. If it had not been that the scholars mentioned it, I would not have been pleased to give it a glance and would not have given it a thought in my heart.' The definition of a journey is not mentioned in the Qur'an or the *Sunnah*. That is because it is an Arabic word which was known by the Arabs whose language is the language of the Qur'an. We know that if someone leaves his house for a few chores, he is not travelling either legally or linguistically, and if he travels for three days, he is definitely travelling.

We judge that someone who walks a day and a night is travelling because the Prophet ﷺ said, 'It is not lawful for a woman who believes in Allah and the Last Day to travel the distance of a day except with a relative who is *maḥram*.' It is sound because it is in the middle between the two states and Mālik relied on that. He did not find that this *ḥadīth* was agreed upon. Sometimes it is related as 'a day and a night' and sometimes as 'three days'. He relied on the action of Ibn 'Umar who shortened the prayer at Ri'm, which is a distance four stages, because he always imitated what the Messenger of Allah ﷺ had done.

All scholars have said that the shortening was prescribed to make things easier, which applies to a long journey in which there is hardship. Mālik, ash-Shāfi'ī and his people, al-Layth, al-Awzā'ī and the *fuqahā'* of *ḥadīth*, Aḥmad ibn Ḥanbal, Isḥāq and others said that it is a full day. Mālik said a day and a night, meaning a full day. It does not mean that he travels the full day and the full night, but means that he travels far enough to spend the night away from his family and cannot return to them.

We find in al-Bukhārī that Ibn 'Umar and Ibn 'Abbās used to break the fast and shorten the prayer for a distance of four *burd*s (mail-stages) which is sixteen parasangs. This is the position of the school of Mālik. Ash-Shāfi'ī and aṭ-Ṭabarī said that the distance is 46 miles. It is reported from Mālik in *al-'Utbiyyah* that he went out to his estate which was 45 miles away and shortened the prayer. It is a similar distance. It is also reported from Mālik that he shortened after thirty-six miles, which is close to a day and a night. Yaḥyā ibn 'Umar said, 'It is always repeated.' Ibn 'Abd al-Ḥakam added, 'within the time!'

The Kufans said that the prayer is not shortened on a journey of less than three days. That is the position of 'Uthmān, Ibn Mas'ūd and Ḥudhayfah. We find in *Ṣaḥīḥ Bukhārī* from Ibn 'Umar that the Prophet ﷺ said, 'A woman should not travel for three days [or more] except with a *maḥram*.' Abū Ḥanīfah said that it is three days and nights by camel, and by walking. Al-Ḥasan and az-Zuhrī said that the prayer is shortened on a two day journey. This view is related from Mālik. Abū Sa'īd al-Khudrī related that the Prophet ﷺ said, 'A woman should not travel for the distance of two nights except with a husband or a *maḥram*.' Ibn 'Umar shortened the prayer at a distance of thirty miles and Anas after fifteen miles. Al-Awzā'ī said, 'Most scholars shorten after a full day. That is my position.'

Abū 'Umar said, 'The *marfū'* reports in this area are indecisive, as you see from their words. In summary, and Allah knows best, is that they come to answer questions. Each of them related the answer of what he heard. It is as if the Prophet ﷺ was asked at a particular time, 'Can a woman travel the distance of a day without a *maḥram*?' and he said, 'No.' Another time he was asked, 'Can a woman travel two days without a *maḥram*?' and he said, 'No.' And yet another time he was asked, 'Can a woman travel three days without a *maḥram*?' and he said, 'No.' The same is true about the meaning of 'night' and '*burd*' as is related. Each conveyed the meaning of what he heard. Allah knows best. Combining the meaning of the reports in this area, even if their literal wording varies, is that it is forbidden for a woman to make a journey, in which trial is feared on it, if she does not have a *maḥram*, be it long or short. Allah knows best.

People disagree about the type of journey on which the prayer may be shortened. There is a consensus among people about *jihād*, *ḥajj* and *'umrah*, and what is similar, such as maintaining ties of kinship and saving life. People disagree about other things. The majority say that it is permitted to shorten the prayer on a permissible journey like one for trade and the like. It is related that Ibn Mas'ūd said, 'The prayer is only shortened for the *ḥajj* or *jihād*.' 'Aṭā' said, 'The prayer is only shortened on a journey of obedience and one of the paths of good.' It is also related from 'Aṭā' that it is shortened on every permissible journey and that is the position of the majority.

Mālik said, 'When someone goes out to hunt, not for the sake of livelihood but for pleasure, or goes to visit a town for amusement and pleasure, they should not shorten the prayer.' The majority of scholars say that there is no shortening on a journey involving disobedience, like that of a rebel or highwayman and other such things. It is related from al-Awzā'ī and Abū Ḥanīfah that it is permitted to shorten for all of that and it is also related from Mālik. The different views of Aḥmad were reported *in al-Baqarah*: sometimes he took the position of the majority and sometimes he said that it may only be shortened for *ḥajj* or *'umrah*.

The sound position is what the majority said because shortening was prescribed as a dispensation for travellers because of the hardships connected to it and helping them during it. All journeys are the same in that respect because Allah says: *'When you are travelling in the land, there is nothing wrong* (meaning any sin) *in your shortening your prayer.'* So it is universal. The Prophet ﷺ said, 'The best of Allah's servants are those who shorten the prayer and break the fast when they travel.' Ash-Sha'bī said, 'Allah loves people to avail themselves of dispensations as He loves them acting with resolve.' As for journeys involving disobedience, it is not permitted to shorten the prayer on those because that is helping people to disobey Allah. Allah says: *'Help each other to goodness and taqwā. Do not help each other to wrongdoing and enmity.'* (5:2)

They disagree about when someone starts to shorten the prayer. The majority of scholars say that they do not shorten the prayer until they have left the houses of the town. Then they are 'travelling in the land'. It is the view of Mālik in the *Mudawwanah* and he did not give a definition for proximity. It is related from Mālik that when the inhabitants of a town live close together, they do not shorten the prayer until they have gone three miles beyond them. That is the same with the return. If the people do not live not close together, they shorten when they go past their gardens.

It is related that when al-Ḥārith ibn Abī Rabī'ah wanted to travel, he led those with him in two *rak'ahs* in his home, and they included al-Aswad ibn Yazīd and more than one of the companions of Ibn Mas'ūd. 'Aṭa' ibn Abī Rabāḥ and Sulaymān ibn Mūsā said that. According to this, the *āyah* would mean: 'when you resolve to travel in the land.' Allah knows best.

It is related that Mujāhid said, 'A traveller does not shorten the prayer on the first day until night.' This is aberrant. It is confirmed from the *ḥadīth* of Anas ibn Mālik that the Messenger of Allah ﷺ prayed *Ẓuhr* in Madīnah with four *rak'ahs* and prayed *'Aṣr* at Dhu-l-Ḥulayfah with two *rak'ahs*. The imams have transmitted it. There are about six or seven miles between Dhu-l-Ḥulayfah and Madīnah.

A traveller must make the intention to shorten when he starts the prayer. If someone starts the prayer with the intention of shortening it and then while they are praying decide they are resident, they should turn it into a voluntary prayer. If that is after they have prayed a *rak'ah*, they add another and say the *salām*. Then they pray the prayer of a resident. Al-Abharī and Ibn al-Jallāb said that this is recommended, and Allah knows best. If they build on what they have prayed and complete the prayer, it satisfies the requirement. Abū 'Umar said, 'I consider this to be as they have both said because they were referring to *Ẓuhr*, whether travelling or resident. The same is true about the rest of the five prayers.'

Scholars disagree about the length of time a traveller intends to remain in a place which requires them to perform the prayer in full. Mālik, ash-Shāfi'ī, al-Layth ibn Sa'd, aṭ-Ṭabarī and Abū Thawr said that if someone intends to remain for four days, then he should perform the prayer in full. That is related from Sa'īd ibn al-Musayyab. Abū Ḥanīfah and his people and ath-Thawrī said that when someone intends to remain for fifteen nights, they should perform the prayer in full. If it is less than that, they continue to shorten the prayers. That is the position of Ibn 'Umar and Ibn 'Abbās and none of the Companions disagreed with them according to what aṭ-Ṭaḥāwī mentioned. It is also related from Sa'īd. Aḥmad said, 'When a traveller intends to remain in a place for twenty-one prescribed prayers, they should shorten. When it is more than that, he does it in full.' That is the position of Dāwūd.

The sound position is what Mālik said based on the *ḥadīth* of Ibn al-Ḥaḍramī that the Prophet ﷺ made the stay of a Muhājir, who stayed in Makkah after finishing his practices, three days and then they would return. Aṭ-Ṭaḥāwī, Ibn Mājah and others transmitted it. It is known that since hijrah became obligatory before the conquest of Makkah, residing in Makkah was not permitted. So the Messenger of Allah ﷺ assigned a Muhājir three days to settle his needs and prepare things. He was not given the ruling of residence and continued to have the ruling of a traveller. He forbade him to stay a fourth day which would have given him the ruling of being a resident. That is a reliable basis. It is like what 'Umar did when he exiled the Jews based on the statement of the Messenger of Allah ﷺ. He assigned them three days to settle their affairs.

Ibn al-'Arabī said, 'I heard one of the eminent Mālikīs say that the three days are outside of the ruling of being in residence because Allah granted a deferment of the descent of the punishment for that period along with the certainty of leaving this world. He says: *"Enjoy yourselves in your land for three more days. That is a promise which will not be belied."* (11:65)' Other things are said about this matter. It is that a traveller always shortens the prayer until they return home or take up residence. It is related that Anas stayed for two years in Nishapur during which he shortened the prayers the whole time. Abū Miljaz said, 'I said to Ibn 'Umar, "I will go to Madīnah and stay there for seven or eight months to take care of something I need to do." He said, "Pray two *rak'ahs*."' Abū Isḥāq as-Sabī'ī said, 'We stayed in Sijistan for two years accompanied by some of the people of Ibn Mas'ūd. We prayed two *rak'ahs*. Ibn 'Umar remained in Azerbaijan in which he prayed two *rak'ahs*. The snow kept us from travelling on.' Abū 'Umar said, 'We believe that these hadiths are based on the fact that none of these people had an intention to remain for this period. This is like when someone says, "I will leave tomorrow. I will leave tomorrow." When it is like that, there is no resolve to reside.'

Muslim related from 'Urwah that 'Ā'ishah said, 'When Allah prescribed the prayer, He prescribed it as two *rak'ahs*. Then He made them complete while resident and the travelling prayer was affirmed on the basis of the first obligation.' Az-Zuhrī said, 'I asked 'Urwah, "Why did 'Ā'ishah do it in full while travelling?" He answered, "She followed the same interpretation as 'Uthmān."' This answer is not complete. People disagree about 'Uthmān and 'Ā'ishah's interpretation in performing the prayer in full and there are various positions. Ma'mar said that az-Zuhrī said, "Uthmān prayed four *rak'ahs* at Minā because he had decided to stay on after the ḥajj.' Mughīrah related from Ibrāhīm that 'Uthmān prayed four *rak'ahs* at Minā because he took it as a place of residence. Yūnus said that az-Zuhrī said, 'When 'Uthmān acquired property at Ṭā'if and wanted to reside there, he prayed four *rak'ahs*.' He said that the imams took that position after him.

Ayyūb said that az-Zuhrī said, "Uthmān ibn 'Affān performed the prayer in full at Minā for the Bedouin because there were many of them that year and he led the people in four *rak'ahs* in order to teach them that the prayer had four *rak'ahs*.' Abū Dāwūd mentioned all of these views in his book in the Book of Hajj Practices about the prayer at Minā. In *at-Tamhīd*, Abū 'Umar mentioned that Ibn Jurayj said, 'I heard that 'Uthmān did the full prayer of four *rak'ah*s at Minā because a Bedouin called to him in the Khayf mosque at Minā: "Amīr al-Mu'minīn! I have continued to pray them as two *rak'ah*s since I saw you the first year!" 'Uthmān was afraid that ignorant people would think that the prayer consisted of two *rak'ahs*.' Ibn Jurayj said that he only prayed it in full at Minā.

Abū 'Umar said, 'As for the opinions about 'Ā'ishah doing the full prayer, nothing about it is related from her. These are opinions and interpretations without any accompanying evidence.' The weakest of what is said about that is that she was the Mother of the Believers, and the people are her sons and so their houses are her houses. Is the Mother of the Believers other than the wife of the Prophet ﷺ, the father of the believers? He is the one who made the sunnah of shortening the prayer on his journeys and expeditions, and during his hajj and *'umrah*. The reading of Ubayy ibn Abī Ka'b includes the words: 'his wives are their mothers, and he is a father to them.' (33:6) Mujāhid said about Allah's words: *'Here are my daughters. They are purer for you'* (11:78): that: 'Lut did not mean his actual daughters, but the women of his community. Every Prophet is a father to his community.'

The objection to this is that the Prophet ﷺ prescribed law and 'Ā'ishah is not like that and so there is a difference. Weaker than this is the position of those who say that it is possible that she did it in full because she was not on a permissible journey. This is absolutely false. She had too much fear of Allah and *taqwā* to go out on a journey not pleasing to Allah. This interpretation attributed to her is one of the ugly lies of the innovating Shi'ites. Glory be to Allah above this great lie! She went out striving, in expectation of a reward, desiring to extinguish the fire of civil war since she was more entitled to be regretful about it. Then things got out of control. This will be explained, Allah willing. It is said that she did it in full because she thought that the prayer was only shortened during the hajj, *'umrah* and on military expeditions. This is false because that has not been transmitted from her and is not known to be her position. She did it in full when she travelled to 'Alī.

The best of what is said about whether she shortened it or did it in full was that she took advantage of a dispensation given by Allah to show people that there is no harm in doing it in full, even if shortening it is better. 'Aṭā' said, 'Shortening is *sunnah* and a dispensation. It is transmitted from 'Ā'ishah that, when travelling, the Messenger of Allah ﷺ both fasted, broke the fast, and did the prayer in full and shortened. Ṭalḥah ibn 'Amr related it. He said, 'The Messenger of Allah ﷺ did all those things: he fasted and broke the fast, shortened the prayer and did it in full.'

An-Nasā'ī related with a sound *isnād* that 'Ā'ishah went on *'umrah* with the Messenger of Allah ﷺ from Madīnah to Makkah, and when she went to Makkah, she said, 'Messenger of Allah, may my father and mother be your ransom! You shorten and pray in full, and break the fast and fast!' He said, 'You have done well, 'Ā'ishah,' without criticizing what she had done. Ad-Dāraquṭnī related from 'Ā'ishah that the Prophet ﷺ used, when travelling, sometimes to shorten the prayer and sometimes do it in full and sometimes fast and sometimes break the fast. It has a sound *isnād.*

'An' is in the position of the accusative in 'in shortening your prayer' and so a *fī* (in) is implied. Abū 'Ubaydah said that there are three dialectical possibilities: *qaṣartu*, *qaṣṣartu* and *aqṣartu*.

Scholars disagree about the interpretation of this *āyah*. One group of scholars believe that the prayer is shortened from four to two when there is fear and on other journeys based on the *ḥadīth* of Ya'lā ibn Umayyah, as will be mentioned. Others believe that two *rak'ahs* is shortened to one, and that two *rak'ahs* on a journey is doing the prayer in full as 'Umar said, 'Completion is not shortening. Shortening it is when it becomes one.' As-Suddī said, 'When you pray two *rak'ahs* on a journey, it is doing the prayer in full. Shortening is only allowed if you are in fear. This *āyah* allows each group to pray one *rak'ah* and no more and the imām prays two *rak'ahs*.'

The same is related from Ibn 'Umar, Jābir ibn 'Abdullāh and Ka'b. Ḥudhayfah did it in Tabaristan. The commander Sa'īd ibn al-'Āṣ asked him about that. Ibn 'Abbās related that the Prophet ﷺ prayed like that in the Dhū Qarad expedition: one *rak'ah* for each group, and they did not make up the other. Jābir ibn 'Abdullāh related that the Prophet ﷺ prayed like that with his Companions on the day against Muḥārib, Khaṣafah and the Banū Tha'labah. Abū Hurayrah related that the Prophet ﷺ prayed like that between Ḍajnān and 'Usfān.

We find in *Ṣaḥīḥ Muslim* that Ibn 'Abbās said, 'Allah prescribed the prayer on the tongue of your Prophet ﷺ as four while resident, two on journeys and one when in fear.' This supports this position, although Qāḍī Abū Bakr ibn al-'Arabī mentioned in his book, *al-Qabas*, 'Our scholars said that this *ḥadīth* is rejected by consensus.' This is not sound. He and others mentioned disagreement and contention. The consensus they claim is not sound. Success is by Allah.

Abū Bakr ar-Rāzī al-Ḥanafī mentioned in *Aḥkām al-Qur'an* that what is meant by shortening here is shortening in the prayer by omitting bowing and prostration in favour of gesture, and leaving standing for bowing. Others said that this *āyah* permits shortening the limits and form of the prayer in face-to-face combat and actual fighting. It is permitted for someone in that situation to pray by indicating with his head and pray one *rak'ah* wherever he turns with the *takbīr* as mentioned in *al-Baqarah*. Aṭ-Ṭabarī prefers this position and says that it is balanced by Allah's words: *'When you are safe again perform the prayer in the normal way.'* (4:103)

These three positions have a similar basis. They are based on the fact that the obligation for a traveller is the shortened prayer, and that the prayer in respect of him was revealed as two *rak'ah*s and so it is not considered to be shortened. You cannot say '*there is nothing wrong*' in respect of a divinely imposed duty, and when two *rak'ah*s are prescribed, you cannot say that it is shortening, just as you do not say that about the *Ṣubḥ* prayer. Allah mentioned shortening with two conditions, and the prayer in which the two conditions are considered is the Fear Prayer. This is what was mentioned by Abū Bakr ar-Rāzī in *Aḥkām al-Qur'ān*. He supports it, and it is refuted by the *ḥadīth* of Ya'lā ibn Umayyah as will be mentioned, Allah willing.

if you fear that those who disbelieve may harass you

This is used for the general state of affairs since on journeys, the general state of affairs for Muslims was fear. Ya'la ibn Umayyah asked 'Umar ibn al-Khaṭṭāb about this, 'Why do we shorten the prayer when we are safe?' 'Umar said, 'I wondered about what you wondered. So I asked the Messenger of Allah ﷺ about that and he said, *"A ṣadaqah* which Allah gives you. Accept His *ṣadaqah*."' The people of ash-Shāfi'ī and others argued against the Ḥanafīs using the *ḥadīth* of Ya'la ibn Umayyah and said that his words, 'Why do we shorten the prayer when we are safe?' is definitive evidence that what is understood from the *āyah* is shortening the number of *rak'ah*s.

Aṭ-Ṭabarī said, 'According to this interpretation, the people of Abū Ḥanīfah did not mention an interpretation equal to what was mentioned. The two conditions are not considered in the Fear Prayer. If someone is not travelling in the land and there is no journey and the unbelievers come and attack our land, then the Fear Prayer is permitted and there is no consideration for the conditions according to what he said.' The reading of Ubayy has the condition 'if you fear'. The meaning of his reading is 'disliking for those who disbelieve to harass you.'

A group believe that this *āyah* only allows someone who fears the enemy to shorten the prayer while travelling. So someone who is safe does not shorten the prayer. It is related that 'Ā'ishah used to say on journeys, 'Do your prayer in full.' They said, 'The Messenger of Allah ﷺ used to shorten it.' She answered, 'He was engaged in war and in fear. Are you in fear?' 'Aṭā' said, 'Among the Companions of the Messenger of Allah ﷺ who did the prayer in full were: 'Ā'ishah and Sa'd ibn Abī Waqqāṣ. 'Uthmān did it in full. That, however, is faulty because of various reasons, some of which have been mentioned.' One group believed that Allah Almighty only allowed shortening in His Book when two conditions are met: travelling and fear. When there is no fear, it is by the *sunnah*. They included ash-Shāfi'ī.

Some believe that Allah's words: '*if you fear*' are not connected to what is before it and the words end at '*your prayer*'. Then there is a new sentence, so it means: 'Muḥammad, establish the Fear Prayer for them' and the words: '*The unbelievers are your clear-cut enemies,*' is interposed as al-Jurjānī said and al-Mahdawī and others mentioned. This view is refuted by al-Qushayrī and Qāḍī Abū Bakr ibn al-'Arabī. Abū Naṣr al-Qushayrī said, 'Applying it in this manner is very forced indeed, and this man – meaning al-Jurjānī – exaggerated in assumption and making examples.' Ibn al-'Arabī said, 'All of this was not needed by 'Umar, nor his son nor Ya'lā ibn Umayyah.'

There is a *ḥadīth* which contains what al-Jurjānī said which Qāḍī Abu-l-Walīd ibn Rushd mentioned in the *Muqaddimāt* as well as Ibn 'Aṭiyyah in his *Tafsīr* from 'Alī ibn Abī Ṭālib. He said, 'Some merchants asked the Messenger of Allah ﷺ, "How should we pray when we are travelling in the land?" So Allah revealed: *"When you are travelling in the land, there is nothing wrong in your shortening your prayer."* A year after that the Messenger of Allah ﷺ went on an expedition and prayed *Ẓuhr*. The idolaters said, "Muḥammad and his companions have given us power over their backs. Shouldn't we attack them?" One of them said, "They have another one after it." Between the two prayers, Allah revealed: *"if you fear that those who disbelieve may harass you…"* about the Fear Prayer.'

If this report is sound, no one can say anything in the face of it. It provides proof that shortening outside of fear is found in the Qur'an. Ibn 'Abbās also related something similar. He said that the words: *'When you are travelling in the land, there is nothing wrong with your shortening the prayer'* were revealed about praying on a journey and then about a year afterwards fear was added to it: *'If you fear that those who disbelieve may harass you.'* According to this, the *āyah* involves two situations and two rulings. The first part has to do with travelling and then there is another obligation in which the condition is put first. It implies: 'If you fear that those who disbelieve will harass you when you are among them, then establish the prayer for them.'

Some people believe that the mention of fear was abrogated by the Sunnah. That comes from the *ḥadīth* of 'Umar when he related that the Prophet ﷺ told him, 'This is *ṣadaqah* which Allah gives you. Accept His *ṣadaqah*.' An-Naḥḥās said, 'Whoever says that the fact that the Prophet ﷺ shortened the prayer when there was no fear abrogates the *āyah* has erred because there is nothing in the *āyah* which prevents shortening it when there is security. It simply gives permission to shorten it in time of fear.'

As for the term *'yaftinakum'* (harass you), al-Farrā' said that the people of the Hijaz use Form I while Rabī'ah, Qays, Asad and all of the people of Najd use Form IV. Al-Khalīl and Sībuwayh distinguish between them. Form I is to make unrest in it and Form IV is to make someone affected by it. Al-Aṣma'ī stated that he did not recognise Form IV. '*Enemy*' [in the singular] means 'enemies'.

وَإِذَا كُنتَ فِيهِمْ فَأَقَمْتَ لَهُمُ ٱلصَّلَوٰةَ فَلْتَقُمْ طَآئِفَةٌ مِّنْهُم مَّعَكَ
وَلْيَأْخُذُوٓا۟ أَسْلِحَتَهُمْ فَإِذَا سَجَدُوا۟ فَلْيَكُونُوا۟ مِن وَرَآئِكُمْ وَلْتَأْتِ
طَآئِفَةٌ أُخْرَىٰ لَمْ يُصَلُّوا۟ فَلْيُصَلُّوا۟ مَعَكَ وَلْيَأْخُذُوا۟ حِذْرَهُمْ وَأَسْلِحَتَهُمْ
وَدَّ ٱلَّذِينَ كَفَرُوا۟ لَوْ تَغْفُلُونَ عَنْ أَسْلِحَتِكُمْ وَأَمْتِعَتِكُمْ فَيَمِيلُونَ عَلَيْكُم
مَّيْلَةً وَٰحِدَةً وَلَا جُنَاحَ عَلَيْكُمْ إِن كَانَ بِكُمْ أَذًى مِّن مَّطَرٍ أَوْ
كُنتُم مَّرْضَىٰٓ أَن تَضَعُوٓا۟ أَسْلِحَتَكُمْ وَخُذُوا۟ حِذْرَكُمْ إِنَّ ٱللَّهَ أَعَدَّ
لِلْكَٰفِرِينَ عَذَابًا مُّهِينًا ﴿١٠٢﴾

102 When you are with them and leading them in the prayer, a group of them should stand with you, keeping hold of their weapons. When they prostrate, the others should guard your backs. Then the other group who have not yet prayed should come and pray with you. They too should be careful and keep hold of their weapons. Those who disbelieve would like you to be negligent of your arms and equipment so that they can swoop down on you once and for all. There is nothing wrong, if you are bothered by rain or you are ill, in laying your weapons down; but take every precaution. Allah has prepared a humiliating punishment for the unbelievers.

When you are with them and leading them in the prayer

Ad-Dāraquṭnī reported from Abū 'Ayyāsh az-Zuraqī, 'We were with the Messenger of Allah ﷺ at 'Usfān when the idolaters under Khālid ibn al-Walīd confronted us. They were between us and the qiblah. The Prophet ﷺ had led us in the *Ẓuhr* prayer. Then they [the idolaters] said, "They are in a state where we could take them unawares." Then they said, "Now the prayer will come on them and they love it more than their sons and their selves." Then Jibrīl descended with this *āyah* between *Ẓuhr* and *'Aṣr.*' The *ḥadīth* will come in full, Allah willing. This was the reason that Khālid became Muslim.

This *āyah* is connected to the one before it by mentioning *jihād*. The Lord made it clear that the prayer is not cancelled by the excuse of travel or the excuse of *jihād* and fighting the enemy, but there is an allowance as was mentioned in *al-Baqarah* and the disagreement of scholars is mentioned here. It is addressed to the Prophet ﷺ and then extends to those who are in command after him until the Day of Rising. That is like Allah's words: *'Take zakāt from their wealth'* (9:103). All scholars say this except for someone with an aberrant view like Abū Yūsuf and Ismā'īl ibn 'Ulayyah who said that the Fear Prayer is not prayed after the time of the Prophet ﷺ since it is addressed particularly to him: *'when you are with them.'* So when he is not with them, they cannot do it because the Prophet ﷺ is not like anyone else in that respect. All of them wanted to emulate him and pray behind him. No one after him has his status in excellence. People after him have similar states to one another. That is why the imam can lead one group in prayer and command another to lead another group, but they do not pray with one imam.

Nevertheless, the majority say that we are commanded to follow and imitate in other *āyahs* and hadiths. Allah says: *'Those who oppose his command should beware of a testing trial coming to them…'* (24:63) The Prophet ﷺ said, 'Pray as you see me praying.' Therefore, it is necessary to follow him in general unless there is clear evidence that it is a specific case. If what they mentioned had indicated that it was specific, it would be necessary to confine instructions to only those to whom they were addressed. Then the Sharī'ah would be confined to those to whom it was addressed. The Companions, however, discarded the illusion that it was specific in this prayer and considered that it applied to other than the Prophet ﷺ. They had better knowledge of what was said and were closer to the situation. Allah Almighty says: *'When you see people engrossed in mockery of Our Signs, turn away from them until they start to talk of other things.'* (6:68) This is addressed to him and yet his community is included in it. There are many examples of that.

Allah says: *'Take zakāt from their wealth'* (9:103) and that is not confined to him alone: those after him took his place in this. The same is true of His words: *'When you are among them.'* Do you not see that Abū Bakr aṣ-Ṣiddīq along with the Companions fought those who took an interpretation of *zakāt* similar to that taken here about the Fear Prayer. Abū 'Umar said, 'The collection of *zakāt*, which the Prophet ﷺ and caliphs did after him, is not like a prayer prayed behind the Prophet ﷺ being like the prayer prayed behind others because the benefit of *zakāt* goes to the poor, and the giver does not obtain excellence in it as the excellence that someone who prays behind the Prophet ﷺ obtains.'

a group of them should stand with you,

This is a group standing with him in the prayer.

keeping hold of their weapons.

This refers to those praying, or it can be those facing the enemy. Allah only mentioned a single *rak'ah* for the group, but hadiths tell us that each group added another to it. The *kasrah* is elided from '*fa-l-taqum*' and '*fa-l-yakūnū*' because it is heavy. Al-Akhfash, al-Farrā' and al-Kisā'ī related that the *lām* of the command, the *lām* of 'in order to' and the *lām* of denial have a *fatḥah*. Sībawayh forbids that because of a necessary reason: it is the difference between the genitive *lām* and the *lām* of stress.

There are different transmissions about the form of the Fear Prayer and scholars differ accordingly. Ibn al-Qaṣṣār mentioned that the Prophet ﷺ prayed it in ten places. Ibn al-'Arabī related that the Prophet ﷺ prayed the Fear Prayer twenty-four times. Imām Aḥmad ibn Ḥanbal, the Imam of Hadith and the preeminent scholar in knowledge of the defects of *ḥadīth* transmission, said, 'I do not know of just one firm *ḥadīth* on the Fear Prayer, but they are all sound and firm. Whichever *ḥadīth* is the basis for praying the Fear Prayer satisfies the requirement, Allah willing.' That is like what Abū Ja'far aṭ-Ṭabarī said.

Mālik and the rest of his people except for Ashhab believe that the Fear Prayer is done according to the *ḥadīth* of Sahl ibn Abī Ḥathmah. He related in his *Muwaṭṭā'* from Yaḥyā ibn Sa'īd from al-Qāsim ibn Muḥammad from Ṣāliḥ ibn Khawwāt al-Anṣārī that Sahl ibn Abī Ḥathmah related that the form of the Fear Prayer is that the imam stands with a group of his companions, while another group faces the enemy. The imam prays one *rak'ah* with them, including the prostration, and then stands. He remains standing while they complete the remaining *rak'ah* by themselves. Then they say the *taslīm*, leave, and form up opposite the enemy while the imam remains standing. Then the others who have not prayed come forward and say the *takbīr* behind the imam and he prays one *rak'ah* with them, including the prostration. He then says the *taslīm* while they stand up and pray the remaining *rak'ah* by themselves. Then they say the *taslīm*.

Ibn al-Qāsim, the companion of Mālik, said, 'The practice with Mālik was based on the *ḥadīth* of al-Qāsim ibn Muḥammad from Ṣāliḥ ibn Khawwāt.' Ibn al-Qāsim said, 'He used to take the *ḥadīth* of Yazīd ibn Rūmān but then returned to this one.' Abū 'Umar said, 'Both the *ḥadīth* of al-Qāsim and that of Yazīd ibn Rūmān come from Ṣāliḥ ibn Khawwāt, although there is a difference between them about the *taslīm*. In the *ḥadīth* of al-Qāsim, the imam says the *taslīm* with the second group who then stand and finish the *rak'ah* by themselves. In the *ḥadīth* of Yazīd ibn Rūmān, he waits for them and says the *taslīm* with them. That is the position of ash-Shāfi'ī. He said, "The *ḥadīth* of Yazīd ibn Rūmān coming from Ṣāliḥ ibn Khawwāt is the most likely of the hadiths about the Fear Prayer based on the literal text of the Book. I take it."'

Part of the argument of Mālik in choosing the *ḥadīth* of al-Qāsim is based on analogy with the other prayers: the imam does not wait for anyone when he has preceded him in part of the prayer. Furthermore the *sunnah* that is agreed upon is that those following the imam make up anything that was done before they joined the prayer after the *salām* of the imam. The position of Abū Thawr in this is like that of Mālik, while Aḥmad took the position of ash-Shāfi'ī in what he preferred. There is no criticism of anyone who follows any of the forms related in respect of the Fear Prayer. Among Mālik's people, Ashhab took the *ḥadīth* of Ibn 'Umar who said, 'The Messenger of Allah ﷺ prayed the Fear Prayer: one *rak'ah* with one group while the other group was facing the enemy. Then they left and took the position of their companions, facing the enemy, and the second group came and the Messenger of Allah ﷺ prayed one *rak'ah* with them. Then the Prophet ﷺ said the *taslīm* and they finished another *rak'ah* as did the other group.' Ibn 'Umar said, 'When the fear was more intense than that, one would pray riding or standing, making indications.' Al-Bukhārī, Muslim, Mālik and others transmitted it.

Al-Awzā'ī believed that this was the form. It is what Abū 'Umar ibn 'Abd al-Barr was content with and said, 'That is because it has the strongest *isnād*. It has been transmitted by the people of Madīnah and they are an argument against those who oppose them. It is also because it most resembles the fundamental principles because the first and second groups only made up the second *rak'ah* after the Prophet ﷺ finished the prayer. That is known in his agreed upon *sunnah* in all the prayers.

The Kufans, Abū Ḥanīfah and his people with the exception of Qāḍī Abū Yūsuf Ya'qūb, took the *ḥadīth* of 'Abdullāh ibn Mas'ūd. Abū Dāwūd and ad-Dāraquṭnī transmitted it: 'The Messenger of Allah ﷺ prayed the Fear Prayer. They stood in two rows: one row behind the Prophet ﷺ and one row facing the enemy. The Prophet ﷺ led them in one *rak'ah*. Then the others came and took their place and the first group faced the enemy. The second group took their places and prayed one *rak'ah* for themselves and then said the *taslīm*.' This is the description and form mentioned in the *ḥadīth* of Ibn 'Umar, although there is a difference between them, which is that it appears that in the *ḥadīth* of Ibn 'Umar those finishing the prayer do it at the same time while the imam remains like a sole guard. In this *ḥadīth* they finish the prayer separately.

Some of them interpret the *ḥadīth* of Ibn 'Umar based on what is found in the *ḥadīth* of Ibn Mas'ūd. Ath-Thawrī followed the *ḥadīth* of Ibn Mas'ūd in one of the three transmissions from him, as did Ashhab ibn 'Abd al-'Azīz in what al-Ḥasan al-Lakhmī mentioned from him. The first was mentioned by Abū 'Umar, Ibn Yūnus and Ibn Ḥabīb from him. Abū Dāwūd related the *ḥadīth* of Ḥudhayfah, Abū Hurayrah and Ibn 'Umar in which the Prophet ﷺ prayed a *rak'ah* with each group and they did not make it up. That is what is demanded by the *ḥadīth* of Ibn 'Abbās: 'one *rak'ah* in fear'. This is the position of Isḥāq. This is indicated in *al-Baqarah* and it is more appropriate in terms of guarding the prayer. The *ḥadīth* of Ibn 'Abbās is not authoritative. His words in the *ḥadīth* of Ḥudhayfah and others, 'they did not make it up' means, as far as the one who related that knew, because it was related that they made up one *rak'ah* in that very prayer and so the testimony of the one added to it is more fitting. It is possible that it means that they did not make it up when they were safe. The point is that when the person who is fearful is safe, he does not make up the prayers he prayed in that form when there was fear. Abū 'Umar said all of that.

We find in *Ṣaḥīḥ Muslim* from Jābir that the Prophet ﷺ prayed two *rak'ahs* with each group and he said that Prophet ﷺ prayed four *rak'ahs* while the others prayed two. Abū Dāwūd and ad-Dāraquṭnī transmitted from al-Ḥasan from Abū Bakrah that the Messenger of Allah ﷺ said the *salām* after each pair of *rak'ahs*. Ad-Dāraquṭnī also transmitted from al-Ḥasan from Jābir that the Messenger of Allah ﷺ prayed two *rak'ahs* with them and said the *salām* and then prayed two *rak'ahs* with the others and said the *salām*. Abū Dāwūd said that al-Ḥasan gave a fatwa on that basis, and it is related from ash-Shāfi'ī. That is the argument used by all those who permit a difference between the intention of the imam and the one following him in the prayer. It is the position of the schools of ash-Shāfi'ī, al-Awzā'ī, Ibn 'Ulayyah, Aḥmad ibn Ḥanbal and Dāwūd. They support this by the *ḥadīth* of Jābir that Mu'ādh prayed *'Ishā'* with the Prophet ﷺ and then went and led his people in the prayer. Aṭ-Ṭaḥāwī said, 'This was in the beginning of Islam when it was permitted to pray the obligatory prayer twice. Then that was abrogated. Allah knows best.' These are the interpretations of scholars about the Fear Prayer.

The Muslims needed this prayer, which is mentioned in the Qur'an, when the Muslims had their backs to *qiblah* and the enemy were facing qiblah. That happened at Dhāt ar-Riqā'. At 'Usfān the Muslims were facing qiblah. What we mentioned about the reason for the revelation in the story of Khālid ibn al-Walīd does not match up with the division of the people into two groups. We find in the *ḥadīth* about this that when the time for the prayer came, the Prophet ﷺ ordered them to take their weapons and line up in two rows behind him. When he bowed, they all bowed. When he came up, they all came up. Then he ﷺ prostrated with the row behind him and the rest stood guarding them. When they finished and rose, the others prostrated in their place. Then they changed rows. When he bowed, they all bowed. When he came up, they all came up. Then he ﷺ prostrated with the row behind him and the rest stood guarding them. When the others sat, they prostrated and then said the *salām*. He said, 'The Messenger of Allah ﷺ prayed twice like that: once at 'Usfān and once in the territory of the Banū Sulaym.' Abū Dāwūd transmitted it from the *ḥadīth* of Abū 'Ayyāsh az-Zuraqī. It is the position of ath-Thawrī and is the most cautious of them.

Abū 'Īsā at-Tirmidhī transmitted from Abū Hurayrah that the Messenger of Allah ﷺ stopped between Ḍajnān and 'Usfān. In it he split them into two groups and prayed a *rak'ah* with each group. The people prayed one *rak'ah* each and the Prophet ﷺ prayed two *rak'ahs*. He said that it is a *gharīb* sound *ḥasan ḥadīth*. It is found in the chapter from 'Abdullāh ibn Mas'ūd, Zayd ibn Thābit, Ibn 'Abbās, Jābir, Abū 'Ayyāsh az-Zuraqī whose name was Zayd ibn aṣ-Ṣāmit, Ibn 'Umar, Ḥudhayfah, Abū Bakr, and Sahl ibn Abī Ḥathmah.

There is no contradiction between these transmissions. It is possible that one time he ﷺ prayed with them together as in the *ḥadīth* of Abū 'Ayyāsh, and another time he led them in separate groups as in the *ḥadīth* of Abū Hurayrah. There is evidence in it for someone who says that Fear Prayer is one *rak'ah*. Al-Khaṭṭābī said, 'There are various types of the Fear Prayer which the Prophet ﷺ prayed on different days and with different forms. Aiming for all of them in it is more encompassing of the prayer and more effective in being cautious.'

They disagree about how the Fear Prayer is performed at *Maghrib*. Ad-Dāraquṭnī related from al-Ḥasan from Abū Bakrah that the Prophet ﷺ led the people in the *Maghrib* prayer with three *rak'ahs* and then they left and the others came and he led them in three *rak'ahs*. So the Prophet ﷺ prayed six and the people prayed in three in two groups. That is what al-Ḥasan said.

The majority position about the *Maghrib* is different. It is that he prays two *rak'ahs* with the first group and one with the second. There is also a question about how they complete it and whether that is before or after the *taslīm* of the imam. This is the position of Mālik and Abū Ḥanīfah because it better preserves the form of the prayer. Ash-Shāfi'ī said that he prays one *rak'ah* with the first group because 'Alī did that in the night of Harīr [in the Battle of Ṣiffīn]. Allah knows best.

They disagree about the Fear Prayer when the fighting is fierce and it is feared that the time will be missed. Mālik, ath-Thawrī, al-Awzā'ī, ash-Shāfi'ī and the bulk of scholars say that people pray however they can since Ibn 'Umar said, 'If the fear is greater than that, then pray riding or sitting, indicating it.' According to the *Muwaṭṭā'*, 'facing *qiblah* or not facing it.' The position of aḍ-Ḍaḥḥāk and Isḥāq was mentioned in *al-Baqarah*.

Al-Awzā'ī said, 'If they are on the point of victory and are unable to pray, each man prays making indications for himself. If they are unable to make indications, then they delay the prayer until the fighting stops and they are safe: they then pray two *rak'ah*s. If they are unable to do so, they pray one *rak'ah* and two prostrations. If they cannot do that, then the *takbīr* is enough and they delay it until they are safe. Makḥūl said that.

Aṭ-Ṭabarī related that in *Aḥkām al-Qur'ān* from Abū Ḥanīfah and his people. He said, 'When the fear is more intense than that and they are in the clash of the battle, the Muslims pray as they can, either facing qiblah or with their backs to it. Abū Ḥanīfah and his three companions agree that they do not pray when the situation is like this, but delay the prayer. They say that if they fight while praying, the prayer is invalid. It is related that ash-Shāfi'ī said that if he follows the thrust and blow, his prayer is invalid.'

This position indicates the soundness of the view of Anas: 'I was present when the fortress of Tustar put up a resistance when dawn was becoming light while the fighting was intense. We could only pray after it was well into the day. Then we prayed it. We were with Abū Mūsā and had victory.' Anas said, 'I would not be happy to exchange that prayer for this world and all it contains.' Al-Bukhārī mentioned it and that is what was believed by our Shaykh, Abū Ja'far Aḥmad ibn Muḥammad al-Qaysī al-Qurṭubī known as Abū Ḥujjah. It is evident that al-Bukhārī preferred it because he followed it with the *ḥadīth* of Jābir: "Umar came on the Day of the Ditch and began to curse the unbelievers of Quraysh. He said, "Messenger of Allah, I could not pray *'Aṣr* until the sun had almost set." The Prophet ﷺ said, "By Allah, I too have not prayed it." He went to Buṭḥān and did *wuḍū'* and prayed *'Aṣr* after the sun had set. Then he prayed *Maghrib* afterwards.'

They disagree about the prayer of the pursuer and the pursued. Mālik and a group of his people said that they are the same. Each of them prays on his animal.

Al-Awzā'ī, ash-Shāfi'ī, the *fuqahā'* of the people of *ḥadīth* and Ibn 'Abd al-Ḥakam said that the pursuer may only pray on the ground, and that is sound, because pursuit is voluntary whereas it is obligatory for the prescribed prayer to be prayed on the ground whenever possible. Someone pursued only prays it in great fear and that is not the case with the pursuer. Allah knows best.

They disagree about when an army sees a darkness and thinks that it is the enemy and pray the fear prayer and then it becomes clear that it was nothing. Our scholars have two views. One is that they repeat the prayer, as Abū Ḥanīfah said, and the other is that they do not repeat it. That is the most evident view of ash-Shāfi'ī. The reason for the first is that they are correcting a mistake and returning to what is correct, in the way that a judge does. The reason for the second view is that they acted on their *ijtihād* and so it is permitted, as when someone errs about the *qiblah*. This is more fitting because they did what they were commanded to do. It is said that they should repeat it within the time but when it is after the time, they do not. Allah knows best.

They too should be careful and keep hold of their weapons.

This commands caution and keeping weapons on the ready so that the enemy do not realise their hope and seize the opportunity. The weapons are those which a person uses to defend himself in war. 'Antarah said:

I wore the curly hair of the sons of Abān
As my weapon (*salāḥ*) after he was divested and disgraced.

He says, 'I divested him of my weapons to prevent him using them to defend himself after being disarmed.'

Ibn 'Abbās said that the words *'keeping hold of their weapons'* apply to the group facing the enemy because the one praying does not fight. Others said that it is those praying, meaning that those who have prayed first should take up their weapons. Az-Zajjāj mentioned it and said, 'It is possible that the group in the prayer are commanded to bear weapons, meaning a group of them should stand with you and keep hold of their weapons. That is more frightening for the enemy.' An-Naḥḥās said, 'It is permitted for all because it causes fear to the enemy. It is possible that it is specific to those who are facing the enemy.'

Abū 'Umar said that most of the people of knowledge recommend that someone who prays in a state of fear should keep hold of his weapons. They interpret the words '*keeping hold of their weapons*' to be a recommendation because if it had not been for fear, they would not have taken them. Therefore, the command is a recommendation.' The literalists say that keeping hold of weapons in the Fear Prayer is obligatory since Allah has commanded it unless there is some harm from rain [or illness]. In that case, one is permitted to put them down. Ibn al-'Arabī said, 'When they prayed, they kept hold of their weapons when there was fear. That is what ash-Shāfi'ī said. It is the text of the Qur'an.' Abū Ḥanīfah said, 'They do not carry them because if it had been obligatory for them to carry them, the prayer would have been invalidated by not doing so.' We say that it is not an obligation to carry them in the prayer but is for the sake of strength and appearance.

The pronoun in *'when they prostrate'* refers to the group praying, and then they leave according to one of the transmitted forms. It is said that it means when they prostrate in the *rak'ah* of completion. This is in the form of Sahl ibn Abī Ḥathmah. This *āyah* indicates that 'prostration' is used to designate the entire prayer as when the Prophet ﷺ says, 'When one of you enters the mosque, he should perform two prostrations,' which means that he should pray two *rak'ah*s as is the sunnah. The pronoun 'they' can refer to those who prostrate or to the group who first stand opposite the enemy.

Those who disbelieve would like you to be negligent

The unbelievers hope and want for you to be negligent about keeping hold of your weapons so they can achieve their desire. Allah explained the wisdom in the command to keep hold of weapons, and He mentioned carefulness in the second group rather than the first because it is more incumbent on them to be careful because the enemy might not delay their attack until the end of the prayer. Furthermore, the enemy might see that you are heavily armed and leave. This *āyah* indicates making use of means which will achieve victory and safety. *'Once and for all'* means suddenly and in such an overwhelming manner that no second attack will be required.

There is nothing wrong, if you are bothered by rain or you are ill,

Scholars have spoken about the obligatory nature of keeping hold of weapons in the prayer as we have indicated. Even if it is not obligatory, it is definitely recommended for caution. Then there is an allowance for rain because it will make the linings wet and heavy and rust iron.

It is said that it was revealed about the Prophet ﷺ who was in a palm wadi when the idolaters had been routed and the Muslims had gained victory. It was a rainy day and the Prophet ﷺ left his weapons and went out for a call of nature.

The idolaters saw him leave his Companions and Ghawrath ibn al-Ḥārith crept down to him with his sword and said, 'Who will defend you from me now?' The Messenger of Allah ﷺ replied, 'Allah.' Then he said, 'O Allah, defend me from Ghawrath ibn al-Ḥārith as You wish!' Ghawrath brought the sword down to strike and he was pushed back and the sword slipped from his hand. Al-Wāqidī reported that it was Jibrīl who pushed him. The Messenger of Allah ﷺ got up and took the sword and said, 'Ghawrath, who will protect you from me now?' 'No one,' he replied. He said, 'Testify that I have the truth and I will give you your sword.' 'No,' he said, 'but I will testify that I will not fight you and will not help anyone against you.' So the Messenger of Allah gave him his sword.

The *āyah* was revealed about the allowance to set aside weapons when it is raining. 'Abd ar-Raḥmān ibn 'Awf was suffering from a wound, as it states in *Ṣaḥīḥ Bukhārī*, and Allah made an allowance for them to leave their weapons and readiness for the enemy because of rain. Then He commands them: '*...but take every precaution,*' in other words be alert, whether or not you lay aside your weapons. This indicates the paramount importance of being prepared and cautious about the enemy in all moments and not surrendering. The army is only afflicted by lack of caution. Aḍ-Ḍaḥḥāk said that it means 'gird on your swords.' That is how warriors are.

فَإِذَا قَضَيْتُمُ ٱلصَّلَوٰةَ فَٱذْكُرُوا۟ ٱللَّهَ قِيَٰمًا وَقُعُودًا وَعَلَىٰ جُنُوبِكُمْ فَإِذَا
ٱطْمَأْنَنتُمْ فَأَقِيمُوا۟ ٱلصَّلَوٰةَ إِنَّ ٱلصَّلَوٰةَ كَانَتْ عَلَى ٱلْمُؤْمِنِينَ
كِتَٰبًا مَّوْقُوتًا ۝١٠٣ وَلَا تَهِنُوا۟ فِى ٱبْتِغَآءِ ٱلْقَوْمِ إِن تَكُونُوا۟ تَأْلَمُونَ
فَإِنَّهُمْ يَأْلَمُونَ كَمَا تَأْلَمُونَ وَتَرْجُونَ مِنَ ٱللَّهِ مَا لَا يَرْجُونَ وَكَانَ
ٱللَّهُ عَلِيمًا حَكِيمًا ۝١٠٤

103 When you have completed the prayer remember Allah standing, sitting and lying on your sides. When you are safe again do the prayer in the normal way. The prayer is prescribed for the believers at specific times. 104 Do not relax in pursuit of the enemy. If you feel pain, they too are feeling it just as you are, but you hope for something from Allah which they cannot hope for. Allah is All-Knowing, All-Wise.

When you have completed the prayer

When you have completed the Fear Prayer. This indicates that 'completing' is used for what is within the time as we see elsewhere (2:200).

remember Allah standing, sitting and lying on your sides.

Most believe that this *dhikr* (remembering) is commanded to be done after the Fear Prayer, meaning when you have completed the prayer, remember Allah with your heart and tongue in every state and continue to mention Him with the *takbīr*, *shahādah* and prayer for victory, especially in battle. This is like the *āyah*: *'When you met a troop, stand firm and remember Allah repeatedly so that hopefully you will be successful.'* (8:46).

It is said that the words: *'When you have completed'* means praying in the Abode of War, when you can pray on mounts, or standing, sitting or on your sides when you cannot stand due to fear or illness. Allah says in another *āyah*: *'If you are afraid, pray on foot or mounted.'* (2:239)

Some people said that this is like the *āyah* in *Āli 'Imrān*. It is reported that 'Abdullāh ibn Mas'ūd saw some people making an uproar in the mosque and asked, 'What is this uproar?' They answered, 'Did not Allah say: *"Remember Allah standing, sitting and lying on your sides?"*' He said, 'By this He meant the prescribed prayer. If you are not able to stand, then sitting. If you cannot do that, then pray on your side.' What is meant is the prayer itself because the prayer is remembering Allah Almighty. It contains prescribed and *sunnah* forms of *dhikr*. The first is more likely, and Allah knows best.

When you are safe again perform the prayer in the normal way.

'Feeling safe' is the soul being free of fear. *'When you are safe,'* then perform the prayer with all its pillars and in its full form on a journey and with its full number of *rak'ahs* when resident.

The prayer is prescribed for the believers at specific times.

These are its obligatory times. Zayd ibn Aslam said that the term *'specific times'* (*mawqūt*) means its appointed times, meaning that you must perform it at its appointed times. The people of language say that it means at its proper time. One says that its time is *'mawqūt'* and *waqqatahu* is to appoint a time for it which is then *mu'aqqat* (appointed). This is also exactly what Zayd ibn Aslam said. He said that *'kitāb'* is a masculine verbal noun which is why Allah says: *'mawqūt'*.

Do not relax in pursuit of the enemy.

'Do not relax' means do not weaken as was already mentioned in *Āli 'Imrān*. It is

said that it was revealed in the Battle of Uḥud when the Prophet ﷺ commanded them to go after the idolaters when many Muslims were wounded. The command was that only those who had taken part in the battle could go with him as was mentioned in *Āli 'Imrān*. It is said that it means in all *jihād*.

If you feel pain, they too are feeling it just as you are, but you hope for something from Allah which they cannot hope for.

The pain is because of their wounds and the enemy also feel pain from their wounds. You, however, have a definitive advantage, which is that you hope for the reward of Allah which they cannot hope for. That is because anyone who does not believe in Allah does not hope for anything from Allah. That is like the *āyah*: *'If you have received a wound, they have already received a similar wound.'* (3:140)

'Abd ar-Raḥmān al-A'raj recited *'an takūnū'*, meaning 'because it'. Manṣūr ibn al-Mu'tamir recited *'in takūnū tīlamūna'*. According to the Basrans, it is not permitted to have a *kasrah* on the *tā'* because it is heavy on it. It is also said that *raja'* (hope) here can mean 'fear because when someone hopes for something that he will not definitely obtain, he must have fear of not getting what he hopes for. Al-Farrā' and az-Zajjāj said, *'Rajā'* is only used with the meaning of "fear" with the negative as in 71:13 and 45:14.' Al-Qushayrī said, 'It is not impossible to mention fear without the words being in the negative, but the two claim that it only exists with the negative. Allah knows best.'

إِنَّآ أَنزَلْنَآ إِلَيْكَ ٱلْكِتَٰبَ بِٱلْحَقِّ لِتَحْكُمَ بَيْنَ ٱلنَّاسِ بِمَآ أَرَىٰكَ ٱللَّهُ
وَلَا تَكُن لِّلْخَآئِنِينَ خَصِيمًا ﴿١٠٥﴾

105 We have sent down the Book to you with the truth so that you can judge between people according to what Allah has shown to you. But do not be an advocate for the treacherous.

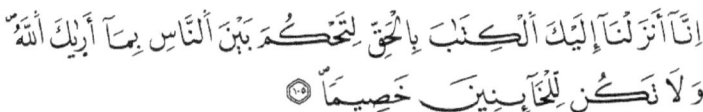

This *āyah c*ontains honour and esteem for the Prophet ﷺ and entrusting the matter to him. It also contains the establishment of the method of judgment and rebuke for what was presented to him in the case of the sons of Ubayraq. They were three brothers: Bishr, Bushayr and Mubashshir. Usayr ibn 'Urwah was their cousin. They went into a room belonging to Rifā'ah ibn Zayd in the night and stole some of his armour and food. He discovered that. It was also said that the thief was only Bushayr who was called Abū Ṭa'imah. It is said that the armour was in a bag with some flour. The flour leaked from a hole in the bag all the way to his house. The nephew of Rifā'ah, Qatādah ibn an-Nu'mān, went to the Prophet ﷺ to lodge a complaint about them. Usayr ibn 'Urwah went to the Prophet ﷺ and said, 'Messenger of Allah, they turned towards the people of a house who are people of righteousness and *dīn* and blamed them for the theft and accused them of it without any evidence.'

He began to argue until the Prophet became angry with Qatādah and Rifā'ah. Then Allah revealed: *'Do not argue on behalf of those who betray themselves'* (4:107) and Allah revealed: *'Anyone who commits an error or an evil action, and then ascribes it to someone innocent...'* (4:112) The innocent man whom they accused of theft was Labīd ibn Sahl or Zayd ibn as-Samīn or a man of the Anṣār. When Allah revealed this, the son of Ubayraq who was the thief fled to Makkah and lodged with Sulāfah bint Sa'd. Ḥassān ibn Thābit then composed a poem about her:

The daughter of Sa'd lodged him
    and the skin of her buttocks fought her and she fought him.

You suppose that what you have done is hidden,
    but among us is a Prophet with revelation.

When she heard it, she said, 'You have given me Ḥassān's poem!' She took his saddle and threw him out. He fled to Khaybar and apostatised. Then he broke through a wall at night to steal and the wall fell on him and he died an apostate. This story is mentioned by at-Tirmidhī. He said that it is a *gharīb ḥasan ḥadīth*. We do not know of anyone who has its *isnād* other than Muḥammad ibn Salamah al-Ḥarrānī. Al-Layth and aṭ-Ṭabarī mentioned it with different wording. Yaḥyā ibn Salām mentioned his death in his *tafsīr*. Al-Qushayrī also has it like that and also mentions his apostasy.

Then it is said that Zayd ibn as-Samīn and Labīd ibn Sahl were Jews. It is said that Labīd was a Muslim as al-Mahdawī mentioned. Abū 'Umar included him in his *Book of Companions*. That indicates that he thought that he was a Muslim. Bushayr was a hypocrite who used to satirise the Companions of the Prophet ﷺ and used poetry against others. The Muslims used to say, 'By Allah, it is only the poetry of a foul person.' He said in his poetry in which he justified himself:

Whenever men utter an ode
    freely given, they say, 'Ibn al-Ubayriq said it.'

Aḍ-Ḍaḥḥāk said, 'The Prophet ﷺ wanted to cut off his hand. The Jews came to complain about weapons and seized him and fled with him, so this was revealed. Allah knows best.

according to what Allah has shown to you.

It means according to the laws of the *Sharī'ah* either by revelation and text or by investigation according to the customs of revelation, which is the basis for analogy. This indicates that when the Prophet ﷺ saw something, he was correct because Allah had showed him it. Allah guaranteed His Prophets protection (*'iṣmah*) from wrong action. When one of us sees and supposes something, there is no definitiveness in what he has seen. Seeing with the physical eye is not meant here because a judgment is not seen by the eye. There is some elision in the words, meaning: 'According to what Allah has shown you.' There is another implication: 'carry out the judgments according to what We have taught you without being deceived by their deduction.'

But do not be an advocate for the treacherous.

Khaṣīm (advocate) is an active participle, like *jalīs* for a sitting companion. The form *fa'īl* here does not have a passive meaning. That is indicated by the words here. *Khaṣīm* is the one who argues. The plural is *khuṣamā'*. It is also said that it is the adversary (*mukhāṣim*). It is an active participle.

Allah forbids His Prophet ﷺ to support the people of suspicion and to defend them. This indicates that it is not permitted to represent the one in the wrong and the suspect in a quarrel, and it is not permitted for anyone to argue on behalf of someone unless he believes he is in the right. The words of the *sūrah* discuss the preservation of the property of orphans and other people and it is clear that the property of the Muslim and the unbeliever is protected except in such circumstances as Allah has made clear.

Scholars say that when the hypocrisy of a people is clear to the Muslims, it is not proper for a group of the Muslims to argue on behalf of a group of them to protect and defend them. When this occurred in the time of the Prophet ﷺ, this *āyah* was revealed about that as well as: *'Do not argue on behalf of those who betray themselves.'* (4:107) It is addressed to the Prophet ﷺ while what is meant are those Muslims who used to do this. There are two reasons for that. One of them is that Allah made that clear afterwards when He said: *'Here you are arguing on their behalf in this world.'* (4:109) The other is that the Prophet ﷺ judged between them and so he should not offer a plea to him or to anyone else. This indicates that what is desired is something else.

وَاسْتَغْفِرِ اللَّهَ إِنَّ اللَّهَ كَانَ غَفُورًا رَّحِيمًا ﴿١٠٦﴾

106 And ask Allah's forgiveness. Allah is Ever-Forgiving, Most Merciful.

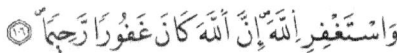

Aṭ-Ṭabarī believed that the meaning is: 'Ask forgiveness of Allah for your error in arguing on behalf of the treacherous.' He was commanded to ask forgiveness for defending them and cutting off the hand of the Jew. This is the position of those who allow minor errors to the Prophets, may Allah's blessing be on all of them.

Ibn 'Aṭiyyah said, 'This is not an error, but the Prophet ﷺ decided on the basis of the apparent, believing in their innocence,' and so the meaning is: 'Ask forgiveness of Allah for the wrongdoers among your community and those who argue for falsehood. Your place is to listen to the claimant and judge according to what you hear and ask forgiveness for the wrongdoer.' It is said that asking forgiveness is glorification. It is as a man says, 'I ask Allah's forgiveness' by way of glorification without intending repentance for an error. It is also said that although it is addressed to the Prophet ﷺ, it is the sons of Ubayraq who are meant as in 33:1 and 10:94.

وَلَا تُجَٰدِلۡ عَنِ ٱلَّذِينَ يَخۡتَانُونَ أَنفُسَهُمۡۚ إِنَّ ٱللَّهَ لَا يُحِبُّ مَن كَانَ خَوَّانًا
أَثِيمٗا ١٠٧

107 Do not argue on behalf of those who betray themselves. Allah does not love any evildoing traitors.

This was revealed about Usayr ibn 'Urwah. Argumentation is disputation, derived from *jadl,* which is twisting rope. A man with trim physique is described as *majdūl.* A hawk is called *ajdal.* It is said that it is derived from *jadālah,* which is the surface of the earth, on which each of the opponents wants to throw down his fellow. Al-'Ajjāj said:

I rode through state after state,
and I left the powerless on the ground (*jadālah*),
covered in dust, boneless.

Jadālah is the earth. It is as you say, 'I left him *mujaddal,*' thrown down on the earth (*jadālah*). *'Allah does not love'* means that Allah is not pleased with them. The word for 'traitor' is *khawwān* rather than *khā'in* to stress how terrible treachery is. Allah knows best.

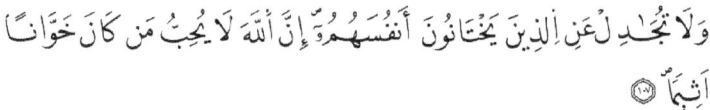

يَسْتَخْفُونَ مِنَ ٱلنَّاسِ وَلَا يَسْتَخْفُونَ مِنَ ٱللَّهِ وَهُوَ مَعَهُمْ إِذْ يُبَيِّتُونَ مَا
لَا يَرْضَىٰ مِنَ ٱلْقَوْلِ وَكَانَ ٱللَّهُ بِمَا يَعْمَلُونَ مُحِيطًا ﴿١٠٨﴾ هَٰٓأَنتُمْ هَٰٓؤُلَآءِ
جَٰدَلْتُمْ عَنْهُمْ فِي ٱلْحَيَوٰةِ ٱلدُّنْيَا فَمَن يُجَٰدِلُ ٱللَّهَ عَنْهُمْ يَوْمَ
ٱلْقِيَٰمَةِ أَم مَّن يَكُونُ عَلَيْهِمْ وَكِيلًا ﴿١٠٩﴾

108 They try to conceal themselves from people, but they cannot conceal themselves from Allah. He is with them when they spend the night saying things which are not pleasing to Him. Allah encompasses everything they do. 109 Here you are arguing on their behalf in this world, but who will argue with Allah on their behalf on the Day of Rising? Who will act as guardian for them then?

Aḍ-Ḍaḥḥāk said, 'When he stole the armour, he put it in a hole in his house and this was revealed. The hiding place of the armour was not hidden from Allah.' The words: *'He is with them'* mean that Allah is watching and observing them and it is said that the words: *'They try to conceal themselves from people'* mean that they try to hide as when Allah says: *'...you hide in the night'* (13:10). It is said that they are ashamed before people, and this is because shame is a reason to seek concealment.

'He is with them' means that He sees them, hears them and knows them. This is what the people of the *Sunnah* say. The Jahmites, Qadarites and Mu'tazilites say that He is in every place, holding to this *āyah* and those like it. They said: 'When He says that *"He is with them"*, it is confirmed that He is in every place because He is confirmed as "being with them".' This is an attribute of physical bodies and Allah is exalted beyond anything like that. Do you not see the argument of Bishr [al-Mārisī al-Jahmī] about His words: *'Three men cannot confer together secretly without him being the fourth of them'* (48:7) when he said, 'He is in every place.' His opponent said to him, 'So He is in your cap, in your intestines and inside your donkey!' Allah is greatly exalted over what they say! Wakī' related that. The words: *'they spend the night'* means that they talk. Al-Kalbī said that from Abū Ṣāliḥ from Ibn 'Abbās.

Here you are arguing on their behalf in this world,

Allah means on behalf of the people of Bushayr the thief when he fled and they argued on his behalf. Az-Zajjāj said that 'these' means 'those'. *'Jādaltum'* is 'you argued'.

Who will act as guardian for them then?

This is a question which implies denial and rebuke. A *wakīl* is the one who undertakes affairs and so Allah Almighty is the one who undertakes to manage His creation. It means that no one will undertake their business when Allah seizes them with His punishment and admits them to the Fire.

وَمَن يَعْمَلْ سُوٓءًا أَوْ يَظْلِمْ نَفْسَهُۥ ثُمَّ يَسْتَغْفِرِ ٱللَّهَ يَجِدِ ٱللَّهَ غَفُورًا رَّحِيمًا ﴿١١٠﴾

110 Anyone who does evil or wrongs himself and then asks Allah's forgiveness will find Allah Ever-Forgiving, Most Merciful.

Ibn 'Abbās said, 'Allah offered repentance to the sons of Ubayriq with this *āyah*: *"Anyone who does evil"* by stealing *"or wrongs himself"* by committing *shirk* *"and then asks Allah's forgiveness"* by repentance.' Asking forgiveness on the tongue without repentance is of no use. We explained this in Āl 'Imran. Aḍ-Ḍaḥḥāk said, 'The *āyah* was revealed about the business of Waḥshī, Ḥamzah's killer. He associated others with Allah and killed Ḥamzah and then went to the Messenger of Allah ﷺ and said, "I regret. Is any repentance possible for me?" Then Allah revealed: *"Anyone who does evil or wrongs himself."*' It is said that what is meant by this *āyah* is not defined and includes all of creation.

Sufyān related from Abū Isḥāq that al-Aswad and 'Alqamah said that 'Abdullāh ibn Mas'ūd said, 'Whoever recites these two *āyah*s of *Sūrat an-Nisā'* and then asks for forgiveness is forgiven: *"Anyone who does evil or wrong himself and then asks Allah's forgiveness will find Allah Ever-Forgiving, Most Merciful"* and *"If only when they wronged themselves they had come to you and asked Allah's forgiveness, and the Messenger had asked forgiveness for them they would have found Allah Ever-Relenting, Most Merciful."* (4:64)' It is related that 'Alī said, 'When I heard a *ḥadīth* from the Messenger of Allah ﷺ, Allah let me benefit from it as He wished. When I heard it from someone else, I made him swear to it. Abū Bakr related to me – and Abū Bakr spoke the truth – "There is no one who commits a wrong action and then does *wuḍū'* and prays two *rak'ah*s and asks for Allah's forgiveness but that He forgives him."' Then he recited this *āyah*.

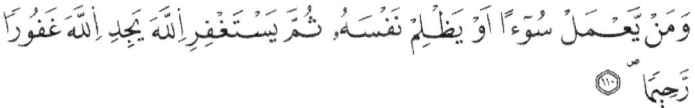

وَمَن يَكْسِبْ إِثْمًا فَإِنَّمَا يَكْسِبُهُۥ عَلَىٰ نَفْسِهِۦ وَكَانَ ٱللَّهُ عَلِيمًا
حَكِيمًا ﴿١١١﴾ وَمَن يَكْسِبْ خَطِيٓـَٔةً أَوْ إِثْمًا ثُمَّ يَرْمِ بِهِۦ بَرِيٓـًٔا فَقَدِ
ٱحْتَمَلَ بُهْتَٰنًا وَإِثْمًا مُّبِينًا ﴿١١٢﴾

111 If anyone commits an evil action, the responsibility for it is his alone. Allah is All-Knowing, All-Wise. 112 Anyone who commits an error or an evil action, and then ascribes it to someone innocent, bears the weight of slander and clear wrongdoing.

If anyone commits an evil action, the responsibility for it is his alone.

'*An evil action*' is a wrong action. Its result reverts only to the one who commits it. The verb '*commits*' here is *kasaba* (earn), which is what a human being does in order to bring to himself benefits or by which he defends himself from harm. That is why the action of the Lord cannot be called 'earning'. The expression is repeated for stress and because of the difference in the words.

Aṭ-Ṭabarī stated that there is a difference because an error can be intentional or unintentional and an evil action is only ever intentional. It is said that an error is unintentional, like accidental homicide, and it is said that an error is minor and an evil action is major. The words of this *āyah* are general and include the individuals referred to and others.

and then ascribes it to someone innocent,

The pronoun '*it*' includes error or evil action or both of them. It is also said that it refers to *kasb*.

bears the weight of slander and clear wrongdoing.

The metaphor is that wrong actions are a burden and so they are 'heavy', and that is used in the Qur'an as when Allah says: *'They will bear their own burdens and other burdens together with them.'* (29:13)

Muslim reports from Abū Hurayrah that the Prophet ﷺ said, 'Do you know what backbiting is?' They replied, 'Allah and His Messenger know best.' He said, 'It is to mention your brother in a manner he dislikes.' It was asked, 'What if my brother is as I say?' He said ﷺ, 'If he is as you said, you have backbitten him. If he is not as you said, you have slandered him.' This is a text that it is slander to falsely accuse the innocent.

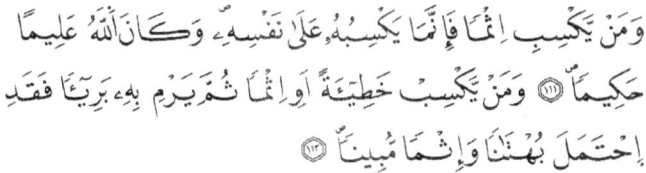

Buhtān (slander) comes from *baht* (false accusation). It is that you slander your brother by accusing him of a wrong action of which he is innocent. The verb is *bahata* with the verbal nouns *buhtān* and *baht* when one attributes something to someone when he did not do it. The person who does that is *bahhāt* and the subject is *mabhūt*. One says *bahita* with a *kasrah* when someone is dumbfounded and bewildered. *Bahuta* means the same, but *buhita* is more eloquent as we see in 2:258 because one describes a man as *mahbūt*. One does not say *bāhit* or *bahīt*. Al-Kisā'ī said that.

وَلَوْلَا فَضْلُ ٱللَّهِ عَلَيْكَ وَرَحْمَتُهُۥ لَهَمَّت طَّآئِفَةٌ مِّنْهُمْ أَن
يُضِلُّوكَ وَمَا يُضِلُّونَ إِلَّآ أَنفُسَهُمْ وَمَا يَضُرُّونَكَ مِن شَىْءٍ وَأَنزَلَ ٱللَّهُ
عَلَيْكَ ٱلْكِتَٰبَ وَٱلْحِكْمَةَ وَعَلَّمَكَ مَا لَمْ تَكُن تَعْلَمُ وَكَانَ
فَضْلُ ٱللَّهِ عَلَيْكَ عَظِيمًا ﴿١١٣﴾

113 Were it not for Allah's favour to you and His mercy, a group of them would almost have managed to mislead you. But they mislead no one but themselves and do not harm you in any way. Allah has sent down the Book and Wisdom to you and taught you what you did not know before. Allah's favour to you is indeed immense.

What follows the words '*were it not*' is in the nominative because of the inceptive according to Sībawayh and the predicate is elided. '*Allah's favour*' may refer to what Allah has informed you of regarding the Truth, or it may refer to Prophethood and protection (*'iṣmah*).

a group of them would almost have managed to mislead you.

They would have misled him from the truth because they asked the Messenger of Allah ﷺ to free the son of Ubayraq from suspicion and to attach it to the Jew. Allah was gracious to His Messenger by informing him of that.

But they mislead no one but themselves and do not harm you in any way.

That is because they do the actions of the misguided and so its consequences rebound on them. '*They do not harm you in any way*' because you are protected. '*Allah has sent down the Book and Wisdom to you*' is the inceptive of the words. It is said that the *wāw* at the beginning is the *wāw* of the *ḥāl*. It is as you say, 'I came while (*wāw*) the sun was rising.' [POEM ILLUS] The words are connected and mean: 'they will not harm you at all when Allah has sent down the Qur'an on you.'

The word '*Wisdom*' here means judging by the revelation and '*He taught you what you did not know before*' refers to laws and rulings. The verb '*know*' is in the position of the accusative because it is the predicate of *kāna* and the *ḍammah* is elided from the *nūn* for the jussive and the *wāw* is elided because of two silent letters meeting.

لَّا خَيْرَ فِي كَثِيرٍ مِّن نَّجْوِيٰهُمْ إِلَّا مَنْ أَمَرَ بِصَدَقَةٍ أَوْ مَعْرُوفٍ أَوْ إِصْلَاحٍ بَيْنَ
النَّاسِ وَمَن يَفْعَلْ ذَٰلِكَ ابْتِغَاءَ مَرْضَاتِ اللَّهِ فَسَوْفَ نُؤْتِيهِ أَجْرًا
عَظِيمًا ﴿١١٤﴾

114 There is no good in much of their secret talk, except in the case of those who enjoin *ṣadaqah*, or what is right, or putting things right between people. If anyone does that, seeking the pleasure of Allah, We will give him an immense reward.

There is no good in much of their secret talk, except in the case of those who enjoin ṣadaqah,

Allah is speaking of the plotting of the family of the sons of Ubayraq. The word *najwā* means secret conversation between two people. It is derived from the verb *nājā*, with the verbal nouns are *munājah* and *nijā'*. People are described as *yuntajūna* and *yatanājawna*. You say *najawtu, anjū najw*, meaning to confide to someone. It is derived from the verb *najā, yanjū* which means 'to rescue something and set it aside'. *Najwā* is an elevation on the earth because it is on its own by its elevation. A poet said:

Whoever is on his hill (*najwah*) is like someone in his own home.
Someone going home is like someone going out uncovered.

Najwā is a verbal noun and can be used for a group as well, as in 'a just people' (*qawm 'adl*) and 'pleasing people (*qawm riḍā*). Allah says: '*when they confer together secretly (najwā).*' (17:47)

According to the first view of *najwā*, the exception of those who enjoin *ṣadaqah* is an exception to other than the genus, and it is a separated exception. This has already been discussed. The pronoun '*man*' (*those who*) is in the position of the nominative, meaning 'but those who enjoin *ṣadaqah*, or what is right, or putting things right between people and calling to it. Then there is good in conferring together secretly.' It is also possible that '*man*' is in the genitive and so it implies: 'There is no good in much of their secret talk except in secret talk which enjoins *ṣadaqah*,' and there is elision.

According to the second view, which is that *najwā* is a noun for a group of individuals, then '*man*' is in the genitive as an appositive. It means: 'There is no good in much of their secret talk except for those who enjoin *ṣadaqah*.' Or it is in the position of the accusative according to the words of those who say, 'I did not pass by anyone but Zayd.'

Some commentators, including az-Zajjāj, said that *najwā* are the words of an isolated group or two people, whether secretly or openly. Allah knows best.

or what is right,

The noun '*ma'rūf*' (*what is right*) is a general term for all types of piety. Muqātil said that *ma'rūf* here means the obligatory practices. The first view is sounder. The Prophet ﷺ said, 'Every right action (*ma'rūf*) is *ṣadaqah*. Part of right action is to meet your brother with a cheerful face.' He ﷺ also said, 'Right action is like its name, and the first of those who enter the Garden on the Day of Rising will be right action and its people.' 'Alī ibn Abī Ṭālib said, 'Do not let the ingratitude of the one who is ungrateful to you make you dispense with right action. The thankful person is thanked many times over by the denial of the ingrate.' Al-Ḥuṭi'ah said:

Someone who does good does not lack its recompense.
Kindness (*'urf*) between Allah and people does not depart.

Ar-Riyyāshī said:

The hand of right action (*ma'rūf*) is benefit whenever it exists.
Both the ingrate and grateful bear it.

The gratitude of the grateful is recompense
and what an ingrate is ungrateful about is found with Allah.

Al-Māwardī said, 'Someone who is able to do what is right should hasten to do it before he misses the chance. He should hurry to do it out of the fear that he will lose the ability. He should know that it is part of what is incumbent in its time and there are benefits from being able to do it. Someone trustworthy who is able to do it should not neglect it. How many a person who has the ability to do it misses the chance and it is followed by regret, and how many a person who has the ability to do it misses it and is ashamed. It is as the poet said:

I continued to hear how many a trustworthy person is ashamed
until I was tested and I was the ashamed trustworthy one.

If he had grasped the calamities of his time and been protected from the results of his actions, then the profits would have been stored up and his debts settled.'

It is related that the Prophet ﷺ said, 'If someone has the door of good opened to him, he should seize hold of it. He does not know when it will be closed to him.' It is related that he ﷺ said, 'Everything has a fruit and the fruit of doing right [*ma'rūf*] is release.' Anūshirwān was asked, 'What do you consider to be the greatest affliction?' He replied, 'That you are able to do something right and do not do it until the opportunity is lost.' 'Abd al-Ḥamīd said, 'If someone delays the opportunity (to do right) beyond its time, he should be confident that he will lose it altogether.' One of the poets said:

When your winds blow, take advantage of them.
    Every flag may be becalmed.

Do not neglect charity then.
    You do not know when the becalming will occur.

Someone with wives wrote to the governor who was lax in attending to his wife (*ḥurmah*):

Do you want to attend to your wife on the road
    or to be favoured with blessings at the Reckoning?

The benefit you desire in this world will vanish
    like the sleep of sleepers.

Al-'Abbās said, 'Doing what is right in giving is only complete when it has three qualities: it is quickly done, one thinks little of it, and it is concealed. When it is quickly done, it is welcomed. When someone thinks it small, it becomes immense. When it is concealed, it is complete.' One of the poets said:

Your right giving increases in greatness in my eye
    when it is concealed and insignificant with you.

You pretend to forget it as if you had not done it,
    but with people it is known and important.

One of the conditions of right giving is not to indebt someone by it and not to be proud about it because that removes gratitude and cancels the reward. This was explained in *al-Baqarah*.

putting things right between people.

This is general to life, property and honour and everything in which there can be conflicting claims and disagreement between Muslims and in everything by which the Face of Allah is desired. We hear in a report, 'The words of the son of Ādam are all against him, except what is commanding the right, forbidding the wrong or remembering Allah.' As for seeking reputation or leadership, that has no reward. 'Umar wrote to Abū Mūsā al-Ash'arī, 'Go back to the litigants until they make peace. The final settlement of judgment may create rancour between them.' In *al-Mujādalah* we will discuss the forbidden and permitted secret talk, Allah willing.

Anas ibn Mālik said, 'If someone puts things right between two people, Allah will grant him the [reward for the] freeing of a slave for every word.' The Prophet ﷺ said to Abū Ayyūb, 'Shall I direct you to a *ṣadaqah* which Allah and His Messenger love? That you put things right between people when they are alienated and bring them near together if they are far apart.' Al-Awzā'ī said, 'There is no step which Allah loves more than a step taken to reconcile disagreement. If someone puts things right between two people, Allah will write for him freedom from the Fire.' Muḥammad ibn al-Munkadir said, 'Two men argued in a corner of the mosque and I went to them and kept at them until they made peace. Abū Hurayrah saw me and said that he had heard the Messenger of Allah ﷺ say, "If someone puts things right between people, the reward of a martyr becomes obligatory for him."' Abū Muṭī' Makḥūl ibn al-Mufaḍḍal an-Nasafī mentioned these reports in *Kitāb al-Lu'lu'yāt*. I found it in the author's handwriting on a page in which he does not state its topic.

The verb '*seeking*' is in the accusative as a direct object.

وَمَن يُشَاقِقِ ٱلرَّسُولَ مِنۢ بَعْدِ مَا تَبَيَّنَ لَهُ ٱلْهُدَىٰ وَيَتَّبِعْ غَيْرَ سَبِيلِ
ٱلْمُؤْمِنِينَ نُوَلِّهِۦ مَا تَوَلَّىٰ وَنُصْلِهِۦ جَهَنَّمَ وَسَآءَتْ مَصِيرًا ﴿١١٥﴾ إِنَّ ٱللَّهَ
لَا يَغْفِرُ أَن يُشْرَكَ بِهِۦ وَيَغْفِرُ مَا دُونَ ذَٰلِكَ لِمَن يَشَآءُ وَمَن
يُشْرِكْ بِٱللَّهِ فَقَدْ ضَلَّ ضَلَٰلًۢا بَعِيدًا ﴿١١٦﴾

115 But if anyone opposes the Messenger after the guidance has become clear to him, and follows other than the path of the believers, We will hand him over to whatever he has turned to, and We will roast him in Hell. What an evil destination! 116 Allah does not forgive anything being associated with Him but He forgives whoever He wills for anything other than that. Anyone who associates something with Allah has gone very far astray.

Scholars say that these two *āyah*s were revealed because of Ibn Ubayraq, who was a thief, when the Prophet ﷺ judged that his hand be cut off and he fled to Makkah and apostatised. Sa'īd ibn Jubayr said, 'When he went to Makkah, he entered a house in Makkah and the idolaters caught him and killed him, and then Allah revealed: *"Allah does not forgive anything being associated with Him..."'*

Aḍ-Ḍaḥḥāk said, 'Some of the Quraysh of Makkah came to Madīnah and became Muslim and then returned to Makkah as apostates and Allah revealed: *"But if anyone opposes the Messenger..."'* If the *āyah* was revealed about the thief of the armour or someone else, then it is general to anyone who opposes the path of the Muslims. 'Guidance' *(hudā)* is right direction and clarification of this has already been given.

We will hand him over to whatever he has turned to,

This is said to be revealed about the one who apostasised. It means: 'We will leave him with what he worships.' Mujāhid said, 'We will hand him over to the idols which neither help nor harm.' Muqātil said that. Al-Kalbī said that it was revealed about Ibn Ubayraq when his situation and theft became clear and he fled to Makkah and apostasised. He made a hole in a wall belonging to a man in Makkah called Ḥajjāj ibn 'Ilāṭ. He fell and remained in the hole until he was found there. They expelled him from Makkah and he went to Syria and stole some property from a caravan and they stoned him and killed him. Then this was revealed. 'Āṣim, Ḥamzah, and Abū 'Amr recited '*nuwallih*' and '*nuṣlih*' while the rest have '*nuwallihi*' and '*nuṣlihi*'. They are two dialects.

Scholars said that the words: *'If anyone opposes the Messenger...'* are proof of the validity of consensus. The sentence: *'Allah does not forgive anything being associated with Him but He forgives whoever He wills for anything other than that.'* is a refutation of the Khārijites since they claimed that one who commits a major wrong action is an unbeliever. At-Tirmidhī reported that 'Alī ibn Abī Ṭālib said, 'There is no *āyah* in the Qur'an more beloved to me than this *āyah*: *"Allah does not forgive anything being associated with Him but He forgives whomever He wills."'* He said that this is a *gharīb ḥadīth*.

Ibn Fūrak said, 'Our people agree that no one will be in the Fire forever except for the unbelievers. When an evildoer of the people of *qiblah* dies without repenting, he will be punished in the Fire, but most will leave it through the intercession of the Messenger or through the mercy of Allah Almighty.' Aḍ-Ḍaḥḥāk said, 'An old man of the Arabs came to the Messenger of Allah ﷺ and said, "Messenger of Allah, I am an old man immersed in sins and wrong actions. But I have not associated anything with Allah since I acknowledged Him and believed in Him. What is my state with Allah?" Allah revealed: *"Allah does not forgive anything being associated with Him but He forgives whoever He wills.'"*

إِن يَدْعُونَ مِن دُونِهِۦٓ إِلَّآ إِنَٰثًا وَإِن يَدْعُونَ إِلَّا شَيْطَٰنًا مَّرِيدًا ﴿١١٧﴾

117 What they call on apart from Him are female idols. What they call on is an arrogant shayṭān

'What they call on apart from Him' means apart from Allah. This was revealed about the people of Makkah when they worshipped idols. In Arabic the particle '*in*' here means the negative '*mā*'. The female idols were al-Lāt, al-'Uzzā and Manāt. Each tribe had an idol which they worshipped. They would say, 'It is the "female idol" of a certain clan.' Al-Ḥasan and Ibn 'Abbās said, 'Each idol had a shayṭān which appeared to the priests and soothsayers and spoke to them using extraordinary words.' The feminine is used to denote abasement. This is the ignorance of someone who associates an inanimate object with Allah and believes that it is female. It is said that '*ināth*' means dead because they have no *rūḥ*, like wood or stone. The dead is reported from as one reports from a female because of the lowliness of their position. You say, 'I liked the stones' as you say, 'I liked the woman.' It is said that they are called *'female'* because, as aḍ-Ḍaḥḥāk said, they called the angels 'the daughters of Allah' and claimed that they were their intercessors with Allah. Ibn 'Abbās recited it in the singular (*wathan*) as a generic noun. He also recited '*wuthun*' which is the plural of *wathan*, and *awthān* is also a plural of *wathan* like *asad* and *āsād*. An-Naḥḥās said, 'That is not recited as far as I know.'

Abū Bakr al-Anbārī mentioned from his father from Naṣr ibn Dāwūd from Abū 'Ubayd from Ḥajjāj from Ibn Jurayj from Hishām ibn 'Urwah from his father that 'Ā'ishah recited 'idols' as '*awthān*' and Ibn 'Abbas recited '*unuth*', as the plural of *wathan* (idol). This is as you say *jamal* and *jimāl*. Then the plural of *wuthun* is *withān*, as you say *muthul*, *mithāl*. Then the *wāw* is changed into a *hamzah* when it has a *ḍammah* as in 77:11. *Uthun* is a plural of plurals. The Prophet ﷺ recited '*illā uthanan*', the plural of *anīth*, like *ghadīr* and *ghudur*. Aṭ-Ṭabarī related that it is the plural of *ināth*, like *thimār* and *thumur*. Abū 'Amr ad-Dānī related this reading from the Prophet ﷺ and said that it was recited by Ibn 'Abbās, al-Ḥasan and Abū Ḥaywah.

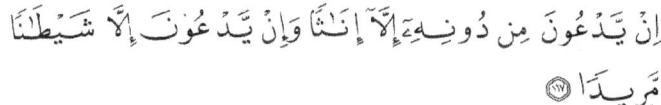

What they call on is an arrogant shayṭān

This means Iblīs because, when they obeyed what he encouraged them to do, they were in effect worshipping him. A similar example is: *'They have taken their rabbis and monks as lords besides Allah'* (9:31), meaning they obeyed them in what they commanded them, not that they actually worshipped them. *'Marīd'* (arrogant) means insolent and violently obstinate. Al-Azharī said that the *marīd* is one who will not obey because of arrogance. Ibn 'Arafah said that it is someone whose evil is apparent. A tree is called *mardā'* when its leaves fall off and its branches show. A man is called *'amrad'* or beardless.

لَّعَنَهُ ٱللَّهُ وَقَالَ لَأَتَّخِذَنَّ مِنْ عِبَادِكَ نَصِيبًا مَّفْرُوضًا ﴿١١٨﴾

118 whom Allah has cursed. He said, 'I will take a certain fixed proportion of Your slaves.

The root of 'to curse' (*la'ana*) means to make distant, as already mentioned. Customarily, making distant is connected to wrath and anger. So it is permitted to curse Iblīs and other dead unbelievers like Pharaoh, Hāmān and Abū Jahl. As for cursing the living, that was discussed in *al-Baqarah.*

I will take a certain fixed proportion of Your slaves.

Shayṭān said this. It means: 'I will select them through my misguiding and misleading of them.' They are the unbelievers and rebels. We find in a tradition, 'Out of every thousand, one is for Allah and the rest for Shayṭān.' This is a sound idea which is supported by the words of the Almighty to Ādam on the Day of Rising, 'Bring forth those who will be sent to the Fire.' He will say, 'Who are those sent to the Fire?' He said, 'Nine hundred and ninety-nine from every thousand.' Muslim transmitted it. Those sent to the Fire are the share of Shayṭān. Allah knows best. It is also said that part of his share is them obeying him in things he suggests to them, including hitting the newborn with a peg when he is born and carrying him around after a week, saying that it was so that the inhabitants would recognise him.

وَلَأُضِلَّنَّهُمْ وَلَأُمَنِّيَنَّهُمْ وَلَءَامُرَنَّهُمْ فَلَيُبَتِّكُنَّ ءَاذَانَ ٱلْأَنْعَٰمِ
وَلَءَامُرَنَّهُمْ فَلَيُغَيِّرُنَّ خَلْقَ ٱللَّهِ ۚ وَمَن يَتَّخِذِ ٱلشَّيْطَٰنَ
وَلِيًّا مِّن دُونِ ٱللَّهِ فَقَدْ خَسِرَ خُسْرَانًا مُّبِينًا ﴿١١٩﴾

119 I will lead them astray and fill them with false hopes. I will command them and they will cut off cattle's ears. I will command them and they will change Allah's creation.' Anyone who takes Shayṭān as his protector in place of Allah has clearly lost everything.

I will lead them astray and fill them with false hopes.

'I will turn them away from the path of guidance and give false hope dominance over them.' The concept of *'false hopes'* is not confined to one hope because everyone has different hopes according to their circumstances. It is said that it is their hope for a long life full of good and repentance and recognition while persisting in their bad actions.

I will command them and they will cut off cattle's ears.

Batk is cutting. A sword is called *batik* (sharp). It means 'I will compel them to cut the ears of the cattle which they called *baḥīrah, sā'ibah* and the like. The verb is *bataka, battaka*. A cut on the hand is *bitkah* ad the plural is *bitak*. Zuhayr said:

It flew and there were cuts (*bitak*) from the feathers on his palm.

I will command them and they will change Allah's creation.

The *lāms* (*li*) in this *āyah* are all used for the oath. Scholars disagree about what change this refers to. One group say that it is castration, gouging eyes and cutting off ears. That is said to be its meaning by Ibn 'Abbās, Anas, 'Ikrimah and Abū Ṣāliḥ. All of that involves torturing an animal and making it lawful or unlawful by transgression and adopting a position without proof or evidence. Ears are useful and something beautiful for cattle as well as other limbs. This is why Shayṭān thought that the creation of Allah should be changed by doing this.

We find in the *ḥadīth* of 'Iyāḍ ibn Ḥimār al-Mujāshi': 'I created all My slaves as natural believers (*ḥunafā'*) and then the shayṭāns came to them and dislodged them from their *dīn* and they forbade them what I made lawful for them and commanded them to associate with Me what I sent down no authority for and commanded them to change My creation.' Qāḍī Ismā'īl and Muslim transmitted it.

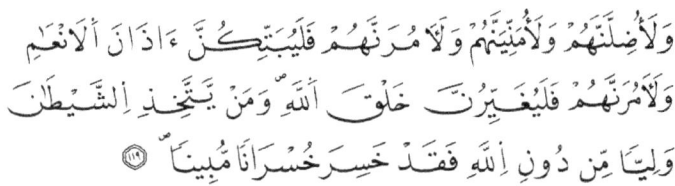

Ismā'īl related from Abu-l-Walīd and Sulaymān ibn Ḥarb from Shu'bah from Abū Isḥāq that Abu-l-Aḥwaṣ said, 'I went to the Messenger of Allah ﷺ when I was squalid in appearance. He asked, "Do you have any wealth?" "Yes," I replied. He said, "What sort of wealth?" "Every sort of wealth," I replied, "horses, camels and slaves." (Abu-l-Walīd added "sheep"). He said ﷺ, "When Allah gives you wealth, its effect should be seen on you." Then he asked, "Do you take the ears of your people's camels, which have sound ears, and, using the razor, slit their ears and say, 'This is *Baḥr,*' and slit the skins and say, 'This is *Ṣirm,*' to make them unlawful for you and your people?" "Yes," I replied. He said ﷺ, "Everything Allah has given you is lawful and the razor of Allah is sharper than your razor and the strength of Allah is stronger than strength." I said, "Messenger of Allah, what do you think about a man I stop with who does not give me hospitality and then camps with me. Should I show him hospitality or do the same to him?" He replied, "Rather give him hospitality."'

Since this is part of the action and effect of Shayṭān, the Messenger of Allah ﷺ commanded us to pay attention to the eyes and ears and not to sacrifice a one-eyed animal, an animal with a slit ear that hangs at the front or the back, one with a perforated ear, or one with the ear slit lengthwise.' Abū Dāwūd transmitted that from 'Alī. *Muqābalah* is an animal which has the front of its ear cut and *mudābarah* is one that has the ear cut from behind. *Sharqā'* is one with ears perforated and *kharqā'* is one with the ear perforated by a branding iron. Most scholars say that one looks for a defect in the ear. Mālik and al-Layth said, 'An animal with a severed ear or most of it severed is not allowed [for sacrifice]. A slit for a brand is allowed.' That is the position of ash-Shāfi'ī and most *fuqahā'*. If it is an animal born without an ear, Mālik and ash-Shāfi'ī said that it will not do [as a sacrifice], but if it has a small ear, it is accepted. The like of that is related from Abū Ḥanīfah.

As for castrating animals, there is an allowance for it made by a group of the people of knowledge, if benefit is intended by it, either fattening or something else. The majority of scholars say that there is no harm in sacrificing a gelding and some of them recommend it when it is fatter than other animals. 'Umar ibn 'Abd al-'Azīz made an allowance for gelding horses. 'Urwah ibn az-Zubayr gelded a mule of his. Mālik allowed the castrating of rams. That is permitted because it does not aim at attaching an animal to an idol nor to a Lord. It is intended to improve the meat which is eaten and to strengthen the animal when it has no hope of finding a female.

Some of them dislike that since the Prophet ﷺ said, 'Those who do not know do that.' Ibn al-Mundhir preferred that because it is confirmed from Ibn 'Umar.

He used to say, 'It is development of the creation of Allah.' 'Abd al-Mālik ibn Marwān disliked that. Al-Awzā'ī said, 'They used to dislike castrating anything which had offspring.' Ibn al-Mundhir said that there are two *ḥadīth*s about it, one from Ibn 'Umar that the Prophet ﷺ forbade castrating sheep, cattle, camels and horses, and the other from Ibn 'Abbās that the Prophet ﷺ forbade confining a person and shooting at him until he dies and castrating beasts. That which is in the *Muwaṭṭā'* is mentioned from Ibn 'Umar who disliked gelding, saying that it is part of full physique. Abū 'Umar said, 'He means that full physique consists of not having gelding.'

Abū Muḥammad 'Abd al-Ghanī transmitted it from 'Umar ibn Ismā'īl from Nāfi' that Ibn 'Umar said, 'Do not geld what Allah has made grow.' His shaykh related it from ad-Dāraquṭnī. He said that Abū 'Umar al-Mu'addil related it from 'Abbās ibn Muḥammad from Abū Mālik an-Nakha'ī from 'Umar ibn Ismā'īl. Ad-Dāraquṭnī said that 'Abd aṣ-Ṣamad ibn an-Nu'mān related it from Abū Mālik.

As for castrating human beings, it is a disaster because it weakens the heart and undermines strength, which is not the case with animals. It prevents procreation which is commanded by the Prophet ﷺ: 'Marry and procreate. I will have the largest community by you.' It also entails great pain and sometimes can cause death and so it is loss of property and loss of life as well as mutilation that the Prophet ﷺ forbade. That is sound [that he forbade that]. A group of the *fuqahā'* of the Hijaz and Kufa disliked buying eunuchs from the Slavs and others. They said, 'If none of them were bought, they would not be castrated.' There is no disagreement that castrating human beings is not lawful or permitted because it is mutilation and altering Allah's creation. The same is true about amputating any of their limbs unless it is for a *ḥadd* punishment or retaliation. Abū 'Umar said that.

As this is confirmed, know that branding (*wasm*) and marking are an exception to this prohibition regarding the alterations of Shayṭān. It was already mentioned that it is forbidden to torture animals with fire, and branding is marking with fire. Its root is a sign. The verb *wasama* means to mark something with a sign by which it is known. Allah says: *'Their mark (sīmā) is on their faces.'* (48:29) *Sīmā* is a mark and *mīsam* is a branding-iron. It is confirmed in *Ṣaḥīḥ Muslim* that Anas said, 'I saw the Prophet ﷺ with a branding-iron in his hand, branding the *zakāt* camels, booty and other animals so that the property would be known and properly dealt with and not go to someone to whom it did not belong.'

Branding is permitted on all limbs except the face since it is reported from Jābir that the Messenger of Allah ﷺ forbade striking the face and branding the face. Muslim transmitted it. That is because it is the noblest of body parts and the place of beauty. The Prophet ﷺ passed by a man who was beating his slave and said, 'Beware of the face. Allah created Ādam on his form,' in other words on the form made so that this face resembles that of Ādam. This is the best of what is said about its interpretation, and Allah knows best.

One group stated that what is indicated by '*change*' in this context is tattooing and what is like it of artifice for beauty. Ibn Mas'ūd and al-Ḥasan said that. Part of that is the sound *ḥadīth* from 'Abdullāh in which the Prophet ﷺ said, 'Allah cursed women who tattoo and are tattooed, women who pluck their eyebrows, and women who join hair together and the person asks for it to be joined, and women who file their teeth to make gaps for beauty, changing Allah's creation!' Muslim transmitted it. It will be fully dealt with in *al-Ḥashr*, Allah willing.

Tattooing can be done on the back of the hands and wrist of a woman by pricking the skin with a needle and then filling that with antimony or ink. The verb is *washama* and the woman does it is a *wāshimah* and the one to whom it is done is a *mustawshimah*. Al-Harawī said that. Ibn al-'Arabī said, 'Men from Sicily and North Africa used to do it, each of them indicating his manliness in his youth.'

Qāḍī 'Iyāḍ said, 'In the transmission of al-Harawī, one of Muslim's transmitters has "*mustawshiyyah*" from *washī* which is adornment. The root of *washī* is weaving cloth with two colours. An ox described as *muwashshī* has black on its legs and face. So the verb describes a woman with respect to what she does by way of plucking her hair and filing her teeth. The pluckers are those who pluck out hair from the face with tweezers.' Ibn al-'Arabī said, 'The people of Egypt pluck the hair of the pubes. This is part of it. The sunnah is to shave the pubic hair and pluck the armpits. Plucking the private parts can cause harm and negate many of its benefits.' Filing the teeth is to make gaps in the teeth. The *ḥadīth* here uses *mutafallajāt* for those who do that. Outside the book of Muslim we find *wāshirāt*, the plural of *wāshirah*, someone who sharpens the teeth to look like the teeth of a younger woman. Hadiths testify that someone who does all these things is cursed and that it is one of the major sins.

There is disagreement about the reason why this is forbidden. It is said that it is part of deception, and it is said that it is part of changing Allah's creation, as Ibn Mas'ūd said, and that is sounder. It contains the first idea. It is said that what is forbidden is that which is permanent because it is part of changing Allah's creation. As for that which does not last, like kohl which women use for adornment, scholars, Mālik and others, permit that. Mālik disliked it for men. Mālik permitted a woman to dye her hands with henna. It is related that 'Umar disliked that and said, 'Either she dyes her whole hand or leaves it.' Mālik did not acknowledge this transmission from 'Umar. The Prophet ﷺ saw a woman who did not use henna and said, 'One of you should not leave her hand like a man's.' She continued to use henna when she was over seventy until her death. Qāḍī 'Iyāḍ said, 'A *ḥadīth* has the prohibition against using black dye which was mentioned by the author of *al-Maṣābīḥ* and it is still operative.' A woman should wear a necklace of a bead on a thong on her neck. It is related that the Prophet ﷺ said to 'Ā'ishah, 'It is not proper for you to be without a necklace, either with a string or a thong.' Anas said, 'It is recommended that a woman wear a necklace in the prayer, even if it is just a thong.'

Abū Ja'far aṭ-Ṭabarī said, 'The *ḥadīth* of Ibn Mas'ūd provides evidence that it is not permitted to change any of Allah's creation by adding to it or decreasing it, seeking beauty for a husband or someone else, whether she files her teeth or makes gaps in them, or has an extra tooth and removes it, or a long tooth and shortens it. Similarly a woman is not permitted to shave a beard or moustache if it grows because that is changing Allah's creation.'

'Iyāḍ said, 'It is mentioned that if someone is born with an extra finger or limb, it is not permitted to amputate it or remove it because that is changing Allah's creation, unless it harms them and then, according to Abū Ḥanīfah and others, it should be removed.'

Part of this is cursing those who add false hair. That is to add someone else's hair to one's own to increase it. A woman who does it is called *wāṣilah* and the one who asks to have it done is called a *mustawṣilah*. Muslim reported that Jābir said, 'The Prophet ﷺ said that a woman should not add any [false hair] to her hair.' It is transmitted that Asmā' bint Abī Bakr said that a woman asked the Prophet ﷺ, 'O Messenger of Allah, my daughter was afflicted by measles and her hair fell out. I have given her in marriage, can I join on other hair to hers?' He replied, 'Allah has cursed anyone who joins hair together and the person to whose hair it is joined.' All of that is a text for forbidding adding false hair. Mālik and most scholars agree on that and forbid adding anything: wool, rags or other things because that has the same aim. Al-Layth ibn Sa'd said that this is aberrant and allowed adding wool, rags and what is other than hair. This resembles the school of the Ẓāhiriyyah.

Others permit placing a wig over the hair since that is not actually adding extensions to hair. This is pure literalism and moving away from the meaning. Some others take an aberrant view and permit adding hair extensions unrestrictedly. That is an absolutely false position refuted by hadiths. It is related from 'Ā'ishah, but it is not sound. It is related that Ibn Sīrīn was asked by a man: 'My mother does women's hair. Can I consume any of her property?' He answered, 'Not if she adds false hair.' The prohibition does not include coloured silk threads that are used to tie it for adornment. Allah knows best.

One group say that what is meant by changing the creation of Allah is that Allah created the sun, moon, stones, fire and other created things for reflection and use, and the unbelievers changed them by making them worshipped idols. Az-Zajjāj said, 'Allah created cattle for riding and eating and they forbade them to themselves, and He made the sun, moon and stones subject to people and they made them gods to worship. So they changed what Allah created.' A group of commentators said that: Mujāhid, aḍ-Ḍaḥḥāk, Sa'īd ibn Jubayr and Qatādah.

It is related from Ibn 'Abbās that it is about changing the *dīn* of Allah, and an-Nakha'ī said that and aṭ-Ṭabarī preferred it. He said, 'If that is what is meant, then it includes doing what Allah has forbidden to do in terms of castration, tattooing and other acts of disobedience, because shayṭān incites to all acts of disobedience, so as to change what Allah created in His *dīn*.' Mujāhid also said that the words: *'they will change Allah's creation'* refer to the natural form on which Allah created people, meaning that they were born in Islam and then Shayṭān commanded them to change it. It is the meaning of the words of the Prophet ﷺ, 'Every child is born on the natural form and then his parents make him a Jew, Christian or Magian.' So the meaning would refer to the faith He created in them on the day when they were atoms: *"Am I not your Lord?" they said, "We testify that indeed You are!"'* (7:172)

Ibn al-'Arabī said, 'It is related that Ṭāwūs would not attend a wedding of a black woman to a white man or a white woman to a black man. He remarked, "This is an aspect of the words of Allah about changing creation."' The Qāḍī commented, 'Even if the words allow this interpretation, it is made specific when the Prophet ﷺ married his freedman Zayd who was white to his wet-nurse Barakah who was Abyssinian and the mother of Usāmah. This was a black person to a white person. This was concealed from Ṭāwūs in spite of his knowledge.' Then Usāmah married Fāṭimah bint Qays who was white and Qurayshī. Bilāl was married to the sister of 'Abd ar-Raḥmān ibn 'Awf az-Zuhrī. This also refines the meaning.

Anyone who takes Shayṭān as his protector in place of Allah

This is the one who obeys him and abandons Allah's command. He has diminished himself and cheated himself by giving what is due to Allah to Shayṭān.

يَعِدُهُمْ وَيُمَنِّيهِمْ وَمَا يَعِدُهُمُ الشَّيْطَٰنُ إِلَّا غُرُورًا ﴿١٢٠﴾ أُولَٰٓئِكَ
مَأْوَىٰهُمْ جَهَنَّمُ وَلَا يَجِدُونَ عَنْهَا مَحِيصًا ﴿١٢١﴾ وَالَّذِينَ ءَامَنُوا
وَعَمِلُوا الصَّٰلِحَٰتِ سَنُدْخِلُهُمْ جَنَّٰتٍ تَجْرِي مِن تَحْتِهَا الْأَنْهَٰرُ
خَٰلِدِينَ فِيهَا أَبَدًا وَعْدَ اللَّهِ حَقًّا وَمَنْ أَصْدَقُ مِنَ اللَّهِ قِيلًا ﴿١٢٢﴾

120 He makes promises to them and fills them with false hopes. But what Shayṭān promises them is nothing but delusion. 121 The shelter of such people will be Hell. They will find no way to escape from it. 122 But as for those who believe and do right actions, We will admit them into Gardens with rivers flowing under them, remaining in them timelessly, for ever and ever. Allah's promise is true. Whose speech could be truer than Allah's?

Shayṭān makes false promises to them and bribes of wealth, rank and leadership and promises that there will be no resurrection or punishment. He makes them fear poverty for themselves so that they do not spend in charity. As for delusion, it is deceit.

Ibn 'Arafah said, 'Delusion is something whose outward aspect a person loves while its inward is disliked or unknown.' Shayṭān deludes because he moves people to what their lower selves desire when evil lies behind that. '*Those*' is an inceptive, '*shelter*' is a second inceptive and '*Hell*' is the predicate. The sentence is a predicate of the first. *Maḥīṣ* (escape) is a refuge. The verb is *ḥāṣa, yaḥīṣu.* The phrase '*Whose speech is truer than Allah's*' is an inceptive and '*qīlan*' is for clarification. *Qīl*, *qawl* and *qāl* mean the same. No one is more truthful than Allah. The ideas contained in these *āyah*s have already been discussed. Praise be to Allah.

لَّيْسَ بِأَمَانِيِّكُمْ وَلَا أَمَانِيِّ أَهْلِ الْكِتَٰبِ مَن يَعْمَلْ سُوٓءًا
يُجْزَ بِهِۦ وَلَا يَجِدْ لَهُۥ مِن دُونِ اللَّهِ وَلِيًّا وَلَا نَصِيرًا ﴿١٢٣﴾

123 It is not a matter of wishful thinking on your part nor of the wishful thinking of the People of the Book. Anyone who does evil will be repaid for it. He will not find any protector or helper besides Allah.

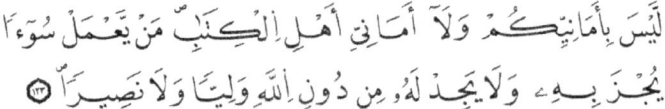

It is not a matter of wishful thinking on your part nor of the wishful thinking of the People of the Book.

Abū Ja'far al-Madanī recited *'amānīkum walā amānī'* with a single *yā'*. Part of the best of what has been reported about the reason for its revelation is what al-Ḥakam ibn Abān related from 'Ikrimah that Ibn 'Abbās said, 'The Jews and Christians said, "None but those who are affiliated with us will enter the Garden" and Quraysh said, "We will not be resurrected."' Then Allah revealed this. Qatādah and as-Suddī said that the believers and People of the Book were exchanging boasts and the People of the Book said, 'Our Prophet was before your Prophet and our Book before your Book and we are more entitled to Allah than you.' The believers said, 'Our Prophet is the Seal of the Prophets and there will be no other Books after our Book,' and the *āyah* was revealed.

Anyone who does evil will be repaid for it.

Evil here is *shirk*. Al-Ḥasan said, 'This *āyah* is about ingrates,' and he recited: *'Are any but the ungrateful repaid like this?'* (34:17) He also said about this *āyah*, 'He is the one whom Allah wants to humiliate. That is not the case for the one He want to honour. Allah mentioned some people and said: *"Those are the people whose best deeds will be accepted and whose wrong deeds will be overlooked. They are among the Companions of the Garden, in fulfilment of the true promise made to them."* (46:16)'

Aḍ-Ḍaḥḥāk said that it refers to the Jews, Christians, Magians and unbelieving Arabs. The majority say that the *āyah* is general. Both believers and unbelievers will be repaid for the evil they do. The repayment of an unbeliever will be the Fire because it his disbelief has destroyed him. A believer is repaid by suffering misfortunes in this world as Muslim reports in the *Ṣaḥīḥ* from Abū Hurayrah that the Messenger of Allah ﷺ said, 'Press together and close the gaps. There is expiation in all that befalls a Muslim, even a stone which bruises him and thorn which pricks him.'

Al-Ḥakīm at-Tirmidhī reports in *Nawādir al-Uṣūl* in Section 95 from Ibrāhim ibn al-Mustamirr al-Hudhalī from Abū Zayd 'Abd ar-Raḥmān ibn Sulaym ibn Ḥayyān from his father that his father said, 'I accompanied of Ibn 'Umar from Makkah to Madīnah and he said to Nāfi', "Do not take me past the crucified," meaning Ibn az-Zubayr. Suddenly in the middle of the night his litter hit that post. He sat up and rubbed his eyes and said, "May Allah have mercy on you, Abū Khubayb, however you were. I heard your father az-Zubayr say that the Messenger of Allah ﷺ said, 'Whoever does evil will be paid back for it either in this world or the Next World.' If this is for that, it is so!"'

Abū 'Abdullāh at-Tirmidhī said that the Revelation is undefined and the words:

'Anyone who does evil will be repaid for it. He will not find any protector or helper besides Allah' include the pious and impious, enemy and friend, believer and unbeliever. Then the Messenger of Allah ﷺ distinguished in this *ḥadīth* between the two abodes, stating that people are repaid either in this world or in the Next. The repayment is not in both places. Do you not see that Ibn 'Umar said, 'If this is for that, it is so!'? It means that he fought in the Ḥaram of Allah and caused a terrible event in it so that the House was burned and the Black Stone struck by a catapult. It was cracked and then put together with silver and it remains like that to this day. The House was heard to moan, 'Oh! Oh!' When Ibn 'Umar had seen what he had done and then saw him killed and crucified, he remembered the words of the Messenger of Allah ﷺ: *'Anyone who does evil will be repaid for it'* and so he said, 'If this killing is for that action it is so!' It means that it is as if he was repaid for that evil by his killing and crucifixion. May Allah have mercy on him!

Then the Messenger of Allah ﷺ distinguished between the two groups in another *ḥadīth*. My father related to us from Abū Nu'aym from Muḥammad ibn Muslim that Yazīd ibn 'Abdullāh ibn Usāmah ibn al-Hād al-Laythī said, 'When the words: "*Anyone who does evil will be repaid for it,*" were revealed, Abū Bakr aṣ-Ṣiddīq said, 'Who among us does not?' He said ﷺ, 'Abū Bakr, a believer will be repaid for it in this world and an unbeliever will be repaid for it on the Day of Rising.' Al-Jārūd related from Wakī', Abū Mu'āwiyah and 'Abdah from Ismā'īl ibn Abī Khālid that Abū Bakr ibn Abī Zuhayr ath-Thaqafī said, 'When the words: "*Anyone who does evil will be repaid for it,*" were revealed, Abū Bakr said, 'How can righteousness co-exist with this, Messenger of Allah? We will be repaid for everything that we do.' He said ﷺ, 'May Allah forgive you, Abū Bakr! Do you not become fatigued? Do you not sorrow? Are you not afflicted by hardship?' 'Yes,' he replied. He said, 'That is part of repayment.' So the Messenger of Allah ﷺ explained what is undefined in the *āyah*.

At-Tirmidhī related from Abū Bakr aṣ-Ṣiddīq that when it was revealed, the Prophet ﷺ said to him, 'You and the believers, Abū Bakr, are repaid for that in this world until you meet Allah with no sins remaining. The others will have it collected for them until they are repaid for it on the Day of Rising.' He said that it is a *gharīb ḥadīth* and its *isnād* is questionable. Mūsā ibn 'Ubaydah weakens the *ḥadīth*. He considered weak by Yaḥyā ibn Sa'īd al-Qaṭṭān and Aḥmad ibn Ḥanbal. The client of Ibn Sibā' is unknown. This is related by a different path from Abū Bakr, but also without a sound *isnād*.

There is something on the subject related from 'Ā'ishah. Qāḍī Ismā'īl ibn Isḥāq transmitted it from Sulaymān ibn Ḥarb from Ḥammād ibn Salamah from 'Alī ibn Yazīd that his mother asked 'Ā'ishah about the *āyah*: *'Whether you divulge what is in yourselves or keep it hidden'* (2:284), and about: *'Anyone who does evil will be repaid for it'* and 'Ā'ishah said, 'No one has asked me about this since I asked the Messenger of Allah ﷺ about it. He said, "'Ā'ishah, this is the transaction of Allah by which He afflicts a person with fever, calamity, thorns, even by some goods that he puts in his sleeve and then misses them and is alarmed and then finds them in his bag, until the believer emerges from his sins like ore emerges from the bellows.'

The noun of '*laysa*' is elided in all of these statements. It implies: 'None of your wishful thinking will be realised. Rather anyone who does evil will be repaid for it. It means: It is said that it means that the reward of Allah is not through your wishful thinking since as has already been mentioned the truth is: *'But as for those who believe and do right actions, We will admit them into the Garden.'* (4:122)

He will not find any protector or helper besides Allah.

This refers to an idolater since Allah says: *'We will certainly help Our Messengers and those who believe, both in the life of this world and on the Day the witnesses appear.'* (40:51) It is said that *'Anyone who does evil will be repaid for it'* unless he repents. If the *āyah* is applied to an unbeliever, he will have neither protector or helper tomorrow. If it is applied to the believer, he has no protector or helper except Allah.

وَمَن يَعْمَلْ مِنَ ٱلصَّٰلِحَٰتِ مِن ذَكَرٍ أَوْ أُنثَىٰ وَهُوَ مُؤْمِنٌ فَأُوْلَٰٓئِكَ
يَدْخُلُونَ ٱلْجَنَّةَ وَلَا يُظْلَمُونَ نَقِيرًا ﴿١٢٤﴾

124 Anyone, male or female, who does right actions and is a believer, will enter the Garden. They will not be wronged by so much as the tiniest speck.

Belief is a made a condition because the idolaters served the Ka'bah, fed the *ḥājjis* and gave hospitality, as did the People of the Book before them. They said, 'We are the sons and beloved ones of Allah.' So Allah made it clear that good actions are not accepted unless accompanied by belief. Abū 'Amr and Ibn Kathīr recite *'enter'* as *'yudkhalūna'* in the passive (be admitted) while the rest have it as *'tadkhulūna'* meaning that they will enter the Garden because of their actions. *Naqīr* is the spot on the back of the date-stone.

وَمَنْ أَحْسَنُ دِينًا مِّمَّنْ أَسْلَمَ وَجْهَهُۥ لِلَّهِ وَهُوَ مُحْسِنٌ وَاتَّبَعَ مِلَّةَ
إِبْرَٰهِيمَ حَنِيفًا وَاتَّخَذَ اللَّهُ إِبْرَٰهِيمَ خَلِيلًا ﴿١٢٥﴾

125 Who could have a better *dīn* than someone who submits himself completely to Allah and is a good-doer, and follows the religion of Ibrāhīm, a man of pure natural belief? Allah took Ibrāhīm as an intimate friend.

Who could have a better *dīn* than someone who submits himself completely to Allah

This propounds the excellence of Islam over all other religions. *'Submits himself'* means to make one's *dīn* sincerely for Allah, be humble to Him, and turn to Him alone in worship. Ibn 'Abbās said that Allah is referring here to Abū Bakr aṣ-Ṣiddīq. The noun '*dīn*' is in the accusative for clarification. The words '*is a good-doer*' are an inceptive and their predicate is in the place of a *ḥāl*. It means that such a person unifies Allah, and so the People of the Book have no way into it because they abandoned faith in Muḥammad ﷺ. *Millah* means the *dīn*. The *ḥanīf* is the Muslim and was already mentioned.

Allah took Ibrāhīm as an intimate friend.

Tha'lab said that he is called *Khalīl* because love pervaded his heart and there was no gap but that it filled it. Bashshār said:

> You pervaded (*takhallaltu*) the path of the *rūḥ* in me,
> and because of it the Khalīl is called Khalīl.

Khalīl is on the form *fa'īl* with the meaning of an active participle, in the same way that *'alīm* (knowing) means *'ālim*. It is also said that it can have a passive meaning, like *ḥabīb* means '*mahbūb*' (beloved). Ibrāhīm loved Allah and was loved by Allah.

It is also said that *khalīl* comes from election, and so Allah selected Ibrāhīm in his time for the Message. An-Naḥḥās preferred that and said, 'The proof is found in the words of the Prophet ﷺ, "Allah took your companion as a friend (*khalīl*)," meaning himself. The Prophet ﷺ also said, "If I were to take a close friend, I would have taken Abū Bakr as a close friend," meaning, "If I were to choose anyone, I would choose Abū Bakr." This refutes anyone who claims that the Prophet ﷺ chose another of his Companions for something special in the *dīn*.' It is also said that *khalīl* means 'in need', and so Ibrāhīm was in need of Allah. It is as if his need was an imbalance (*ikhtilāl*). Zuhayr said when he praised Zuhayr ibn Sinān:

> When a friend (*khalīl*) comes on a day of need,
> he says, 'My property is not absent nor denied.'

Az-Zajjāj said that the meaning of *Khalīl* is the one who has no gaps in his love, and so it is possible that he is called a *Khalīl* of Allah since He loved him and chose him for complete love and it is possible that he is called that because he needs Allah since his poverty and need are for Allah alone, and he is sincere in that. *Ikhtilāl* is poverty. It is related that when he was shot out of the catapult, while he was in the air Jibrīl came to him and asked, 'Do you need anything?' He replied, 'As for from you, no.' Therefore Allah's friendship towards Ibrāhīm was Him helping him. It is also said that he was called that because he went to a friend (*khalīl*) of his in Egypt or Mosul to get some food from him. He did not find his friend and so he filled his bag with sand and gave it to his family and went to sleep. His family opened it and found that it was flour and they prepared food from it. When they brought it to him, he asked, 'Where did you get this?' They said, 'It is from that which you brought from your Egyptian friend.' He said, 'It is indeed from my Friend,' meaning Allah, and so Allah called him that.

It is said that he gave hospitality to the leaders of the unbelievers and gave them gifts and they asked him, 'What do you need?' He answered, 'I need you to prostrate once.' So they prostrated and he prayed to Allah and said, 'O Allah, I have done what you enabled me to do, so do what You are entitled to!' Allah gave them success in adopting Islam and because of that Allah took him as a Friend.

It is said that when the angels visited him in human form and he brought them a fattened calf and they did not eat from it and said, 'We do not eat anything without paying for it.' He told them, 'Then pay its price and eat.' They asked, 'What is its price?' He said, 'That you say at the beginning, "In the name of Allah" and at the end, "Praise be to Allah."' They said between themselves, 'It is right for Allah to take him as a Friend,' so Allah took him as a Friend.

Jābir related that the Messenger of Allah ﷺ said, 'Allah took Ibrāhīm as an intimate friend because he fed people, gave the greeting widely, and prayed at night while people were sleeping.' 'Abdullāh ibn 'Amr ibn al-'Āṣ reported that the Prophet ﷺ asked, 'Jibrīl, why did Allah take Ibrāhīm as an intimate friend?' He replied, 'Because of his feeding people, Muḥammad.'

It was said that the meaning of *Khalīl* is the one who makes enemies for the sake of Allah and friends for the sake of Allah. *Khullah* (close friendship) between human beings is *ṣadaqah*, derived from the interpenetration (*takhallala*) of secrets between friends. It is said that it comes from *khallah*, and each of the two *khalīls* blocks the need (*khallah*) of his fellow. Abū Dāwūd reports in his collection that the Prophet ﷺ said, 'A man follows the *dīn* of his intimate friend, so let each of you look to see who he takes as a friend.' Excellent are the words of the one who said:

If someone's friendship (*khullah*) is not for the sake of Allah,
then his friend is in danger from him.

Another said:

When you do not have a friend (*khalīl*),
do not entrust brotherhood to every brother.

If you choose between them,
cling to the people of intelligence and modesty among them,

There is no substitute for intelligence
when virtues are compared.

Hassan ibn Thābit said:

The friends of men are many,
but few in affliction.

Do not be deluded by the friendship of brothers.
You have no friend in calamity.

Every brother says, 'I am faithful!'
but he does not do what he says.

Except a friend of his with lineage and *dīn*.
That is the one who does what he says.

وَلِلَّهِ مَا فِي ٱلسَّمَٰوَٰتِ وَمَا فِي ٱلْأَرْضِ وَكَانَ ٱللَّهُ بِكُلِّ شَيْءٍ مُّحِيطًا ﴿١٢٦﴾

126 Everything in the heavens and in the earth belongs to Allah. Allah encompasses all things.

It all belongs to Him in respect of both dominion and origination. He took

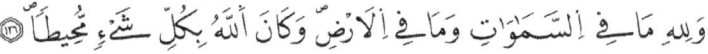

Ibrāhīm as an intimate friend because of his excellent obedience, not out of need of friendship nor for more of it. How could that be when everything in the heavens and the earth is His? He honoured him because he obeyed Him. Allah's knowledge encompasses all things.

وَيَسْتَفْتُونَكَ فِي النِّسَاءِ قُلِ اللَّهُ يُفْتِيكُمْ فِيهِنَّ وَمَا يُتْلَىٰ عَلَيْكُمْ فِي
الْكِتَابِ فِي يَتَامَى النِّسَاءِ اللَّاتِي لَا تُؤْتُونَهُنَّ مَا كُتِبَ لَهُنَّ
وَتَرْغَبُونَ أَن تَنكِحُوهُنَّ وَالْمُسْتَضْعَفِينَ مِنَ الْوِلْدَانِ وَأَن تَقُومُوا
لِلْيَتَامَىٰ بِالْقِسْطِ وَمَا تَفْعَلُوا مِنْ خَيْرٍ فَإِنَّ اللَّهَ كَانَ بِهِ عَلِيمًا ﴿١٢٧﴾

127 They will ask you for a fatwa about women. Say, 'Allah gives you a fatwa about them; and also what is recited to you in the Book about orphan girls to whom you do not give what they are owed, while at the same time desiring to marry them; and also about young children who are denied their rights: that you should act justly with respect to orphans.' Whatever good you do, Allah knows it.

This was revealed about a question asked by some of the Companions about women and their rulings with respect to inheritance and other things. Allah commanded His Prophet ﷺ to tell them: 'Allah makes clear what you have asked about.' This *āyah* refers to what was said about women at the beginning of the *sūrah*. There were still rulings concerning them that they did not know about and so they asked and were told, 'Allah gives you a *fatwa* about them.'

Ashhab reported that Mālik said, 'The Prophet ﷺ was asked and did not answer until he received revelation. That is referred to several times in the Book of Allah: *"They will ask you for a fatwa about women. Say, 'Allah gives you a fatwa about them,'"* and: *"They will ask you about orphans"* (2:220), and: *"They will ask you about wine and gambling"* (2:219), and: *"They will ask you about the mountains."* (2:105).'

In the phrase *'what is recited to you,'* the *mā* is in the position of the nominative, added to the name of Allah. It means: the Qur'an gives you a *fatwā* about them. That is in His words: *'then marry other permissible women.'* (4:3) This was discussed earlier. Allah's words, *'targhabūna an tankiḥūhunna'* can mean 'desiring to marry them' and the *"an'* is elided. It is also said that it means 'desiring to marry them' and the *'fī'* is elided. Sa'īd ibn Jubayr and Mujāhid said, 'desiring to marry her when she is very wealthy.' The *ḥadīth* of 'Ā'ishah strengthens the elision of *"an'*.

She says 'this means the desire of one of you to (*'an*) marry the orphan girl in his care when she has little wealth and beauty.' This was mentioned at the beginning of the *sūrah*.

وَإِنِ ٱمْرَأَةٌ خَافَتْ مِنۢ بَعْلِهَا نُشُوزًا أَوْ إِعْرَاضًا فَلَا جُنَاحَ عَلَيْهِمَآ
أَن يُصْلِحَا بَيْنَهُمَا صُلْحًا ۚ وَٱلصُّلْحُ خَيْرٌ ۗ وَأُحْضِرَتِ ٱلْأَنفُسُ ٱلشُّحَّ ۚ وَإِن
تُحْسِنُوا۟ وَتَتَّقُوا۟ فَإِنَّ ٱللَّهَ كَانَ بِمَا تَعْمَلُونَ خَبِيرًا ﴿١٢٨﴾

128 If a woman fears cruelty or aversion on her husband's part, there is nothing wrong in the couple becoming reconciled. Reconciliation is better. But people are prone to selfish greed. If you do good and are godfearing, Allah is aware of what you do.

If a woman fears cruelty or aversion on her husband's part,

The noun '*woman*' is in the nominative by an implied verb which explains what follows. The verb '*fears*' here means 'anticipates'. Az-Zajjāj says that the meaning is that a woman fears constant bad behaviour from her husband. An-Naḥḥās says that the difference between cruelty (*nushūz*) and aversion is that *nushūz* is estrangement and aversion is shown by not speaking to her or being intimate with her. Most recite '*an yaṣṣāliḥā*' and the Kufans recite '*an yuṣliḥā*'. Al-Jaḥdarī and 'Uthmān al-Battī recite '*an yuṣṣliḥā*'. It means to agree between themselves, and there is *idghām*.

The *āyah* was revealed about Sawdah bint Zam'ah. At-Tirmidhī reported from Ibn 'Abbās: 'Sawdah feared that the Messenger of Allah ﷺ would divorce her and said, "Do not divorce me. Keep me and I will give my day with you to 'Ā'ishah," She did that and this was revealed." If they are reconciled on the basis of something, it is allowed. This is a *ḥasan gharīb ḥadīth*. Ibn 'Uyaynah related from az-Zuhrī that Sa'īd ibn al-Musayyab reported that Rāfi' ibn Khadīj was married to Khawlah bint Muḥammad ibn Maslamah. He disliked something about her, either age or something else, and wanted to divorce her. She said, 'Do not divorce me and allot me what you wish.' So this was revealed. Al-Bukhārī reported from 'Ā'isha that it was about a man who was married to a woman who he did not care for much and wanted to leave. She said, 'I put you in the lawful in regard to me,' and this was revealed.

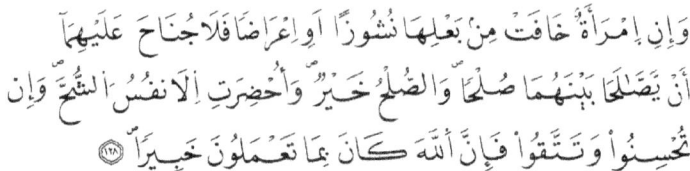

In *fiqh*, this question refutes foolish, ignorant people who think that when a man takes a young woman and she becomes old, he may not replace her. Ibn Abī Mulaykah said, 'When Sawdah bint Zam'ah became old, the Prophet ﷺ wanted to divorce her but she preferred to remain with him and said, "Keep me and I will give my day to 'Ā'ishah." The Prophet ﷺ did so and she died as one of his wives.'

That is what the daughter of Muḥammad ibn Maslamah did. Mālik related from Ibn Shihāb that Rāfi' ibn Khadīj married Khawlah bint Muḥammad ibn Maslamah and she was married to him until she was old and then he married a young woman with her. He preferred the young woman to her and she asked him for a divorce. He divorced her once and then took her back. The same thing happened again and he took her back again. Again he preferred the young woman and she asked for a divorce and he said, 'There is one left. If you wish, you can agree to the preference you see, or, if you wish, I will divorce you.' She agreed to that and he kept her on that basis. Rāfi' did not think that he incurred a wrong action when she remained with him on that basis. Ma'mar related it in word and meaning from az-Zuhrī and added, 'That reconciliation which we conveyed is that about which the *āyah*: *"If a woman fears cruelty or aversion on her husband's part, there is nothing wrong in the couple becoming reconciled. Reconciliation is better."* was revealed.' Abū 'Umar ibn 'Abd al-Barr said, and Allah knows best, that that preference refers to his personal inclination and activities with her, not preferring her in food, clothing or lodging because such a thing cannot be imagined of someone like Rāfi' ibn Khadīj. Allah knows best.

Abū Bakr ibn Abī Shaybah mentioned from Abu-l-Aḥwaṣ from Simāk ibn Ḥarb from Khālid ibn 'Ar'arah that a man asked 'Alī ibn Abī Ṭālib about this *āyah* and he said, 'It is about a man who is married to a woman and his eyes turn away from her because of her ugliness, poverty, old age or bad character, but he does not want to divorce her. If she gives him any of her dower, he is allowed to take it. If she gives him some of her days, there is no harm.' Aḍ-Ḍaḥḥāk said, 'There is nothing wrong in lessening her due when he marries a younger and more attractive woman than her.' Muqātil ibn Ḥayyān said that it refers to a man who is married to an old woman and then marries a young woman. He says to the old woman, 'I will give you some of my wealth if you let me allot more time to this young woman than I give to you in the night and day.' If she accepts, they are reconciled. If she does not accept that, then he must be fair in the division.

Our scholars say that this means that all sorts of reconciliation are permitted in this case. It is permitted that reconciliation be based on the wife being patient, her allowing preference of another wife, or preferring and keeping the tie of marriage, or there is reconciliation based on patience and preference without a gift. All of this is permitted. It is permitted for reconciliation to be based on her giving her day to another, as the wives of the Prophet ﷺ did. That was when the Messenger of Allah ﷺ was angry with Ṣafiyyah and she told 'Ā'ishah, 'Reconcile me with the Messenger of Allah ﷺ and I will give my day to you.' Ibn Khuzayzimandād mentioned it from 'Ā'ishah in *al-Aḥkām*. She said, 'The Messenger of Allah ﷺ was cross with Ṣafiyyah about something and Ṣafiyyah said to me, "Can you make the Messenger of Allah ﷺ pleased with me and then you can have my day?" I put on a long head covering which was dyed with saffron and sprinkled it. Then I went and sat down beside the Messenger of Allah ﷺ and he said, "Move away from me. It is not your day." I said, "That is Allah's favour which He gives to whomever He wishes." She told him about it and he was pleased with her.' This story contains the permission to not be equal between wives and prefer some over others when it is with the consent of the one less favoured.

The Kufans recite *'yuṣilaḥā'* while most recite *'yaṣṣālaḥā'*. Al-Jaḥdarī recited *'yaṣṣalaḥā'*. If someone recites *'yaṣṣālaḥā'*, its form is that it is known in Arabic that when there is a dispute between people, one says *taṣālaḥa* for the people reconciling and not *aṣlaḥa*. If it had been *aṣlaḥa*, the verbal noun would be *iṣlāḥ*. If someone recites *'yuṣilaḥā'*, the like is used in 2:182 where *aṣlaḥa* is used. *'Ṣulḥ'* is in the accusative in this reading as the object. It is a noun, like *'aṭā* from *a'ṭā*. So you say, *'aṣlaḥtu ṣulḥan'* (I made peace) as you say, *'aṣlaḥtu amran'* (I put a matter right). It is also the object according to the reading of *'yaṣṣālaḥā'* because Form VI can be transitive. It is possible that it is a verbal noun whose augments have been elided. If someone recites *'yaṣṣālaḥā'*, its root is *yaṣliḥā* which has become *yaṣṭaliḥā* and then the *ṭā'* changed into a *ṣād* and the *ṣād* is elided into it. The *ṣād* is not changed into a *ṭā'* because of the extension of exhalation in it.

Reconciliation is better.

This is a general expression which demands that true reconciliation, which is that in which selves are satisfied and disagreement is resolved, is always better. That includes all forms of reconciliation between a man and wife regarding property, sexual intercourse and other things. *'Better'* means better than separation. Continuing disagreement, rancour and hatred are the triggers of evil. The Prophet ﷺ said about hatred, 'It is the shaver,' in other words it shaves away the *dīn* rather than shaving hair.

But people are prone to selfish greed.

This is information that greed exists in everyone and that people are greedy on the basis of their natural disposition and character which moves a person to some of what he dislikes. Ibn Jubayr said, 'It is the desire of a woman for maintenance from her husband and allotment of days.' Ibn Zayd said, 'Greed here exists in both him and in her,' and Ibn 'Aṭiyyah said, 'This is better. Generally a woman is greedy for her share from her husband and a husband is greedy for his portion with the young woman.' Greed can be directed to belief, will, aspirations and property and the like of that. Greed devoted to the *dīn* is praiseworthy but greed devoted to something else entails some blame. It is that about which Allah says: *'It is the people who are safe-guarded from the avarice of their own selves, who are successful'* (64:16), and that which leads to denying legal rights or what chivalry demands or miserliness which are blameworthy. Since miserliness is one of these blameworthy qualities, it is not accompanied by good which is hoped for or desired goodness.

It is related that the Prophet ﷺ asked the Anṣār, 'Who is your master?' They said, 'Al-Jadd ibn Qays, although he has some miserliness in him.' The Prophet ﷺ said, 'What sickness could be worse than miserliness!' They asked, 'How is that, Messenger of Allah?' He said, 'Some people camped by the shore and because of their miserliness disliked guests staying with them. They said, "Our men should be far from the women so that the men can excuse themselves by the distance of the women and the women will have an excuse by the distance of the men." So they did that and it went on for a long time and the men became involved with the men and the women with the women.' It was already mentioned by al-Māwardī.

If you do good and are godfearing, Allah is aware of what you do.

This is addressed to husbands since a husband should not be greedy and should do good and fear Allah in how he treats women by staying with them in spite of disliking of their company and avoiding wronging them. That is better for you.

وَلَن تَسْتَطِيعُوٓاْ أَن تَعْدِلُواْ بَيْنَ ٱلنِّسَآءِ وَلَوْ حَرَصْتُمْ ۖ فَلَا تَمِيلُواْ كُلَّ ٱلْمَيْلِ فَتَذَرُوهَا كَٱلْمُعَلَّقَةِ ۚ وَإِن تُصْلِحُواْ وَتَتَّقُواْ فَإِنَّ ٱللَّهَ كَانَ غَفُورًا رَّحِيمًا ﴿١٢٩﴾

129 You will not be able to be completely fair between your wives, however hard you try. But do not be completely partial so as to leave a wife, as it were, suspended in mid-air. And if you make amends and are godfearing, Allah is Ever-Forgiving, Most Merciful.

You will not be able to be completely fair between your wives, however hard you try.

Allah negates anyone's ability to be completely fair between their wives. That is because of natural inclination where love, intercourse and share of one's heart is concerned. Allah described the state of human beings and the fact that they are subject to their innate character and cannot control the direction of their hearts. That is why the Prophet ﷺ said, 'O Allah, this is the part of me that is under my control. Do not take me to task for what I do not control.' Then the prohibition follows: *'But do not be completely partial.'* Mujāhid says that it means do not intend maltreatment. Try to be equitable in division and maintenance because this is something one can do. This will be further discussed in *Sūrat al-Aḥzāb*, Allah willing.

Connected to this is what Qatādah related from an-Naḍr ibn Anas from Bashīr ibn Nahīk from Abū Hurayrah who related that the Messenger of Allah ﷺ said, 'Anyone who has two wives and is not fair between them will come with one shoulder sloping down on the Day of Rising.'

so as to leave a wife, as it were, suspended in mid-air.

This means she is neither divorced nor does she really have a husband. Al-Ḥasan said that. This is making something resemble something else because it is not firm on the ground nor supported by what suspends it. This is general in what they said in the adage: 'Be content with sending the camel to bring corn (*ta'līq*).' [meaning to be content with hanging the corn on the camel rather than also riding it.] The grammarians refer to the *ta'līq* of the verb. Another example is found in the *ḥadīth* of Umm Zar' when the woman said, 'My husband is a tall man. If I speak, I am divorced. If I am silent, I am left hanging.' Qatādah said that it means, 'like a woman imprisoned,' which is how Ubayy recited it: *'masjūnah'*. Ibn Mas'ūd recited *'ka-annahā mu'allaqah'*. *'Leave her'* is in the accusative as the apodosis of the prohibition and the *kāf* (*as it were*) is also in the accusative.

وَإِن يَتَفَرَّقَا يُغْنِ ٱللَّهُ كُلًّا مِّن سَعَتِهِۦ وَكَانَ ٱللَّهُ وَٰسِعًا
حَكِيمًا ﴿١٣٠﴾ وَلِلَّهِ مَا فِي ٱلسَّمَٰوَٰتِ وَمَا فِي ٱلْأَرْضِ وَلَقَدْ وَصَّيْنَا
ٱلَّذِينَ أُوتُوا۟ ٱلْكِتَٰبَ مِن قَبْلِكُمْ وَإِيَّاكُمْ أَنِ ٱتَّقُوا۟ ٱللَّهَ وَإِن
تَكْفُرُوا۟ فَإِنَّ لِلَّهِ مَا فِي ٱلسَّمَٰوَٰتِ وَمَا فِي ٱلْأَرْضِ وَكَانَ ٱللَّهُ غَنِيًّا
حَمِيدًا ﴿١٣١﴾ وَلِلَّهِ مَا فِي ٱلسَّمَٰوَٰتِ وَمَا فِي ٱلْأَرْضِ وَكَفَىٰ بِٱللَّهِ وَكِيلًا ﴿١٣٢﴾

130 If a couple do separate, Allah will enrich each of them from His boundless wealth. Allah is All-Encompassing, All-Wise. 131 Everything in the heavens and in the earth belongs to Allah.

We have instructed those given the Book before you, and you yourselves, to have taqwā of Allah, but if you disbelieve, everything in the heavens and in the earth belongs to Allah. Allah is Rich Beyond Need, Praiseworthy. 132 Everything in the heavens and in the earth belongs to Allah. Allah suffices as a Guardian.

If a couple do separate, Allah will enrich each of them from His boundless wealth.

If it is not possible to reconcile them, then they should both have a good opinion of Allah that He will give the man a wife who pleases him and the woman someone who will be generous to her. It is related from Ja'far ibn Muḥammad that a man complained to him of poverty and he ordered him to marry. The man went and married and then came to him and complained of poverty. He told him to divorce. He was asked about this *āyah* and said, 'I commanded him to marry because he might be one of the people of the *āyah*: *"If they are poor Allah will enrich them from His bounty."* (24:32) Since he was not one of the people of that *āyah*, I commanded him to divorce since he may be one of the people this *āyah*: *"If a couple do separate Allah will enrich each of them from His boundless wealth."*'

We have instructed those given the Book before you, and you yourselves, to have taqwā of Allah,

This is a command to have *taqwā*, and that is general to all communities. *Taqwā* has already been discussed. Al-Akhfash said, 'It is a command to have *taqwā* of Allah.' One of the gnostics said that this *āyah* is the millstone of the *āyah*s of the Qur'an because all the rest revolves around it.

But if you disbelieve, everything in the heavens and in the earth belongs to Allah.

If it is asked what the point of the repetition of '*everything in the heavens and earth belongs to Allah*' is, there are two responses to that. One is that it is repeated for stress to call attention to it and so that people reflect on Allah's domain and kingdom and that He has no need of the worlds. The second is that it is repeated to make different points. In the first, Allah reports that He enriches each from His wealth because everything in the heavens and what is in the earth is His and His treasures will never run out. Then He says, 'He instructed you and the People of the Book to have *taqwā*, but if you reject, He has no need of you because everything in the heavens and the earth belongs to Him.' Then in the third He informs us that He preserves His kingdom and manages it.

Allah suffices as a Guardian.

That is because everything in the heavens and earth belongs to Him. He says 'what' is in the heavens rather than 'who' because that then becomes generic. The heavens and earth contain both sentient and non-sentient beings.

إِن يَشَأْ يُذْهِبْكُمْ أَيُّهَا ٱلنَّاسُ وَيَأْتِ بِـَٔاخَرِينَ ۚ وَكَانَ ٱللَّهُ عَلَىٰ ذَٰلِكَ قَدِيرًا ﴿١٣٣﴾

133 Mankind, if He wanted, He could remove you altogether, and produce others instead. Allah certainly has the power to do that.

He could remove you by death. '*Mankind*' here means the idolaters and hypocrites. When this was revealed, the Messenger of Allah ﷺ tapped Salmān's back and said, 'They are the people of this one.' It is also said that the *āyah* is universal: 'If you disbelieve, He will remove you and bring people who obey Allah more than you.' This is like another *āyah*: *'If you turn away, He will replace you with a people other than yourselves and they will not be like you are.'* (47:38).

The *āyah* also alarms and warns all who have position, authority or leadership not to deviate regarding their subjects, or scholars who do not act by their knowledge or advise people, that He will remove such people and bring others.

Allah certainly has the power to do that.

Power is a pre-eternal attribute and its effects do not end in the same way that there is no end to what Allah knows. In relation to Him, past and future are the same. The past tense is used here so that it should not be imagined that anything has an effect on His Essence or Attributes. The power is that by which action occurs and it is not possible for lack of power to exist together with it.

مَّن كَانَ يُرِيدُ ثَوَابَ ٱلدُّنْيَا فَعِندَ ٱللَّهِ ثَوَابُ ٱلدُّنْيَا وَٱلْـَٔاخِرَةِ ۚ وَكَانَ ٱللَّهُ سَمِيعًۢا بَصِيرًا ﴿١٣٤﴾

134 If anyone desires the reward of this world, the reward of both this world and the Next World is with Allah. Allah is All-Hearing, All-Seeing.

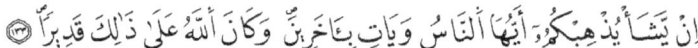

If someone acts by what Allah has made obligatory for him, seeking the Next World, Allah will give him that in the Next World. Whoever acts seeking just this world, Allah will give him what He has prescribed for him in this world and he will have no reward in the Next World, because he acted for other than the sake of Allah, as He says: *'He will have no share in the Next World'* (42:20) and: *'Such people will have nothing in the in the Next World but the Fire.'* (11:16). This is when the hypocrites and unbelievers are meant in this *āyah,* as aṭ-Ṭabarī prefers.

It is related that the idolaters did not believe in the Resurrection and tried to approach Allah in order to obtain more of this world and for Him to remove from them what they disliked. So Allah revealed this. He hears what they say and sees what they conceal.

يَٰٓأَيُّهَا ٱلَّذِينَ ءَامَنُوا۟ كُونُوا۟ قَوَّٰمِينَ بِٱلْقِسْطِ شُهَدَآءَ لِلَّهِ وَلَوْ عَلَىٰٓ
أَنفُسِكُمْ أَوِ ٱلْوَٰلِدَيْنِ وَٱلْأَقْرَبِينَ ۚ إِن يَكُنْ غَنِيًّا أَوْ فَقِيرًا فَٱللَّهُ أَوْلَىٰ بِهِمَا ۖ
فَلَا تَتَّبِعُوا۟ ٱلْهَوَىٰٓ أَن تَعْدِلُوا۟ ۚ وَإِن تَلْوُۥٓا۟ أَوْ تُعْرِضُوا۟ فَإِنَّ ٱللَّهَ كَانَ بِمَا
تَعْمَلُونَ خَبِيرًا ﴿١٣٥﴾

135 You who believe, be upholders of justice, bearing witness for Allah alone, even against yourselves or your parents and relatives. Whether they are rich or poor, Allah is well able to look after them. Do not follow your own desires and deviate from the truth. If you twist or turn away, Allah is aware of what you do.

You who believe, be upholders of justice,

Allah uses the intensive form (*qawwām*) here for emphasis, implying that you should always uphold justice when bearing witness against yourselves. A person bearing witness against himself is by affirming the rights he owes to others. Then He mentions parents, since it is mandatory to respect and esteem them. Then He coupled that with relatives since they are where love and partisanship are likely. So one is more likely to establish justice against a non-relative and testify against him, and so in the *sūrah* Allah speaks about preserving people's rights with regard to property.

There is no disagreement among the people of knowledge about the validity of the rulings of this *āyah.* The testimony of a child against his parents is effective and that does not prevent his respect for them, and indeed it is out of his respect for them that he testifies against them and frees them of what is false which is the meaning of Allah's words: *'Protect yourselves and your family from a Fire.'* (66:6)

As for testimony by you for them or by them for you, there is disagreement about it, and scholars say various things. There has been disagreement about it in the past and present. Ibn Shihāb az-Zuhrī said, 'Among the righteous early ones, they allowed the testimony of parents and brothers. They took that interpretation from the words of Allah: *"Be upholders of justice, bearing witness for Allah alone."* None of the early generations are suspect in that. May Allah be pleased with them. Then matters arose among people which led the governors to suspect them and they abandoned the testimony of those who were suspect. Then it was not allowed from a child, parent, brother, husband, or wife. That is the school of al-Ḥasan, an-Nakhaʿī, ash-Shaʿbī, Shurayḥ, Mālik, ath-Thawrī, ash-Shāfiʿī and Ibn Ḥanbal.'

Some people allow them to testify for one another if they have integrity. It is related that ʿUmar ibn al-Khaṭṭāb allowed it. That was also related from ʿUmar ibn ʿAbd al-ʿAzīz, and it was stated by Isḥāq, Abū Thawr and al-Muzanī. The position of the school of Mālik is that a brother is permitted to testify for his brother, as long as he has integrity, except regarding lineage. It is related from him by Ibn Wahb that it is not allowed when it is about dependants or a portion of property that he will inherit.

Mālik and Abū Ḥanīfah said that the testimony of a husband for his wife is not accepted because of the mutual connection of their financial interests which is the subject of the testimony. Ash-Shāfiʿī said that spouses are permitted to testify for one another because they are not related. A marriage contract exists between them, but it can be removed. The fundamental principle is that testimony is accepted and, unless there is something specific to alter it, it remains on its basic principle. This is weak. The nature of marriage obliges kindness, mutual connection, intimacy and love. Therefore there is strong apparent suspicion.

Abū Dāwūd related from Sulaymān ibn Mūsā from ʿAmr ibn Shuʿayb from his father from his grandfather that the Messenger of Allah ﷺ rejected the testimony of a man who is treacherous, someone with a grudge against his brother, and rejected the testimony of one who beseeches for his own household, but not for others. Al-Khaṭṭābī said that 'a grudge' is when there is clear enmity between him and the one against whom he testifies: his testimony is rejected because of suspicion. Abū Ḥanīfah said that testimony against an enemy is accepted if the witness has integrity. The one who beseeches (*qāniʿ*) is someone who begs and asks for food or any other type of asking. It is said that it is someone who devotes himself to a people to serve them and attend to their needs. That is like a hireling, trustee or the like.

The reason that the testimony of such a person is rejected is because of suspicion of him trying to bring himself benefit because he is seeking benefits for the people of a house. Anyone who accrues benefit for himself by his testimony has his testimony rejected. This is like when someone testifies that a man has purchased a house when he has the right of pre-emption, or like someone who is bankrupt and says that a man owes him a debt. Al-Khaṭṭābī said, 'If someone rejects the testimony of a beseecher for the people of a house because he is accruing a benefit, then by analogy he must reject the testimony of a husband for his wife because there is more suspicion regarding them with regard to accruing benefit. That is what Abū Ḥanīfah believes.' The *ḥadīth* provides evidence against the one who permits a father to testify on behalf of his son because that brings him benefit because of his natural disposition to love him and be biased in his favour and because he controls his property. The Prophet ﷺ said, 'You and your property belong to your father.'

One of those whose testimony is rejected according to Mālik is that of a desert Arab against a city person unless he is in a desert or town. As for summoning a desert Arab as a witness in a town while not calling someone's neighbours in the town, I think that it is doubtful. Abū Dāwūd and ad-Dāraquṭnī related that Abū Hurayrah heard the Messenger of Allah ﷺ say, 'The testimony of a desert Arab against a townsperson is not allowed.' Muḥammad ibn 'Abd al-Ḥakam said, 'Mālik interpreted this *ḥadīth* as meaning testimony regarding rights and property. It is not rejected in cases of bloodshed and similar matters which may take place in secluded spots.' Most scholars said, 'When a desert Arab is reputable, his proper testimony is allowed.' Allah knows best. This was discussed in *al-Baqarah* and will be completed in *at-Tawbah*, Allah willing.

bearing witness for Allah alone,

This is in the accusative, describing the *'upholders of justice'*. It can also be a predicate after a predicate. An-Naḥḥās said, 'The better of these two is in that it is in the accusative for the *ḥāl*, modifying what is in *'upholders of justice'* about mentioning those who believe because it has the same meaning. It means: "Bear witness for Allah with justice in your testimony."' Ibn 'Aṭiyyah said, 'The adverbial sense in it is weak in meaning because it refines upholding justice, making it refer to giving testimony. The plural noun *'shuhadā''* is not inflected because it contains the *alif* of the feminine. *'For Allah'* means for the sake of Allah, and for His pleasure and reward.

even against yourselves, or your parents and relatives.

This is connected to '*bearing witness*' and is the apparent meaning used by people in its interpretation. It refers to people testifying against rights owed by their family. That is people testifying against themselves. Allah instructs the believers in the proper way to do this as Ibn 'Abbās explains: 'They were commanded to speak the truth, even against themselves.' It is also possible that the words *'bearing witness for Allah alone'* mean to testify to His oneness. The first interpretation is clearer.

Whether they are rich or poor,

There is an implied elision in the words, which is the noun of '*kāna*', meaning that if the claimant or the one testified against is rich, do not consider his wealth or fear him and if he is poor, do not be moved by compassion for him. Allah is the One who chooses wealth or poverty for them. As-Suddī stated that a rich man and poor man took a dispute to the Messenger of Allah ﷺ and he inclined to the poor man and he thought that the poor man would not wrong a wealthy man and the *āyah* was revealed.

Allah is well able to look after them.

Allah uses the dual (*bihimā*) and not the singular (*bihi*), even though the 'or' indicates that result will benefit only one of them because it means that Allah is better entitled to look after each of them. Al-Akhfash said that 'or' can mean 'and', in other words, 'Both if they are rich and poor, Allah is more entitled to the two litigants whatever their circumstances.' It is said that He says '*bihimā*' because they were both already mentioned as Allah says in 4:12.

Do not follow your own desires and deviate from the truth.

This is prohibited because following desires is ruinous. Allah Almighty says elsewhere: *'Judge between people with truth and do not follow your own desires, letting them misguide you from the Way of Allah.'* (38:26) Following desires leads to perjury and injustice in judgment and other things. Ash-Sha'bī said, 'Allah imposes three things on judges: Not to follow desires, not to fear people but rather to fear Him, and not to sell His signs for a cheap price.'

If you twist or turn away,

It is recited '*in talwū*'. This is from *lawā*, and when you 'twist' someone's right, you dismiss it. The verb is *lawā* and the root is *lawā* and the *yā'* has been changed into an *alif* because of its vowel and the vowel before it. The verbal noun is *layy* and its root is *lawy* and *layyān* whose root is *lawyān* and the *wāw* is assimilated into the *yā'*. Al-Qutabī said that '*talwū*' is from *layy*, which in testimony, it is to incline towards one of the two litigants. Ibn 'Āmir and the Kufans recite '*talū*' which means, 'When you undertake the matter and turn away.' It is from your words, '*walaytu'l-amr*' (I undertook the matter) and the words contain rebuke for not carrying out the command.

It is said that 'twist' also means 'to turn away'. If it is recited with a *ḍammah* on the *lām*, that gives both meanings: undertaking and turning away. When it is read with two *wāws*, then it gives one meaning, which is turning away. Some grammarians claimed that '*talū*' is incorrect because there is no sense of undertaking here. An-Naḥḥās and others said that this is not necessary, but both readings mean the same. That is because the root is '*talwū*' and the *ḍammah* is heavy on a *wāw* followed by another *wāw* and so the vowel is given to the *lām* and one of the two *wāws* is elided because of the meeting of two silent letters. It is like the reading with a *sukūn* on the *lām* and two *wāws* which Makkī mentioned. Az-Zajjāj said that the meaning is based on the reading, '*in talwū*' and then there is a *hamzah* on the first *wāw* and it becomes '*tal'ū*' and then the *hamzah* is lightened by putting the vowel on the *lām* and it becomes '*talū*'. Its root is '*talwū*'. So the two readings agree based on this assumption. It was mentioned by an-Naḥḥās, Makkī, Ibn al-'Arabī and others.

Ibn 'Abbās said, 'The *āyah* is about two litigants who sit before the *qāḍī* and the *qāḍī* twists and turns from one to the other.' According to this, *layy* is dragging things out through talking until the possibility of accurate judgment is lost and that to which the *qāḍī* inclines is carried out. Ibn 'Aṭiyyah said, 'I have seen some judges who did that. Allah will call everyone to account.' Ibn 'Abbās, as-Suddī, Ibn Zayd, aḍ-Ḍaḥḥāk and Mujāhid said, 'In respect of testimony, it is that a witness twists the testimony with his tongue and alters it so that he does not speak the truth, or turns away from performing the duty inherent in it.' The expression in the *āyah* includes both judgment and testimony and every human being is commanded to be just. We find in a *ḥadīth*: 'The twisting of its originator makes his honour and punishment lawful.' Ibn al-A'rābī said that his punishment is imprisonment and his honour is suspect.

Some scholars use this *āyah* as proof for rejecting the testimony of a slave. They say that Allah made the judge a witness in the *āyah* and that is the most evident proof that a slave is not one of the people of testimony because what is meant is to independently assume this task when there is need for it. That condition not met in a slave at all and so his testimony is rejected.

يَا أَيُّهَا الَّذِينَ آمَنُوا آمِنُوا بِاللَّهِ وَرَسُولِهِ وَالْكِتَابِ الَّذِي نَزَّلَ عَلَىٰ
رَسُولِهِ وَالْكِتَابِ الَّذِي أَنزَلَ مِن قَبْلُ ۚ وَمَن يَكْفُرْ بِاللَّهِ وَمَلَائِكَتِهِ
وَكُتُبِهِ وَرُسُلِهِ وَالْيَوْمِ الْآخِرِ فَقَدْ ضَلَّ ضَلَالًا بَعِيدًا ﴿١٣٦﴾

136 You who believe! Believe in Allah and His Messenger and in the Book He sent down to His Messenger, and the Books He sent down before. Anyone who rejects Allah and His angels and His Books and His Messengers and the Last Day has gone very far astray.

This was revealed about all believers. It means: 'O you who affirm, establish your affirmation and confirm it.' '*The Book*' here is the Qur'an. It is said that it was revealed about every Book revealed to the Prophets.

Ibn Kathīr and Ibn 'Āmir recite '*nuzzila*' and '*unzila*' while the rest have '*nazzala*' and '*anzala*'. It is said that it was revealed about those who believed in the Prophets before Muḥammad ﷺ and it is also said that it was addressed to the hypocrites. According to this, it means: 'O you who believe in the outward, be sincere to Allah.' It is said that it is addressed to the idolaters and means: 'You who believe in al-Lāt, al-'Uzzā and Tāghūt, believe in Allah, in other words affirm Him and His Books.'

إِنَّ الَّذِينَ آمَنُوا ثُمَّ كَفَرُوا ثُمَّ آمَنُوا ثُمَّ كَفَرُوا ثُمَّ ازْدَادُوا كُفْرًا لَّمْ يَكُنِ اللَّهُ
لِيَغْفِرَ لَهُمْ وَلَا لِيَهْدِيَهُمْ سَبِيلًا ﴿١٣٧﴾

137 As for those who believe and then return to unbelief, and then again believe and then return to unbelief, and then increase in unbelief, Allah will not forgive them or guide them on any path.

It is said that it means: They believed in Mūsā and rejected 'Uzayr and then believed in 'Uzayr and rejected 'Īsā and then their disbelief in Muḥammad ﷺ increased. It is said that it is those who believed in Mūsā and then believed in 'Uzayr and then rejected the Messiah after 'Uzayr. The Christians rejected what Mūsā brought and believed in 'Īsā and then increased in disbelief in Muḥammad ﷺ and what the Qur'an brought.

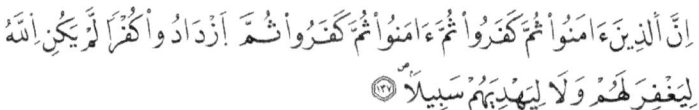

If it is said that Allah does not forgive any disbelief, so how can He say this? The answer is that when an unbeliever believes, he is forgiven his disbelief. If he recants and disbelieves again, his first disbelief is not forgiven, as we find in *Ṣaḥīḥ Muslim* where 'Abdullāh said, 'Some people asked the Messenger of Allah ﷺ, "Messenger of Allah, will we be punished for what we did in the *Jāhiliyyah*?" He replied, "As for those of you with sound Islam, they will not be punished. But as for the one whose Islam is unsound, he will be punished for his actions in the *Jāhiliyyah* and Islam."' One version has, 'Whoever is bad in Islam will be punished for the first and the last.'

Evil here means *kufr*. It is not valid for this to refer to committing wrong action. That is not necessary because Islam wipes out what was before it unless someone is protected from all wrong actions until death, and that is false by consensus. *'Increase in unbelief'* means persisting in it. *'Any path'* means here a path to the Garden. It is said that He will not select them for success as He does His friends.

The *āyah* is refutation of the people who espouse *Qadar*. Allah makes it clear that He goes not guide unbelievers to the path of good, so that the slave knows that guidance is granted only by Allah. Denial of guidance is by the will of Allah. The *āyah* also contains the ruling on apostates. They were already discussed in *al-Baqarah* (2:217).

بَشِّرِ ٱلْمُنَٰفِقِينَ بِأَنَّ لَهُمْ عَذَابًا أَلِيمًا ﴿١٣٨﴾

138 Give news to the hypocrites that they will have a painful punishment.

It is called good news *(tabshīr)* because its effect is seen on the skin. This was also discussed in *al-Baqarah*.

ٱلَّذِينَ يَتَّخِذُونَ ٱلْكَٰفِرِينَ أَوْلِيَآءَ مِن دُونِ ٱلْمُؤْمِنِينَ أَيَبْتَغُونَ عِندَهُمُ
ٱلْعِزَّةَ فَإِنَّ ٱلْعِزَّةَ لِلَّهِ جَمِيعًا ﴿١٣٩﴾

139 Do those who take the unbelievers as protectors, rather than the believers, hope to find power and strength with them? Power and strength belong entirely to Allah.

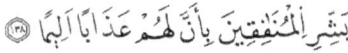

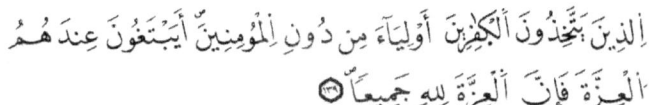

The pronoun '*those*' here refers to the hypocrites. This is an indication that a believer who disobeys is not a hypocrite because he takes unbelievers as friends. It also contains the prohibition against taking unbelievers as a friends and helpers in matters connected to the *dīn*. It is reported in the *Ṣaḥīḥ* from 'Ā'ishah that one of the idolaters joined the Prophet ﷺ to fight with him and he told him, 'Go back. We do not seek the help of an idolater.'

The words *'power and strength'* (*'izzah*) mean victory. All victory and strength belong to Allah. Ibn 'Abbās said about: *'hoping to find with them,'* that it is a reference to the Banū Qaynuqā' whom Ibn Ubayy took as friends.

وَقَدْ نَزَّلَ عَلَيْكُمْ فِي الْكِتَابِ أَنْ إِذَا سَمِعْتُمْ آيَاتِ اللَّهِ يُكْفَرُ بِهَا
وَيُسْتَهْزَأُ بِهَا فَلَا تَقْعُدُوا مَعَهُمْ حَتَّىٰ يَخُوضُوا فِي حَدِيثٍ غَيْرِهِ إِنَّكُمْ
إِذًا مِثْلُهُمْ إِنَّ اللَّهَ جَامِعُ الْمُنَافِقِينَ وَالْكَافِرِينَ فِي جَهَنَّمَ جَمِيعًا ﴿١٤٠﴾
الَّذِينَ يَتَرَبَّصُونَ بِكُمْ فَإِنْ كَانَ لَكُمْ فَتْحٌ مِنَ اللَّهِ قَالُوا أَلَمْ نَكُنْ مَعَكُمْ وَإِنْ
كَانَ لِلْكَافِرِينَ نَصِيبٌ قَالُوا أَلَمْ نَسْتَحْوِذْ عَلَيْكُمْ وَنَمْنَعْكُمْ مِنَ الْمُؤْمِنِينَ
فَاللَّهُ يَحْكُمُ بَيْنَكُمْ يَوْمَ الْقِيَامَةِ وَلَنْ يَجْعَلَ اللَّهُ لِلْكَافِرِينَ عَلَى الْمُؤْمِنِينَ سَبِيلًا ﴿١٤١﴾

140 It has been sent down to you in the Book that when you hear Allah's Signs being rejected and mocked at by people, you must not sit with them till they start talking of other things. If you do you are just the same as them. Allah will gather all the hypocrites and unbelievers into Hell. 141 Those who anticipate the worst for you say, 'Were we not with you?' whenever you gain a victory from Allah, but if the unbelievers have a success they say, 'Did we not have the upper hand over you and yet in spite of that keep the believers away from you?' Allah will judge between you on the Day of Rising. Allah will not give the unbelievers any way against the believers.

It has been sent down to you in the Book that when you hear Allah's Signs being rejected and mocked at by people,

This is addressed to all who show faith, truly or as hypocrites, because a display of faith obliges the person concerned to obey the commands of the Book of Allah. Allah revealed elsewhere: *'When you see people engrossed in mockery of Our Signs, turn away from them until they start to talk of other things.'* (6:68) The hypocrites used to sit with the Jewish rabbis and mock the Qur'an.

'Āṣim and Ya'qūb recited *'nazzala'* (He sent down) referring back to the name of Allah already mentioned. Ḥumayd read it *nazala*. The rest read it *nuzzila* (It has been sent down). *'Being mocked'*: when you hear unbelief and mocking of Allah's signs, it is listening to unbelief and mockery. The position of *'when you hear Allah's Signs'*, according to the reading of 'Āṣim and Ya'qūb is accusative because of the effect of the verb, and according to the reading of the rest, it is nominative because it is a passive noun. The subject of *'being rejected'* is in reality the hearing of unbelief and mockery of the Signs of Allah, and so it is not Allah's Signs that are being heard but rather unbelief and mockery. It is as you say, 'I heard 'Abdullāh blamed,' meaning 'I heard blame about 'Abdullāh.'

You must not sit with them till they start talking of other things

This is until they talk about other than unbelief.

If you do you are just the same as them.

This indicates the obligation to avoid the people who commit acts disobedience when they are doing them because, if someone does not avoid them, it indicates that he is content with their actions, and contentment with unbelief is in itself unbelief. If someone sits in a circle of people of disobedience and does not object, he shares the burden equally with them. He must object to the disobedience when he speaks to them and they act on it. If he is not able to object to it, then he must leave them so that he is not one of the people of this *āyah.*

It is related that 'Umar ibn 'Abd al-'Azīz seized some people who were drinking wine. He was told that one of those present was fasting but he punished him as well, reciting this *āyah.* It means that acquiescing to disobedience is, in itself, disobedience. That is why he punished both the one who did it and the one who acquiesced to it with the punishment of disobedience so that they were all beaten. This resemblance does not exist in all qualities, but obliges likeness based on judging by what is apparent by being directly connected to it as the poet says:

Every comrade imitates the one who he is associated with.

Since it is confirmed that one must avoid the people of disobedience, as we have made clear, then it is better to avoid the people of sects and innovations. Al-Kalbī said that Allah's words here are abrogated by His words: *'Their reckoning is in no way the responsibility of those who are godfearing.'* (6:69). Most commentators say that it is an *āyah* of judgment. Jubaybir related that aḍ-Ḍaḥḥāk said, 'Every innovator in the *dīn* is included in this *āyah* until the Day of Rising.'

Those who anticipate the worst for you say

These are the hypocrites and means that they hope that disasters will befall you.

When you win a victory over the Jews and booty, they ask for some of the booty, and if the unbelievers win, they say this to the unbelievers, telling them that they protected them from the believers. The verb *istaḥwadha* means to overcome something as we see in 58:19. It is said that the root is *ḥawṭ*. The verb *ḥādha* is to encompass something. The phrase: *'keep the believers away from you'* means that we disappointed them in respect of you and made them fail to do what they wanted to do to you.

The *āyah* shows that the hypocrites used to go on expeditions with the Muslims demonstrated by their words: *'Were we not with you?'* It also indicates that they were not given booty and that is why they asked for it, saying, *'Were we not with you?'* It is possible that their words are trying to make the Muslims indebted to them, implying, 'We knew your reports and we are your helpers.'

Allah will not give the unbelievers any way against the believers.

There are three points in this. The first is that scholars have five interpretations of it. One is related from Yusayʿ al-Ḥaḍramī who said, 'I was with ʿAlī ibn Abī Ṭālib when a man said to him, "Amīr al-Mu'minīn, what do you think about the words of Allah: *'Allah will not give the unbelievers any way against the believers'* when they fight us and sometimes defeat us?" ʿAlī replied, "That refers to the Day of Rising, the Day of Judgment."' That is what Ibn ʿAbbās said. Ibn ʿAṭiyyah said, 'This is the position of all the people of interpretation.'

Ibn al-ʿArabī said that it is weak since it is not reported that it is about the Day of Rising even though it might be imagined from His words: *'Allah will judge between you on the Day of Rising.'* So the judgment is delayed until the Day of Rising and the business in this world goes in turns: sometimes you defeat the unbelievers and sometimes you are defeated based on what is seen of wisdom and prior decree.

The second is that Allah did not give them a way to eradicate the state of the believers and remove their traces and violate their territory, as we find in *Ṣaḥīḥ Muslim* from the *ḥadīth* of Thawbān in which the Prophet ﷺ said, 'I asked my Lord not to destroy it by general famine, and not to give an enemy other than themselves power over them to plunder their territory. My Lord said, "Muḥammad, when I make a judgment, it is not retracted. I have granted that your community will not be destroyed by famine, and that an enemy other than themselves will not have power over them to plunder their territory, even if they gather against them from the ends of the earth. However, they will kill one another and imprison one another."'

The third is that Allah has not given unbelievers a way against the believers unless the believers command each other to falsehood and do not give up doing wrong and do not repent. So the overpowering in fact originates from them, as Allah says: *'Any disaster that strikes you is through what your own hands have earned.'* (42:30) Ibn al-'Arabī said, 'This is very valuable.' This is indicated by the words of the Prophet ﷺ in the *ḥadīth* of Thawbān which we find in *Ṣaḥīḥ Muslim*: '… they will kill one another and imprison one another.' That exists now in these times with the internecine wars between Muslims and when the power of the unbelievers has become great and they have taken control of Muslim lands so that there is only the very minimum of Islam left. We ask Allah to grant us His pardon, help and kindness.

The fourth is that Allah will not give the unbelievers a way against the believers in respect of legal rulings. If that exists, it is contrary to the Sharī'ah.

The fifth is that there is no logical or legal argument by which they can overcome the believers.

The second point is that Ibn al-'Arabī said, 'Our scholars use this *āyah* as evidence that an unbeliever cannot own a Muslim slave. Ashhab and ash-Shāfi'i said that because Allah said that Allah does not give the unbeliever a way, and owning by purchase is a way and so the contract is not legal.'

Ibn al-Qāsim reported from Mālik, and it is also the position of Abū Ḥanīfah, that the meaning is constant ownership because we find that he may have that through the conversion of a slave and by inheritance. Such a case would be when an unbelieving slave converts to Islam while owned by an unbeliever. Then there must be a ruling that he sell, and then if he dies before the ruling that he must be sold, if an unbeliever is the heir of the Muslim slave. This is a way which is confirmed by force and is not intended. If he owns him by purchase, then it is confirmed by the aim of the intention. The unbeliever wanted to own him by choice. If the ruling of the contract is confirmed and ownership established, then the aim is realised in him and there is no way against him.

Abū 'Umar said, 'The consensus of the Muslims is that setting free a Muslim slave belonging to a Christian or Jew is necessary and should be carried out. They agree that when the slave of an unbeliever becomes Muslim, he is made to sell him and given his price. That indicates that his property is sold and it is confirmed that his property is emancipated, unless it is property that it is not confirmed that he is obliged to sell. Allah knows best, but that is based on the words of the Almighty: *"Allah will not give the unbelievers any way against the believers."* This means enslavement, ownership and slavehood by confirmed constant ownership. Scholars disagree about an unbeliever buying a Muslim slave. One view is that the sale is void, and the other is that the sale is sound and the buyer is made to sell him.

The third point is that scholars disagree about a Christian man who gives a *tadbīr* to a Christian slave of his who then becomes Muslim. Mālik and ash-Shāfi'ī in one of his two positions say that there is a barrier between him and the slave and that he is removed from his Christian master and he is not sold until his business is clear. If the Christian master dies with a debt, his debt is settled from the price of the *mudabbar* slave unless his estate contains what will bear the price of the *mudabbar* slave. Then the *mudabbar* slave is set free. In another position ash-Shāfi'ī said that he is made to sell him as soon as he becomes Muslim. Al-Muzanī prefers that because the *mudabbar* is a bequest and it is not permitted to leave a Muslim in the ownership of an idolater so that he can humiliate him and impose on him. Islam has made him his enemy.

Al-Layth ibn Sa'd said, 'The Muslim is purchased from the Christian and set free and his *walā'* goes to the one who buys him and sets him free and the Christian receives his price. Sufyān and the Kufans said that when a *mudabbar* slave of a Christian becomes Muslim, his price is estimated and he strives to pay his price. If the Christian dies before the *mudabbar* has managed to do that, then the slave is free and the imposed work is voided.

إِنَّ ٱلْمُنَٰفِقِينَ يُخَٰدِعُونَ ٱللَّهَ وَهُوَ خَٰدِعُهُمْ وَإِذَا قَامُوٓا۟ إِلَى ٱلصَّلَوٰةِ قَامُوا۟
كُسَالَىٰ يُرَآءُونَ ٱلنَّاسَ وَلَا يَذْكُرُونَ ٱللَّهَ إِلَّا قَلِيلًا ﴿١٤٢﴾

142 The hypocrites think they deceive Allah, but He is deceiving them. When they get up to pray, they get up lazily, showing off to people, and only remembering Allah a very little.

The hypocrites think they deceive Allah, but He is deceiving them.

The deceit of hypocrites was already mentioned at the beginning of *al-Baqarah*. Allah's deceiving of them is their repayment for their deceiving His friends and Messengers. Al-Ḥasan said, 'Every believer and hypocrite will be given a light on the Day of Rising and the hypocrites will rejoice, thinking that they are saved. When they come to the *Ṣirāṭ*, the light of every hypocrite will be extinguished. That is when they say: *"Wait for us so that we can borrow some of your light."* (57:13)'

When they get up to pray, they get up lazily, showing off to people

They pray to show off and they are lazy and sluggish. They do not hope for a reward nor believe that there is any punishment for leaving it. We find in the sound *ḥadīth*, 'The heaviest prayers for a hypocrite are *'Ishā'* and *Ṣubḥ*.' *'Ishā'* comes after the work of the day and it is hard for them to get up for it and *Ṣubḥ* comes when they prefer to sleep. Had it not been for the sword, they would not have got up.'

Showing off (*riyā'*) is to put on a good appearance so that people see them, not to follow the command of Allah. Allah described them as having little remembrance of Him, as showing off and as being in fear. The Prophet criticised those who delayed the prayer and said three times, 'The prayer of the hypocrites, the prayer of the hypocrites, the prayer of the hypocrites is that one of them sits until the sun becomes yellow and is between the horns of Shayṭān, or on the horn of Shayṭān, and then gets up and rattles off four *rak'ahs,* hardly remembering Allah in them at all.' Mālik and others related it. It is said that they are described with little remembrance because while they do not remember Allah by recitation or glorification, they remember Him by *takbīr.* It is said that it is lack of acceptance or lack of sincerity.

There are two points here. The first is that in this *āyah* Allah describes the prayer of the hypocrites and His Messenger Muḥammad ﷺ explained it. If someone prays like them and his remembrance is like theirs, he joins them in not being accepted and fails to fulfil what is demanded by the words of Allah: *'It is the believers who are successful: those who are humble in their prayer.'* (23:1) This is unless the person has an excuse and confines himself to the obligatory according to what the Prophet ﷺ taught the bedouin when he saw him with defects in his prayer. He said, 'When you stand for the prayer, perform *wuḍū'* fully, them face *qiblah,* say the *takbīr* and then recite what is easy for you of the Qur'an. Then bow until you are at rest in *rukū'.* Then rise until you are standing upright. Then prostrate until you are still in prostration. Then come up until you are still in sitting. Then do that in all of your prayer.' The Imāms related it. The Prophet ﷺ said, 'There is no prayer for the one who does not recite the *Umm al-Qur'an.*' He said, 'A prayer in which a man's back is not straight in bowing and prostration is not sufficient.' At-Tirmidhī transmitted it and said that it is a sound *ḥasan ḥadīth.*

According to the people of knowledge among the Companions of the Prophet ﷺ and those after them, the normative practice is based on this. They thought that a man should have his back straight in bowing and prostration. Ash-Shāfi'ī, Aḥmad and Isḥāq said, 'If someone does not have his back straight in bowing and prostration, his prayer is invalid based on the *ḥadīth* of the Prophet ﷺ, "A prayer in which a man's back is not straight in bowing and prostration is not sufficient."' Ibn al-'Arabī said, 'Ibn al-Qāsim and Abū Ḥanīfah believed that being still is not an obligation. It is an Iraqi transmission which none of the Mālikīs should occupy themselves with.' This was mentioned in *al-Baqarah*.

The second is that Ibn al-'Arabī said, 'If someone prays a prayer so that people see it and they see him doing it and testify that he has faith, or he wants position and appearance so that his testimony is accepted and his leadership is allowed, that is not the showing-off which is meant. There is no deprecation of his character. What is meant is the disobedience which he covers to trap people and lead to consumption of property. Such an intention is not permitted and he must repeat the prayer.'

His words, 'he wants position and appearance so that his testimony is accepted' are debatable. This was already explained in this *sūrah*. This *āyah* indicates that showing off can occur in both obligatory and supererogatory prayers since Allah's words are general. Some people say that it is only possible in the supererogatory because the obligatory is obligatory for all people and it is the supererogatory that is subject to showing off. The reverse is also said because if he does not perform the supererogatory, he is not punished for it.

مُّذَبْذَبِينَ بَيْنَ ذَٰلِكَ لَآ إِلَىٰ هَٰٓؤُلَآءِ وَلَآ إِلَىٰ هَٰٓؤُلَآءِ ۚ وَمَن يُضْلِلِ ٱللَّهُ فَلَن تَجِدَ لَهُۥ سَبِيلًا ﴿١٤٣﴾

143 They vacillate between the two – not joining these or joining those. If Allah misguides someone, you will not find any way for him to go.

Mudhabdhab is someone who vacillates between two matters and *dhabdhabah* is being unsettled. Part of that is the words of an-Nābighah:

Do you not see that Allah has given you strength
and you see every kingdom unsettled before it?

Another said:

A spectre of Umm as-Salsabīl when before [where she is]
Is a distance of a month for the fluctuating riding camel.

That is how it is related with a *kasrah* as *mudhabdhib*. Ibn Jinnī said that it is shaking with pretended fear which is not firm nor does it last. Those are the hypocrites who vacillate between the believers and idolaters, neither sincere in faith nor openly espousing disbelief. In *Ṣaḥīḥ Muslim*, Ibn 'Umar reported that the

Prophet ﷺ said, 'A hypocrite resembles a stray sheep between two flocks, going one moment to this flock and then to the other.' One variant has '*kakurru*' instead of '*ta'īru*'.

Most recite '*mudhabdhabīna*' with *fatḥahs* on both *dhāls*. Ibn 'Abbās recited '*mudhabdhibīna*' and the mode of Ubayy has '*mutadhabdhibīna*'. *Idghām* is permitted in this reading as '*madhdhabdhibīna*'. Al-Ḥasan has '*madhabdhabīna*'.

يَٰٓأَيُّهَا ٱلَّذِينَ ءَامَنُوا۟ لَا تَتَّخِذُوا۟ ٱلْكَٰفِرِينَ أَوْلِيَآءَ مِن دُونِ ٱلْمُؤْمِنِينَ
أَتُرِيدُونَ أَن تَجْعَلُوا۟ لِلَّهِ عَلَيْكُمْ سُلْطَٰنًا مُّبِينًا ﴿١٤٤﴾

144 You who believe! do not take the unbelievers as friends rather than the believers. Do you want to give Allah clear proof against you?

Do not make them your close friends. Do you want to give Allah clear evidence for punishing you by establishing the proof against you since He has forbidden you to do that?

إِنَّ ٱلْمُنَٰفِقِينَ فِى ٱلدَّرْكِ ٱلْأَسْفَلِ مِنَ ٱلنَّارِ وَلَن تَجِدَ لَهُمْ نَصِيرًا ﴿١٤٥﴾

145 The hypocrites are in the lowest level of the Fire. You will not find any one to help them,

'*Level*': the Kufans read it as '*dark*'. [Warsh has '*darak*'.] *Darak* is more eloquent because the plural is *adrāk* or *adruk*. Abū 'Alī said that they are two dialectical forms. The Fire has seven levels and stations, although the Arabs use that word for all that goes down and would say, for instance, that a well has 'levels'. The Garden's levels are called *daraj*. This has already been discussed. The hypocrites will be in the lowest level, which is Hāwiyah, because of their intense disbelief and deceit and the ability to harm the believers. The highest level is Jahannam, then Laẓā, then Ḥuṭamah, then Sa'īr, then Saqar, then Jahīm and then Hāwiyah. It is all called Jahannam after the first level. May Allah give us refuge from its punishment.

Ibn Mas'ūd reported about its interpretation that it consists of 'sealed boxes of iron in the midst of the fire.' Ibn 'Umar said, 'Three will have the worst punishment of the Day of Rising: the hypocrites, those who denied among the People of the Table and the people of Pharaoh.' He cited this *āyah* as evidence for the first group. Allah said about the People of the Table: *'I will punish him with a punishment the like of which I will not inflict on anyone else in all the worlds'* (5:115) and about the people of Pharaoh*: 'Admit Pharaoh's people to the harshest punishment.'* (40:46)

إِلَّا ٱلَّذِينَ تَابُوا۟ وَأَصْلَحُوا۟ وَٱعْتَصَمُوا۟ بِٱللَّهِ وَأَخْلَصُوا۟ دِينَهُمْ لِلَّهِ
فَأُو۟لَٰٓئِكَ مَعَ ٱلْمُؤْمِنِينَ ۖ وَسَوْفَ يُؤْتِ ٱللَّهُ ٱلْمُؤْمِنِينَ
أَجْرًا عَظِيمًا ١٤٦

146 except those who repent and put things right and hold fast to Allah and dedicate their *dīn* to Allah alone; they are with the believers. Allah will give the believers an immense reward.

This is the exception from the hypocrites. Among the conditions of repentance is to put things right in action and word, hold fast to Allah as a refuge and retreat, and be sincere in one's *dīn*, as this *āyah* states. Otherwise there is no true repentance. This why Allah uses the future tense for the reward of the believers so that the hypocrites have a chance to join them, and Allah knows best.

Al-Bukhārī reported that al-Aswad said, 'We were in the circle of 'Abdullāh [ibn Mas'ūd] when Ḥudhayfah came and stood before us, greeted us and then said, "Hypocrisy befell people who were better than you." Al-Aswad said, "Glory be to Allah! Allah says: *'The hypocrites are in the lowest level of the Fire'!*" 'Abdullāh smiled and Ḥudhayfah sat down in a corner of the mosque. 'Abdullāh got up and his companions split up. He threw some pebbles at me and I went over to him. Ḥudhayfah said, "I was surprised at his smile although he understood what I said. Hypocrisy befell people who were better than you and then they repented and Allah turned to them."'

Al-Farrā' said that the words *'they are with the believers'* means they are among the believers. Al-Qutabī said that this indicates anger, because Allah did not say, 'They are believers.'

The *yā'* is elided from *'yu'ti'* in writing as it is in the expression because it has a *sukūn* and the *lām* after it has a *sukūn*. The like of this is seen in 50:41, 96:18 and 54:6. The two *wāws* are elided because of the meeting of two silent letters.

مَّا يَفْعَلُ ٱللَّهُ بِعَذَابِكُمْ إِن شَكَرْتُمْ وَءَامَنتُمْ ۚ وَكَانَ ٱللَّهُ شَاكِرًا
عَلِيمًا ١٤٧

147 Why should Allah punish you if you are thankful and believe? Allah is All-Thankful, All-Knowing.

This is a question which implies confirmation. It means: 'What use is it to punish you if you are thankful and believe?' Allah points out that He will not punish the thankful believer and that His punishment of His slaves does not increase His kingdom and not punishing them for their actions does not decrease His power.

Makḥūl said, 'Four things which are hidden in it are for him, and three which are hidden in it are against him. The four that are for him are thankfulness, faith, supplication and asking forgiveness. Allah says: *"Why should Allah punish you if you are thankful and believe?"* and He says: *"Allah would not punish them while you were among them. Allah would not punish them as long as they sought forgiveness,"* (8:33) and He says: *"Say: 'What has My Lord to do with you if you do not call on Him?'"* (25:77) The three which are against him are evil plotting, rebelliousness and breaking contracts. Allah says: *"He who breaks his pledge only breaks it against himself"* (48:10) and: *"But evil plotting envelops only those who do it"* (35:43) and: *"Your rebelliousness is only against yourselves."* (10:23)'

Allah is All-Thankful, All-Knowing.

He thanks His slaves for obeying Him. The meaning of 'thanking' here is praising them. So He accepts a small action and gives an immense reward for it. That is His 'thanking' for worship. Linguistically *shukūr* is 'showing' as when the animal shows fat from only a little fodder. This has already been discussed

لَّا يُحِبُّ ٱللَّهُ ٱلْجَهْرَ بِٱلسُّوٓءِ مِنَ ٱلْقَوْلِ إِلَّا مَن ظُلِمَ وَكَانَ ٱللَّهُ سَمِيعًا
عَلِيمًا ﴿١٤٨﴾ إِن تُبْدُوا۟ خَيْرًا أَوْ تُخْفُوهُ أَوْ تَعْفُوا۟ عَن سُوٓءٍ فَإِنَّ ٱللَّهَ كَانَ
عَفُوًّا قَدِيرًا ﴿١٤٩﴾

148 Allah does not like evil words being voiced out loud, except in the case of someone who has been wronged. Allah is All-Hearing, All-Knowing. 149 Whether you reveal a good act or keep it hidden, or pardon an evil act, Allah is Ever-Pardoning, All-Powerful.

Allah does not like evil words being voiced out loud, except in the case of someone who has been wronged.

This means that someone who is wronged can say, 'So-and-so has wronged me.' Allah does not like anyone disclosing wrongdoing unless he has himself been wronged. Most recite '*ẓulima*'. It is also permitted with *sukūn* (*ẓulma*). Those who recite '*ẓalama*', namely Zayd ibn Aslam, Ibn Abī Isḥāq and others, are not permitted to give the *lām* a *sukūn* because of the lightness of the *fatḥah*. According to the first reading, it means that Allah does not like anyone speaking evil words aloud except for someone wronged but it is not disliked for him to speak them aloud.

Then they disagree about how such evil words should be voiced out loud, and what is permitted of it. Al-Ḥasan said, 'It is when a man wrongs another man in speech. He may not curse him, but he may say, "O Allah, help me against him! O Allah, bring out my due! O Allah, come between me and the one who wants to wrong me!"' This supplication for self-defence is the least of the levels of evil words. Ibn 'Abbās and others said, 'It is permitted for someone who is wronged to pray against the one who wronged him but it is better for him to be patient.' This is general to supplication against someone who wrongs you. He and as-Suddī also said, 'There is nothing wrong in someone who is wronged asking for help against the one who wronged him in the same manner and expressing that aloud.'

Ibn al-Mustanīr said that it means: 'Someone who is compelled to voice evil words openly, unbelief or the like. That is allowable.' It is said, according to this, that the one wronged is the one forced. Quṭrub said that the one forced is the one wronged. That is not a felony for him, even if it is tantamount to unbelief. He said, 'It is possible that the meaning of "except in the case of someone who has been wronged" is an appositive. It is as if Allah were saying, "Allah only loves the one wronged," when it means "Allah does not love the wrongdoer."' It is as if Allah were saying, 'He loves someone who has been wronged,' meaning that He protects the one who is wronged. According to this view, it implies: 'Allah does not love the one who openly speaks evil unless he is someone who is wronged.'

Mujāhid said that this *āyah* was revealed about lack of hospitality and the person who experienced it is allowed to speak about it. Ibn Jurayj said that Mujāhid said that it was revealed about a man who asked for hospitality in a wilderness and he was not given it and so the *āyah* was revealed. Ibn Abī Najīḥ related from Mujāhid that the *āyah* was revealed about a man who passed by another man who did not give him hospitality. So he was allowed to say, 'He does not give good hospitality.' Those who say that hospitality is mandatory use this *āyah* as evidence for that. They said that is because injustice is forbidden and so it indicates that hospitality is obligatory. That is the position of al-Layth ibn Sa'd. The majority say that it is part of good character. It will be explained in *Sūrat Hūd*.

The apparent meaning of the *āyah* is that someone wronged can seek help against the person who wronged him, but in moderation, if he is a believer, as al-Ḥasan said. But as for meeting slander with slander and the like, he may not do that, as is mentioned in *al-Baqarah*. If it is an unbeliever, however, then let your tongue go and invoke destruction against him if you wish, as the Prophet ﷺ did when he prayed against Muḍar and certain individuals whom he named when he said, 'O Allah, be hard on Muḍar and impose on them years like the famine years of Yūsuf,' and he said, 'O Allah, deal with so-and-so and so-and-so.' He named them.

If someone is open with his injustice, then the person he is unjust to can pray against him openly and he does not have respect his honour, his body or his property. Abū Dāwūd related about 'Ā'ishah: 'Something of hers was stolen and she began to invoke against the person. The Messenger of Allah ﷺ said, "Do not lighten it for him."' This means not to lighten the penalty against him by invoking against him.

It is also related from 'Amr ibn ash-Sharīd from his father that the Messenger of Allah ﷺ said, 'If anyone who can afford to pay delays repayment, his honour and punishment is lawful.' Ibn al-Mubārak said, 'His honour is subject to abuse and the punishment is that he can be detained for it.' We find in *Ṣaḥīḥ Muslim*: 'The procrastination of a wealthy person is injustice.' When a wealthy person is asked to pay and is able to do so, his procrastination is injustice. That makes it legitimate to impugn his honour. People may say, 'He puts people off and keeps what is due to them.' The ruler is permitted to punish and discipline him in order to deter him. That idea is related from Sufyān. It is also the sense of what Ibn al-Mubārak said.

This topic does not include what is found in *Ṣaḥīḥ Muslim* where al-'Abbās said about 'Alī in the presence of 'Umar, 'Uthmān, az-Zubayr and 'Abd ar-Raḥmān ibn 'Awf, 'Amīr al-Mu'minīn! Judge between me and this lying, sinful, treacherous, perfidious person!' No one replied to him because it was arbitration and each of them believed he was right until 'Umar settled it. Ibn al-'Arabī said that.

Our scholars say, 'This happens when the positions are equal or close. When there is great disparity between them, there is no possible advantage in being presumptuous towards the excellent. The right is sought by the mere claim without any explicit statement of injustice or anger. This is sound and it is indicated by reports. Another possibility is that anger moved al-'Abbās to say this and to attack like an uncle does. An uncle is the father's brother. There is no doubt that when a father uses these words to his child, that is undersstod to be harshness and deterrence in disciplining them. It does not mean that they are really described by what he says. Furthermore, they were involved in a religious argument. Al-'Abbās believed that it is was not permitted to oppose him and that opposing him in it would lead to describing the opponent with these qualities. So he released his anger in this way. Since those who were present knew that, they did not object to him doing it. This is indicated by al-Māzirī, Qāḍī 'Iyāḍ and others.'

The reading *ẓalama* was that of Zayd ibn Aslam, of some of the Qur'anic scholars in Madīnah after Muḥammad ibn Ka'b al-Quraẓī and of Ibn Abī Isḥāq, aḍ-Ḍaḥḥāk, Ibn 'Abbās, Ibn Jubayr, and 'Aṭā' ibn as-Sā'ib. It means: except against the one who wrongs in action or words and they publicly expose his evil in order to reprove his action, rebuke him and refute him. It means that Allah does not like it to be asked of someone who has repented of hypocrisy, 'Are you a hypocrite?' except in the case of someone who has done evil, in other words remained in hypocrisy. This is indicated by His words: *'except those who repent'*. Ibn Zayd said, 'That is because when Allah reports that the hypocrites will be in the lowest level of the Fire, that is an open statement about evil. Then after that He tells them: *"Why should Allah punish you?"* (4:147) This has a sense of solace and calling for thankfulness and faith. Then the believers are told: *"Allah does not like evil words being voiced out loud, except in the case of someone who has done wrong (ẓalama)"* in remaining in hypocrisy. It can be said to him, "Are you not the unbelieving hypocrite who will have the lowest level in the Fire in the Next World?" or similar words.'

Some people say that the meaning of the words is: 'Allah does not like anybody to voice evil out loud' and then makes an exception for the someone who does wrong. His evil in respect of injustice and aggression can be voiced. This frequently occurs with wrongdoers and their continuing habit. In spite of their injustice, they release their tongues and attack the honour of those they have wronged in a way that is forbidden for them to do. Abū Isḥāq az-Zajjāj said, 'It is possible that it means, "except those who have done wrong" and spoken evil. He should be stopped. So it is not an exception to the first part.' Hadiths indicate this, including the words of the Prophet ﷺ, 'Take hold of the hands of your fools to stop them' and 'Help your brother, wronging or wronged.' They asked, 'We can help someone wronged? But how do we help the one who wrongs?' He answered, 'Restrain him from wrongdoing.' Al-Farrā' said that 'except those who have done wrong' means 'not those who have done wrong'.

Allah is All-Hearing, All-Knowing.

Allah warns the wrongdoer not to do wrong and the wronged person not to exceed the limits in seeking help.

Whether you reveal a good act or keep it hidden, or pardon an evil act, Allah is Ever-Pardoning, All-Powerful.

Then He follows that with His words: *'Whether you reveal a good act or keep it hidden, or pardon an evil act...'* It is a recommendation to pardon and that is desirable. Pardon is one of Allah's attributes, exercised when He has the power to take revenge, and the excellence of those who pardon was discussed in *Āli 'Imrān*. These few words contain many ideas for someone who reflects. It is said, 'If you pardon, Allah will pardon you.' Ibn al-Mubārak related from someone who heard al-Ḥasan say, 'When the Muslim nation comes before the Lord of the Worlds on the Day of Rising, a call will be given for those, whose wage is with Allah, to come. Only those who pardoned in this world will rise to respond.' This is confirmed by the words of the Almighty: *'But if someone pardons and puts things right, his reward is with Allah.'* (42:40)

إِنَّ ٱلَّذِينَ يَكْفُرُونَ بِٱللَّهِ وَرُسُلِهِۦ وَيُرِيدُونَ أَن يُفَرِّقُوا۟ بَيْنَ ٱللَّهِ
وَرُسُلِهِۦ وَيَقُولُونَ نُؤْمِنُ بِبَعْضٍ وَنَكْفُرُ بِبَعْضٍ وَيُرِيدُونَ أَن يَتَّخِذُوا۟
بَيْنَ ذَٰلِكَ سَبِيلًا ﴿١٥٠﴾ أُو۟لَٰٓئِكَ هُمُ ٱلْكَٰفِرُونَ حَقًّا ۚ وَأَعْتَدْنَا لِلْكَٰفِرِينَ
عَذَابًا مُّهِينًا ﴿١٥١﴾

150 Those who reject Allah and His Messengers and desire to cause division between Allah and His Messengers, saying, 'We believe in some and reject the others,' wanting to take a pathway in between, 151 such people are the true unbelievers. We have prepared a humiliating punishment for the unbelievers.

Those who reject Allah and His Messengers and desire to cause division between Allah and His Messengers,

After the idolaters and hypocrites have been mentioned, the unbelievers among the People of the Book are mentioned – the Jews and Christians – since they rejected Muḥammad ﷺ. Allah explains that rejection of him is rejection of all the Prophets since there was no Prophet who did not bring his people belief in Muḥammad ﷺ and in every one of the Prophets, peace be upon them all. The words: *'They desire to cause division between Allah and His Messengers'* means between belief in Allah and belief in His Messengers. Allah states that making division between Allah and His Messengers is disbelief and it is disbelief because Allah has obliged people to worship Him by what He prescribed for them on the tongues of the Messengers. If they deny the Messengers, they reject their laws and do not accept them, when they are obliged to worship as they were commanded. So it is like the denial of the Maker, and the denial of the Maker is rejection of Him by not obeying Him and worshipping Him. So, in the same way, dividing His Messengers, by believing in some and not others, is itself disbelief.

saying, 'We believe in some and reject the others,' wanting to take a pathway in between,

They are the Jews, who believed in Mūsā and rejected 'Īsā and Muḥammad. This was already mentioned in *al-Baqarah*. They told the common people that they did not find Muḥammad mentioned in their Scriptures. The phrase: '… *wanting to take a pathway in between'* means in between belief and unbelief, in other words an innovated *dīn* between Islam and Judaism. Allah says here '*dhalika*' (m. plural) and not '*dhaynika*' (dual) which is used for two. If He had used '*dhaynika*', that would be permitted.

such people are the true unbelievers.

This removes any illusions about them being believers because of their belief in some of the Prophets. That does not help them since they rejected Allah's Messenger. When they rejected His Messenger, they rejected Him and they also rejected every Messenger who gave the good news of that Messenger, which makes them truly unbelievers. The word '*unbelievers*' takes the place of the second object of '*prepared*,' implying 'We have prepared for all of them.'

وَالَّذِينَ ءَامَنُوا۟ بِاللَّهِ وَرُسُلِهِۦ وَلَمْ يُفَرِّقُوا۟ بَيْنَ أَحَدٍ مِّنْهُمْ أُو۟لَٰٓئِكَ
سَوْفَ نُؤْتِيهِمْ أُجُورَهُمْ ۗ وَكَانَ اللَّهُ غَفُورًا رَّحِيمًا ﴿١٥٢﴾

152 Those who believe in Allah and His Messengers and do not differentiate between any of them, We will pay them their wages. Allah is Ever-Forgiving, Most Merciful.

This refers to the Prophet ﷺ and his community.

يَسْـَٔلُكَ أَهْلُ ٱلْكِتَٰبِ أَن تُنَزِّلَ عَلَيْهِمْ كِتَٰبًا مِّنَ ٱلسَّمَآءِ فَقَدْ سَأَلُوا۟ مُوسَىٰٓ
أَكْبَرَ مِن ذَٰلِكَ فَقَالُوٓا۟ أَرِنَا ٱللَّهَ جَهْرَةً فَأَخَذَتْهُمُ ٱلصَّٰعِقَةُ بِظُلْمِهِمْ ثُمَّ
ٱتَّخَذُوا۟ ٱلْعِجْلَ مِنۢ بَعْدِ مَا جَآءَتْهُمُ ٱلْبَيِّنَٰتُ فَعَفَوْنَا عَن ذَٰلِكَ وَءَاتَيْنَا
مُوسَىٰ سُلْطَٰنًا مُّبِينًا ﴿١٥٣﴾

153 The People of the Book will ask you to bring down a Book from heaven to them. They asked Mūsa for even more than that. They said, 'Let us see Allah with our own eyes.' So the lightning-bolt struck them down for their wrongdoing. Then they adopted the Calf after the Clear Signs had come to them, but We pardoned them for that and gave Mūsa clear authority.

The Jews asked Muḥammad ﷺ to rise up to heaven while they were watching and to bring them down a written Book confirming his claim of truthfulness all at once in the way Mūsā had brought down the Torah from Allah. This arose from their obstinacy regarding the Prophet ﷺ. Allah informs us that their fathers asked Mūsā for more than that. The meaning of the words: *'Let us see Allah with our own eyes'* was mentioned in *al-Baqarah*. They were punished by the lightning bolt for the outrageousness of their request and their wrongdoing after the miracles they had seen.

Then they adopted the Calf after the Clear Signs had come to them,

There is some elision: 'We brought them to life and then they adopted the Calf.' This is also mentioned in *al-Baqarah* and will be further mentioned in *Ṭaha*, Allah willing. *'The Clear Signs'* are proofs, evidence and clear miracles manifested in the white hand, the staff, the parting of the sea and other things, since none should be worshipped but Allah. They were pardoned for their obstinacy and Mūsā's *'clear authority'* was a clear proof, consisting of the Signs he brought. It had authority because it overpowered the hearts, since it is known that it is not in the power of a human being to produce anything like them.

وَرَفَعْنَا فَوْقَهُمُ الطُّورَ بِمِيثَٰقِهِمْ وَقُلْنَا لَهُمُ ادْخُلُوا الْبَابَ سُجَّدًا
وَقُلْنَا لَهُمْ لَا تَعْدُوا فِي السَّبْتِ وَأَخَذْنَا مِنْهُم مِّيثَٰقًا غَلِيظًا ﴿١٥٤﴾

154 We lifted up the Mount above their heads in accordance with the covenant they had made, and We said to them, 'Enter the gate prostrating,' and We said to them, 'Do not break the Sabbath,' and We made a binding covenant with them.

This was on account of their breaking of the covenant which Allah had made with them, which was to act by what is in the Torah. This was also discussed in *al-Baqarah*. Imam Warsh alone recited *'ta'addū'* from *'adā, ya'dū, 'adw, 'udwān, 'udhuw, 'adā'*. It means by catching fish as was mentioned in *al-Baqarah*. An-Naḥḥās said, 'It is not permitted to recite this with a *sukūn* on the *'ayn* and two silent letters are not joined in this. The one who recites it is in error.' The '*binding covenant*' is the covenant made with them by Allah in the Torah. It is said that a covenant reinforced by an oath is called '*binding*' (*ghalīẓ*).

فَبِمَا نَقْضِهِم مِّيثَٰقَهُمْ وَكُفْرِهِم بِـَٔايَٰتِ اللَّهِ وَقَتْلِهِمُ الْأَنۢبِيَآءَ بِغَيْرِ حَقٍّ
وَقَوْلِهِمْ قُلُوبُنَا غُلْفٌۢ بَلْ طَبَعَ اللَّهُ عَلَيْهَا بِكُفْرِهِمْ فَلَا يُؤْمِنُونَ إِلَّا قَلِيلًا ﴿١٥٥﴾
وَبِكُفْرِهِمْ وَقَوْلِهِمْ عَلَىٰ مَرْيَمَ بُهْتَٰنًا عَظِيمًا ﴿١٥٦﴾

155 Because of the fact that they broke their covenant, and rejected Allah's Signs, and killed the Prophets without any right to do so and said, 'Our hearts are covered over,' Allah has stamped them with unbelief, so they do not believe except for very few. 156 And on account of their unbelief, and their utterance of a monstrous slander against Maryam,

Because of the fact that they broke their covenant,

The conjunction *mā* is redundant and used for emphasis, as is seen in 3:159, and the *bā'* is connected to something elided. It implies: 'We cursed them because of the fact that they broke their covenant.' Qatādah and others said that. This elision takes place because the listener already knows what is meant. Abu-l-Ḥasan 'Alī ibn Ḥamzah al-Kisā'ī says that it is connected to what is before it and means, 'The lightning-bolt struck them down for their breaking the covenant, etc.' So the wrong they did, on account of which the lightning-bolt struck them, was their breaking of their covenant, their killing of the Prophets and the other matters by which they wronged themselves. Aṭ-Ṭabarī and others said that was not the case, because those struck by the lightning-bolt were in the time of Mūsā and those who killed the Prophets and slandered Maryam were after the time of Mūsā and were not struck by a thunderbolt.

Al-Mahdawī and others point out that the report can mention them when, in fact, it is their ancestors that are meant, as was mentioned in *al-Baqarah*. Az-Zajjāj said, 'Because of their breaking of their covenant, We forbade them the good things which were lawful for them.' This narrative continues until *āyah* 160. They broke their covenant by reneging on their agreement to make clear the description of the Prophet ﷺ. It is also said that it was by their breaking of contracts and because of that Allah stamped their hearts with disbelief. It is said that it means that only a few believe because of their breaking of the covenant. The *fā'* is redundant (*muqḥamah*). The '*Signs*' are their Books in which they made changes.

Our hearts are covered over.

Ghulf is the plural of *ghilāf*. It means: 'Our hearts are vessels of knowledge and we have no need of any knowledge other than our own.' It is said that it is the plural of *aghlaf* which is a cover, meaning: 'Our hearts are covered and so we do not understand what you say,' as in: *'Our hearts are covered up.'* (41:5) This was discussed in *al-Baqarah*. Their aim in that was to parry the proof of the Messengers.

Allah has stamped them with unbelief.

The verb *tab'* means to seal as was mentioned in *al-Baqarah*. The words *'with their unbelief'* means that it is the repayment for their disbelief referred to in Allah's words: *'Rather, Allah has cursed them for their unbelief. What little faith they have!'* (2:88) *'So they do not believe except for very few'* can also mean that they only believe in some Prophets and that will not benefit them.

and on account of their unbelief, and their utterance of a monstrous slander against Maryam.

This reports that they disbelieved after their belief. Their unbelief is their rejection of the Messiah. This is indicated by what follows it. 'Slander' (*buhtān*) is an excessive lie which astonishes. The slander was to accuse Maryam of fornication. Allah knows best.

وَقَوْلِهِمْ إِنَّا قَتَلْنَا ٱلْمَسِيحَ عِيسَى ٱبْنَ مَرْيَمَ رَسُولَ ٱللَّهِ وَمَا قَتَلُوهُ وَمَا
صَلَبُوهُ وَلَٰكِن شُبِّهَ لَهُمْ وَإِنَّ ٱلَّذِينَ ٱخْتَلَفُوا۟ فِيهِ لَفِى شَكٍّ مِّنْهُ مَا لَهُم بِهِۦ
مِنْ عِلْمٍ إِلَّا ٱتِّبَاعَ ٱلظَّنِّ وَمَا قَتَلُوهُ يَقِينًۢا ﴿١٥٧﴾ بَل رَّفَعَهُ ٱللَّهُ إِلَيْهِ وَكَانَ ٱللَّهُ
عَزِيزًا حَكِيمًا ﴿١٥٨﴾

157 and their saying, 'We killed the Messiah, 'Īsā son of Maryam, Messenger of Allah.' They did not kill him and they did not crucify him but it was made to seem so to them. Those who argue about him are in doubt about it. They have no real knowledge of it, just conjecture. But they certainly did not kill him. 158 Allah raised him up to Himself. Allah is Almighty, All-Wise.

and their saying, 'We killed the Messiah, 'Īsā son of Maryam, Messenger of Allah.'

'*Innā*' at the beginning has a *kasrah* because it is inchoative after the words. Having it with a *fatḥah* is a dialect. This was discussed in *Āli 'Imrān*. '*Messenger of Allah*' is an appositive, or, if you wish, it means: 'I mean the …'.

They did not kill him and they did not crucify him but it was made to seem so to them.

Their statement is refuted. They are told that his likeness was cast on someone else as was already stated in *Āli 'Imrān*. It is also said that they did not recognise him and killed another person other than 'Īsā as they were unsure about who he was, as Allah says here: '*Those who argue about him are in doubt about it.*' This reports about all of them. It is said that only their common people differ about it.

Their disagreement is that some believe he is God and some that he is the son of God. Al-Ḥasan said that. It is said that their disagreement is that the common people said, 'We have killed 'Īsā.' and those who saw him ascend said, 'We did not kill him.' It is said that the disagreement is that the Nestorians said, 'The crucifixion of 'Īsā was of his *nāsūt* (human nature), not his *lāhūt* (divine nature).' The Melkites said, 'The crucifixion of the Messiah was of both his *nāsūt* and his *lāhūt*.' It is said that their disagreement was that they said, 'If this is our companion, where is 'Īsā? If this is 'Īsā, where is our companion?' It is said that their disagreement is that the Jews said, 'We killed him' because Yahūdhā, the leader of the Jews, is the one who strove to kill him. A group of the Christians said, 'We killed him.' Another group of them said, 'Allah raised him to heaven while we were looking at him.'

They have no real knowledge of it, just conjecture.

The conjunction *'min'* is redundant and the words end at *'knowledge.'* Then *'just conjecture'* is an exception to the first phrase in the position of the accusative. It can also be in the nominative for an appositive. It means: 'they have no knowledge other than following conjecture.' Sībawayh said:

> A town in which there is no close friend
> other than gazelles, except for camels.

But they certainly did not kill him.

Ibn 'Abbās and as-Suddī said that it means they did not actually do as they thought. It is like, 'I killed him knowingly,' i.e. 'I knew it fully' and so the pronoun *hā'* refers to *'conjecture'*. Abū 'Ubayd said, 'If it means: "They certainly did not kill 'Īsā," it is saying, "They did not kill 'Īsā at all."' It is said that it means: 'They did not kill what appeared to them was certainly 'Īsa.' According to this, the stop is at *'yaqīnan'* (*certainly*). It is said that it means: 'They did not kill 'Īsā', and the stop is at 'him' and *'certainly'* is an adjective of an elided verbal noun. There are two possibilities. One is that they said this with certainty or that Allah says the true words. The second view is that it means: they did not really know that. An-Naḥḥās said that.

If you assume that the meaning is: 'Rather Allah raised him to Him certainly,' that is a mistake because what follows the word *'bal'* does not effect what is before it because of its weakness. Ibn al-Anbārī permitted that one stop at *'him'* on the basis that *'certainly'* is in the accusative by the effect of an elided verb which is the apodosis of the oath. It implies: 'You affirmed with certainty,' i.e. with a true certainty.

Allah raised him up to Himself.

This begins a new sentence. This means to heaven as Allah is above having a place. The manner of raising him was mentioned in *Āli 'Imrān*.

Allah is Almighty, All-Wise.

'Allah is Almighty', in other words strong enough to take revenge on the Jews by giving the Romans power over them and *'All-Wise'* in judging them worthy of the curse and Divine wrath.

وَإِن مِّنْ أَهْلِ ٱلْكِتَٰبِ إِلَّا لَيُؤْمِنَنَّ بِهِۦ قَبْلَ مَوْتِهِۦ ۖ وَيَوْمَ ٱلْقِيَٰمَةِ يَكُونُ عَلَيْهِمْ
شَهِيدًا ﴿١٥٩﴾

159 There is not one of the People of the Book who will not believe in him before he dies; and on the Day of Rising he will be a witness against them.

Ibn 'Abbās, al-Ḥasan, Mujāhid and 'Ikrimah said, 'The meaning is that they will all believe in the Messiah.' The first '*him*' refers to 'Īsā and the second '*he*' to the Kitābī. So all the People of the Book – the Jews and Christians – will believe in 'Īsā when they see the angel (of death), but that will not help them when they are dying and despairing of life. The Jews will state that he is the Messenger of Allah as well as the Christians.

It is reported that al-Ḥajjaj asked Shahr ibn Ḥawshab about this *āyah*. Al-Ḥajjāj said, 'I was brought a Jewish or Christian captive and I commanded that he be beheaded. I looked at him at that moment and did not see any faith in him.' Shahr said to him, 'When he sees the Next World, he will affirm that 'Īsā is the slave and Messenger of Allah. He will believe but it will not help him.' Al-Ḥajjāj asked him, 'Where did you get this from?' He answered, 'From Muḥammad ibn al-Ḥanafiyyah.' Al-Ḥajjāj said, 'You took it from a pure source.'

Mujāhid also said, 'There is not one of the People of the Book who will not believe in 'Īsā before he dies.' He was asked, 'And if he is drowned, burned or eaten by a wild animal, will he believe in 'Īsā?' 'Yes!' he answered. It is also said that both pronouns refer to 'Īsā. It means that those who are alive when he descends on the Day of Rising will believe in him. Qatādah, Ibn Zayd and others said that, and it is what aṭ-Ṭabarī preferred. Yazīd ibn Zuray' related from a man from al-Ḥasan about this *āyah* that it means before the death of 'Īsā since he is now alive with Allah. When he descends, they will all believe in him. Something similar is related from aḍ-Ḍaḥḥāk and Sa'īd ibn Jubayr.

It is also said that the 'him' refers to Muḥammad ﷺ even if he has not been mentioned here because these stories were revealed to him and the aim is to believe in him. Belief in 'Īsā contains belief in Muḥammad ﷺ since it is not permitted to differentiate between them. It is said that it means that he believes in Allah before he dies but that that belief is of no use to him when he is directly facing death. The first two interpretations are more evident.

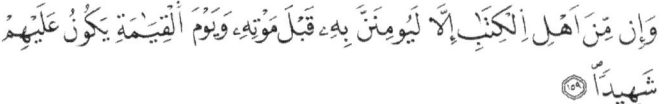

Az-Zuhrī related from Sa'īd ibn al-Musayyab from Abū Hurayrah that the Messenger of Allah ﷺ said, 'The son of Maryam will descend as a just judge and will kill the Dajjāl, kill pigs, and break crosses and all prostration will be to Allah, the Lord of the Worlds.' Then Abū Hurayrah said, 'Recite, if you wish: *"There is not one of the People of the Book who will not believe in him before he dies."'* Abū Hurayrah said, 'Before the death of 'Īsā,' and he repeated it three times. According to Sībawayh the *āyah* implies: 'There is no one from the People of the Book who will not believe in him.' The Kufan view implies: 'There are none among the People of the Book except those who believe in him.' This is ugly because it contains the elision of the relative pronoun and making the relative clause part of the relative pronoun. So it is as if part of the noun were elided. *'He will be a witness against them'*, against those who denied him and for those who affirmed him.

فَبِظُلْمٍ مِنَ الَّذِينَ هَادُوا حَرَّمْنَا عَلَيْهِمْ طَيِّبَاتٍ أُحِلَّتْ لَهُمْ وَبِصَدِّهِمْ عَن سَبِيلِ اللَّهِ كَثِيرًا ۝ وَأَخْذِهِمُ الرِّبَوٰا۟ وَقَدْ نُهُوا۟ عَنْهُ وَأَكْلِهِمْ أَمْوَٰلَ النَّاسِ بِالْبَٰطِلِ وَأَعْتَدْنَا لِلْكَٰفِرِينَ مِنْهُمْ عَذَابًا أَلِيمًا ۝

160 Because of wrongdoing on the part of the Jews, We made unlawful for them some good things which had previously been lawful for them; and because of their obstructing many people from the Way of Allah, 161 and because of their practising usury when they were forbidden to do it, and because of their consuming people's wealth by wrongful means, We have prepared for the unbelievers among them a painful punishment.

Because of wrongdoing on the part of the Jews, We made unlawful for them some good things which had previously been lawful for them;

Az-Zajjāj said that the phrase: *'Because of wrongdoing on the part of the Jews'* is an appositive for the words: *'their breaking their covenant.'* The *'good things'* that were made unlawful are what is mentioned in *al-An'ām*: *'We made unlawful for the Jews every animal with an undivided hoof….'* (6:146) *'Wrongdoing'* as causing the prohibition is what is meant by this. It is the reason for the prohibition.

and because of obstructing many people from the Way of Allah…

This is by preventing themselves and others from following Muḥammad ﷺ. The rest explains their wrongdoing. This is similar to what was already mentioned about their breaking of the covenant and what follows it. It was mentioned in *Āli 'Imrān* that scholars take three different positions about the reason for this making things unlawful. Ibn al-'Arabī said, 'There is no disagreement in the school of

Mālik that the unbelievers are addressed and Allah makes it clear in this *āyah* they were forbidden usury and from consuming people's wealth by wrongful means. That tells us that what was revealed to Muḥammad in the Qur'an also applied to them and that it was part of what Allah revealed to Mūsā in the Torah and that they changed and altered and disobeyed and opposed. So is it permitted to do business with them after this corruption of their wealth in their *dīn* or not?

One group believe that dealings with them are not permitted since their wealth entails this corruption. The sound view, however, is that it is permitted, in spite of their usury and doing what Allah has made forbidden for them. There is definitive evidence for that in the Qur'an and the *Sunnah*. Allah says: *"And the food of those given the Book is also lawful for you."* (5:5) This is a text. Furthermore, the Prophet ﷺ had dealings with the Jews and died while his armour was in pawn to a Jew in return for some barley for his family. The disagreement is settled by the agreement of the Community that it is permitted to trade with the People of War and the Prophet ﷺ travelled to them as a merchant.

If it is observed that took place before he was a Prophet, we reply that he was not sullied by the *ḥarām* before he was a Prophet, as is confirmed by multiple transmissions, nor after He was sent and became a Prophet. None of his Companions stated it during his lifetime nor did any of the Muslims after his death. They used to travel to ransom captives which was mandatory, and for truces, as he sent 'Uthmān and others, and that is obliged by recommendation. Travelling to them for trade is permitted.

لَّٰكِنِ ٱلرَّٰسِخُونَ فِي ٱلْعِلْمِ مِنْهُمْ وَٱلْمُؤْمِنُونَ يُؤْمِنُونَ بِمَآ أُنزِلَ إِلَيْكَ وَمَآ أُنزِلَ
مِن قَبْلِكَ وَٱلْمُقِيمِينَ ٱلصَّلَوٰةَ وَٱلْمُؤْتُونَ ٱلزَّكَوٰةَ وَٱلْمُؤْمِنُونَ بِٱللَّهِ
وَٱلْيَوْمِ ٱلْءَاخِرِ أُو۟لَٰٓئِكَ سَنُؤْتِيهِمْ أَجْرًا عَظِيمًا ﴿١٦٢﴾

162 But those of them who are firmly rooted in knowledge, and the believers, believe in what has been sent down to you and what was sent down before you: those who establish the prayer and pay *zakāt*, and believe in Allah and the Last Day – We will pay such people an immense wage.

But those of them who are firmly rooted in knowledge, and the believers,

This excludes the believers of the People of the Book from those mentioned previously. That is because the Jews denied and said, 'These things were originally unlawful and you allow them. We were not forbidden them because of our wrongdoing.' So this was revealed. The adjective '*firmly-rooted* (*rāsikh*)' means possessing extensive and firm knowledge of the Book. *Rusūkh* means firmness. This was mentioned in *Āli 'Imrān*. Those who are meant are 'Abdullāh ibn Salām, Ka'b al-Aḥbār and their likes. '*The believers*' are the Muhājirun and Anṣār, the Companions of Muḥammad ﷺ.

those who establish the prayer

Al-Ḥasan, Mālik ibn Dīnār and a group recited '*muqīmūn*' as added to what is before it. That is how it is in the variant of 'Abdullāh. As for the mode of Ubayy it is '*muqīmīn*' as it is in other copies of the Qur'an. Various things are said about it being in the accusative, the soundest of which is that of Sībawayh that it is for praise. It means those who establish the prayer. Sībawayh said that this is the area of what is in the accusative for esteem. He quoted:

All the people obey the command of their Master
except for Numayr who obey their enticer to error.

An-Naḥḥās said that this is the soundest of what is said about '*muqīmūn*'. Al-Kisā'ī said that it is added to *mā*. An-Naḥḥās said that al-Akhfash said, 'This is unlikely because then the meaning would be: 'they believe in those who establish'.

Muḥammad ibn Jarīr stated that it is related that it is the angels who are referred to here because they are constant in prayer, glorification and asking forgiveness. He preferred this position. It is related that it is unlikely for it to be in the accusative for praise, because praise comes after the end of the predicate, and the predicate of '*those who are firmly rooted … an immense wage.*' So '*muqīmīn*' is not in the accusative for praise.

An-Naḥḥās said, 'The position of Sībawayh is that the word "*pay*" is in the nominative by the inceptive.' Others said that it is in the nominative by an implied inchoative, i.e. 'They are those who pay…' It is said that '*muqīmīn*' is added to the *kāf* in '*qablika*'. It is said that it is added to '*hum*', i.e. 'from them and from those who establish'. These are three responses which are not permitted because they add an explicit pronoun to an implied genitive pronoun.

It is related that 'Ā'ishah was asked about this *āyah* and Allah's words: '*These two magicians*' (20:63) and: '*and Sabaeans*' (2:62). She said to the asker, 'Cousin, the scribes erred.' Abān ibn 'Uthmān said, 'The scribe was dictated to and then wrote: "*But those of them who are firmly rooted in knowledge, and the believers.*" Then he asked, "What should I write?" and he was told: "*those who establish the prayer.*" That is how this occurred.' Al-Qushayrī said, 'This is false because those who collected the Book were models of language. It is impossible that they would have incorporated into the Qur'an anything that was not revealed.' The soundest of these positions is what Sībawayh said. It is the position of al-Khalīl. Al-Qaffāl and aṭ-Ṭabarī preferred the position of al-Kisā'ī. Allah knows best.

إِنَّآ أَوۡحَيۡنَآ إِلَيۡكَ كَمَآ أَوۡحَيۡنَآ إِلَىٰ نُوحٖ وَٱلنَّبِيِّـۧنَ مِنۢ بَعۡدِهِۦۚ وَأَوۡحَيۡنَآ إِلَىٰٓ
إِبۡرَٰهِيمَ وَإِسۡمَٰعِيلَ وَإِسۡحَٰقَ وَيَعۡقُوبَ وَٱلۡأَسۡبَاطِ وَعِيسَىٰ وَأَيُّوبَ وَيُونُسَ
وَهَٰرُونَ وَسُلَيۡمَٰنَۚ وَءَاتَيۡنَا دَاوُۥدَ زَبُورٗا ١٦٣

163 We have revealed to you as We revealed to Nūḥ and the Prophets who came after him. And We revealed to Ibrāhīm and Ismā'īl and Isḥāq and Ya'qūb and the Tribes, and 'Īsā and Ayyūb and Yūnus and Hārūn and Sulaymān. And We gave Dāwūd the Zabūr.

This is connected to *āyah* 154: *'The People of the Book will ask you to bring down a Book from heaven to them.'* Know that Allah commanded Muḥammad ﷺ as He did earlier Prophets. Ibn Isḥāq quotes Ibn 'Abbās as saying, 'It was revealed about some of the Jews, including Sukayn and 'Adī ibn Zayd, who said to the Prophet ﷺ, "Allah has not given revelation to anyone after Mūsā," and Allah refuted them.' Revelation (*waḥy*) is conveying information in a hidden manner. The verb is *waḥā* and *awḥā*.

Nūḥ is mentioned because he was the first Prophet who was given a Sharī'ah. Other things are said. Az-Zubayr ibn Bakkār mentioned from Abu-l-Ḥasan 'Alī ibn al-Mughīrah from Hishām ibn Muḥammad ibn as-Sā'ib that his father said, 'The first Prophet sent by Allah to the earth was Idrīs, whose name was Enoch, and then there was a break in the Messengers until Allah sent Nūḥ ibn Lamik ibn Mutawshlakh ibn Ukhnūkh. Sām, the son of Nūḥ, was a Prophet. Then there was another break until Allah sent Ibrāhīm and took him as a Close Friend. He is Ibrāhīm ibn Tārikh, and Tārikh's name was Āzar. Then He sent Ismā'īl ibn Ibrāhīm who died in Makkah, and then Isḥāq ibn Ibrāhīm who died in Syria, then Lūṭ, Ibrāhīm's nephew, then Ya'qūb, who is Isrā'īl ibn Isḥāq, then Yūsuf ibn Ya'qūb, then Shu'ayb ibn Yawbab, then Hūd ibn 'Abdullāh, then Ṣāliḥ ibn Asaf, then Mūsā and Hārūn, the sons of 'Imrān, then Ayyūb, then al-Khiḍr, who is Khiḍrūn, then Dāwūd ibn Īshā, then Sulaymān ibn Dāwūd, then Yūnus ibn Mattā, then Ilyās, then Dhu-l-Kifl whose name was 'Awīdanā, from a tribe of Yahūdhā ibn Ya'qūb.' He said, 'There were 1700 years between Mūsā ibn 'Imrān and Maryam bint 'Imrān, the mother of 'Īsā, neither of whom was from a tribe (*sibṭ*). Then came the Prophet, Muḥammad ibn 'Abdullāh ibn 'Abd al-Muṭṭalib ﷺ.' Az-Zubayr remarked, 'Every Prophet mentioned in the Qur'an is from the descendants of Ibrāhīm, except for Idrīs, Nūḥ, Lūṭ, Hūd and Ṣāliḥ. The Arabs only had five Prophets: Hūd, Ṣāliḥ, Ismā'īl, Shu'ayb, and Muḥammad, may Allah bless all of them. They are called "Arabs" because they were the only ones to speak Arabic.'

and We revealed to Ibrāhīm

Certain individuals are singled out for mention to honour them as when Allah says: *'and His angels and His Messengers, and Jibrīl and Mīkā'īl.'* Then He says: *"Īsā and Ayyūb.'* 'Īsā is mentioned before the people who came before him because the *wāw* does not necessitate chronological order. It also singles him out to refute the Jews who denied him. This *āyah* points out the worth and honour of our Prophet ﷺ since he is mentioned first, before the other Prophets. Another example of this is Allah's words: '*We made a covenant with all the Prophets – with you and with Nūḥ.*' (33:7)

The name Nūḥ is derived from *nawḥ*, lamentation. That was already adequately discussed in *Āli 'Imrān,* and the fact that it is declined, in spite of being a foreign name, because it has three letters. Ibrāhīm, Ismā'īl, and Isḥāq are foreign and definite and so they are not inflected. The same is true of Ya'qūb, 'Īsā and Mūsā, although 'Īsā and Mūsā may have an *alif* in them for feminine, and so they are not inflected in either the definite or indefinite. As for Yūnus and Yūsuf, it is related that al-Ḥasan recited 'Yūnis' and 'Yūsif' and made then come from *ānasa* and *āsafa*. According to this, it is necessary for them to be inflected and take a *hamzah*, and their plurals are Yānis and Yāsif. Without a *hamzah*, it is Yawānis and Yawāsif. Abū Zayd said that it is Yūnas and Yūsaf. Al-Mahdawī said, 'It is as if the root of Yūnis is *fi'l* based on the active participle and Yūnas is based on the passive, and that is the source of the names.

And We gave Dāwūd the Zabūr.

The *Zabūr* (Psalms) is the book of Dāwūd. It contained 150 chapters but did not contain any judgments or the lawful and unlawful, but rather wisdoms and admonition. *Zabr* means writing. *Zabūr* is what is written, like *rasūl*, *rakūb* and *ḥalūb*. Ḥamzah recited '*zubūr*', the plural of *zabr*, like *fals* and *fulūs*. *Zabr* can mean written, as you say, 'This dirham was struck (*ḍarb*) by the amīr.' The root meaning of the word is to bind something. A well which is *mazbūrah* is cased in with stones. The Book is called *Zabūr* because of the strength of its security.

Dāwūd had a beautiful voice and when he began to recite the Zabūr, people, jinn, birds and wild animals would gather round him because of the beauty of his voice. He was humble and ate from what he earned through his own work. Abū Bakr ibn Abī Shaybah related from Abū Usāmah from Hishām ibn 'Urwah that his father said, 'Dāwūd would address people with a basket full of plaited palm-leaves in his hand. When he finished speaking, he would sell some of them to those beside him. He used to make armour as well. The *ḥadīth* said, 'Blueness of the eye is a blessing.' Dāwūd was blue-eyed.

وَرُسُلًا قَدْ قَصَصْنَٰهُمْ عَلَيْكَ مِن قَبْلُ وَرُسُلًا لَّمْ نَقْصُصْهُمْ عَلَيْكَ
وَكَلَّمَ ٱللَّهُ مُوسَىٰ تَكْلِيمًا ١٦٤

164 There are Messengers We have already told you about and Messengers We have not told you about; and Allah spoke directly to Mūsā –

There are Messengers We have already told you about

in Makkah. The word '*Messengers*' is in the accusative by the effect of an implied verb, in other words, 'We sent Messengers', because the words: '*We revealed to Nūḥ*' (4:163) means 'We sent Nūḥ.' It is said that it is in the accusative by a verb which is indicated: 'We have told you about them,' i.e. 'We have told you about the Messengers.' It is like the words of Sībawayh:

I accompanied but did not carry weapons
  and I do not control the head of the camel when it shies away.

I fear the wolf when I pass by it alone,
  and I fear the spears and rain,

It means: 'I fear the wolf.' The mode of Ubayy has '*rusulun*' in the nominative, implying, 'among them are Messengers.'

It is said that when Allah recounted in His Book some of the Names of His Prophets without mentioning the names of others – and those who are mentioned have precedence over those not mentioned – the Jews said, 'Muḥammad mentioned the Prophets but did not mention Mūsā,' and so Allah revealed: '*Allah spoke directly to Mūsa*'. *Taklīm* is a verbal noun which is for emphasis. This *āyah* indicates the falsity of the position which holds that Allah created words in the Bush which Mūsā heard. It was actual words spoken by Allah Himself. An-Naḥḥās said,

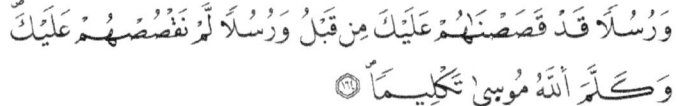

'Grammarians agree that when a verb is reinforced with a verbal noun, it cannot be metaphorical, so when Allah says *'taklīman'* here, it is understood that actual words were spoken.'

Wahb ibn Munabbih said, 'Mūsā said, "Lord, why did You select me to be spoken to directly?" He was asking what was the action that he had done for which Allah had made him so fortunate so that he could do more of it. Allah Almighty said to him, "Do you remember the day when a billy-goat ran off and you followed it for most of the day and then it came to you and you took it, kissed it and held it to your chest and said, 'Will you now follow me when before you followed your own way?' You were not angry at it. That is why I selected you to speak directly to you."'

رُّسُلًا مُّبَشِّرِينَ وَمُنذِرِينَ لِئَلَّا يَكُونَ لِلنَّاسِ عَلَى ٱللَّهِ حُجَّةٌۢ
بَعْدَ ٱلرُّسُلِ ۚ وَكَانَ ٱللَّهُ عَزِيزًا حَكِيمًا ﴿١٦٥﴾

165 Messengers bringing good news and giving warning, so that people will have no argument against Allah after the coming of the Messengers. Allah is Almighty, All-Wise.

The phrase: *'Messengers bringing good news and giving warning,'* is in the accusative as an appositive for: *'...Messengers We have already told you about.'* It can also be in the accusative by the action of an implied verb, and it can be in the accusative for the *ḥāl*, in other words, 'As We revealed to Nūḥ and the Messengers after him.'

so that people will have no argument against Allah.

So that they will not be able to say, 'You did not send us a Messenger or send down a Book to us.' We find in the Revelation: *'We never punish until We have sent a Messenger'* (17:15) and: *'If We had destroyed them with a punishment before this, they would have said, "Our Lord, why did You not send us a Messenger, so we could follow Your Signs?"'* (20:134) All of this is clear evidence that it is not obliged logically. It is related that Ka'b ibn Aḥbar said, 'There were 1,200,000 Prophets.' Muqātil said that there were 1,424,000 Prophets. Anas ibn Mālik reported that the Messenger of Allah ﷺ said, 'I was sent after 8000 Prophets, 4000 of whom were from the tribe of Israel.' Abu-l-Layth as-Samarqandī mentioned it in his *Tafsīr.* Then there is an *isnād* from Shu'bah from Abū Isḥāq from al-Ḥārith al-A'war that Abū Dharr al-Ghifārī said, 'I asked, "Messenger of Allah, how many Prophets were there and how many Messengers?" He replied, "There were 124,000 Prophets and 313

Messengers." The latter is the soundest of what is reported on that. Al-Ajurrī and Abū Ḥātim al-Bustī transmitted it in his sound *Musnad.*

لَٰكِنِ ٱللَّهُ يَشْهَدُ بِمَآ أَنزَلَ إِلَيْكَ أَنزَلَهُۥ بِعِلْمِهِۦ وَٱلْمَلَٰٓئِكَةُ يَشْهَدُونَ
وَكَفَىٰ بِٱللَّهِ شَهِيدًا ﴿١٦٦﴾

166 But Allah bears witness to what He has sent down to you. He has sent it down with His knowledge. The angels bear witness as well. And Allah suffices as a Witness.

The phrase: *'But Allah bears witness'* is in the nominative by the inceptive. If you wish, the *nūn* can be doubled and in the accusative. There is some elision here. It is that the unbelievers said, 'What will testify for you, Muḥammad, regarding what you say?' and this was revealed. The words: *'He has sent it down with His knowledge'* mean He knows that you are worthy of receiving the revelation. The *āyah* indicates that Allah knows by knowledge. He mentioned the testimony of the angels as a counterpoise to negate their testimony. The *bā'* in *'Allah suffices'* (*kafā bi-llāhi*) is redundant.

إِنَّ ٱلَّذِينَ كَفَرُوا۟ وَصَدُّوا۟ عَن سَبِيلِ ٱللَّهِ قَدْ ضَلُّوا۟ ضَلَٰلًۢا بَعِيدًا ﴿١٦٧﴾

167 Those who reject and bar access to the Way of Allah have gone very far astray.

'Those who reject' here are the Jews, indicating that they are wrongdoers. They '*bar access to the Way of Allah*' by preventing people from following the Messenger Muḥammad ﷺ saying, 'We do not find him mentioned in our Book. Prophethood is only among the descendants of Hārūn and Dāwūd. The Torah contains the Law of Mūsā which is not abrogated.' *'They have gone very far astray'* because they denied and kept people from Islam.

إِنَّ ٱلَّذِينَ كَفَرُوا۟ وَظَلَمُوا۟ لَمْ يَكُنِ ٱللَّهُ لِيَغْفِرَ لَهُمْ وَلَا لِيَهْدِيَهُمْ طَرِيقًا ﴿١٦٨﴾
إِلَّا طَرِيقَ جَهَنَّمَ خَٰلِدِينَ فِيهَآ أَبَدًا وَكَانَ ذَٰلِكَ عَلَى ٱللَّهِ يَسِيرًا ﴿١٦٩﴾

168 Allah will not forgive those who reject and do wrong or guide them on any path, 169 except the path of Hell, remaining in it timelessly, for ever and ever. That is easy for Allah.

'*Those who reject and do wrong*' are the Jews, meaning they wrong Muḥammad ﷺ by concealing his description. They wrong themselves when they reject and wrong other people when they conceal things from them. '*Allah will not forgive*' those who die unbelievers without repenting.

يَٰٓأَيُّهَا ٱلنَّاسُ قَدۡ جَآءَكُمُ ٱلرَّسُولُ بِٱلۡحَقِّ مِن رَّبِّكُمۡ فَـَٔامِنُواْ
خَيۡرٗا لَّكُمۡۚ وَإِن تَكۡفُرُواْ فَإِنَّ لِلَّهِ مَا فِي ٱلسَّمَٰوَٰتِ وَٱلۡأَرۡضِۚ وَكَانَ ٱللَّهُ
عَلِيمًا حَكِيمٗا ١٧٠

170 Mankind, the Messenger has brought you the truth from your Lord, so it is better for you to believe. But if you reject, everything in the heavens and the earth belongs to Allah. Allah is All-Knowing, All-Wise.

This is addressed to all human beings. The Messenger is Muḥammad ﷺ. '*The truth*' is the Qur'an. It is said that it is the true *dīn*, and it is said that it is the testimony that 'There is no god but Allah'. It is said that the *bā'* makes the verb transitive, meaning, 'He has come to you bringing the Qur'an.'

In the words: '*...it is better for you to believe*' there is some elision and the meaning is: 'Come to what is better for you.' This is the position of Sībawayh. According to the position of al-Farrā', it is an adverb of an elided verbal noun, meaning: 'belief is better for you.'

يَٰٓأَهۡلَ ٱلۡكِتَٰبِ لَا تَغۡلُواْ فِي دِينِكُمۡ وَلَا تَقُولُواْ عَلَى ٱللَّهِ إِلَّا ٱلۡحَقَّۚ
إِنَّمَا ٱلۡمَسِيحُ عِيسَى ٱبۡنُ مَرۡيَمَ رَسُولُ ٱللَّهِ وَكَلِمَتُهُۥٓ أَلۡقَىٰهَآ إِلَىٰ مَرۡيَمَ
وَرُوحٞ مِّنۡهُۖ فَـَٔامِنُواْ بِٱللَّهِ وَرُسُلِهِۦۖ وَلَا تَقُولُواْ ثَلَٰثَةٌۚ ٱنتَهُواْ
خَيۡرٗا لَّكُمۡۚ إِنَّمَا ٱللَّهُ إِلَٰهٞ وَٰحِدٞۖ سُبۡحَٰنَهُۥٓ أَن يَكُونَ لَهُۥ وَلَدٞۘ لَّهُۥ
مَا فِي ٱلسَّمَٰوَٰتِ وَمَا فِي ٱلۡأَرۡضِۗ وَكَفَىٰ بِٱللَّهِ وَكِيلٗا ١٧١

171 People of the Book! do not go to excess in your *dīn*. Say nothing but the truth about Allah. The Messiah, 'Īsā son of Maryam, was only the Messenger of Allah and His Word, which He cast into Maryam, and a Spirit from Him. So believe in Allah and His Messengers. Do not say, 'Three.' It is better that you stop. Allah is only One God. He is too Glorious to have a son! Everything in the heavens and in the earth belongs to Him. Allah suffices as a Guardian.

People of the Book! do not go to excess in your *dīn*.

This forbids excess. Excess is exceeding the limits. The verb *ghalā* is used for excessive prices as well as going to excess in something. It is used for a young woman becoming plump at the rapid onset of adolescence in a manner beyond what is usual. Commentators mentioned that the Jews went to excess regarding 'Īsā in their slandering of Maryam, and the Christians went to excess regarding him in making him into their Lord. Both excessiveness and negligence are all evil and disbelief. Muṭarrif ibn 'Abdullah said:

Do not go to excess in anything. Be moderate.
Either of the furthermost ends of a matter is blameworthy.

A poet said:

You must have the middle of things.
It is salvation. Do not embark on the abased or the difficult.

We find in *Ṣaḥīḥ Bukhārī*: 'Do not extol me as the Christians extolled 'Īsā. Say, "The slave of Allah and His Messenger."'

Say nothing but the truth about Allah.

Do not say that Allah has a partner or a son. Then Allah goes on to clarify the state and description of 'Īsā, and there are three points made. The first is that *"Īsā son of Maryam'* is evidence: if someone is ascribed to his mother, how can he be a god? God must be timeless, not bound by time. The second is that Allah does not name any woman in His Book except for Maryam, the daughter of 'Imrān. Her name is mentioned in about thirty places. This is a place for a wisdom mentioned by some shaykhs. Kings and nobles do not mention their wives in gatherings and are not free with regard to mentioning their names. Rather they veil their wife and her, family, dependants and the like of that. They do mention slave-girls and do not conceal them or prevent their names from being mentioned. Whereas the Christians said what they said about Maryam and her son, Allah states her name openly and does not conceal her quality of being a mother and servant. The third point is that it is mandatory to believe that 'Īsā has no father. When it is repeated that he is ascribed to his mother, the hearts are aware of what they must believe in denying that he had a father and elevating his pure mother above what the Jews say. Allah knows best.

and His Word, which He cast into Maryam,

He was formed from the word 'Be!' He was a mortal without a father. The Arabs call something by the name of the thing from which it issues. It is said that *'His Word'* means the good news from Allah to Maryam and His message to her on the tongue of Jibrīl. That is: *'And when the angels said, "O Maryam! Allah gives you the good news of a Word from Him."'* (3:45) *'Word'* here means 'sign'. Allah says: *'She confirmed the Words of her Lord...'* (66:12) and: *'...Allah's words still would not run dry.'* (31:27) 'Īsā has four names: the Messiah, 'Isā, Word and Spirit (*Rūḥ*). Other things are said which do not relate to the Qur'an. The words *'He cast into Maryam'* means 'He commanded it for Maryam.'

a Spirit from Him.

This is what caused the Christians to go astray. They said, "Īsā is a part of Him,' and so they were ignorant and misguided. There are eight rejoinders to this assertion. The first is what Ubayy ibn Ka'b said: 'Allah created the spirits of the children of Ādam when he took the covenant from them. Then He returned them to the loins of Ādam but kept the spirit of 'Īsā with Him. When He wanted to create him, He sent that spirit to Maryam and 'Īsā came from it. That is why Allah says: *"a Spirit from Him."'*

It is said that this ascription is out of preference, although all spirits are created by Him. It is like His words: *'Purify My House for those who circle it.'* (22:26)

It is said that things which appear in an extraordinary way are called 'spirit', and that is ascribed to Allah since it is His creation as one ascribes blessing to Allah. 'Īsā used to heal the blind and lepers and bring the dead to life and so he deserved that appellation.

It is said that he is called a Spirit because he is from the breath of Jibrīl. The breath is called '*rūḥ*' because it is a wind (*rīḥ*) which emerges from the *rūḥ*. A poet, Dhu-r-Rummah, said:

I said to him, 'Make it rise to you and revive it
with your breath (*rūḥ*) and feed it accordingly.

It is reported that Jibrīl blew into Maryam's garment and she conceived by Allah's permission. Therefore *'a Spirit from Him'* is added to what is implied: the Name of Allah in '*He cast*'. It implies: Allah and Jibrīl cast the Word into Maryam.

It also said that it means, 'It is a spirit Allah created' as in His words: *'He has made everything in he heavens and everything on the earth subservient to you'* (45:13), meaning in His creation.

It is said that it means 'a mercy from Him,' as 'Īsā was a mercy from Allah to those who followed him. Part of that is His words: '*...reinforce them with a Rūḥ from him*'. (58:22) That means 'by a mercy'.

It is said that it means 'a proof from Him.' 'Īsā was a proof against his people.

So believe in Allah and His Messengers.

Believe in Allah alone, the Creator of the Messiah and the One who sent him. Believe in His Messengers, including 'Īsā, and do not turn him into a god.

Do not say, 'Three.'

Az-Zajjāj said that Ibn 'Abbās said, 'Three means: Allah, a consort and a son.' Al-Farrā' and Abū 'Ubayd said, 'Do not say, "They are three."' That is like Allah's words: '*They will say, "There were three of them."*' (18:22) Abū 'Alī said, 'Do not say, "He is one of three."' So there is some elision.

In spite of their doctrinal disagreements, the Christians agree on the trinity and say that Allah is one essence with three elements. They call each element a god and consider the elements to be existence, life and knowledge, and they designate the elements as the Father, the Son and the Holy Ghost. By 'Father' they mean existence, by the Holy Ghost life and by the son knowledge.

There is confusion in the fundamental doctrines of their religion, but their deliberations led to holding that 'Īsā is a god because of the miracles which Allah made occur at his hands. They claim that since these miracles are beyond the power of a mortal to perform, then the one who performs them must necessarily be a god. It is pointed that if he had possessed such power, he would have had free use of it and saved himself from his enemies and averted their evil. That did not happen.

If the Christians admit that, then their claim that he did that independently is negated. If they do not agree to that, they still have no proof because they are countered with the miracles and other tremendous things that occurred at the hand of Mūsā, such as turning his staff into a serpent, splitting the sea, the white hand, manna and quail and other things. Such matters also occurred at the hands of other Prophets as well. If they deny that, then we deny what they claim about that for 'Īsā. They cannot confirm any of that for 'Īsā. We believe that the method of affirmation is through the text of the Qur'an and they deny the Qur'an and reject the one who brought it. Therefore, they cannot affirm their claim through reports which have multiple transmission.

It has been said that the Christians followed the *dīn* of Islam for eighty-one years after the ascent of 'Īsā and prayed towards the qiblah and fasted the month of Ramadan until there was fighting between them and the Jews. The Jews had a bold man called Paul who killed a group of 'Īsā's companions. He stated, 'If 'Īsā has the truth, then we have disbelieved and denied and will go to the Fire and we will be deceived if they enter the Garden while we enter the Fire. I will deceive them and misguide them and they will enter the Fire.' He had a horse called al-'Uqāb. He made an appearance of regret and put dust on his head and said to the Christians, 'I was your enemy, Paul. I received a call from heaven saying, "You have no repentance unless you become a Christian."' So they brought him inside a room in the church and he stayed there for a year during, which he did not leave either night or day, until he had learned the Gospel. He came out and said, 'I received a call from heaven saying, "God has accepted your repentance."' People believed him and loved him.

Then he went to Jerusalem and put Nusṭūr in charge of them and told him that 'Īsā the son of Maryam was a god. Then he went to Rome and taught them about divine nature and human nature. He said, "Īsā was not human being but took on human form, nor did he have a physical body but took on corporeal form. He was the son of God.' He taught this to a man called Ya'qūb. Then he summoned a man who was called al-Malik and told him, 'God still exists and 'Īsā still exists.' When he had control of these three men, he summoned them one by one and said, 'You are my deliverer. I saw 'Īsā in a dream and he is pleased with me.' He told each of them, 'I will sacrifice myself tomorrow and use that to draw near to God. Call people to your creed.' Then he entered the abattoir and killed himself. On the third day each of them called people to his creed. A group followed each of them and they fought and disagreed until today. All Christians follow one of the three groups. This is said to be the reason for their associating others with Allah. Allah knows best.

This story is what lies behind Allah's words in *Sura al-Ma'ida*: *'We stirred up enmity and hatred between them until the Day of Rising.'* (5:14) It will be discussed there, Allah willing.

It is better that you stop.

The word '*better*' is in the accusative according to Sībawayh by an implied verb. It is as if He were saying, 'Bring what is better for you, because when they were forbidden *shirk* they were commanded to bring what was better than that. Sībawayh said, 'One of the reasons that things may be in the accusative because of an abandoned implied verb is to make what is mentioned clear as is the case in "It is better that you stop," because if you were to you say, "Stop it" [in the imperative], you [immediately] bring someone out of one matter and make him enter into another.' [POEM]

The position of the school of Abū 'Ubaydah is that the meaning is: 'Stopping will be better for you.' Muḥammad ibn Yazīd said that this is an error because it implies a precondition and its apodosis. This is not found in the Arabic language. The position of the school of al-Farrā' is that it is an adjective modifying an elided verbal noun. 'Alī ibn Sulaymān said, 'This is a gross error because it would mean: "Stop in a manner of stopping which is better for you."'

Allah is only one God.

This is an inceptive and predicate. 'One' is its adjective. 'God' can also be an appositive for the name Allah Almighty with 'one' as its predicate. It implies: the One Who is worshipped is one.

He is too Glorious to have a son!

He is too transcendent to have a child. When the preposition '*'an*' is omitted [as it is here], then the particle '*an*' is in the position of the accusative by the removal of the genitive [which would follow *'an*]. It means: 'How can He have a son? A person's child resembles him, and nothing resembles Allah.'

Everything in the heavens and in the earth belongs to Him.

He has no partner. 'Īsā and Maryam are part of what is in the heavens and in the earth and everything in them is created. So how can 'Īsā be a god when he is created? If it were possible for Allah to have a child, then multiple children would be permitted [for Him] in which case anyone who displayed a miracle would be His child. Allah is a sufficient Guardian for His friends.

لَّن يَسْتَنكِفَ ٱلْمَسِيحُ أَن يَكُونَ عَبْدًا لِّلَّهِ وَلَا ٱلْمَلَٰٓئِكَةُ ٱلْمُقَرَّبُونَ ۚ وَمَن
يَسْتَنكِفْ عَنْ عِبَادَتِهِۦ وَيَسْتَكْبِرْ فَسَيَحْشُرُهُمْ إِلَيْهِ جَمِيعًا ﴿١٧٢﴾ فَأَمَّا ٱلَّذِينَ
ءَامَنُوا۟ وَعَمِلُوا۟ ٱلصَّٰلِحَٰتِ فَيُوَفِّيهِمْ أُجُورَهُمْ وَيَزِيدُهُم مِّن فَضْلِهِۦ ۖ وَأَمَّا
ٱلَّذِينَ ٱسْتَنكَفُوا۟ وَٱسْتَكْبَرُوا۟ فَيُعَذِّبُهُمْ عَذَابًا أَلِيمًا وَلَا يَجِدُونَ لَهُم مِّن
دُونِ ٱللَّهِ وَلِيًّا وَلَا نَصِيرًا ﴿١٧٣﴾

172 The Messiah would never disdain to be a slave to Allah nor would the angels near to Him. If any do disdain to worship Him, and grow arrogant, He will in any case gather them all to Him.
173 As for those who believe and do right actions, He will pay them their wages in full and will give them increase from His favour. As for those who show disdain and grow arrogant, He will punish them with a painful punishment. They will not find any protector or helper for themselves besides Allah.

The Messiah would never disdain to be a slave to Allah nor would the angels near to Him.

He would not refuse and would not be ashamed to be a slave. Al-Ḥasan recited '*in yakūnu*' with a *kasrah* on the *hamzah* (as *in* instead of *an*) as a negative meaning *mā*. So it would mean: 'He does not have a child', and so it should be '*yakūnu*' (instead of *yakūna*) while the transmitters are not mentioned.

The word '*near*' in the phrase: '*...nor would the angels near to Him*' means near to His mercy and pleasure. This indicates that the angels are better than all the Prophets, as is the case in Allah's words: '*I do not say that I am an angel.*' (11:31) This was discussed in *al-Baqarah*.

He will in any case gather them all to Him.

Everyone will be gathered before Him in the place of Gathering and repaid according to what they deserve as is explained in the following *āyah*. The root of the verb *'yastankif'* (disdain) is *nakafa* and the *ya'*, *sīn* and *tā'* are added to it. *Nakafa* and *istankafa* are used for spurning a thing. *Ankafa* is to free oneself of what is spurned. An example of that is the *ḥadīth*: 'He was asked about "Glory be to Allah" and said, "It is freeing (*inkāf*) Allah of everything bad."' It means to declare Allah independent and exalted and free of any likenesses or children. Az-Zajjāj said that *istankafa* means *anifa* (disdain). It is taken from wiping (*nakafa*) tears from the cheek with a finger. Part of it is the *ḥadīth*: 'Sweat is not wiped (*yunkafu*) from his brow.' There is also the *ḥadīth*: 'He brought an army whose end was not broken (*yunkafu*).' It is also said that it comes from *nakaf* which is a fault. It is said: 'It has no *nakf* or *kaff* in this business,' meaning no fault. So it means: 'The Messiah would not refuse and would not disdain to be a slave and would not stop being one nor find any fault with that.'

يَٰٓأَيُّهَا ٱلنَّاسُ قَدْ جَآءَكُم بُرْهَٰنٌ مِّن رَّبِّكُمْ وَأَنزَلْنَآ إِلَيْكُمْ
نُورًا مُّبِينًا ﴿١٧٤﴾

174 Mankind! a clear proof has come to you from your Lord. We have sent down a Clear Light to you.

The clear proof is Muḥammad ﷺ according to ath-Thawrī. He is called a proof because the actual proof, which was the miracle, was performed by him. Mujāhid said that proof is the definitive evidence. It is a similar idea. The miracles he performed are the proof of the Prophet ﷺ. The *'Light'* sent down with him was the Qur'an according to al-Ḥasan. It is called a light because it makes judgments clear and guides people from misguidance. So it is a clear and clarifying light.

فَأَمَّا ٱلَّذِينَ ءَامَنُوا۟ بِٱللَّهِ وَٱعْتَصَمُوا۟ بِهِۦ فَسَيُدْخِلُهُمْ فِى رَحْمَةٍ
مِّنْهُ وَفَضْلٍ وَيَهْدِيهِمْ إِلَيْهِ صِرَٰطًا مُّسْتَقِيمًا ﴿١٧٥﴾

175 As for those who believe in Allah and hold fast to Him, He will admit them into mercy and favour from Him and will guide them to Him on a straight path.

'Hold fast to Him' means to 'it', to the Qur'an, away from acts of disobedience. When people cling to His Book, they hold to Him and to His Prophet ﷺ. It is said that it means 'Hold fast to Allah.' *'Iṣma* (from 'hold fast', *'iṣtaṣama*) means inviolability. *'Guide them'* means 'He will guide them' and 'He' is implied on the

basis that the words are separate from what precedes them. '*To Him*' can also mean 'to His reward' or 'to the Truth so that they recognise it.' '*A Straight path*' is the straight *Dīn*. '*He will guide them*' implies: 'He will inform them of the Straight Path.' It is said that it is a *ḥāl*.

'*Ilayhi*' can mean to His reward, to the Qur'an, to favour, or to favour and mercy. That is because favour and mercy are part of the reward. It is said that it means 'to Allah' based on the elision of the *muḍāf*, as it was already mentioned that it means 'He will guide them to His reward.' Abū 'Alī said that it means 'to Allah' and He guides to His Path. If we make '*straight path*' accusative for the *ḥāl*, the *ḥāl* is elided in that. The noun '*favour*' indicates that it is Allah who bestows His reward on His servants since there is no action that fully merits it. Therefore, it is truly a favour, and Allah knows best.

يَسْتَفْتُونَكَ قُلِ اللَّهُ يُفْتِيكُمْ فِي الْكَلَالَةِ إِنِ امْرُؤٌا هَلَكَ لَيْسَ لَهُ وَلَدٌ
وَلَهُ أُخْتٌ فَلَهَا نِصْفُ مَا تَرَكَ وَهُوَ يَرِثُهَا إِن لَّمْ يَكُن لَّهَا وَلَدٌ فَإِن
كَانَتَا اثْنَتَيْنِ فَلَهُمَا الثُّلُثَانِ مِمَّا تَرَكَ وَإِن كَانُوا إِخْوَةً رِّجَالًا
وَنِسَاءً فَلِلذَّكَرِ مِثْلُ حَظِّ الْأُنثَيَيْنِ يُبَيِّنُ اللَّهُ لَكُمْ أَن تَضِلُّوا وَاللَّهُ
بِكُلِّ شَيْءٍ عَلِيمٌ ﴿١٧٦﴾

176 They will ask you for a fatwa. Say: 'Allah gives you a fatwa about people who die without direct heirs: If a man dies childless but has a sister she receives half of what he leaves, and he is her heir if she dies childless. If there are two sisters they receive two-thirds of what he leaves. If there are brothers and sisters the males receive the share of two females. Allah makes things clear to you so you will not go astray. Allah has knowledge of all things.'

Al-Barā' ibn 'Āzib said, 'This was the last *āyah* of the Qur'an to be revealed,' as is stated in Muslim. It is said that it was revealed while the Prophet ﷺ was preparing for the Farewell Ḥajj and it was revealed because of Jābir. Jābir ibn 'Abdullāh was ill and the Messenger of Allah ﷺ came to him on foot with Abū Bakr to visit him. Jābir fainted and the Messenger of Allah ﷺ did *wuḍū'* and then poured the water over him and he recovered. He asked, 'Messenger of Allah, how should I settle my property?' Jābir said, 'He did not reply to me until the *Āyah* of Inheritance was revealed.' Muslim related it. He said, 'It was the last of the Qur'an to be revealed.'

It is also said that the last revelation was an *āyah* in *al-Baqarah*: *'Show fear of a Day when you will be returned to Allah.'* (2:281)

Kalālah was discussed adequately at the beginning of the *sūrah*. What is meant by brothers here are full or paternal brothers. Jābir had nine sisters.

If a man dies childless but has a sister she receives half of what he leaves,

This is when he has neither child nor parent. It is enough to mention only one of the categories and that implies the other category. Al-Jurjānī said, 'The term "child" is applied to both parent and child. The father is called *'wālid'* because he procreated (*walada*), and a child is called *'walad'* because he was born (*wulida*). Similarly, *dhurrīyah* (progeny) comes from *dhara'a* (to sow) and is used for the child and the parent. Allah says: *"A Sign for them is that We carried their children (dhurrīyah) in the laden ship."* (36:41)'

Most scholars among the Companions and *Tābi'ūn* make the sisters agnates of the daughters, even if they have no brother, except for Ibn 'Abbās who does not. That is the position of Dāwūd and a group. Their argument is evident from the words of Allah: *'If a man dies childless but has a sister she receives half of what he leaves.'* The sister only inherits when the deceased has no children. They said, 'It is known that a daughter is a child and so a sister cannot inherit when she exists.' Ibn az-Zubayr took the position of Ibn 'Abbās in this matter until al-Aswad ibn Yazid informed him that Mu'ādh gave a judgment in the case of a daughter and sister, dividing the property equally between them.

This *āyah* is called the *Āyah* of Summer because it was revealed in the summer. 'Umar said, 'By Allah, I do not leave anything more important to me than the case of someone who dies with heirs. I asked the Messenger of Allah ﷺ about it and he was not as harsh to me about anything as he was about it until he poked me in the chest or the side with his finger and said, "'Umar! Is it not enough for you that the *Āyah* of Summer was revealed at the end of *Sūrat an-Nisā'*?"' 'Umar also said, 'There are three things which are dearer to me than this world and everything it contains because the Messenger of Allah ﷺ clarified them to me himself: a person who dies without an heir, usury and the caliphate.' Ibn Mājah transmitted it in the *Sunan*. Some Rāfiḍites attack what 'Umar said, 'By Allah, I do not leave...'.

Allah makes things clear to you

Al-Kisā'ī says that it means: 'Allah makes things clear to you so that you do not go astray.' Abū 'Ubayd said, 'Al-Kisā'ī related a *ḥadīth* from Ibn 'Umar in which the Prophet ﷺ said, 'None of you should invoke against his child lest Allah answer it.' So it is recommendation. An-Naḥḥās said, 'According to Abū 'Ubayd, it means, "lest the answer from Allah coincide with it."' The Basrans say that this is a clear error and they do not permit the implication of '*lā*' (no). They say that it means, 'Allah makes things clear to you because of His dislike of you going astray.' Then there is elision as when He says: '*Ask the town*'. (12:82) That is similar to the meaning in the *ḥadīth* of the Prophet ﷺ: 'Out of dislike of it coinciding with an answer from Allah.'

Table of Contents for *Āyats*

23 Forbidden for you are: your mothers and your daughters ... 1
24 And also married women, except for those you own as slaves... 15
25 If any of you do not have the means to marry free women ... 31
26 Allah desires to make things clear to you and to guide you ... 42
27 Allah desires to turn towards you ... 43
29 You who believe, do not consume one another's property ... 44
30 As for anyone who does that out of enmity and wrongdoing... 51
31 If you avoid the serious wrong actions you have been forbidden ... 52
32 Do not covet what Allah has given to some of you in preference ... 56
33 We have appointed heirs for everything ... 59
34 Men have charge of women because Allah has preferred ... 62
35 If you fear a breach between a couple, send an arbiter ... 68
36 Worship Allah and do not associate anything with Him ... 73
37 As for those who are tight-fisted and direct others to be tight-fisted ... 85
38 and also for those who spend their wealth to show off to people ... 86
39 What harm would it have done them to have believed in Allah ... 87
40 Allah does not wrong anyone by so much as the smallest speck ... 87
41 How will it be when We bring a witness from every nation ... 89
42 On that day those who disbelieved and disobeyed the Messenger ... 91
43 You who believe! do not approach the prayer when you are drunk ... 92
44 Do you not see those who were given a portion of the Book ... 129
45 Allah knows best who your enemies are. Allah suffices as a Protector ... 129
46 Some of the Jews distort the true meaning of words ... 129
47 You who have been given the Book! believe in what We have sent ... 129
48 Allah does not forgive anything being associated with Him ... 129
49 Do you not see those who claim to be purified? ... 130
50 Look how they invent lies against Allah. ... 130
51 Do you not see those who were given a portion of the Book ... 130
52 Those are the ones Allah has cursed. And if someone is cursed ... 130
53 Or do they indeed really own a portion of Allah's kingdom? ... 130
54 Or do they in fact envy other people for the bounty ... 139
55 Some of them believe in him, and some bar access to him ... 139
56 As for those who reject Our Signs, We will roast them in a Fire ... 142

57 But as for those who believe and do right actions … 142
58 Allah commands you to return to their owners … 144
59 You who believe, obey Allah and obey the Messenger and … 147
60 Do you not see those who claim that they believe … 151
61 When they are told, 'Come to what Allah has sent down … 151
62 How will it be when a disaster strikes them because of what they … 153
63 Allah knows what is in such people's hearts so turn away from them … 153
64 We sent no Messenger except to be obeyed by Allah's permission … 154
65 No, by your Lord, they are not believers until they … 154
66 If We had directed them to kill themselves or leave their homes … 158
67 In that case We would have given them an immense reward from Us … 158
68 and We would have guided them on a straight path. 158
69 Whoever obeys Allah and the Messenger … 159
70 That is favour from Allah. Allah suffices as a Knower. 159
71 You who believe, take all necessary precautions … 162
72 Among you there are people who hang back … 164
73 But if you meet with favour from Allah they say … 164
74 So let those who sell the life of this world for the Next World fight … 166
75 What reason could you have for not fighting in the Way of Allah … 167
76 Those who believe fight in the Way of Allah … 169
77 Do you not see those who were told: 'Hold back from fighting … 169
78 Wherever you are, death will catch up with you, even if you … 171
79 Any good thing that happens to you comes from Allah … 173
80 Whoever obeys the Messenger has obeyed Allah … 176
81 They have the word, 'Obedience!' on their tongues … 177
83 When news of any matter reaches them they spread it about … 180
84 So fight in the way of Allah – you are only answerable for yourself … 181
85 Those who join forces for good will receive a reward for it … 183
86 When you are greeted with a greeting, return the greeting … 185
87 Allah, there is no god but Him. He will gather you … 193
88 How is it that you have become two parties regarding the hypocrites … 193
89 They would like you to disbelieve as they disbelieve … 195
90 except for those who seek shelter with people with whom … 195
91 You will find others who desire to be safe from you … 198
92 A believer should never kill another believer unless it is by mistake … 199
93 As for anyone who kills a believer deliberately … 215
94 You who believe, when you go out to fight in the Way of Allah … 222
95 Those believers who stay behind – other than those forced to … 227
96 high ranks conferred by Him as well as forgiveness and mercy … 227

97 The angels ask those they take while they are wrongING themselves … 230
98 Except for those men, women and children who really are oppressed … 230
99 It may well be that Allah will pardon them. Allah is Ever-Pardoning … 230
100 Those who make hijrah in the Way of Allah will find … 233
101 When you are travelling in the land, there is nothing wrong … 237
102 When you are with them and leading them in the prayer, a group … 248
103 When you have completed the prayer remember Allah standing … 257
104 Do not relax in pursuit of the enemy. If you feel pain, they too … 257
105 We have sent down the Book to you with the truth so that … 259
106 And ask Allah's forgiveness. Allah is Ever-Forgiving, Most Merciful … 261
107 Do not argue on behalf of those who betray themselves … 262
108 They try to conceal themselves from people … 263
109 Here you are arguing on their behalf in this world … 263
110 Anyone who does evil or wrongs himself and then asks … 264
111 If anyone commits an evil action, the responsibility for it is his alone … 265
112 Anyone who commits an error or an evil action, and then … 265
113 Were it not for Allah's favour to you and His mercy … 266
114 There is no good in much of their secret talk, except in the case … 267
115 But if anyone opposes the Messenger after the guidance … 270
117 What they call on apart from Him are female idols … 272
118 whom Allah has cursed. He said, 'I will take a certain fixed … 273
119 I will lead them astray and fill them with false hopes … 274
120 He makes promises to them and fills them with false hopes … 280
121 The shelter of such people will be Hell. They will find no way … 280
122 But as for those who believe and do right actions … 280
123 It is not a matter of wishful thinking on your part … 280
124 Anyone, male or female, who does right actions and is a believer … 283
125 Who could have a better *dīn* than someone who submits himself … 284
126 Everything in the heavens and in the earth belongs to Allah … 286
127 They will ask you for a fatwa about women … 287
128 If a woman fears cruelty or aversion on her husband's part … 288
129 You will not be able to be completely fair between your wives … 291
130 If a couple do separate, Allah will enrich each of them … 292
131 Everything in the heavens and in the earth belongs to Allah … 292
132 Everything in the heavens and in the earth belongs to Allah … 292
133 Mankind, if He wanted, He could remove you altogether … 294
134 If anyone desires the reward of this world … 294
135 You who believe, be upholders of justice … 295
136 You who believe! Believe in Allah and His Messenger … 300

137 As for those who believe and then return to unbelief … 300
138 Give news to the hypocrites that … 301
139 Do those who take the unbelievers as protectors … 301
140 It has been sent down to you in the Book that when you hear … 302
141 Those who anticipate the worst for you say, 'Were we not with you?' … 302
142 The hypocrites think they deceive Allah, but He is deceiving them … 306
143 They vacillate between the two – not joining these or joining those … 308
144 You who believe! do not take the unbelievers as friends … 309
145 The hypocrites are in the lowest level of the Fire … 309
146 except those who repent and put things right and hold fast to Allah … 310
147 Why should Allah punish you if you are thankful and believe? … 311
148 Allah does not like evil words being voiced out loud … 311
149 Whether you reveal a good act or keep it hidden … 311
150 Those who reject Allah and His Messengers … 315
151 such people are the true unbelievers … 315
152 Those who believe in Allah and His Messengers … 316
153 The People of the Book will ask you to bring down a Book … 317
154 We lifted up the Mount above their heads … 318
155 Because of the fact that they broke their covenant … 318
156 And on account of their unbelief … 318
157 and their saying, 'We killed the Messiah, 'Īsā son of Maryam … 320
158 Allah raised him up to Himself. Allah is Almighty, All-Wise … 320
159 There is not one of the People of the Book … 322
160 Because of wrongdoing on the part of the Jews … 323
161 and because of their practising usury when they were forbidden … 323
162 But those of them who are firmly rooted in knowledge … 324
163 We have revealed to you as We revealed to Nūḥ and the Prophets … 326
164 There are Messengers We have already told you about … 328
165 Messengers bringing good news and giving warning … 329
166 But Allah bears witness to what He has sent down to you … 330
167 Those who reject and bar access to the Way of Allah … 330
168 Allah will not forgive those who reject and do wrong … 330
170 Mankind, the Messenger has brought you the truth from your Lord … 331
171 People of the Book! do not go to excess in your *dīn* … 332
172 The Messiah would never disdain to be a slave to Allah … 337
173 As for those who believe and do right actions … 337
174 Mankind! a clear proof has come to you from your Lord … 338
175 As for those who believe in Allah and hold fast to Him … 338
176 They will ask you for a fatwa. Say: 'Allah gives you a fatwa … 339

Glossary

Abū al-'Abbās: Muḥammad ibn Yazīd al-Mubarrad, a leading philologist and grammarian of the school of Basra. He died in Baghdad in 285/898. He wrote many books, including *al-Kāmil* and *al-Kitāb*.
Abū Ḥātim: Sahl ibn Muḥammad al-Jushanī as-Sijistānī, d. 255/869, a prominent Basran philologist.
Abū Ḥaywah: Shurayḥ ibn Yazīd al-Ḥaḍramī, the Qur'an reciter of Syria from Homs. He has a *shādhdh* reading, and died in 203/818.
Abū Isḥāq: Ibrāhīm ibn as-Sarī az-Zajjāj, author of *I'rab al-Qur'ān*.
Abū Ja'far: aṭ-Ṭabarī.
Abū Jahl: 'Amr ibn Hishām, one of the important men of Quraysh who was violently opposed to Islam.
Abū Lahab: One of the Prophet Muhammad's uncles, who was a great enemy of Islam.
Abū 'Ubayd: al-Qāsim ibn Sallām al-Harawī or al-Baghdādī, d. 224/838.
Abū 'Ubaydah: Ma'mar ibn al-Muthanna at-Taymī, d. 209/824, author of *Majāz al-Qur'ān*, the first book on the linguistic analysis of the Qur'an.
Al-Abwā': a place between Makkah and Madīnah.
'Ād: an ancient people in southern Arabia to whom the Prophet Hūd was sent.
adab: correct behaviour, inward and outward.
adhān: the call to prayer.
Al-Akhfash: Abū al-Khaṭṭāb 'Abd al-Ḥamīd ibn 'Abd al-Majīd al-Akhfash al-Kabīr, a grammarian in Basra, one of the first to study Arabic poetry as well as contributing to philology, a lexicography and recording Bedouin vocabulary. He revised *Kitāb*, the first book on Arabic grammar, written by his student Sībawayh. He was a client of the Qays tribe and died in 177/793.
Amīr al-Mu'minīn: 'the Commander of the Believers', the caliph.
Anṣār: the "Helpers", the people of Madīnah who welcomed and aided the Prophet ﷺ.
'āqilah: the paternal kinsmen of an offender who are liable for the payment of blood money.
'arīyah: a kind of sale by which the owner of an *'arīyah* is allowed to sell fresh dates while they are still on the palms by means of estimation, in exchange for dried picked dates.

'aṣabah: male relatives on the father's side.
Al-Aṣma'ī: Abū Sa'īd ibn 'Abd al-Malik ibn Qurayb, 122/740-213/820, an early philologist and Arabic grammarian of Basra. He also wrote on genealogy, natural science and zoology and was a scholar of Arabic poetry in the court of Hārūn ar-Rashīd. He spent a great deal of time recording the language of desert Bedouins.
'Aṣr: the mid-afternoon prayer.
awliyā': the plural of *walī.*
Awṭās: a location between Makkah and Ta'if, about fifteen miles from Makkah, the site of a battle.
āyah: a verse of the Qur'an.
Ayyūb: the Prophet Job.
Badr: a place near the coast, about 95 miles to the south of Madīnah where, in 2 AH in the first battle fought by the newly established Muslim community, the 313 outnumbered Muslims led by the Messenger of Allah overwhelmingly defeated 1000 Makkan idolaters.
Banū: lit. sons, meaning a tribe or clan.
Ḍajnān: a mountain 25 km north of Makkah.
ḍammah: the Arabic vowel 'u'.
Dāwud: the Prophet David.
Dhāt ar-Riqā': an expedition to Najd led by the Prophet ﷺ. They had to bandage their feet with rags (*riqā'*).
Dhāt as-Salāsil: a site with a well to the north of Madīnah. In 8 AH the Prophet ﷺ sent an expedition led by 'Amr ibn al-'Āṣ against the Banū Quḍā'ah which was victorious. He camped at Dhāt as-Salāsil.
dhikr: lit. remembrance, mention. Commonly used to mean invocation of Allah by repetition of His names or particular formulae.
dhimmah: obligation or contract, in particular a treaty of protection for non-Muslims living in Muslim territory.
dhimmī: a non-Muslim living under the protection of Muslim rule.
Dhu-l-Ḥijjah: the twelfth month of the Muslim calendar, the month of the hajj.
Dhu-l-Ḥulayfah: the *mīqāt* of the people of Madīnah.
Dhu-l-Qa'dah: the eleventh month of the Muslim calendar.
Dhū Qarad: an expedition in 6/627, also called the al-Ghābah expedition, to re-capture from Quraysh some milk camels taken by Ghaṭafān.
dīn: the life-transaction, lit. the debt between two parties, in this usage between the Creator and created.
Dīwān: originally the register of soldiers and pensions under 'Umar.

Subsequently it became a governmental department for the finance and records of the government.

Fajr: the dawn prayer.

faraq: a kind of large pot used as a measure in Madīnah, containing about three *ṣā*'s (approx. 10 l.) of water.

farḍ kifāyah: a collective obligation, something which is obligatory for the community as a whole and is satisfied if one adult performs it.

Al-Farrā': Abū Zakariyyā Yaḥyā ibn Ziyād, ca. 144/761- 207/882, a noted grammarian of Kufa. Al-Farrā' means 'he who skins/scrutinises language'. He wrote *Majāz al-Qur'an*.

al-Fārūq: a name for the second caliph, 'Umar ibn al-Khaṭṭāb, It means someone who makes a distinction between truth and falsehood, or between cases.

faqīh: pl. *fuqahā'*, a man learned in knowledge of fiqh who by virtue of his knowledge can give a legal judgment.

fatḥah: the Arabic vowel 'a'.

Fātiḥah: "the Opener," the first sūrah of the Qur'an.

fatwa: an authoritative statement on a point of law.

fidyah: a ransom, compensation paid for rites or acts of worship missed or wrongly performed because of ignorance or ill health. Also the amount paid by a woman in the *khul'* divorce.

fiqh: the science of the application of the Sharī'ah. A practitioner or expert in fiqh is called a *faqih*.

fiṭrah: the natural form on which man was created.

fuqahā': plural of *faqīh*.

gharīb: a hadith which has a single reporter at some stage of the *isnād*.

Ghaṭafān: a very large tribal grouping who lived east of Madīnah and Makkah in the land between the Hijaz and the Shammar mountains.

ghurrah: a high value slave.

ghusl: major ablution of the whole body with water required to regain purity after menstruation, lochia and sexual intercourse.

ḥadd: Allah's boundary limits for the lawful and unlawful. The *ḥadd* punishments are specific fixed penalties laid down by Allah for specified crimes.

ḥadith: reported speech of the Prophet ﷺ.

ḥāfiẓ: pl. ḥuffāẓ, someone who has memorised the Qur'an.

hajj: the annual pilgrimage to Makka which is one of the five pillars of Islam.

ḥakam: an arbiter.

ḥāl: In Arabic grammar, a circumstantial adverb in the accusative case which describes something happening at the same time as the action or event mentioned in the main clause.
hamzah: the character in Arabic which designates a glottal stop.
harām: unlawful in the Sharī'ah.
al-Ḥarrah: a stony tract of black volcanic rock east of Madīnah where a terrible battle took place in 63 AH (26 August 683) between the forces of Yazīd I and 'Abdullāh ibn az-Zubayr which ended in Madīnah being sacked and plundered.
Hārūn: the Prophet Aaron, the brother of Mūsā.
ḥasan: good, excellent, often used to describe a hadith which is reliable, but which is not as well authenticated as one which is *ṣaḥīḥ*.
Ḥawwā': Eve, the first woman.
Hijrah: emigration in the way of Allah. Islamic dating begins with the Hijrah of the Prophet Muḥammad ﷺ from Makkah to Madīnah in 622 AD.
ḥisbah: the function of market inspection.
Hūd: the Prophet sent to the people of 'Ād.
Ḥudaybīyah: a well-known place ten miles from Makkah on the way to Jiddah where the Homage of ar-Riḍwān took place.
ḥudūd: plural of *ḥadd*.
ḥuffāẓ: plural of *ḥāfiẓ*.
'Ibādiyyah: the remnants of the Khārijites who were the followers of 'Abdullāh ibn 'Ibād.
Iblīs: the personal name of the Devil. He is also called Shayṭān or the 'enemy of Allah'.
Ibrāhīm: the Prophet Abraham.
'Īd: a festival, either the festival at the end of Ramadan or at the time of the Hajj.
iḍāfah: a possessive construction in Arabic in which the first noun is indefinite and the second usually definite. It is used to indicate possession. The first word is called '*muḍāf*' and the second is '*muḍāf ilayhi*'.
'iddah: a period after divorce or the death of her husband for which a woman must wait before re-marrying.
Idrīs: a Prophet, possibly Enoch.
iḥṣān: the state of having been validly married.
ijtihād: to exercise personal judgment in legal matters.
īlā': a vow by a husband to abstain from sexual relations with his wife. If four months pass, it is considered a divorce.

'Illiyūn: 'the High Places', a name for the upper part of the heavens, where the register of people's good actions is kept, or the register itself.
imālah: a vowel shift in Arabic where an open vowel rises, *ā* towards *ī*, and short *a* towards *i*.
imam: Muslim religious or political leader; leader of Muslim congregational worship.
īmān: belief, faith.
iqāmah: the call which announces that the obligatory prayer is about to begin.
'Īsā: the Prophet Jesus.
'Ishā': the obligatory evening prayer.
Isḥāq: the Prophet Isaac.
Ismā'īl: the Prophet Ishmael.
isnād: a hadith's chain of transmission from individual to individual.
istibrā': the waiting period for slave-girls.
i'tikāf: seclusion, while fasting, in a mosque, particularly in the last ten days of Ramadan.
Jāhiliyyah: the Time of Ignorance before the coming of Islam.
janābah: major ritual impurity requiring a ghusl: brought about by sexual intercourse, sexual discharge, menstruation, childbirth.
Jibrīl: the angel Gabriel.
jihad: struggle, particularly fighting in the way of Allah to establish Islam.
jinn: inhabitants of the heavens and the earth made of smokeless fire who are usually invisible.
Juhaynah: a large nomadic tribe from the Hijaz whose territory covered the routes between Syria and Makkah.
Jumādā al-Ākhir: the sixth month of the Muslim calendar.
Jumādā al-Ulā: the fifth month of the Muslim calendar.
Jumu'ah: the day of gathering, Friday, and particularly the Jumu'ah prayer which is performed instead of *Ẓuhr* by those who attend it.
Ka'bah: the cube-shaped building at the centre of the Ḥaram in Makkah, originally built by the Prophet Ibrāhīm. Also known as the House of Allah.
kaffārah: atonement, prescribed way of making amends for wrong actions, especially missed obligatory actions.
kāfir: (pl. *kāfirūn* or *kuffār*): an unbeliever, a person who rejects Allah and His Messenger. The opposite is believer or *mu'min*.
kasrah: the Arabic vowel i.
Al-Khalīl: Abū 'Abd ar-Raḥmān ibn 'Amt al-Farāhidī, 110/718-170/786, born in Oman, a leading grammarian, philologist and lexicographer of

Basra. He compiled the first Arabic dictionary: *Kitāb al-'Ayn*, and was the first to codify the metres of Arabic poetry. His students included Sībawayh and al-Aṣma'ī.

Khārijites: the earliest sect, who separated themselves from the body of the Muslims and declared war on all those who disagreed with them, stating that a wrong action turns a Muslim into an unbeliever.

Khaṣafah: a sub-tribe of Qays 'Aylān.

Khaybar: a Jewish colony to the north of Madina which was laid siege to and captured by the Muslims in the seventh year after the Hijra because continual treachery on the part of the Jewish clans.

Khayf Mosque: the mosque at the eastern end of Minā.

Khuzā'ah: an Azdī tribe who were concentrated around Makkah.

khul': a form of divorce initiated by the wife from her husband by giving him a certain compensation, or by returning back the dowry (*mahr*) which he gave her.

kitābah: a contract for a slave to buy his freedom in instalments.

Kitābī: Someone who is one of the People of the Book, i.e. a Jew or Christian.

kufr: disbelief, to cover up the truth, to reject Allah and refuse to believe that Muhammad ﷺ is His Messenger.

kunyah: a respectful but intimate way of addressing people as "the father of so-and-so" or "the mother of so-and-so."

Lūṭ: the Prophet Lot.

maddah: prolongation. There are three letters which are subject to prolongation in recitation of the Qur'an: *alif*, *wāw* and *yā'*.

Madyan: Midian, the people to whom the Prophet Shu'ayb was sent.

Maghrib: the sunset prayer; also the western part of Muslim lands. Today it also means Morocco.

maḥram: a male relative of a woman, with whom marriage is forbidden.

Maqām of Ibrāhīm: the place of the stone on which the Prophet Ibrāhīm stood while he and Ismā'īl were building the Ka'bah, which marks the place of the two *rak'ah* prayer following *ṭawāf* of the Ka'bah.

marfū': 'elevated', a narration from the Prophet ﷺ mentioned by a Companion, e.g. 'The Messenger of Allah ﷺ said...'

Maryam: Mary, the mother of 'Īsā.

mawālī: plural of *mawlā*.

mawlā: a person with whom a tie of *walā'* has been established, usually by having been a slave and then set free.

mawqūf: 'stopped', a narration from a Companion without mentioning the Prophet ﷺ.
Minā: a valley five miles on the road to 'Arafah where the three *jamrah*s stand. It is part of the hajj to spend four or possibly three nights there over the course of the hajj.
Mīqāt: the principal boundary point of an area, within which Muslims on the Hajj must be in the state of *ihram*.
mudabbar: a slave who has been given a *tadbīr*, a contract that he be freed after his master's death.
Muḍar: the ancestor of the Arabs.
mudd: a measure of volume; approximately a double-handed scoop.
Mudlij: an Arab tribe which was a branch of Kinānah.
Mufaṣṣal: the shorter *sūrah*s at the end of the Qur'an starting from *Sūrat al-Hujurāt* (49) or *Sūrat Qāf* (50) to the end of the Qur'an.
mufti: someone qualified to give a legal opinion or fatwa.
Muhājirūn: Companions of the Messenger of Allah ﷺ who accepted Islam in Makkah and made hijrah to Madīnah.
muḥārib: a brigand, someone involved in armed robbery.
Muḥarram: the first month of the Muslim lunar year.
muḥkam: perspicuous, a word or text conveying a firm and unequivocal meaning.
muḥṣan (or *muḥṣin*): a person who has been previously legally married.
mukātab: a slave who has been given a *kitābah*, a contract to buy his freedom.
munkar: "denounced", a narration reported by a weak reporter which goes against another authentic hadith.
Al-Muraysī': a battle between the Prophet ﷺ and the Banū al-Muṣṭaliq in 6/627.
mursal: a hadith where a man in the generation after the Companions quotes directly from the Prophet without mentioning the Companion from whom he got it.
Mūsā: the Prophet Moses.
musnad: a collection of hadiths arranged according to the first authority in its *isnād*; also a hadith which can be traced back through an unbroken *isnād* to the Prophet.
Muṣṭaliq: a tribe that is a sub-clan of Khuzā'ah who were allied with Quraysh. The Muslims defeated them at al-Muraysi' in 5/626.
mu'tah: a temporary marriage.
mutashābih: intricate, unintelligible, referring to a word or text not

immediately clear, whose meaning needs explanation.
Mu'tazilite: someone who adheres to the school of the Mu'tazilah which is rationalist in its approach to existence. Originally they held that anyone who commits a sin is neither a believer nor an unbeliever. They also held the Qur'an to be created.
nabīdh: a drink made by soaking grapes, raisins, dates, etc. in water without allowing them to ferment to the point of becoming intoxicating. Once it is intoxicating, it is *nabīdh*.
nāfilah: (plural *nawāfil*): supererogatory act of worship.
An-Naḥḥās: Abū Ja'far Aḥmad ibn Muḥammad an-Naḥḥās, d. 338/949, an Egyptian scholar of grammar and *tafsīr* in the Abbasid period.
Najd: the region around Riyadh in central Arabia.
Nūḥ: the Prophet Noah.
People of the Book: principally the Jews and Christians whose religions are based on the Divine Books revealed to Mūsā and 'Īsā; a term also used to refer to any other group who claim to be following a Book revealed prior to the Qur'an.
People of Hadith: 'the adherents of Hadith', the movement who considered only the Qur'an and hadith to be valid sources of fiqh.
People of Opinion (*ra'y*): a term used to describe those who use personal opinion to deduce judgment. It was a term used particularly to describe the early Ḥanafīs.
Qābīl: Cain.
Qadariyyah: sect who said that people have power (*qadar*) over their actions and hence free will.
qāḍī: a judge, qualified to judge all matters in accordance with the Sharī'ah and to dispense and enforce legal punishments.
Qādisīyah: a decisive four day battle fought against the Persians in Iraq in 15/636.
Qārūn: the Biblical Korah who was famed for his incredible wealth and became arrogant on account of it. The earth swallowed him up.
qasāmah: an oath taken by fifty members of a tribe or locality to refute or establish accusations of complicity in unclear cases of homicide.
Qaynuqā': one of the Jewish tribes of Madīnah.
qiblah: the direction faced in the prayer which is towards the Ka'bah in Makkah.
Qudayd: a large town with wells located between Makkah and Madīnah.
Quraysh: one of the great tribes of Arabia. The Prophet Muḥammad ﷺ belonged to this tribe, which had great powers spiritually and financially

both before and after Islam came. Someone from this tribe is called a Qurashī.

Qurayẓah: one of the Jewish tribes of Madīnah.

ar-Rabadhah: a luxuriant oasis about 200 km northeast of Madīnah, located on a pilgrimage route.

Rabī' al-Awwal: the third month of the Muslim calendar.

Rabī' al-Ākhir: the fourth month of the Muslim calendar.

Rajab: the seventh month of the Muslim calendar.

rak'ah: a unit of the prayer consisting of standing, bowing, prostration and sitting.

Ramadan: the month of fasting, the ninth month in the Muslim lunar calendar.

Rāshidūn: 'Rightly Guided', the title given to the first four caliphs in Islam: Abū Bakr, 'Umar, 'Uthmān and 'Alī.

ra'y: opinion, personal discretion. (see also People of Opinion.)

Ri'm: or Rīm, a wadi belonging to Muzaynah near to Madīmah.

ṣā': a measure of volume equal to four *mudd*s.

ṣadaqah: charitable giving in the Cause of Allah.

Ṣafar: the second month of the Muslim lunar calendar.

ṣaḥīḥ: healthy and sound with no defects, used to describe an authentic hadith.

Ṣaḥīḥ: "the Sound", the title of the hadith collections of al-Bukhārī and Muslim.

Salaf: the early generations of the Muslims.

salām: the expression, '*as-salāmu 'alaykum*,' or 'Peace be upon you,' used as a greeting and to end the prayer.

Ṣāliḥ: the Prophet sent to the people of Thamūd.

Sha'bān: the eighth month in the Muslim calendar.

shahādah: bearing witness, particularly bearing witness that there is no god but Allah and that Muhammad is the Messenger of Allah. It is one of the pillars of Islam. It is also used to describe legal testimony in a court of law.

Sharī'ah: The legal modality of a people based on the revelation of their Prophet. The final Sharī'ah is that of Islam.

Shawwāl: the tenth month of the Muslim calendar.

Shayṭān: the devil, particularly Iblīs, one of the jinn.

shirk: the unforgiveable wrong action of worshipping something or someone other than Allah or associating something or someone as a partner with Him.

Shu'ayb: the Prophet Jethro.
ṣiddīq: a man of truth; the *ṣiddīq* is the one who believes in Allah and His Messenger by the statement of the one who reports it, not from any proof except the light of belief which he experiences in his heart and which prevents him from hesitating and prevents any doubt entering him about the word of the Messenger who reported.
Ṣiffīn: a place in Syria near Raqqa where in 38/657 a battle took place between 'Alī ibn Abī Ṭālib and Mu'āwiyah. Part of it was the Night of Ḥarīr (Clamour) where the two armies fought into the night and all that could be heard was the sound of the clashing of swords.
Aṣ-Ṣiḥāḥ: the famous dictionary *Tāj al-'Arūs wa's-Ṣiḥāh al-'Arabīyah*, by Ismā'īl ibn Ḥammād al-Jawharī.
Sīrah: biography, particularly biography of the Prophet ﷺ.
siwāk: a small stick, usually from the arak tree, whose tip is softened and used for cleaning the teeth.
Ṣubḥ: dawn prayer
Sulaymān: the Prophet Solomon.
sunan: plural of sunnah.
Sunnah: the customary practice of a person or group of people. It has come to refer almost exclusively to the practice of the Messenger of Allah ﷺ.
sūrah: a chapter of the Qur'an.
Tābi'ūn: the second generation of the early Muslims who did not meet the Prophet Muhammad ﷺ but learned the *dīn* of Islam from his Companions.
Tabūk: a town in northern Arabia close to Jordan.
tafsīr: commentary or explanation of the meanings of the Qur'an.
tahajjud: voluntary prayers performed at night.
taḥiyyah: the greeting recited in the *tashahhud* of the prayer.
takbīr: saying *'Allāhu Akbar,'* 'Allah is greater'.
Tan'īm: a place to the north of Makkah outside the Ḥaram.
tanwīn: nunation, indicating indefinite nouns.
taqiyyah: concealment of one's views to escape persecution.
taqwā: awe or fear of Allah, which puts a person on guard against wrong action and eager to do actions which please Allah.
tashahhud: lit. to pronounce the *shahādah*. In the context of the prayer, it is a formula which includes the *shahādah* and is recited in the final sitting position of each two *rak'ah* cycle.
taslīm: giving the Islamic greeting of *'as-salāmu 'alaykum,'* 'Peace be upon you.' The prayer ends with a *taslīm*.
tawḥīd: the doctrine of Divine Unity.

ta'wīl: allegorical interpretation.
tayammum: purification for the prayer with clean dust, earth, or stone, when water for *ghusl* or *wuḍū'* is unavailable or would be detrimental to health.
Taym: a sub-tribe of Quraysh.
Tihāmah: the Red Sea coastal plain of Arabia.
Tustar: Shustar, a fortress town in Khuzestan.
Uḥud: a mountain just outside of Madīnah where five years after the Hijrah, the Muslims lost a battle against the Makkan idolaters. Many great Companions, and in particular Ḥamzah, the uncle of the Prophet, were killed in this battle.
Umm al-Mu'minīn: literally 'Mother of the Believers', an honorary title given to the wives of the Prophet.
Umm al-Qur'ān: literally 'the Mother of the Qur'an', the opening *sūrah* of the Qur'an, *al-Fātiḥah.*
umm walad: a slavegirl who has had a child by her master.
Ummah: the body of Muslims as one distinct Community.
'umrah: the lesser pilgrimage to the Ka'bah in Makkah performed at any time of the year.
ūqiyyah: unit of measurement equal to a 12th of a *raṭl.*
'urbūn: non-refundable down payment.
'Usfān: a place on the route between Makkah and Madīnah.
uṣūl: plural of *aṣl*, the basic principles of any source used in fiqh.
uṣūlī: someone well-versed in the study of the fundamental principles (*uṣūl*) of Islamic law.
'Uzayr: Ezra.
wakīl: a person who is an authorized representative, agent or proxy.
walā': the tie of clientage established between a freed slave and the person who frees him, whereby the freed slave becomes integrated into the family of that person as a client (*mawlā*).
walī: (plural *awliyā'*) someone who is a 'friend' of Allah, thus possessing the quality of *wilāyah.* Also a relative who acts as a guardian.
wasq: a measure of volume equal to sixty *ṣā*'s.
wuḍū': ritual washing to be pure for the prayer.
Yaḥyā: the Prophet John the Baptist, the son of Zakariyyā.
Ya'qūb: the Prophet Jacob, also called Isrā'īl (Israel).
Yathrib: the ancient name for Madīnah.
Yūnus: the Prophet Jonah.
Yūsuf: the Prophet Joseph.

Zabūr: the Psalms of Dāwud.
Ẓāhiriyya: a school of *fiqh* which derived its judgments from the literal text of the Qur'an and Sunnah, and rejected the use of other legal principles like analogy.
Zakariyyā: the Prophet Zachariah, the father of Yaḥyā, John the Baptist, and guardian of Maryam.
zakat: a wealth tax, one of the five pillars of Islam.
zakat al-fiṭr: a small obligatory head-tax imposed on every Muslim who has the means for himself and his dependents. It is paid at the end of Ramadan.
Zamzam: the well in the Ḥaram of Makka.
ẓihār: an oath by a husband that his wife is like his mother's back to him, meaning she is unlawful for him. It was a form of divorce.
zindīq: a term used to describe a heretic whose teaching is a danger to the community or state.
Ẓuhr: the midday prayer.

www.ingramcontent.com/pod-product-compliance
Lightning Source LLC
Chambersburg PA
CBHW060309240426
43661CB00059B/2709
9781908892898